William Stone

The Story of the Garden of Eden

William Stone

The Story of the Garden of Eden

ISBN/EAN: 9783337089993

Printed in Europe, USA, Canada, Australia, Japan

Cover: Foto ©Lupo / pixelio.de

More available books at **www.hansebooks.com**

THE STORY

OF

THE GARDEN OF EDEN.

BY

WILLIAM STONE,

RETIRED SOLICITOR IN CHANCERY, ATTORNEY-AT-LAW, ETC.

Author of 'Benefit, Building, and Freehold Land Societies,' &c.

PUBLISHED BY THOMAS SCOTT,
NO. 11 THE TERRACE, FARQUHAR ROAD, UPPER NORWOOD,
LONDON, S.E.

1873.
Price Threepence.

THE STORY OF THE GARDEN OF EDEN.

THE primitive and interesting story of the Garden of Eden in the Book of Genesis is contained in the second account, or tradition of the creation, which is evidently quite distinct and at variance with that which precedes it.

After relating how man was formed and the trees and plants were made to grow, it is stated that man was placed in the Garden of Eden planted by the Lord God (*Jehovah Elohim*), "to dress it and to keep it." And that " the Lord God commanded the man, saying, Of every tree of the garden thou mayest freely eat; but of the tree of the knowledge of good and evil thou shalt not eat of it." Every beast of the field and fowl of the air are said to have been formed out of the ground and brought to Adam to be named, "and whatsoever Adam called *every living creature* that was the name thereof." Then woman is said to have been formed out of one of Adam's ribs as a "help meet for him." It being supposed to be necessary for Jehovah to cause "a deep sleep to fall upon Adam" to effect that object.

The idea intended to be conveyed appears to be that Adam and Eve were to abide in the Garden in a state of ease and comfort, feeding on fruit, and having for their only occupation " to dress it and to keep it;" every creature living there with them; but for what purpose, or under what conditions respecting their food and natural habits, is left to the imagination; and that this state was to have continued indefinitely, if the alleged command had been obeyed not to eat of the fruit of the tree of the knowledge of good and evil.

This abode, with the incidents surrounding it, has been called "*Paradise*," equivalent to "*Eden*" in the original, and is so designated by the translators of the Bible in their concise statement of the contents of the third chapter of Genesis. The words being intended to convey a state of exceptional happiness, far superior to anything which could have been enjoyed elsewhere by human beings under any circumstances; and so blissful as to have been in itself a powerful inducement to the supposed progenitors of the human race to obey the one only command which would enable them to ensure its continuance.

But can any state be imagined more unnatural, and less calculated to produce contentment for any length of time, consistently with the character of man and woman? According to the actual story, as plainly and simply told in Genesis,—and the literal meaning of the words, without either being added to or taken from—it is the most unnatural and artificial condition that could well be conceived, so far as we know of the nature of humanity, either from observation, or from what is said of them before or afterwards in Genesis.

In the previous account by the Elohist of the creation of man and woman, their natural character is clearly indicated by the comprehensive utterance, "Be fruitful, and multiply, and replenish the earth,

the Garden of Eden.

and subdue it." Not confining them to one spot, however delightful, but contemplating their abode in all the earth, to be subdued by them for their own benefit; all which has been accomplished according to the law of Nature and the object of their creation. How could it have come to pass in the marvellous manner in which history and passing events teach us, if the earthly happiness of man and woman could have consisted in remaining in the supposed Paradise of the Garden of Eden in the uneventful kind of life alone suggested by the story? And what was to have become of their children and children's children? They could not have "multiplied" and remained there for any length of time; neither could they have remained there, or elsewhere on the earth, leading the kind of life described, so as to " replenish the earth and subdue it;" for it would have been not only unnatural, but impossible.

It is in vain to suggest, as some commentators have done, that Adam and Eve in Paradise were in a supernatural state of happiness which they were formed to enjoy, and at the same time had the free will to obey or disobey the alleged command; not only because the story itself does not justify such a strained interpretation, but because of the difficulty of supposing a supernatural state with the possibility of disobeying a command of the Creator. And such a state would surely have conveyed to the mind, if it had existed, a higher idea of happiness than to live in a garden, however beautiful, "to dress it and to keep it." Thereby to have rendered unnecessary and useless all the energy and talent which has been actually displayed by man in extending his sphere of usefulness in this world, which has formed the largest portion of his happiness, to the praise and glory of God! and prepared his spirit for greater bliss hereafter.

Even the genius of Milton, which enabled him to

depict in most glowing poetical language a Paradise of a more attractive character than the short description in Genesis could accomplish, does not convey to the mind anything sufficiently desirable to make us think that all the happiness of which mankind were capable, even when first created, could have been enjoyed in such a state; so as to prevent that love of change and variety of occupation, and to keep in constant employment those numerous other propensities, physical rather than moral, which must always have been a part of human nature, and could only be satisfied in a more extended sphere and more useful employments.

In Patriarchal times in a hot country, some men of quiet, contemplative dispositions might have considered such a state paradisaical; as we have known many such men have lived and done some good in their generation; and probably the originator of this story was of that character; but it is far from conveying the impression of an inspired revelation through the Divine Omniscient Spirit, foreseeing the wonderful variety of human minds and bodies; and knowing what they were destined to accomplish in this beautiful world, so full of the treasures of a bountiful Providence, which have been, and still will be, discovered and rendered useful, "to replenish the earth and subdue it."

There is no suggestion in Genesis that after the expulsion of Adam and Eve from the Garden of Eden their natural qualities, or their power of imparting varieties of gifts mental and physical to future generations, were changed. The one idea, of what is called orthodox theology, has been that they conveyed to all mankind, in some mysterious way, the condemnation to which they themselves are represented to have been subjected. But how extremely difficult it is to find in all or any of the words of this story the enormous proportions attached to the doctrine of

the Garden of Eden. 9

"*original sin;*" and how inadequate the disobedience and condemnation are to account for the great variety of temptations peculiar to each individual, which are the causes of sin, and arise from the temperament and disposition which form a part of the nature of every human being born into the world, no two alike.

Can it be said that, if Adam and Eve had remained obedient, all their descendants would have been free from those passions and appetites which create temptation, or that they would have been more within control? If not, what difference did the supposed disobedience make in the character of their children? Nothing can be found in the story itself to elucidate these questions; notwithstanding the host of comments which have appeared since the days of St Paul, founded on words attributed to him, referring to this subject, but which may be better interpreted in a more rational way.

How different is the voice of Nature from the beginning of history.

We find that Cain and Abel, the first children of Adam and Eve according to the Jehovistic tradition, differed materially in their inclinations and characters, one being "a tiller of the ground," the other "a keeper of sheep," and one murdering the other. The chase is soon spoken of in Genesis—Nimrod being "a mighty hunter." Other occupations and acquirements are named, attractive to men of different dispositions—Jabal being the father "of such as dwell in tents, and of such as have cattle;" Jubal being the father "of such as handle the harp or the organ;" and Tubal-Cain "an instructor of every artificer in brass and iron."

All these natural varieties of disposition, and many more which prevailed in the primitive world, are inconsistent with the notion that man could have remained in the Garden of Eden in the fanciful state of uneventful indolence which the possible obedience to the command would have entailed on him and his posterity. And they are also inconsistent with the supposition on which this story is founded that man and woman were not originally created with passions and appetites similar, though not alike in kind or degree, to what they imparted to their descendants, which led to the prevalence of evil as well as good conduct in the various relations of life from the beginning until now.

In very many instances the food of man would depend on his skill in first inventing means to entrap and kill his fish and game, and, by practice, to become more skilful in their use. Some would exceed others in skill, either by being more powerful or agile, or by greater perseverance or superior mental capacity; which last would often ensure success with even less physical strength. Thus emulation and excitement would arise, perfectly natural and desirable in the early state of society after man began to be fruitful and multiply according to the fiat of his Maker.

Flocks and herds appear to have been the greatest source of wealth in patriarchal times, requiring large tracts of country and a constant change for their maintenance. There is the clearest evidence in the early Scriptural history of the expansions of territory rendered necessary as population increased, as well as evidences of degrees of skill, both mental and physical, and of good and evil passions in a variety of ways.

The ideas connected with love, joy, hate, jealousy, ambition, emulation, hope, fear, hunger, enmity, strife, envyings, and such like, are all in conjunction with the blessing and direction, "Be fruitful and multiply, and replenish the earth, and subdue it." Man could not have had " dominion over the fish of the sea, and over the fowl of the air, and over every living

the Garden of Eden.

thing that moveth upon the earth," without the exertion and commotion occasioned by those passions and feelings. The exercise of them is natural to mankind, and they are, and always were, the causes and promoters of the chequered state of happiness and misery in this world—the former prevailing to much the greater extent.

Think of what man has done, and is still doing, to replenish the earth and subdue it, and to have the dominion which, in God's providence, was intended from the beginning. In reference to hunger and food, man has followed the universal law of Nature. He has used his intellect, and thereby aided his physical powers, in pursuing, killing, and subjecting animals and other creatures to his will, and obtaining the dominion intended for him. Whilst the fish of the sea, the fowl of the air, the beast of the field, the insect, and creeping things, each in their respective ways, have done likewise; and, in so doing, have followed the same universal law. It was instituted before the advent of man on the earth, as shown by the fossil remains of bygone eras, and has continued ever since.

How could these natural events have taken place, and the varieties of human character have found a scope for action, if it had been possible for man to have remained in the supposed Paradise, living the kind of life which the description in Genesis, or any comment upon it, conveys to the mind. Is it consistent with any revelation of the character of man found in the Bible, or obtained from Natural History? In the former, one tradition contradicts the other; in the latter, all is in clear harmony with present natural facts and those obtained from undoubted history, including the whole history of man in the Bible, except the interlude of the Garden of Eden.

The alleged punishment of man for disobedience

in eating of the fruit of the forbidden tree has already been alluded to as, in fact, a blessing, so far as the necessity for bodily labour is concerned,—"In the sweat of thy face shalt thou eat bread,"—a blessing in the way of promoting health and providing an occupation, with the attainment of an object, so desirable to prevent the weariness constantly besetting those to whom labour is unnecessary, or with whom indolence becomes a habit. But, if labour was to be a punishment, why was mental labour excluded, which has become more important to man in providing food and clothing and comforts and luxuries of every description—such labour at times having been far more exhausting than bodily labour. Yet that also has ever been, and will be, a blessing, so long as man shall remain on earth. Without it how much less completely, if at all, could he have accomplished the supposed command, but in truth the natural law, "to replenish the earth and subdue it." With it what wonders have been performed in multiplying power and obtaining the "dominion," and in finding out more truly some of the ways of God in the earth and in the heavens, and His more perfect Laws in regard to the moral and physical government of man and of the Universe.

These things could not have been done without persevering labour, which has its reward in this life; and who can doubt that mental improvement, with the fruits of righteousness, will lead to greater blessing in the world to come! The talent was not given to be laid up in a napkin, but to be used and improved for purposes here and hereafter which we cannot fathom; but we may be sure that, if we use it well, we shall hear spiritually the blessed words, "Well done, good and faithful servant, enter thou into the joy of thy Lord."

It is further said, "Cursed is the ground for thy sake, in sorrow shalt thou eat of it all the days of

the Garden of Eden. 13

thy life. Thorns also and thistles shall it bring forth to thee, and thou shalt eat the herb of the field." The first suggestion of this passage is that Jehovah *cursed* the ground in consequence of Adam's disobedience. But geology has revealed to us that the surface soils throughout the world were gradually formed by natural laws from the component parts of the pre-existing rocks or crust of the earth before man was created, and that the same component parts exist now as were in existence from time to time throughout the various geological eras of the world.

And chymistry has taught us that the ground, so far from having been *cursed*, has been productive or unproductive in exact accordance with the chymical composition of the soil, agreeing always with the adjacent rocks and substratum, sometimes very fertile in its original state, at others less so, and in many localities sterile. Proper cultivation has been found to consist in applying to less fertile soils such artificial and other dressings as contain the necessary chymical qualities to make them productive.

Then it is said, "In *sorrow* shalt thou eat of it." But is this so? Or has it ever been so since the world began? On the contrary, man has always enjoyed the fruit of his labour; the more so because the toil has produced the harvest and an increased appetite, the very expression of enjoyment being praise to God of a sweet savour. From the earliest days to the present time the "*joy of harvest*" has been a poetical and appropriate image to express great happiness, often used in Scripture. "They joy before Thee according to the joy of harvest, and as men rejoice when they divide the spoil" (Isaiah ix. 3). The reversed picture is thus beautifully described by the same Prophet:—"I will water thee with my tears, O Heshbon and Elealah; for the shouting for thy summer fruits and the harvest is fallen. And gladness is taken away, and joy out of the plentiful field; and in the vineyards there shall be no more singing neither shall there be shouting. The treaders shall tread out no wine in their presses; I have made their vintage shouting to cease " (Isaiah xvi. 9). The harvest home of Old England has changed in character. The utilitarian spirit has somewhat depressed the earnest manifestations of former days; but the hymn of praise still ascends, and ever will, throughout the earth, so long as it endures.

It is, moreover, natural and not a *curse*, that the ground brings forth " thorns also and thistles " which have their allotted task as all other productions have; and one of the necessities of cultivation or replenishing the earth is, that man should not only undergo the comparatively slight labour of removing the "thorns and thistles," but also the large trees, roots, and stubs of the virgin forests. It was a blessing and not a curse when the early emigrants finding labour poorly rewarded at home, because the people multiplied so fruitfully, followed the example of the Patriarchs of old, according to the Law of Nature, and the Law of God, by going forth to "*replenish*" another portion of the earth, and "*subdue*" it. With their hatchet in hand, a bold heart, and determined perseverance, they entered the virgin forests, and by hard labour, day after day, felled and grubbed the luxuriant growth of trees; knowing that the ground which produced such magnificent forests would soon bear abundant harvests of a more useful kind; and they obtained the reward of comparative wealth, instead of their previous penury and want. In the meantime,—exercise, good health, good appetite, and, above all, the conscientious conviction that they were doing their duty in the state of life in which it had pleased God to place them, caused as much earthly happiness as man was ever intended to enjoy. Where

the Garden of Eden.

can the *curse* be found in all this; and much more? For from such small and apparently insignificant beginnings, have sprung up great and wealthy nations, and wise and happy peoples in America, Australia, and elsewhere,—fulfiling the command, or natural law to "be fruitful and multiply and replenish the earth and subdue it" to the praise and glory of God! The blessing, and the praise are manifest, but where is the *curse*?

Again,—the punishment of the woman is said to have been—"I will greatly multiply thy sorrow, and thy conception, in sorrow shalt thou bring forth children." Now is this so? Is it not rather a joy unspeakable to every woman when she has the hope, and then the fruition of the very object of her creation, that a child, and children should be born into the world? The Psalmist uttered a more reliable revelation when he said—" Lo, children are an heritage of the Lord: and the fruit of the womb is His reward" (blessing), Psalm cxxvii. 3. It is quite true that the pains and perils of childbirth do exist; and science tells us that woman's natural form, which it is not stated was altered, causes her necessarily to have *pain*, the absence of it would occasion greater peril: but bodily pain is not always sorrow, although the latter word is used by St John xvi. 21. "A woman when she is in travail hath sorrow because her hour is come; but so soon as she is delivered of the child she remembers no more the anguish for joy that a man is born into the world." And Jesus Christ is represented to have used that interesting illustration to show more clearly what he wished to convey to his disciples, that his leaving them for "a little while" was only for their good—"Ye now, therefore, have sorrow; but I will see you again, and your heart shall rejoice, and your joy no man taketh from you" (St John xvi. 22). The natural truth is, that from first to last, children are a crown of rejoicing both to man and woman; and to woman especially there is always heartfelt joy and no sorrow. It may happen that in straightened circumstances doubts and fears arise respecting the means of providing food and clothing, but even then the little stranger is always welcomed by affection, and fostered by maternal love. Truly has the poet written—

> "The cherubs well might envy thee
> The pleasures of a parent."

There is no love more refined, or less tinctured with selfishness, save the love of God. And if there be an exception occasionally to this universal law, from the "beginning" so well expressed by the Elohist—"Be fruitful and multiply"—it is reprobated as unnatural. Where, then, is the punishment, if all that has been would have been, whether the alleged disobedience occurred or not?

Again, it is stated as a part of the woman's *curse*, "thy desire shall be to thy husband, and he shall rule over thee." As if the *desire* of woman to her husband was thenceforth to change and be more overpowering than that of man to his wife! The beautiful description in 'Paradise Lost' conveying a contrary impression is more true to nature, for it was, doubtless, a law from the beginning that man should seek the woman, although it may be true that she "flys to be pursued." *Mutuality* approaches nearest to what is observed in nature; which sentiment applies also to the remaining portion of the supposed *curse* "and he shall rule over thee"—for woman has had her peculiar powers over man, and in her sphere has always possessed the *rule*.

The whole spirit of this story is to represent woman as inferior; that she was created subsequently, merely as "a help meet" and an inferior adjunct to man; that she was formed of one of man's

the Garden of Eden.

ribs; that she fell *first* into temptation and sin, and was the cause of the fall of man from "original righteousness;" by whose offence "judgment came upon all men to condemnation." The command having been given to him *alone*, according to the account, Adam is said to have excused himself by saying: "The woman whom Thou gavest me, she gave me of the tree, and I did eat." What a representation is this of the first parent of mankind! What an unmanly and ungrateful excuse for a supposed result, magnified by commentators into such enormously doctrinal importance!

Such depressing inferiority of woman characterises the Jewish legislation, and literature, relating to her; and also of other Eastern nations; and is the unjust masculine tone of judaising teachers now. But the more truthful idea of the Elohist was that man and woman were *both* created by the Almighty Father at the same time " in his own image;" "Male and female created He *them,* and called *their* name Adam in the day when they were created." This name, Adam, signifying *Earth born*, synonymous in the original language with the term *man*, as the collective designation of the human race, male and female. (Gen. v. 1-2). There is, therefore, no sign in this more perfect Elohistic tradition of inequality between the sexes, nor could anything of that kind have been intended by their Creator. This is also the teaching of the Gospel; and the effect of Christian knowledge and civilisation, when mere brute force ceases to predominate, has been to place man and woman in their respective spheres, on a complete equality, as it most surely was in " the beginning." Mutual love, mutual respect, mutual forbearance, mutual sympathy, mutual confidence, mutual rule in their several occupations, mutual certainty of their high vocation as the children of God, and temples of the spirit He has implanted within them ; mutual aspirations of spiritual happiness in Eternity !

Again, it is stated of the serpent that it was " more subtle than any beast of the field ; " and that it said unto the woman, " Yea, hath God said ye shall not eat of every tree of the garden ? " and afterwards, " Ye shall not surely die, for God doth know that in the day ye eat thereof, then your eyes shall be opened, and ye shall be as gods, knowing good and evil." (Gen. iii.) It is not indicated that the serpent was made to speak miraculously, yet natural history teaches us that its mouth and tongue are not formed in a way to enable it to speak. Neither is it here mentioned that the Satan of Scripture took on him the form of a serpent for the purpose of tempting Eve. It is all related as a natural occurrence founded on the serpent's subtlety ; and Jehovah is represented as having, by way of punishment, said to the serpent —" Because thou hast done this thou art cursed above all cattle, and above every beast of the field ; upon thy belly shalt thou go, and dust shalt thou eat all the days of thy life." (Gen. iii. 14.)

The words " because thou hast done this " imply that the serpent had power to do it or not,—opposing the supposition of Satanic influence in the temptation. Yet the Bishop of Ely, in the 'New Bible Commentary' (Vol. I. 44), observes, in support of the old Satanic theory, that " the reason why Satan took the form of a beast so remarkable for its subtlety *may* have been that so Eve *might* be the less upon her guard. New as she was to all creation, she *may* not have been surprised at speech in an animal which apparently possessed almost human sagacity." (!) The Bishop assumes that Satan took the serpent's form, without any distinct scriptural authority, either in this story or elsewhere, beyond the occasional vague expressions of its subtlety founded on this

the Garden of Eden.

story, and the reference in Rev. xii. 9, "That old serpent called the Devil." But how painfully inconsistent such an assumption is with the supposition that Jehovah would punish the animal if Satan had power to take its form for the purpose of deceiving Eve! Moreover, it is the merest fancy of olden times, and not natural truth, that the serpent was "remarkable for its subtlety," although Jesus Christ, adopting the Jewish notion, is said to have used the words, "Be ye, therefore, wise as serpents and as harmless as doves." Much less did it ever "*apparently*" possess "almost human sagacity" as imagined by the Bishop. Where can anything be found, either in the Bible or in natural history, to justify such expressions?

The Jewish impression was probably based on the statement in Genesis, "that the serpent was more subtle than any beast of the field"—but even in the time of Moses the slightest observation would have shown that many other animals were far more sagacious—capable of knowing, recollecting, and obeying in a remarkable way, and in a manner beneficial to man, showing in their conduct and habits a subtlety which could not fail to attract attention; whereas the ideas respecting the serpent were fictitious, and its real habits so little known to the Jewish writers that they thought, in accordance with the supposed curse, that it fed on dust! We find in Isaiah lxv. 25, "*Dust shall be the serpent's meat;*" and in Micah vii. 17, "They shall lick the *dust* like a serpent."

The Bishop of Ely further observes (p. 45), "The most natural interpretation of the curse *might* indicate some change of form." It would appear that he leans towards the old cherished notion, that before the supposed fall of man serpents moved in an erect attitude, and were doomed by the curse to go on their belly! But this or any other change of form is opposed to science, which reveals to us that serpents lived long before the advent of man on earth, and always had the same mode of locomotion (on their bellies) as at present.

In this passage and others in Scripture, *the* serpent is spoken of, as if only of one kind; but natural history teaches us that there are, and always were, many kinds of serpents in different parts of the world—being most numerous in warm latitudes. They are classed under the order *Ophidia*, and distinguished from reptiles which go on legs, because of their (the serpents) eel-like bodies and absence of external limbs; having been so formed with two to three hundred flexible vertebræ along their spinal column, for the express purpose of enabling them, as "creeping things," to go "on their belly," with an undulatory motion. Above five hundred kinds have been specified, venomous and non-venomous. None of them ever fed on *dust*, but chiefly on small or large animals, according to their size and offensive powers, which they swallow entire after covering them first with a slippery saliva provided them for that purpose by Nature; whilst others live on worms, frogs, grubs, and insects. The non-venomous serpents are provided with an extraordinary power of dilating their jaws, and of coiling themselves round their prey so as to crush it to death by a succession of powerful muscular contractions. One species of serpent found in Brazil can move both ways, backwards and forwards, and created the popular but erroneous impression that it was double-headed. It usually coils, and conceals itself in the large ant mounds, on which insect it feeds.

These few and concise references to facts in natural history teach us that what is spoken of as a punishment to the serpent in this story is not really so; but perfectly natural. They are not cursed in any

the Garden of Eden.

proper sense of the term; but are as providence made them from "the beginning." They have all enjoyed life in their ways quite as much as other "beasts of the field" and "creeping things." And the "enmity" referred to between the serpent and the woman, and "thy seed and her seed," is nothing more than the natural fact, that, human beings must fear, and be at enmity with venomous and powerful serpents like the vipers and boas, in the same way, and no further, than they are with wild "beasts of the field" such as the lion, tiger, and bear, when fear of danger causes enmity. On the other hand, serpents have no special enmity against human beings more than other wild creatures, or so much as against their ordinary victims for food.

It is, therefore, very manifest that the whole of this interlude of the story of the garden of Eden by the Jehovist is inconsistent with the previous Elohistic narrative of creation, and also with the actual facts revealed by natural science. It is also in antagonism with our just impressions of the Omniscient to believe that He would create man and woman, and place them in a garden to be so easily tempted against His express command to eat of the forbidden fruit, " pleasant to the eye;" and that such a venial offence should bring death and woe into the world, and subject all mankind to eternal torments. That this disobedience which He foreknew caused so much wrath in the Creator that it could only be appeased by God the Son, " co-equal and co-eternal " with Himself, appearing long afterwards as man on earth to perform the whole law, and suffer death upon the Cross as an an atonement,—" not by the conversion of the Godhead into flesh, but by taking of the manhood into God," as the Athanasian Creed asserts. All which " except a man believe faithfully, he cannot be saved," but must go into " everlasting fire." And that those who went before were to believe by anticipation!

Moreover, that the eating of this fruit by man caused the Lord God to say—"Behold the man is become *as one of us* to know good and evil: and now lest he put forth his hand and take also of the tree of life, *and live for ever.* Therefore the Lord God sent him forth from the Garden of Eden." What interpretation can be put on these words consistently with our present notions of God and of man, as so clearly revealed to us through nature and nature's laws? And how is it possible to reconcile the appearance of the Lord God "*walking* in the garden in the cool of the day," and *speaking* to Adam, and Eve, and the Serpent, with our higher faith, and conscientious conviction that "God is a Spirit" pervading all creation? Not appearing in it to man's outward vision, but always near—seen and felt, and known only by the soul of man in a way to rouse his deepest love and reverential awe!

At the same time this story is interesting as conveying to us the primitive ideas of our race respecting the origin of sin and death and the many woes of this mortal life; more especially when they are compared with records of a similar character of many other ancient religions, some of them still in existence. We know that sin entered into the world, and that from the beginning until the end of time there has been, and will be, a constant conflict between good and evil. We need not look beyond ourselves for the origin of evil, when our consciences tell us that it is within, constantly striving for and too often obtaining the victory. It is a part of this probationary state and a law of Nature. There must, therefore, be "a new birth unto righteousness," through faith in that which is good and holy, as taught in the Bible and elsewhere, and especially by Jesus Christ.

Without such an arousing of the conscience and earnest desire for sanctification of the spirit in this life, how is a nearer approach to perfection in eternity to be enjoyed? With it and all its blessed accompaniments, how perfect will be the bliss! And how thoroughly can our minds, even through the present veil of humanity, comprehend and appreciate such thoughts and aspirations as Divine Truths from everlasting to everlasting!

CHRIST AND OSIRIS.

BY

J. S. STUART-GLENNIE, M.A.

Reprinted by permission from

'IN THE MORNINGLAND.'

PUBLISHED BY THOMAS SCOTT.

11 THE TERRACE, FARQUHAR ROAD, UPPER NORWOOD,

LONDON, S.E.

1876.

Price Threepence.

LONDON:
PRINTED BY C. W. REYNELL, LITTLE PULTENEY STREET,
HAYMARKET.

CHRIST AND OSIRIS.

"Thou hast conquered, O pale Galilean; the world has grown grey from thy breath;
We have drunken of things Lethean, and fed on the fulness of death.
O lips that the live blood faints in, the leavings of racks and rods!
O ghastly glories of saints, dead limbs of gibbeted gods!
Though all men abase them before you in spirit, and all knees bend,
I kneel not, neither adore you, but standing, look to the end.
 * * * * *
Though before thee the throned Cytherean be fallen, and hidden her head,
Yet thy kingdom shall pass, Galilean, thy dead shall go down to the dead." *

REFLECTING here, on the Temple-roof at Karnak, on the general results of our Egyptian studies, we are first of all struck with what I may call the Christian character of Osirianism. But before proceeding to point this out, and to state the hypothesis which this Christian character of Osirianism suggests, it may be desirable to offer a few remarks on the outward, and hence more vulgarly appreciated characteristics of the Egyptian religion. For, in amazement at any likening of Osirianism to Christianism, or of Christianism to Osirianism, many readers may, as if in

---

* Swinburne, *Poems and Ballads*, *Hymn to Proserpine*, pp. 79-80.

settlement of any suggestion even of a causal relation between Osirianism and Christianism, ask, ' Were not the Egyptians, as a matter of fact, idolaters, and worshippers, indeed, of the most grotesque and monstrous idols?' But let us understand what idolatry means. Possibly, you who put this question may be more of an idolater than were the ancient Egyptians when they first created their Gods. Idolatry is ceremonial worship when the meaning of the ceremonies and symbols is lost. We are helped to the understanding of this by the study of language, in its first formations. Names, as a class of signs,* are themselves but a kind of symbols. In the formation of a language, they are at first uttered certainly not without a meaning; they certainly are the attempt to denote some thing, or express some want, hitherto nameless, unutterable. Yet these names, at first so meaningful, may in time so completely lose their original meaning, as to become the terminations of a declension.† So symbols, animal-headed deities, and others. What if the symbol, in later times, so lost its meaning as to be itself worshipped? Originally it had carried the mind from itself to that which it signified. And as, in Language, ' the formation of substantive nouns is the first stage of personifying God;'‡ so, in Religion, the creation of symbols is the first stage of idolatry. We shall hereafter have occasion to consider idol-creation more fully, and from other points of view. Here I will only remark, that a reference to the idolatry of the Egyptians is unfortunate, if it is intended thereby to disprove the likeness of Osirian-

---

* ' A name is a word taken at pleasure to serve for a *mark* which may raise in our mind a thought like to some thought we had before, and which, being pronounced to others, may be to them a *sign* of what thought the speaker had, or had not, before in his mind.'—Hobbes, *Computation or Logic*, ch. ii., cited by Mill, *System of Logic*, vol. II. p. 23.
† See Müller, *Lectures on the Science of Language*.
‡ Bunsen, *Egypt's Place*, vol. IV. p. 566.

ism to Christianism. For we shall find that it is just in comparing these two Creeds in this matter of idolatry, that — when we set Yahvehism between them—their likeness comes out most strongly—the religion of Abraham, whether as Judaism, or as Mohammedanism, acting as a foil, and bringing out with startling clearness, at once, the Osirian character of Christianism, and the Christian character of Osirianism.

2. But is the Animal-worship of the Egyptians next objected against any comparison of Osirianism with Christianism, or any hypothesis with respect to the origination of the latter in a transformation of the former? Well, it is admitted that that exaggerated care for animals which becomes a superstitious worship of them is not a feature of Christian religious emotion. But in the Animal-worship which—probably derived from an aboriginal African element in the population[*] — was, soon after the time of Menes, incorporated with Osirianism throughout the Empire, there should seem to have been an idea which modern Science tends more and more clearly to establish—the identity, namely, of the principle of life in all its manifestations.[†] 'And what is this,' asks Bunsen, ' but a specific adaptation of that consciousness of the divinity of Nature, which is implied in all the religious consciousness of the Old World?'[‡] The doctrine of transmigration thus became a sacred link between animal and human life. And ' the community between the human and animal soul being once admitted, we can understand how the Egyptians at last arrived at the idea of worshipping in animals a living manifestation of Divinity.'[§] But if a similar doctrine is not found in Christianism,

---

[*] Bunsen, *Egypt's Place*, vol. IV. p. 637
[†] See Spencer, *Principles of Biology*, and *Principles of Psychology*.
[‡] Bunsen. *Egypt's Place*, vol. IV. p. 640.
[§] *Ibid.* vol. IV. p. 641.

one is tempted to say that the want of it is much to be regretted. For there have been, and even still are, few worse features in Christian Civilization than its apathy to animal suffering.* And it is very noteworthy that it was the great Apostle of the Utilitarian School of Moralists who, in that very year from which dates a new period of the Modern Revolution, 1789, introduced into European Ethics the consideration of ' the interests of other animals.'† So likewise, a new care for, and new appreciation of animals is one of the characteristic features of Comte's conception of the New Religion of Humanity.‡ And if, at length, men are beginning *again* to become sympathetically aware that other animals also besides themselves feel pain, and that it is shameful and dastardly to inflict pain unnecessarily upon them ; if there is now some hope that Christian 'sports' may, at length, be done away with, and animal-barbarities generally ; and if, in realising that fact of physical kinship with our Elder Brethren, which Science affirms, and Christianity scouts, there is being devoloped some nobler sympathy also with them—this, at least, it must be admitted, is certainly not owing to any doctrine in Christianism that can be paralleled in Osirianism.

3. The considerations thus suggested on the 'Idolatry' and on the 'Animal-worship' of the Egyptians may, I trust, prepare us candidly now to consider the more essential doctrines of Osirianism—those doc-

---

* As to Christian cruelty generally, we must not recall the gladiatorial combats of the Roman amphitheatre, without recalling also the heretic burnings of every chief town in Christendom. Nor is Classic civilization to be judged by the days of its decline ; but rather, as also Christian civilization, by the days of its prime. And that the Middle Ages were the prime of Christian civilization is proved by the fact, that the movement which has, since then, modified Christianity has tended more and more to sweep it, both as a doctrinal and as a social system, away.

† Bentham, *Principles of Morals and Legislation*, ch. XVII.

‡ See Mill, *Comte and Positivism*.

Christ and Osiris. 9

trines which are so remarkably similar to the great dogmas of Christianism. And with respect to what the great religious doctrines of the Egyptians really were, we are not now in any doubt. For one of the grandest achievements of Modern Science* has been the translation of their Funeral Ritual, the 'Todtenbuch,' or 'Book of the Dead,' as Lepsius called it, or as it calls itself, the ' Departure into Light.'† It belongs to Bunsen's fourth class of those Sacred Books which would form collectively the Bible of the ancient Egyptians, and is scarcely posterior to 3,000 years before our era.‡ For, as Bunsen points out, we have a very remarkable proof that the origin of the prayers and hymns of this Ritual belongs probably to the Pre-Menite Dynasty of Abydos, between 3100 and 4500 B.C., in the fact that we find one of these hymns,§ not in its original simplicity, but already mixed up with glosses and commentaries, inscribed on the coffin of Queen Mentuhept of the eleventh dynasty. This monumental text agrees with the printed text of the Turin papyrus. And though the first year of the eleventh dynasty, which lasted forty-three years, cannot be placed earlier than 2782 B.C.;¶ yet, if we consider the many stages

---

* 'The interpretation of the extinct languages of Egypt and Central Asia will ever rank as one of the distinguishing features of the nineteenth century.'—Birch, in Bunsen's *Egypt's Place*, vol. v. p. IX.
† Or ' Manifestation to Light,' according to Champollion and Dr. Birch. The complete translation by the latter was only published with the fifth volume of Bunsen's *Egypt* in 1867. But I had with me at Thebes the previous volumes, besides Wilkinson's *Ancient Egyptians* and other works ; and I had the advantage of perusing and making copious extracts from the translation of an American Egyptologer who was residing at Luxor. Even Dr. Birch's translation, however, must be considered as representing the state of hieroglyphical knowledge rather twenty years ago than now—so long was its publication, owing to various causes, delayed. The translation of the 'Todtenbuch,' to which students must now refer, is that by Brugsch, now in course of publication. My references, however, here, will be to Dr. Birch's Translation. as probably more accessible to the majority of readers.
‡ Bunsen, *Egypt's Place*, vol. IV. p. 646.
§ It forms chapter XVII. of the Ritual. See Birch's translation in *Egypt's Place*, vol. v. pp. 172-80.
¶ Compare *Egypt's Place*, vol. v. pp. 29, 88, and 94.

that must have been passed through, before the original hymn, learned by heart, and recited from memory, became mixed-up with scholia in an undivided sacred text, we cannot but date its composition and primitive use many centuries anterior to that dynasty in which we find it thus embedded in explanations. This hymn implies not only the worship of Osiris, but the whole system of doctrines connected with his redeeming life on Earth, and judicial office in Heaven. Yet an antiquity, even greater than is thus witnessed-to, we are obliged to assign to Osirianism, by the fact that the Osiris-myth itself mentions 'Byblus (Gebal in Phœnicia) as the place where Isis brought up the young Osiris.'* And this derivation from Asia is further confirmed by the universally admitted identity of 'the fundamental ideas of the worship, and sacred ceremonials of Adonis and Osiris.'† To the very earliest period, then, of the history of Humanity, as the history of Thought, we must carry back the ideas of the Osirian Faith. And yet, we may possibly find in the sequel, that it is but a transformed Osirianism that, to this day, dominates Christendom.

4. Considered as a whole, the 'Departure into Light' is a revelation in something of an epic, and even occasionally dramatic form of the departure of the Soul into the Other-world, of its judgment, and of what is required of it, in order to its final beatific reception by its Father Osiris. Its formularies may, perhaps, best be arranged under such heads as the following:—I. General Address. II. Address to each of the Forty-two Assessors. III. Announcement of Justification. IV. Telling the names of different parts of the Temple. V. Blessings, &c.‡ According to Egyptian notions, it was 'essentially an inspired

---
* *Egypt's Place*, vol. IV. p. 347. † *Ibid.*
‡ Compare Birch's introduction to his translation, *Egypt's Place*, vol. V.

work; and the term Hermetic, so often applied by profane writers to these books, in reality means inspired. It is Thoth himself who speaks, and reveals the will of the Gods, and the mysterious nature of divine things to man.'* Portions of them are expressly stated to have been written by the very finger of Thoth himself, and to have been the composition of a great God.† And in this, it may be noted by the way, that we see an illustration of what, in the Introduction, was pointed out as one of the general characteristics of the First Age of Humanity, namely, the authorlessness, for the most part, of its Literature, and its attribution, to supernatural sources. But sacred this Ritual was also esteemed as ' assuring to the soul a passage from the Earth; a transit through the purgatory and other regions of the Dead; the entrance into the Empyreal Gate, by which the souls arrived at the presence of God, typified by the Sun; the admission into the Bark, or Orb of the Sun, ever traversing in brilliant light the liquid ether; and protection from the various Liers-in-wait, or Adversaries, who sought to accuse, destroy, or detain it in its passage, or destiny.'‡ In this most ancient book of the Osirian Scriptures there is, no doubt, not only a vast mass of unintelligible ritualistic allusions, but evidence of gross superstition. Not, however, without evidence of this, are also the Christian Scriptures. And it must be borne in mind that the Osirian Bible had not the good fortune to be, in the formation of its canon, purged, as was the Christian, of impurer, apocryphal elements. Yet, notwithstanding this misfortune, the religious tone of the Osirian Ritual is such as the following brief extracts may serve, though inadequately, to illustrate.

---

* *Ibid.* p. 133.
† See chapter lxiv., Rubric.
‡ Birch in *Egypt's Place*, vol. v. p. 134.

5. Very touching are some of the expressions in which the Departed calls on Osiris to save him from his Accusers, from the Lake of Fire, and from the Tormentors. Addressing these with the noble boldness of great faith, 'says Osiris Anfanch . . . while you strive against me, your acts against me are against Osiris. . . . . To strive against me, is as against Osiris.' Again : ' Let me come, having seen and passed, having passed the Gate to see my Father Osiris. I have made way through the darkness to my Father Osiris. I am his beloved. I stab the heart of Sut. I do the things of my Father Osiris. I have opened every door in heaven and earth. I am his beloved son. I have come from the mummy, an instructed spirit.' And again : ' says Osiris Anfanch, save me, as thou savest what belongs to thy word ; catch me up; the Lord is God, there is but one God for me (or, before the Lord of Mankind, there is but one Lord for me).' A passage, this, which is but one of many* proving the monotheism of the better instructed, or more deeply thinking, of those whom the narrow ignorance of that Creed propagated by the Galilæan Fishermen sets down as ' idolatrous heathens.' He who is thus represented as speaking in a certain stage of his progress to the region of ' Sacred Repose,' is more particularly described in the beginning of some papyri as ' Osiris Anfanch of the true faith, born of the lady Souhenchem of fair fame.' The prefix to the man's name of that of God himself is the ' new name ' which every true believer receives after death. In other passages the good man is even spoken of as an Osiris. ' The Osiris lives, after he dies, like the sun daily ; for as the sun dies, and is born in the morning, so the Osiris dies.' And finally, as to that immortality which is so ignorantly imagined to have

---

* See chap. IV. sect. iii.

Christ and Osiris. 13

been 'brought to light by the Gospel,' the Osiris exclaims in another passage : ' I do not die again in the Region of Sacred Repose.' And again. 'Whosoever does what belongs to him, visibly (individually ?) his soul participates in Life Eternal.' And again. 'Plait for thyself a garland . . . thy life is everlasting.'

6. But it is the central doctrine of Osirianism that more particularly claims our attention. 'The peculiar character of Osiris,' says Sir Gardner Wilkinson, 'his coming upon Earth for the benefit of mankind, with the title of "Manifester of Good" and "Revealer of Truth ;" his being put to death by the Malice of the Evil One; his burial and Resurrection, and his becoming the Judge of the Dead, are the most interesting features of the Egyptian Religion. This was the great mystery; and this myth and his worship were of the earliest times and universal in Egypt.'* And, with this central doctrine of Osirianism, so perfectly similar to that of Christianism, doctrines are associated precisely analogous to those associated in Christianism with its central doctrine. In ancient Osirianism, as in modern Christianism, the Godhead is conceived as a Trinity, yet are the three Gods declared to be only one God. In ancient Osirianism, as in modern Christianism, we find the worship of a Divine Mother and Child. In ancient Osirianism, as in modern Christianism, there is a doctrine of Atonement. In ancient Osirianism, as in modern Christianism, we find the vision of a Last Judgment, and Resurrection of the Body. And finally, in ancient Osirianism, as in modern Christianism, the sanctions of morality are a Lake of Fire and tormenting Demons, on the one hand, and on the other, Eternal Life in the presence

---

* *Ancient Egyptians* (Popular Edition), vol. i. p. 331. Compare Second Series of the larger work, vol. I. p. 320.

of God. Is it possible, then, that such similarities of doctrines should not raise the most serious questions as to the relation of the beliefs about Christ to those about Osiris; as to the cause of this wonderful similarity of the doctrines of Christianism to those of Osirianism; nay, as to the possibility of the whole doctrinal system of Modern Orthodoxy being but a transformation of the Osiris-myth? But if so—you logically argue with amazed incredulity—all the most sacred dogmas of the Christian faith would be proved to have originated but in the influence of a 'heathen' religion—a religion over the scenes of which we Christians ordinarily pass with the most complacent contempt? Nay, if so; if the doctrines of Christianism had but such an origin; must not the Christian 'Revelation' be acknowledged utterly worthless to prove the reality of any one of the supernatural facts which its doctrines affirm—even a Personal Immortality, for instance, or a Personal God?

7. Well, be the consequences what they may, we must find out what is the fact. And there is certainly no escape in the desperate hypothesis to which the manifestly Christian character of Osirianism has driven some to have recourse—the hypothesis that these doctrines of Osirianism were, somehow or other, themselves a 'supernatural revelation.' For the discovery of Osirianism is the discovery of the missing link between Christianism and Heathenism generally, the religions of the First Age of Humanity, or what I have termed Naturianism. It has hitherto appeared not only a crime but a blunder, not merely a blasphemy but a frivolity, to compare the Christian doctrines of the Trinity, of the Incarnation, and of the Death and Resurrection of Christ with the similar doctrines of Naturian Religions. But the doctrines of a Trinity, of an Incarnation, and of the Death and Resurrection of a God-man are

Christ and Osiris. 15

developed in Osirianism with such gravity, such moral purity, and such splendour, that we cannot hesitate to honour them by a comparison with these doctrines as developed in Christianism. Yet, from Osirianism the gradation is so gentle through the whole series of Nature-worships down to the lowest, that, having compared the story and worship of Christ with the worship and myth of Osiris, we find ourselves necessarily comparing the Christian story and worship with the worship and myth of Dionysus, nay, of Adonis, and of Thammuz,—of Thammuz,

> Whose annual wound in Lebanon allured
> The Syrian damsels to lament his fate,
> In amorous ditties all a summer's day.*

And hence if, to support the common belief in the supernatural origin of Christianism, it is concluded that the manifestly similar and unquestionably earlier doctrines of Osirianism had a supernatural origin; then, as we thus find it impossible to draw a line separating the highest of the Heathen religions from the lowest, a supernatural origin must also be supposed for all those Heathen religions in which we find—and where do we not find?—the story of a divine man dying, and—though but to rise again—' in amorous ditties' annually lamented.† But so great are the interests at stake, that even an hypothesis so wild as this, it may be attempted to defend. For, as has just been suggested, if these Heathen beliefs in the incarnation of a God-man, and in Heaven and Hell, have no sort of supernatural authority; and if Osirianism is, indeed, the missing link that connects Christianism with every one of

---

* Milton, *Paradise Lost.*
† Λῆγε γόων, Κυθέρεια, τὸ σήμερον ἴσχεο κομμῶν.
Δεῖ σε πάλιν κλαῦσαι, πάλιν εἰς ἔτος ἄλλο δακρῦσαι.
Bion, *Epitaph. Adon.*

these religions; what authority is there for the objective reality of any one of those supernatural existences, belief in which is thus found to be common to Christianism, and Heathenism generally? An attempt, therefore, will doubtless be made to prove the supernatural and divine origin of Heathenism. And truly, when we recall Christian denunciations of, and missions to the 'Heathen;' when we find that the essential doctrines of 'Heathenism' are, just as in Christianism, a Trinity, an Incarnation, and a Future State of Reward and Punishment; hence that—as such doctrines can have no guarantee of objective reality, except they have had a supernatural origin—*all* must have had such an origin, or none; and hence that, to guarantee the validity of their own beliefs, Christians must maintain the divine origin of those of Heathenism; there is seen such a profound and tragic irony in the situation that we become more than ever attached to the study of that sublime drama—the history of Man.

8. Any hope, however, of establishing a theory of the supernatural origin of the doctrines of Osirianism, how 'Christian' soever they may be, has had, I trust the ground cut from under it, by the facts, in the foregoing chapter brought together, in explanation of these doctrines as *myths*. For, before any theory of the supernatural origin of these doctrines can be maintained, the facts must be met which were in the foregoing chapter summarised as explanatory of the *origin* of the myths of Naturianism. These facts were, as will be remembered, first, those which define the character of the spontaneity of Mind; secondly, the facts of the conditions under which that spontaneity worked in primæval societies; and thirdly, those explanations of modern spiritist conceptions which confirm the theory by which we explain the origin of primitive spiritist conceptions. Before any rational attempt, therefore, any attempt worthy of

Christ and Osiris. 17

scientific notice, can be made to account for the Christian character of the doctrines of Osirianism, and of the other 'Heathen' religions, by attributing to them some sort of supernatural origin in a 'primitive revelation;' those three great classes of facts, psychological, economical, and physio-psychological, in the foregoing chapter summarised, must be shown to be, not only severally, but jointly inadequate to explain, as not only of a natural, but as of a very low natural origin, the formation of such doctrines as those which give to Osirianism its Christian character. Nor are these the only facts which must be met before a scientific hearing even can be gained for any hypothesis that would give to the doctrines, whether Christian or Osirian, of a Trinity, a life, death, and resurrection of a God-man, and an Other-world of Reward and Punishment, any sort of supernatural origin, and hence any degree of authoritative sanction. For besides the great classes of facts just specified, those also must be met which, in proving the conception of Mutual Determination to be the true and ultimate conception of Causation, show such hypotheses, as this of a supernatural origin of these doctrines, to belong properly only to, or to be derived from, the earlier, and more ignorant stages of men's knowledge of the relations of things. But these facts have not as yet been met by any of the arguers for the supernatural origin, and therefore authoritative truth of theological doctrines. We must conclude, therefore, that if, similar though the doctrines of Christianism are to the myths of Osirianism, and of Naturianism generally, a special and independent origin *cannot* be proved for them; they were but derived from, or but transformations of these myths. And if so, then, belief in them has, at bottom, no diviner sanction than the labour-driven ignorance, and priest-ridden servility which—resulting from the economical conditions under which mental spontaneities originally worked—led to what were but the mere subjective fictions of the myth-creating imagination being taken for objective realities. Our hypothesis, as it first presented itself, was simply, that the similarity of the doctrines of Osirianism to those of Christianism was such as to be naturally explained only by showing that the earlier importantly influenced the development of the later Creed. We now, however, see that, if it is to such an origin that the doctrines of Christianism are to be traced, we cannot stop here. If the Christian doctrines of the Trinity, Incarnation, and Other-world, are in any way to be derived from the myths of Osirianism, or generally, of Naturianism; they had in these myths but their proximate origin. Their ultimate origin must, therefore, have been identical with the origin of these myths; and, like that, to be found but in those base conditions, in the foregoing chapter set forth, of primitive spiritist conceptions.

9. Unquestionably, the verification of an hypothesis which, to such an origin as this, would trace the myths of Christianity, is of the very gravest import. For it is almost incredibly tragical, that the sorrow of a Milton, for instance, in meditating on the death of Christ, had—so far as that sorrow was occasioned by the thought of a divine person, an incarnate God, who had come voluntarily on earth for the good of mankind—no more ground of actual objective fact than had the lamentations of the Syrian damsels, whom the great Christian poet, all unconscious of being himself the victim of a similar bitter-sweet delusion, scornfully represents as, 'in amorous ditties,' bewailing such a fiction of their own imaginations as a Thammuz or Adonis. And yet, if we consider the hypothesis here suggested, on the Temple-roof at Karnak, in relation to our Ultimate Law of History, we shall see that such an origin as we have here been led to suppose for the doctrines of Christianism—we

shall see that a transformation of the myths of Naturianism in such doctrines as those of Christianism—is but a deduction from our Ultimate Law, and a deduction, the verification of which will be one of the most important verifications of that Law. For, of that Law the great central affirmation is, that the passage from the earlier to the later mode of conceiving Causation is through a transitional age marked by the differentiation of Subjective and Objective; a differentiation implying a great development of individuality, of subjectivity, of morality; but not a differentiation implying anything more than greater abstractness merely in the primitive spiritist conception of Causation. But if so, then it will evidently follow that the spiritist beliefs which have dominated the First Age of Humanity, will not be destroyed, but only undergo a *moral* transformation. And what is it that we find in the doctrines of Christianism but just this—all the old myths of Osirianism revived in such an identical fashion *intellectually*, that,—put but Christ for Osiris,—and the general description of the one creed is an accurate description of the other? Only in the moral spirit of Christianism is there a change. But this is just what, from our Ultimate Law of History, we should expect to find; and the fact, therefore, which can be for it but a most important verification. This changed moral spirit, however, in no way affects the objective validity of the myths in which it is expressed. These continue to be but a *language;* a language in which other sentiments were expressed before Christianity; and a language which, after Christianity, will still survive for the expression of ideal emotion. And shocking though to some may be the thought of the utter unreality of the supernatural beings affirmed by Christianism, as by Osirianism; such is the spectacle here, at Karnak, presented, of the sublime tragedy of Human Existence; that, if it is in any degree duly felt, it will be impossible for one to shrink from clearly stating to oneself the truth, however destructive it may be. As other Ideals have perished, so,—it would be presumptuous to deny,—may ours. Very far are we from being the first who have experienced the agony of discovered delusion.

ORIGIN OF THE LEGENDS

OF

ABRAHAM, ISAAC, AND JACOB.

CRITICALLY EXAMINED

BY

A. BERNSTEIN.

TRANSLATED FROM THE GERMAN.

PUBLISHED BY THOMAS SCOTT,

NO. 11 THE TERRACE, FARQUHAR ROAD,
UPPER NORWOOD, LONDON, S.E.

Price One Shilling.

NOTICE BY THE EDITOR.

WE publish this very ingenious and somewhat extraordinary little work, for the sake of the many valuable suggestions it contains.

We cannot, however, do so without at the same time expressing our regret, that the author has not availed himself of the assured results of modern criticism on the language of Genesis.

He has thus allowed himself to drift into theories respecting the harmonisation of the legends of the patriarchs, which we cannot regard as conclusive.

On the other hand, it is satisfactory to see that, though arrived at through a very different process, the author gives the time of Rehoboam and Jeroboam as that of the principal actors in the legends; thus agreeing very nearly with the time ascribed to their composition by the Bishop of Natal, namely, the early part of the reign of David and Solomon.

NOTICE BY THE TRANSLATOR.

THE translator of this little work knows well that she has to ask the forbearance of its readers for many defects of style and inelegancies of expression.

In performing her task, however, she preferred a literal translation to the chance of weakening, by freedom, many of the subtle ideas of the author.

She hopes she will be sufficiently excused when she signs herself

A GERMAN LADY.

PREFACE.

THE scientific examination of the Bible-text, and particularly of the first Book of Moses, has long ago put beyond doubt the fact, that that Book is not an original work, the composition of one author, but an adaptation and agglomeration of *earlier writings* upon the like subject, which have been lost; we can, however, in its present form, appreciably discern the earlier writings. The most gifted and learned critics of our time have endeavoured, with extraordinary zeal and talent, to draw this distinction, even now a great task, the conclusion of which is still far in the distance.

The examination of the Text, however, has left almost untouched one preliminary question, which, in our opinion, is of essential influence upon the final result. This preliminary question is, whether the lost original writings, which are the foundation of the present Text, were consistent with each other, or whether they were not rather writings of a partisan character, which originally *conflicted*, and were, only later, at the termination of the contest, *moulded* into consistent history. We are led to make this preliminary enquiry by reason of important historical facts.

The Hebrew people, the remains of whose literature we have before us in the shape of the Old Testament, not only was, like every people, split into parties, but up to a thousand years before our Chronology, consisted of ten or twelve Republican Cantons which often warred with each other. These Cantons, however, were united into a complete Monarchy, first under Saul, then under David and his son Solomon: but after the death of Solomon (about a hundred years after the Union), the monarchy split into *two* kingdoms which engaged in sanguinary wars with each other. Now, the first Book of Moses is a work which evidently was not written till after kings existed in Israel. Without referring to innumerable scientific proofs of this fact, verse 31, chapter xxxvi., is so convincing, that all attempts of orthodoxy to prove the Book to be *older*, are and must remain mere subterfuges. The verse runs thus, "*And these are the kings that reigned in the land of Edom, before there reigned any king over the children of Israel.*" The author of Genesis, therefore, was well aware of the Monarchical period in Israel. As that period, comprising two centuries and a half, was, with few exceptions, replete with sanguinary wars and violent conflicts, between the two kingdoms of Judah and Israel, it is probable, that the lost original writings, which are at the foundation of our present Text, may have reflected these continuous feuds in their polemics.

During the examination of this question, possibility has grown with us to certainty. We believe we shall be able to prove in the history now before us of the Patriarchs, Abraham, Isaac, and Jacob, that the traditions upon which it is based, have been of a most conflicting nature. And this proof is the subject of the present work.

In publishing this, we are fully aware, that in elucidating the truth, many hard struggles will be necessary. Not, indeed, with Orthodoxy, which has long become too self-satisfied to care for the results of mere science. Now and then it puts its feelers out of its snail's shell of Belief, to see if science, as prophesied by the luminaries of theology, has mended its ways, and become a convert to Faith. But as that is not the case, and, as Orthodoxy knows very well, *never* will be, it withdraws its feelers piously, and retreats self-contented into its well-furnished little shell. The struggle which this work will have to maintain, is with traditional views, which obstinately sway even severely-searching science, and which are conquered with the greatest difficulty, when they are already fitted into a successful system of research.

One of these views, is the division into *Elohistic* and *Jehovistic* portions, the happy results of which we fully acknowledge. In the following work, we have, upon principle, avoided this division, not that we think it unnecessary, but that we wish to point out a separation of older date. The *Legends* are *older* than the *Writings*. The severing and separating of the *Legends* must practically *precede* the severing and separating of the Writings. Should we succeed in establishing a firm position for this preliminary work, the further task of separating the Writings may, we hope, the way being cleared, be continued with better success.

A. BERNSTEIN.

BERLIN, *January* 1871.

ORIGIN OF THE LEGENDS OF ABRAHAM, ISAAC, AND JACOB.

I.

LEGEND AND HISTORY.

POPULAR Legend is not the history of the nation, but in its wonderful accounts it reflects the wishes and hopes of a people, which form the basis of their history. The tales about the origin of a people embody the poetical conceptions of the race concerning their past—conceptions framed in accordance with the notions and prevailing tendencies of the time, in which they originated. The description of the lives and deeds of our forefathers, in the dim past, have their true value, only as revelations of the tendencies whence those descriptions sprang. They do not enlighten the darkness of the primitive period they trace, but they cast an interesting light upon the times in which they were thought out and written down.

This applies, in common with other peoples, also to the Hebrews, and to their cycle of legends about the supposed ancestors of their nation. The family history of Abraham, Isaac, and Jacob, though not historical in itself, affords us a historic insight into that period, during which those legends first originated, and were ultimately collected and written down. Although a critical review of these family stories, of their origin and development, destroys the current assumption, that we can know anything about the times thirty-five hundred years ago, it still yields rich results, as it throws light upon the social and intellectual condition of the people out of which these legends arose about twenty-five hundred years ago. To clear up the subject from this latter point of view is the purpose of the following examination.

II.
The Names of the Patriarchs.

It may be suitable to devote a few words to a consideration of the names of the three Patriarchs.

The names of "Abram" or "Abraham," "Isaac," properly "Itzchak," or "Ischak," and "Jacob" occur but once in the Bible. Although the Bible comprises a period of thousands of years in history, and presents thousands of names of historical persons, yet the hypothetical names of the Patriarchs are exclusively appropriated to these hypothetical personages, and are given to no one else. This isolation of names, recurs, however, with other persons, as, for instance, with the sons of Jacob, and with Moses and Aaron, and is, therefore, not so much a matter of surprise with the Patriarchs. Still, with some exceptions, this occurs only in the case of persons who do not belong to history, but to legend. Such names, therefore, must not be regarded as accidental but as premeditated, and so to say, provisory, indicating the fate of the persons to whom they belong. Care is also taken in the legendary reports of them, to *supply motives* for the names, and thus to indicate that persons are mentioned, whose names have had to be invented along with their deeds. This remark refers to the names of the three Patriarchs alike; though there are essential differences in the meaning and origin of them. The name of "Abram" has a very suitable significance. It means "high Father," and, for a Patriarch, is certainly very appropriate. Possibly it may have the signification of "Father of Aram," or "Father from Aram," in Mesopotamia, whence the Patriarch is said to have migrated to Palestine. This signification fully agrees with the character of the person as legend has created it. The legend tells us too, that at a certain time of his life he received a new name from Jehovah, the name of "*Abraham*," as a sign that he was destined to be the "Father of many nations," a signification which, with some ingenuity, may be given to the name. It is self-evident, however, that one would not designate a new-born infant, as "High Father," or "Father of many people." Nor has the human mind the power to foresee in the lifetime of a man, whether his descendants will constitute a great people. Entirely impossible was this, in the lifetime of Abraham, as one hundred and fifteen years after his death, according to Biblical chronology, his supposed grandson, Jacob, undertook the migration to Egypt, accompanied by only seventy persons, who were all the family he had. The name of Abram or Abraham being uncommon, we must conclude, that the Patriarch, even if he had existed, as the first Book of Moses describes him, never could have borne this name in his lifetime.

The name of Isaac, properly Itzchak or Ischak, although uncommon, has a signification, which renders its bestowal less improbable. Its meaning is very unpretending, and as it is more probable that a remarkable man should bear an insignificant name, than that the greatness of a man should coincide with the pregnant import of his name, we cannot very well raise a doubt as to the name of Itzchak, or Ischak, provided, of course, the existence of the Patriarch can be established. The more striking is the fact, that in the first Book of Moses, uncommon pains are taken to throw, directly and indirectly, a light upon the signification of this name. Literally, the name means "he laughs," "he jokes," "he kisses," "he rejoices," or, as a proper name, "the laughing one," "the joking one," "the joyful one," &c. To give such a name to a child requires no explanation. Still the author introduces a variety of incidents, with no other purpose than to justify this harmless name. First of all, God (Elohim) (Gen. xvii. 17, &c.) announces to Abraham the birth of a son, whereupon Abraham falls upon his face and "laughs," in consequence of which Elohim commands him to call the son "Itzchak" (Isaac). Soon after, (Gen. xviii. 10) one of the guests predicts to Abraham the event, already sufficiently guaranteed by a higher authority. Sarah, the wife of Abraham, standing inside the door of the tent, hears the prophecy, and "*she laughs.*" Jehovah calls Abraham to account about this incredulous laughter, and Scripture tells us that he reproaches his wife, but she denies the fact absolutely, and Abraham, evidently indignant, exclaims, "Nay, but thou didst laugh." In due course, we are further told (Gen. xxi. 1-10), that the Son is born, and called Isaac, Itzchak. Again Sarah says, "God hath made me to *laugh*, so that all that hear will laugh with me." These direct allusions and interpretations are followed by many a story, alluding to laughter and sport in connection with Isaac. Thus Sarah sees with jealousy, that Ishmael, the son of Abraham and the bond-woman Hagar, *laughs and sports*, a gaiety which she considers the exclusive privilege of her son. Later on, (Gen. xxvi. 8) King Abimelech of Gerar, perceives that Isaac *laughs or sports* with Rebekah, his wife. Now, when we consider how few are the events in the Patriarch's life transmitted to us, subtracting what belongs to the history of Abraham and Jacob, how little remains, we are inclined to say, that there is nothing peculiar to Isaac, but his name and its conspicuously frequent interpretation. We are thus constrained to think that there is a more serious reason for this name than appears on the surface.

The strangest name is that of "Jacob." If "Abraham" is suspicious, because it agrees too well with a Patriarch's position in history, the name of Jacob, on the other hand, startles us by its *dishonour-*

Abraham, Isaac, and Jacob. 11

able signification. Jacob means, "impostor," somebody who catches hold of his neighbour's heel to trip him up. The latter meaning is illustrated by the political narrator himself. (Gen. xxv. 26). In the metaphorical signification, the narrator represents Esau as explaining the name by the apparently well-founded exclamation "is he not rightly named *Jacob*, for he hath supplanted me these two times"? A name of such dishonourable meaning may have been accidentally given to a child, who afterwards grew up to importance, supposing that name to be so common, as to have lost all implication of insult. When however, as in this instance, the name is quite uncommon, one has reason to suspect other motives for its origin. Now, had Jacob's life been free from any moral blame, one might still believe he had come by his name accidentally. But there are recorded in the history of his life, so many incidents which prove him worthy of his name, that one cannot help supposing that it was designedly given. Inquiry into the origin of the appellation is therefore justified. Besides, there is the circumstance, that another name "Israel," which evidently has a glorifying signification, is also given to Jacob. Whether Israel may mean "Conqueror of a God" or "Champion for God," or "El rules," it unmistakeably points to the intention to substitute a sublime name for an ignoble one. Two distinct versions are given of the bestowal of the name of Israel, (Gen. xxxii. 28, xxxv. 10), it being particularly enjoined on either occasion " thy name shall be called no more Jacob." The name of Israel is also phonetically so widely different from that of Jacob, that one cannot at all place this change of name in analogy with the change from Abram into Abraham. The more surprising therefore is it, that the narrator in the first book of Moses entirely drops the name of Abram after its change, and only speaks of "Abraham," whilst he scarcely heeds the change of Jacob's name, although it is so much more important, and so evidently designed to glorify the patriarch. Notwithstanding the two-fold injunction against the use of the old name "Jacob," it is, except in some trifling matters, employed throughout. Yes, the same Elohe, who had twice prohibited the name of "Jacob" and imposed "Israel" in its stead, is represented by the narrator (Gen. xlvi. 2) as calling Israel with particular stress "Jacob, Jacob." Thus, the names of the Patriarchs offer many a puzzle, for the solution of which we are compelled to look more closely into the accounts given of their lives.

III.

THE TERRITORIAL HOME.

The enquiry leads us next to another point which is of essential influence upon the origin of the legends; we mean, the question of territory, where the legends sought their theatre, and where they also as a rule originated.

Although the scene of the lives and deeds of the Patriarchs seems, in general, to be one and the same, it is in particular, thoroughly different. Abraham, migrating from Mesopotamia, and at Jehovah's bidding, "walking through the land in the length of it and in the breadth of it," (Gen. xiii. 17), settled down finally about Hebron, the oldest town in what was later the kingdom of Judah. He is said though, to have sojourned many days in the land of the Philistines (Gen. xxi. 34), but this assertion, which we shall consider further on, does not alter the fact, that Hebron was his chief abode. There he obtained, after his return from Egypt and his particularly defined separation from Lot, the promise of property for his progeny, and there he built an altar to Jehovah. There he received the news of the defeat of the kings of the land and of the imprisonment of Lot, and thence proceeded with his men to beat the enemy, but far beyond the most northern frontier of the land (Gen. xiv. 13). There also the promise of issue was vouchsafed to him. The narrator, however, (Gen. xx. 1) lets him set out on a journey towards the south, and sojourn there in the land of the Philistines in Gerar. There apparently Isaac was born; there also Abraham concluded an agreement with Abimelech, in whose country he sojourned for a long time, but did not settle, as is evidently purposely indicated by the word ויגר (Gen. xxi. 34), in antithesis to וישב (Gen. xx. i.; xxii. 19). One abode of Abraham was also in the vicinity of Gerar, in Beersheba, which belonged to the kingdom of Judah. Thence he began his journey to Moriah, where Isaac was to be immolated. Abraham also returned there, to dwell. Still, even the abode in Beersheba was not the real one of the patriarch. We find it mentioned that his wife Sarah died in *Hebron*, and that Abraham called himself a "stranger and a sojourner in the place," גר ותושב a stranger, though a resident, (Gen. xxiii. 4.) Then the purchase of a hereditary burying-place was concluded with great formality, and particular stress is laid upon its possession being honestly acquired by purchase. There also, in all probability, Abraham died, and there, as is specially mentioned, was buried. From all these facts we are justified in concluding that Hebron was the chief abode of Abraham, and that only peculiar circumstances made his timely appearance in other countries necessary.

The scene in which Isaac appeared and always remained, was the utmost south of the kingdom, where the land of the Philistines, the land of Edom, the desert, and the frontier town Beersheba, border upon each other. There he was born. After his wanderings with Abraham, who intended to sacrifice him on a mountain in the land of Moriah, he returned with him (Gen. xxii. 19) to Beersheba. Not far off, in the desert near the well Lachai-roi, was his abode, where his wife was introduced to him. (Gen. xxiv. 62.) There also his sons Esau and Jacob were born to him. A famine, which caused him to migrate, did not carry him further than Gerar in the land of the Philistines (xxvi. 1), whence he returned home to Beersheba and there he lived in his old age, stricken blind (xxvii. 1.) If Isaac had ever left this locality, it can, according to the narrator, have been only temporarily, and for the purpose of burying Abraham. (Gen. xxv. 9.) The more remarkable is it that the narrator further on (Gen. xxxv. 27), still shows Isaac living in *Hebron*, even with this addition, contrary to all former statements, "*where Abraham and Isaac sojourned.*" Excepting this passage, we see in Isaac a patriarch whose whole life was passed in a small district, with Beersheba, which is situated on the very frontier of Palestine, as a centre.

The narrative about the patriarch Jacob leads us into very different territory. He started from Beersheba, the alleged abode of his father, and went to Haran in Mesopotamia, where he remained for about twenty years. But already, on his journey there, his elaborately related dream (Gen. xxviii. 10, &c.) caused him to consecrate a place, and even to endow it with the name of "Bethel," a place which was destined to be the centre of worship in Israel. On his return—the history of his life says—a meeting with Laban caused him to give the name of Gilead to the frontier mountains of Israel. The town of Mizpah also received its name from Jacob, and so did Mahanaim. Crossing the Jabbok an event occurred which caused him to call the place Peniel. Not far from thence he built booths for his cattle, and called the place Succoth. He afterwards reached Shechem (Gen. xxxiii. 18), where he bought part of a field for current money. There he erected an altar, calling it "El, God of Israel." Later on we find a double scene related with many essential differences, in which, however (xxxv. 1-15), it is agreed that Jacob again went to Bethel and gave that place its historical name. In the one narrative (Gen. xxxv. 1) God commanded Jacob to *dwell** in Bethel. Notwithstanding, we soon hear that he wandered from Bethel to a place called "Ephrath" (xxxv. 16), where Rachel, Jacob's wife, is said to have died and to have been buried after the birth of his son Benjamin. Another place where Jacob pitched his tent is called Migdal-Eder. (xxxv. 21.) At last, we hear (Gen. xxxv. 27) that Jacob came to Hebron, and there (Gen. xxxvii. 14), where Joseph separated from him, Jacob seems to have dwelt until, in accordance with Joseph's wish, he migrated to Egypt. Again, he halted at Beer-sheba, and travelled to Egypt, where he ended his life. Considering all these wanderings, we observe that with Jacob's history there is connected a series of new places, which are said to have gained importance only through him. Most prominent amongst them is Bethel, which no less than three times was invested by him with that solemn name, so that one sees at once that in this place, geographically, the point of his life lay. Remarkably enough, all the places which date their names from Jacob's visit, are, like Bethel, situated in the territory of what was, later on, the *Israelitic* kingdom.

Characterising the three patriarchs, externally, after the chief geographical places which are given as scenes of their existence, we must say that Abraham was the patriarch of Hebron, consequently of the *Judaic* territory; Jacob, as decidedly the patriarch of Bethel, consequently of the *Israelitic* territory; whilst, on the other hand, Isaac held a most limited geographical territory, in the south of the country, in Beer-sheba.

It is true, however, that the narrative brings Abraham in his migration unto the place of Shecem. (Gen. xii. 6.) Bethel and Ai are also mentioned, as the two places *between* which Abraham pitched his tent, and where he erected altars and invoked the name of "Jehovah," but it can certainly not be without intention that

* וישב שם, and dwell there.

the narrator does not let Abraham visit these places, and only lets him take his principal abode in Hebron. (Gen. xiii. 18.) Equally characteristic is it in the history of Jacob, that he gives names and importance to the places only whilst he is travelling in *Israelitic* territory, but that this *influence instantly ceases* when he is on *Judaic* ground.

After all, taking the places Hebron, Beer-sheba, and Bethel to be the three ancestral seats of the three patriarchs, Abraham, Isaac, and Jacob, we have reason to suppose that upon a closer view of these ancestral homes many an enigma about the narrative of the patriarchs may be solved.

IV.

INFERENCES ABOUT THE ORIGIN OF THE LEGENDS.

In order to find a solution of the problem, we must, first of all, oppose the idea, that the narratives of the lives of the Patriarchs were founded on traditions of the times in which they are assumed to have existed. On the contrary, an unbiassed critic can have no doubt, that all so-called *historical* representations of ancestors, Patriarchs of a people, belong to legend. This legend is not, by any means, as old as the people, but only develops itself, when a people has long existed as such, and has a particular interest, political or religious, to date their origin, in the most simple manner possible, from one family, and from one highly-praised ancestor. In truth, a people never can issue from one ancestral couple immigrating into a country. It needs a thousand years of completely undisturbed multiplication of the descendants of one couple, to form a population. A tranquillity like that, has never been, nor will ever be enjoyed by a people. The changes of destiny, on the contrary, push multitudes through multitudes, annihilate old families, and bring new ones forward, which commingle and never can trace their origin upwards to

Abraham, Isaac, and Jacob.

the first genealogical point. Even in modern times, when America shows an example of immigration entering at once into civilization, and where historical documents are able to prove the course of development, there is not a single instance when a family, even in a small way, has developed into a separate people. In times of old, however, where only tradition records family history, and especially in countries where there was immigration into densely peopled territories, and where wars of centuries have not yet extinguished the original inhabitants, there, any tradition of ancestors, whose descendants form one people, is nothing but a fancy, which was fostered and nursed by the people and ornamented according to want and local conditions, to be then accepted and believed as history.

This view, founded on unprejudiced hypotheses, leads us to think, that the histories of the three patriarchs, alleged to have dwelt in three different parts of Palestine, had not originally their *present coherence*. Every circle of legends about the life of a patriarch seems to us rather to have originated *separately*, and in the very place which pretends to have been the chief abode of the patriarchs. Consequently each of these legends has developed itself separately, and borrowed its colouring from its locality, and from the tendencies circulating there. The particular legends are of very different dates, and have only by degrees amplified and formed into cycles. In order to understand the present setting of the legends which have been worked into one family history, we must, first of all, divide them into their original forms, and doing so, we arrive at the following results, for which we will furnish proofs, as far as they can be gained from the existing material.

The results of our enquiries are the following :—
1. Each of the patriarchal legends stands in politically religious connexion with the place where its hero is said to have lived.

2. Between the three legends there exists no such harmony as would appear from their present form; on the contrary, each of the three patriarchs formed, originally, a strongly marked politically religious contrast to the other.
3. By the side of a worship and a patriarch, originating in the republican time of the Hebrew people, and particularly of local duration in Beersheba, there developed itself a worship, and a legend adorning such worship, in each of the two kingdoms under which the Hebrew people lived for a long time.
4. As long as there were conflicts between the kingdom of Judah, and the kingdom of Israel, a violent conflict was also kept alive in the mouth of the people, at the two chief places of worship, concerning the true patriarch, whilst the spurious one was designated an impostor.
5. The contest about the real patriarch subsided when the violent wars, and the jealousies of the kingdoms terminated, and when the populations were more and more animated by a consciousness of their connexion with each other. When the kingdom of Israel had perished entirely, the legends began to blend, and finally formed a family history of harmonious coherence. *Abraham*, *Isaac*, and *Jacob*, who had originally been contrasts to each other, grew by degrees to be *Father*, *Son* and *Grandson*. Thus sprang through narrative and ingenious journeys from place to place, the coherence, which now presents itself as "history."

We intend to introduce, in order, the detailed proofs of these views.

Abraham, Isaac, and Jacob. 19

V.

WORSHIP AND PATRIARCH IN BEER-SHEBA.

It is a long acknowledged truth, that the places of worship are also the native places of the legends of a people. At the same time, it is in the interest of the guardians of the worship, to give to those places the holiness and sanctity of great age, and to throw the legends into the greatest possible depths of antiquity, when an ancestor of the present people had ascertained or even founded the holiness of the place.

"Hebron," "Beer-sheba," and "Beth-el," are such places of worship; they did *not even* harmonise, but disputed about precedence. If in each place a separate legend of a patriarch was developed, intended to make the place sacred, it is natural, that the patriarchs also should have presented contrasts.

Beersheba appears to be the oldest of the three places of worship, although Hebron claims a greater age. (Numb. xiii. 22). First of all, the situation of Beersheba was very suitable for such a place. At the most southern point of Palestine, near to the desert which bordered upon the land of the Philistines, the territory of Edom, and the abode of the Bedouin races, such a place was one of necessity to all travellers, where they could find protection and counsel in misfortune, comfort and hope before impending dangers, and opportunity for thanksgivings and sacrifices, after past dangers. The name of the place is also explained in such a way, that Abraham and Abimelech, the king of the Philistines, vowed to each other, with an oath, "that child and child's child should not make war upon each other." It was a sort of city of covenant, consecrated by the holy number of *seven*, as it is said in one passage (Gen. xxi. 28) that Abraham made Abimelech a present of *seven ewe lambs*, and in another, that Isaac digged, or digged up again, *seven wells* in this part. (Gen. xxvi. 33). A circumstance which indicates the great age of Beer-sheba as a place of worship, is, that its specific patriarch Isaac, when he makes his appearance, is scarcely recognisable. Not one of his actions is his incontestable property. Of the occurrences in his life, there is not one especially traceable to him. Subtracting from the scenes before us, what belongs to Abraham's and to Jacob's history, nothing remains for Isaac but an empty name, for which the narrator continually gives new motives.

Such a pallid representation of a patriarch is most likely to show a higher antiquity than that of the others. But there are further circumstances added, which make this age more probable.

What kind of worship was reigning there can no more be ascertained. The old prophet Amos from Tekoa, a town only a few miles distant from Beersheba, declaims against the pilgrimage to Beersheba. (Amos v. 5.) He exhorts them to avoid this place of idolatry, and not to consult its oracle: "But seek not Beth-el, nor enter into Gilgal, and pass not to Beer-sheba." Further on: (Amos viii. 13, 14.) "In that day," when the judgment of God will arrive, "shall the fair virgins and young men faint for thirst, they that swear by the sin of Samaria, and say: Thy God, oh Dan, liveth, and the manner of Beer-sheba liveth—even they shall fall and never rise up again." This prophet, the oldest, whose words have come down to us, is the only one who knows anything of the worship reigning in Beer-sheba, but he is also the only one who mentions the name of Isaac. (יִשְׂחָק Ischak). He prophesies that the high places of Isaac shall be desolate." (Amos vii. 9) He is indignant, because the priest of Bethel tries to induce the king to forbid him inveighing against the "*house of Isaac.*" Not without importance for our subject is the fact, that the priest of Bethel says to Amos: "O thou seer, go flee thee away into the land of Judah, and there eat bread, and prophesy there." (Amos vii. 12). The advice of the priest indicates to the prophet the land of Judah, where such speeches against the heights of worship, against the house of Isaac, and the sanctuary of Jacob in Beth-el, would be listened to with favour, and would earn the prophet a living.

From all this we may conclude that, at the time of Amos, the worship in Beer-sheba was still practised and gave support to the legends of an ancestor Isaac. But the flowery period of this worship must have soon passed away, because the other prophets who lived and worked scarcely half a century after Amos, speak only of Beth-el and do not mention Beer-sheba, and because they do not refer to a knowledge of the patriarch Isaac. This fact is not astonishing with Isaiah, because this most sublime prophet avoids throughout, all traditional allusions, and mentions neither Abraham nor Jacob as patriarchs, nor Moses and his guidance. But his contemporary, the prophet Micah, who is full of traditional reminiscences of legends, who speaks of Moses, Aaron, and Miriam as the heralds of God, who reminds us of the peculiar events between Balak and Balaam, finishes with bright hopes for a better future, when Jehovah will take compassion and "perform the truth to *Jacob* and the mercy to *Abraham*, which thou hast sworn unto our fathers from the days of old." (Micah vii. 20). *That no reference is made here to Isaac is certainly not accidental.*

Thus we are only limited to speculation about the worship in Beer-sheba. Perhaps the God who was worshipped there bore the name of " Pachad" פחד " fear," " terror." Anyhow, it is remarkable that in one and the same scene between Jacob and Laban, the God of Isaac is twice designated by the word " Pachad." (Gen. xxxi. 42 and 53). As Itzchak or Ischak expresses the contrary of terror, viz., " joy," " laughter," it is possible that the worship in Beer-sheba was founded on the very contrast of these sensations. *The fear, the terror of the Desert, and the rejoicing, the laughter, on returning thence to the inhabited places of Beersheba, may* very appropriately have been symbolised by a God and a protecting patriarch.

The part which legend assigns to Isaac is also quite appropriate to the position of Beer-sheba. The terrors of the adjacent desert consisted in want of water, and in warlike and rapacious attacks by neighbouring people, such as the Philistines, the Edomites, and the Ishmaelites, who roved through the desert in hordes. The legend equips Isaac well for a protector against all those evils. It ascribes to him the merit of having dug seven wells. Beer-sheba is said to have been the seventh of these wells, and therefore to have received the name of "Seven wells." (Gen. xxvi. 33.) Isaac is also said to have been the brother of Ishmael and the father of Esau (Edom), and to have *loved the latter particularly well*. He is said to have concluded treaties of intimate friendship with the Philistines, and, upon a wish of the king Abimelech, to have sworn mutual peace. The traveller, therefore, who had shewn reverence to the "Pachad" of Isaac, and legitimated himself as belonging to the house of Isaac, was justified in the belief that he would be protected in the desert from the faintness of thirst, and shielded against attacks.

We are well justified in a further hypothesis about the age and the disappearance of the worship in Beer-sheba, when we consider the fate of Beer-sheba itself.

According to the dates in the book of Joshua, it follows that in the old republican times the town of Beer-sheba belonged to the canton of Simeon. This canton, or tribe of Simeon, which is stated to have undertaken the war of conquest against the original inhabitants, jointly with the canton of Judah, disappears, however, very soon from history. One does not know what became of the tribe of Simeon, whether they were banished in a war, annihilated, or whether they migrated of their own accord as chronicles indicate. (1 Chron. iv. 42.) Anyhow, the canton of Judah succeeded as heir to Simeon, and in all historical dates

Abraham, Isaac, and Jacob. 23

Beer-sheba is from that time considered as an uncontested possession of the canton of Judah.

Such a change of political fate brings at all times, and in all cases, a change of traditions and worship. When in legends, gods lead and direct the fate of a war, the gods of the conquerors invariably hurl down the gods of the conquered from their height. Even to Jehovah are ascribed such conquests over the gods of other nations. (Exod. xii. 12.) The change of *power* always goes hand in hand with a change of ideas as to the *rights* of the ruler, and, if not directly, yet by degrees, the new idea absorbs the old and impotent one, or modifies it, and new views imperceptibly permeate.

Thus we may suppose that the god "Pachad" and the patriarch "Isaac" in Beer-sheba descended from old Simeonic times, when the Edomites, the Philistines, and the Ishmaelites, no less than the Simeonites, worshipped the sanctuaries of Beer-sheba. When Beer-sheba fell into the possession of Judah, the authority of the worship necessarily suffered, and Pachad, as well as Isaac, were half forgotten. But as local worship and as local patriarch they continued to exist, and only a prophet, like Amos, who was born near Beer-sheba in Tekoa, and who as "herdsman" may have visited the heaths of Beer-sheba, knew something of this worship, and inveighed against it as against Bethel, although it was in importance much inferior to the latter.

If we have in this way justified the view that the legend of Isaac is the oldest of the three, we hope to tread on more certain ground in considering the patriarch of Hebron, who, as the *Judaic* and reigning one, was, under the name of Abraham, so grandly equipped by legend that he must necessarily put Isaac in the shade.

VI.

HEBRON AND ITS PATRIARCH.

When the hero of a younger legend is destined to surpass the hero of an older one, it is generally effected by appropriating to the former everything laudable which was related of his predecessor. This plan has been so fully carried out with reference to the legend of Abraham against Isaac, that even the harmonist, who attempted to reconcile them and keep Isaac at the side of Abraham, found it impossible to preserve one *special* trait for Isaac.

The younger legend forthwith ascribes the benefit of the wells round Beer-sheba to Abraham, so that it only leaves to Isaac the praise of having re-opened these Abrahamic wells when they were choked up. (Gen. xxvi. 18.)

The predilection of the legend of Isaac for an ancestress, who from her beauty is in danger of being taken into the harem of the king (Gen. xxvi. 6, &c.), is surpassed by the legend of Abraham to such a degree, that not only the insignificant king Abimelec of Gerar (Gen. xx. 1-18), but also the great Pharaoh, king of Egypt, actually take the ancestress Sarah into their harems. (Gen. xii. 14, &c.). But while the wife of Isaac is not touched by the danger, and needs no providential intervention, Abraham's wife is saved in both cases by the *direct* interference of Providence when she was in imminent danger.

The treaty also which Isaac concluded with the king of the Philistines, is repeated to a stronger degree in Abraham's case. Abimelec and his general, Picol, who merely ask friendship from Isaac (Gen. xxvi. 28), entreat their friend Abraham to confer this friendship upon "*son, and son's son.*" (Gen. xxi. 23).

The town of Beer-sheba, which is said to have derived its name from *Isaac* (Gen. xxvi. 33), receives its name in the legend of Abraham in a much more solemn way,

Abraham, Isaac, and Jacob. 25

on account of the vow of eternal friendship which *Abraham* and Abimelec mutually swear. (Gen. xxi. 31).

Isaac, who is represented to be the *brother* of Ishmael, is outflanked by the younger legend through the much more important fact that Abraham is the *father* of Ishmael.

The only uncontested deed of Isaac's is the erection of an altar in Beer-sheba where he invoked the name of Jehovah. The younger legend certainly does not place so holy an altar in Beer-sheba; probably it begrudges the town this honour, still an action of Abraham is related which derogates from the deed of Isaac. Abraham planted a tamarisk* in Beer-sheba—probably a specimen, the sacredness of which was firmly established in the belief of the people—and he there invoked the name of Jehovah, the eternal God. יהוה אל עולם

Only upon one point the legend of Abraham is unable to surpass that of Isaac. Edom, the son of Isaac, "*whom he loveth*," stands in no special relation to Abraham. But this advantage of Isaac, the Judaic hero *could* not possibly touch; because at the time when the legend of Abraham appeared, there was enmity between Judah and Edom which could not be kept under by legends of peace.

But the legend of Abraham did not spring up simply in mere competition with that of Isaac. It was devised with a deeper intention and a more comprehensive political and national significance. The figure of the local patriarch of Beer-sheba stands to the imposing form of the patriarch of Hebron, as the local patriotism of a small republican canton to the national patriotism of a state which puts itself at the head of a kingdom.

In fact, the birth of the legend of Abraham is *not older but younger than the Judaic kingdom.* In the guise of the private life of a wandering patriarch, we have before us the picture of a governor of the whole

* אשל, אשר, פחד, are in a certain sense, nearly synonyms.

country, with full powers. The point of the life of this patriarch shows but too clearly the bold idea of King David to form here an intervening kingdom of great dimensions, which would be able to ward off from both sides the threatening conflict of Mesopotamia and Egypt.

The legend makes Abraham migrate from Mesopotamia, and keep throughout his life, with zealous logic, the consciousness of his relationship to his Asiatic home. The intention is, to prove that *animosity against Mesopotamia could never take root in the kingdom of Judah*, as the ancestor was a blood relation. Scarcely had he become acquainted with the land into which he had wandered, when a famine drove him to Egypt, where he had the adventure most flattering to Sarah's beauty, but rendered harmless by the intervention of Jehovah. Thereupon he left Egypt, loaded with *riches*, and returned to Canaan. Thus the patriarch had, at the very beginning of his migration, measured the boundaries of his power, *which he became entitled to claim for his descendants*. "Unto thy seed will I give the land from the river of Egypt, unto the great river, the river Euphrates," (Gen. xv. 18) a proud word, which could only have been spoken *after the bold deeds of David who verified them*. Before him in the dissensions of the republican cantons which often had fought against, and ruined each other, even the boldest imagination of legend could not assign such a task to the Hebrews.

Another instance of entirely *Davidic* tendency, is the relation to Ammon and Moab, which represents Abraham in his family relation to Lot, the ancestor of those peoples. Abraham is represented as guardian to and protector of Lot, whose father, a brother of Abraham, had died early. Lot wanders with Abraham into Canaan, goes with him to Egypt, returns enriched with Abraham to Canaan, where the pasture is not sufficient for their large flocks herding together. Abraham, with

Abraham, Isaac, and Jacob. 27

more than paternal benevolence, advises a separation (Gen. xiii. 8), and gives Lot the choice of the direction. Lot chooses the flourishing fields around Sodom, whilst Abraham takes up his abode in the plains of Hebron. After the separation Abraham continues to be Lot's benefactor and preserver. He delivers him from captivity and saves his entire possessions from the hands of foreign conquerors (Gen. xiv. 16). Abraham's compassion for Lot also extends to his abode in Sodom, for which he implores Jehovah's mercy. (Gen. xviii. 23). To this intercession Lot evidently owes his preservation from the ruin of Sodom. The intention of the legend to win the sympathy of the population of Moab and Ammon for the patriarch and his descendants is undeniable, and is the more striking as another legend is added to it, (Gen. xix. 30-38), which creates these nations in drunkenness, incest and immorality of the female sex.

To win these people by sympathy and to claim the old blood relationship between Abraham and Lot, notwithstanding a hatred, which is clearly shown in the latter legend, is an endeavour, which could only be made at a time, *when Moab and Ammon had already been conquered by David, when clever politicians deemed it necessary to reconcile people to their fate and to comfort them for the loss of their independence, by the flattering knowledge, that they were of one and the same descent with the conqueror.*

If those traits of the legend of Abraham show the Judaic patriarch to be of a stamp very different to the local Simeonic patriarch of Beer-sheba, everything else, which is related of Abraham, tends to complete the picture of a hero, who, in all directions, is richly endowed with the attributes of a "high father" (Abram,) or a "Father of many people." (Abraham.)

He migrated into the country at Jehovah's bidding. He entered neither Shecem nor Bethel: those were places, hostile to Judah; but with a true Judaic feeling, he erected "altars" in their neighbourhood, and invoked the name of Jehovah. After his return from Egypt, he wandered again through the country, even to its geographical centre between Bethel and Ai, and again invoked Jehovah; a fact *which meant the religious occupation of the country for Jehovah!* After Lot had separated from him, (Gen. xiii. 14.) and Abraham's tribe had been in a way purified of the later worshippers of "Cemosh" and "Milcom" he received the command to walk through the land, northward and southward, eastward and westward, "in the length of it and the breadth of it," because all that country was to be his. Such a man is not the hero of a republican canton, but rather a monarchical hero, who suffers *no* division of government, and who supports David's principle of unity in the name of Jehovah.

Abraham took up his abode in Hebron. This is the city which boasts of having been built seven years before Zoan in Egypt (Numb. xiii. 22). That city, as legend tells us, was governed by a race of giants: it was the primeval city, the city which Caleb, of the tribe of Judah, desired as an inheritance for all his descendants, because of his faithfulness (Joshua xiv. 6, &c.). Moreover, it is the city to which Judah owes its origin. This city, as the history of David relates, (2 Sam. ii. 1.) was *directly recommended* by Jehovah to David, after Saul's death, as his abode. This city was also the residence of David during the first seven years of his reign.

There the patriarch again built an altar, and invoked the name of Jehovah: but not in the way he was accustomed to do, as a passing guest, but as a stranger and an inhabitant, preserver, and ally of the former possessors, who recognized his mission as a "Prince of God." (Gen. xxiii. 6.) But Hebron was not only the ancestral seat of the Judaic kingdom, whence the Elders of Israel fetched David to give him the crown of the whole undivided realm, but it was also the *seat of the Judaic worship at the time when David already resided in Zion.*

Abraham, Isaac, and Jacob. 29

Absolom, his son, pretended to have to go there, *in order " to fulfil a pious vow to Jehovah"* (2 Sam. xv. 7-10,) and there he began his rebellion and was crowned. The patriarch in Hebron, with the prospect of possessing as his inheritance all the land northward and southward, eastward and westward, formed, as we see, a fit model for the legend of *David's state-unity*.

From this place, the legend makes its hero, Abraham, undertake a triumphal march (Gen. xiv.), which is thoroughly *in keeping with David's character*. Four great kings of Asia make war against the people of five small kingdoms, supposed to have existed in the territory of the Dead Sea. The Asiatic kings conquered all around, slew, in the valley of Sidim, the native kings, among whom was the king of Sodom, and took the prisoners and all the booty with them. A fugitive reported these facts to Abraham, who forthwith armed all his allies, followed the conquerors, overtook them in the extreme north, in Dan, fought with them and pursued them even beyond the boundaries of the land, as far as Hoba on the left hand of Damascus, retook the booty and brought back all the prisoners.

This unparalleled triumph of our hero, to whom the whole land was to owe life and property, is further enhanced by the disinterestedness with which Abraham refused any portion of the spoil. Only the combatants, the allies and the inhabitants of the environs of Hebron, took their portion. Abraham solemnly lifted his hand unto Jehovah, the most High God, the possessor of heaven and earth, and swore that he would take neither a thread nor a shoe-latchet.

To the moral and religious occupation in the name of Jehovah, to whom Abraham erected altars at the most celebrated places, whom he everywhere invoked and from whom he everywhere received promises of proprietorship, were superadded *martial reconquest* and with it *legal right*. *A better claim for the annexation of the whole land to Judah, could certainly not be made.*

The constant partisanship, with which the legend presents the figure of Abraham, is still more decidedly shown in the point, that he was the one with whom Elohe made a covenant, and to whom He ordained the circumcision as an indestructible sign in the flesh. The circumcision is, according to all conscientious enquiries, by no means of *Hebrew origin*. It existed and still exists with many peoples who bear no relation whatever to the Hebrews. The Hebrews themselves, when they immigrated into Palestine, were all *not circumcised*, (Joshua, v. 2-8), and most probably accepted the custom from the original inhabitants of Palestine, who are nowhere designated as not circumcised. This remark is only made about the Philistines, who had only just immigrated, and it is unremittingly repeated with them, (עֲרֵלִים).*

From the fact that the name of "uncircumcised" was an insulting one in David's time (1 Sam. xvii. 26, &c.), we may conclude that to the circumcision was ascribed a sanctifying, consecrating power adhering to entire tribes. To attribute the origin of this ceremony to Abraham was consequently a strong argument to *concentrate universal veneration upon this patriarch by all tribes who thought the custom holy.*

However, all this was not sufficient for the Judaic legend. The patriarch from Hebron must also be entitled to possession *by civil right*. Divine promises may be denied by sceptics, conquests may be annulled by defeats, and moral victories of ancestors invalidated by immoral actions of descendants. *Nothing, therefore, would suffice but a civil proceeding before princes and assemblies of people, when a real purchase was concluded for ready weighed silver, in open negotiation before all who went in and out.* Only such an action could procure the never-to-be-doubted possession, which nobody had a right to touch, and which gave a char-

---

* We shall give details about the original inhabitants of Shecem later on.

acter, never to be extinguished, to the sovereign power of the ancestral seat.

The legend of Abraham presents to us this civil proceeding with special elaboration and precision. The name of Hebron (Chebron) has too much affinity of sound with Kibron (burial-place) to remain unexplored by legend. Whose burial-place could be more worthy of adorning this very ancient city than that of the ancestor Abraham ! The burial-place of an ancestor, a saint, or more particularly of the founder of a religion, is known to offer always the most pious and welcome pretext for the conquest of it, and of the whole country around, *at any price*. It could not be imagined that *such* an argument in favour of possession would not be noticed by a venerator of Davidic conquest.

By means of the sword Abraham would not gain anything for himself. Presents and rewards he refused disinterestedly in Palestine : a burial-place, first for his wife and afterwards for himself, he would only buy for current money (Gen. xxiii. 9), and then, indeed, only in a public manner, which has no parallel for subtlety and diplomatic precision. The whole of the 23rd chapter of the first book of Moses is a masterpiece, rarely seen, but admirably fitted for its purpose.

Even with all this, the hero of Hebron would not be a universal patriarch were one trait wanting in his history which could glorify the *real* central seat of David's united kingdom. It was not right that the modern Jerusalem should surpass the ancient Hebron, particularly in the *cultivation of legends*, which always need the dark soil of high antiquity. But legend could not leave the new central seat unconsidered, especially as the grandeur of young Jerusalem excited the jealousy of the old religious and political places,—a jealousy which, in the time of David's grandchildren, led to separation from the united kingdom, and to the formation of the separate kingdom of Israel. Popular report is not critical. It does not avoid anachronisms, and thereby often betrays its youth and arbitrariness to the scrutinizing eye; but it possesses, as a rule, enough critical tact to conceal the fault against chronology by a vague description of time and locality. The legend of Abraham shews this critical tact, relative to Jerusalem, in two points. First of all, there arrives, on his return from the great war of deliverance, one "Malci Tzedek" (a king of justice), king of Salem (Gen. xiv. 18), in order to greet the preserver of the country with bread and wine. That Salem means Jerusalem cannot be *proved*, and yet cannot be *doubted*, as the psalmist (Ps. lxxvi. 3) particularly designates Jerusalem by that name. Its king bears the honourable title of "king of justice," and is, still more than that, "the priest of the most high God." This priest of the most high God not only *greets* Abraham, but *blesses him*, "and he gave him tithes of all." Who is the receiver? It cannot be proved, but yet cannot well be doubted, that the priest must be the receiver of the tithes. Thus Abraham already beforehand *knew the King of Jerusalem as the King of Justice, and brought the tithes to Jerusalem*. This was sufficient for legend *to glorify Jerusalem, and to annihilate the competition of any other place of royalty or of worship*.

Legend, however, knows how to date another great progress of civilization from Abraham, and with the vagueness which legend loves in anachronistic statements, it is transferred to a place which is doubtlessly, though not provably, *meant to be Jerusalem*.

Human sacrifice existed in Palestine up to the historical period. Legend relates (Gen. xxii.) that Elohe asked from Abraham the sacrifice of his son, and that Abraham was ready to make it, but that when the son lay upon the altar, already bound, and the knife to slay him was raised, an angel of "Jehovah" bade him stop, and that *Abraham* offered instead a ram caught in the thicket by its horns.

In all legends a deep meaning is hidden behind the

Abraham, Isaac, and Jacob. 33

simplicity of a plain representation, and such is undoubtedly the case here, when the reversion from human to animal sacrifice is represented in the homely shape of legend. As unassumingly as the narrative alters from Elohe to Jehovah, letting the former *claim* the sacrifice while the latter *prevents* it, so unassumingly would legend place this great progress in civilization to the credit of *the great patriarch of Judah*. Not less does the legend endeavour to remove the related event *to the mountain of the temple in Jerusalem*, although the anachronism is carefully concealed, so that we may still doubt whether Moriah (verse 2) and Mount of Jehovah (verse 14) really mean the place of the temple in Jerusalem.

Looking at the whole round of separate legends which unroll the picture of a universal Patriarch, under the popular guise of a simple family history, we may well say that, with uncommon mastery, it knows how to fulfil its partisan purpose under the plain cover of simplicity. In the materials for legends of the Hebrews, Abraham takes as prominent a place as is due to the ancestor of so powerful a conqueror and king as David.

VII.

THE LEGENDS OF ABRAHAM AND THE PROPHETS.

Although we know that legends grow only very slowly and imperceptibly, and that through entire generations traditions may continue unaltered, and often, as we shall soon show, undergo a great change through political events, which deeply affect the life and views of the people, and thereby, when complete, frequently seem insolvable riddles—still, we believe, from all that has preceded, we are justified in arriving at the following conclusions.

First of all, we may accept as probable that the patriarch Abraham was not a *direct invention of Davidic*

c

partisanship. At the place where he was venerated, and particularly at his supposed burial-place in Hebron, an Abraham, may already, at the time of the republic, have been known, named, and poetically adorned. The legends at first as harmless as the history of Isaac, grew with the fate of Hebron; but they did not receive their universally grand character, before the enthusiasm about David's mission was at its height. This bloom of enthusiasm did not however coincide with the blooming period of David's reign, but was developed later, when under the splendour and weakness of Solomon's reign, the hero-king stood in an ideal light before the nation, and in the fancy of the people grew higher and higher as an object of national enthusiasm. The weaker his successors were, the less they understood how to keep up the unity of the kingdom, and the more violently did blame attach itself to those royal houses *which did not walk " in the ways of Father David."*

If in that way, the circle of the Abrahamic legend, beginning in the simple time of the republic, gradually acquired in Solomon's time a national, political, and religious importance, we may still suppose that it reached the height of development, only *after the division of Israel from Judah* and after jealousy and wars between the two kingdoms had, during the following decennial period, lifted legendary fancy to an important height.

The next impulse was given by the legend of *the Patriarch of Bethel*, which appeared in the kingdom of Israel. But before considering this rival patriarch, we must answer two questions which might excite doubt in reference to our already proclaimed views.

The first question is, why should Shiloh (1 Sam. i. 3, &c.), which, approaching the Davidic time, was the place of worship, be silently passed by in the Abrahamic legend? Why should not the Davidic legend have drawn Shiloh into the circle of Abraham's

Abraham, Isaac, and Jacob. 35

activity, when it was the intention of those legends to bring the patriarch, significantly at least, *into the neighbourhood* of all places of worship, in order to proclaim Jehovah, as was the case for instance with Shecem and Bethel? The second question is of a different nature, although akin to the first. If Abraham be really a figure intended to glorify the Davidic Judah, why, with the exception of the concluding verses in Micah, which we have already quoted, do the old Judaic prophets not mention him, either figuratively or personally?

We answer these two questions in one sentence: that the Davidic aim, viz., *universal monarchy*, and the aim in Shiloh, *a strong Republic*, necessarily conflicted with each other. But it was as decidedly in the interest of the monarchical party to crush Shiloh down to insignificance, as it was in the interest of the Shilonites to make the strongest opposition to royalty, even to David's kingdom

In Shiloh lived the prophet and judge Samuel, a staunch republican, than whom no one could be found more firm and inflexible. His words (1 Sam. viii. 2), in which he describes the kingdom, are as bitter as they are just. It is certainly stated that Samuel secretly anointed the shepherd boy as king (1 Sam. xvi. 13), but this is a mere invention of Davidic historians, who want to bring Samuel's authority into action for their ideal monarch. He who could think of kings as Samuel did, would not voluntarily anoint them. It is a subject too of no doubt, that the disciples of Samuel, the prophet's pupils, were no more royalists than their teacher. Shiloh, on the contrary, was the place where the demagogic conspiracy against the Davidic universal monarchy was initiated. It was the prophet and demagogue Ahijah of Shiloh (1 Kings xi. 29) who directly incited Jeroboam to rebellion. As a fact, one might say, that *Ahijah was the destroyer of the Davidic kingdom!* There really existed scarcely any monarchically minded prophets. They were all, according to circumstances, democrats, republicans, theocrats, and in many cases, demagogues. Isaiah and Micah, who saw their ideal in a better future, painted it (Isaiah ii., etc., and Micah iv., etc.,) as a time of everlasting peace, when God would reign and kings be superfluous. "Nation shall not lift up a sword against nation, neither shall they learn war any more." This hope for eternal peace between people and people, is thoroughly anti-monarchical. Although Isaiah, in cases of danger for the state, and of national sufferings, addresses consolation to reigning kings, still he is, and remains, thoroughly the true man of the people, who with glowing ire makes princes and their accessories feel the weight of his words, and harshly criticises the debauchery of princes and the passion for dress of the ladies of the court. Between the true prophetdom and the kingdom, there existed a conflict such as could only exist between absolutism and democracy. Therefore it is not surprising, that suddenly with David's appearance the importance of Shiloh should vanish; that again at the time of David's grand-son, Rehoboam, a Shilonite should stir up a powerful conspiracy, and that Shiloh, after the revolution, separated from the kingdom of Judah, should rise in war against the *Israelitic* kingdom; and that in the end, after the prophets dispersed in all directions, it should fall into entire ruin.

Thus it is easily explained, why the Davidic development of legends, lets Abraham pass Shiloh by in silence, and why the prophets, the Shilonites and their successors, attach no value to the legend of Abraham.

VIII.

THE PATRIARCH OF BETH-EL.

The legends of the patriarch of *Beth-el* form a most striking contrast to those of Abraham.

One need only picture to oneself the part that Bethel played in the division of the Israelitic tribes from

Abraham, Isaac, and Jacob. 37

the Davidic kingdom, to see at once, that the patriarch of the name of "*Israel*" or "*Jacob*" *was only invented for the sake of glorifying Beth-el*, in order to give to that new place of worship a popular nimbus, which enabled it to compete with Jerusalem.

A glance at the causes and the effects of this great revolution will prove what we say.

The new capital of Jerusalem was, under the gorgeous reign of Solomon, the centre of the Davidic monarchy. It was a fatal error of this king, that he wanted to raise a young state, formed through mighty and successful wars, to a splendour only fit for the great old monarchies, between which it was situated. Jerusalem, the capital, united in itself all the luxury and wantonness of the age. The people, accustomed to plain republican ways, felt the yoke of monarchy grievously (1 Kings xii. 4), and yielded only with reluctance to the central state, which was governed from a new centre, and which obscured the old traditional places of worship and government. Temples, gorgeous buildings, fleets, harems, gold, ivory, peacocks, monkeys, statues, images, singers, dancers, and literary fancies might well flatter the inhabitants of Jerusalem, and might even call forth enthusiasm for the monarchy in the canton of Judah; but they could dazzle a strong republican simple people only for a short time. The old towns were filled with violent anger against the new Jerusalem, eating up the country. Therefore Solomon's death was the signal for the breaking out of the conspiracy, which the prophet Ahijah, the Shilonite, and Jeroboam, the Ephraimite, had already initiated in King Solomon's lifetime (1 Kings xi. 26-40). Rehoboam, the foolish son of Solomon, was obliged to go to Shecem, the old chief place, in order to be crowned at the assembly of States. There, through Rehoboam's pride, the revolution broke out. Its leader, Jeroboam, became king of the new realm, and the *whole* people acknowledged him, with the exceptions of the canton of

Judah, and the canton of Benjamin, which had been humiliated through David's sanguinary persecutions. The new king resided in Shecem. But afraid that the people in pilgrimage to Jerusalem might again turn to David's house, Jeroboam by way of competition erected two *new* places of worship: one *at the frontier of Benjamin in Beth-el*, the other at the most northern end of the kingdom, *in the city of Dan* (1 Kings xii. 26-30).

Whilst the worship at Dan, in the furthest north, does not seem to have been of more importance than the one in Beer-sheba, in the furthest south, the worship in Beth-el was potent enough, to do the most complete damage to the pilgrimages to Jerusalem. All the prophets accuse Beth-el of the worst apostasy. But the priest in Beth-el called it "*the king's chapel,*" "*the king's court,*" (Amos vii. 13) *which nobody was to speak against!*

Is it conceivable that such a place of worship could be successfully established without an endeavour to give it the prestige of great antiquity? If we look at the tales of Jacob, which are related in the first Book of Moses, keeping to the fundamental thought, that these tales are before us in a form which systematically harmonises, and are intended to harmonise, the historical dissention of the kingdoms of Judah and Israel, the result is clear that Jacob was equipped by the legend to be *specifically a patriarch of Beth-el, and a rival of Abraham*. After the division of the kingdom a Jeroboamite patriarch is opposed to the David-like patriarch, as fit to surpass the latter, as Beth-el was to outdo old Hebron and Jerusalem.

Let us look closer at the new patriarch. We pass over, at first, the history of Jacob's youth, which we shall have to consider at a later stage, and begin with the scene which forms an introduction to his patriarchal mission. Jacob arrived after travelling (Gen. xxviii. 10, 22) at a place called "Luz;" there the sun had set,

Abraham, Isaac, and Jacob. 39

and he took one of the stones of that place, put it for his pillow, and lay down to sleep. He dreamed and behold! a ladder was set up on the earth and the top of it reached to heaven and the angels of Elohe were ascending and descending on it. And behold! Jehovah stood above it and said : "I am Jehovah, the God of Abraham thy father, and the God of Isaac ; the land whereon thou liest, to thee will I give it and to thy seed. And thy seed shall be as the dust of the earth (in quantity), and thou shalt spread abroad to the west and to the east, to the north and to the south, and in thy seed shall all the families of the earth be blessed." And behold, "I am with thee and will keep thee whithersoever thou goest, and will bring thee again into this land ; for I will not leave thee until I have done that which I have spoken to thee of." And Jacob awakened out of his sleep and he said : "Surely Jehovah is in this place and I knew it not" (up to the present). Then he was afraid and said : "How fearful is this place! this is none other but the house of God, and this is the gate of heaven." And Jacob rose up early in the morning and took the stone that he had put for his pillow and set it up for a pillar (מצבה), and poured oil on the top of it, and he called the name of that place Beth-el (house of God). Luz had been the name of the city in former times. And Jacob made a vow saying : "If Elohe will be with me and will keep me in this way that I go, and will give me bread to eat and raiment to put on, so that I come again to my father's house in peace ; then shall Jehovah be my God, and this stone, which I have set for a pillar (מצבה) shall be God's house, *and of all that thou wilt give me I will surely give the tenth unto thee.*"

A greater glorification of Beth-el could scarcely be imagined ! How welcome it must have been to King Jeroboam, who erected there the house of God, and had the door of heaven put in the same place ! How particularly welcome this legend must have been to the priests in Beth-el "whom Jeroboam had made of the lowest of the people and not of the sons of Levi," (1 Kings xii. 31)—who did not wish that the tenth should be brought to Jerusalem, to which, according to the Hebron legend, Abraham had already given it, but to Beth-el, where the new patriarch had expressly engaged to bring it! From those concluding words relative to the tithe, and which, without any motive, speak to God in the second person, whilst until then God has always been mentioned in the third person, we judge that particular value was attached to the point *that the tenth should appear for Bethel as a personal and very intimate obligation, vowed face to face, an obligation which could never be got rid of!*

The competition with Abraham is fully expressed in the promise of the whole land as a possession to the descendants of Jacob. That promise so entirely comprises all that gave a providential value to Abraham's mission, that the patriarch of Judah becomes quite superfluous.

Certainly the basis of all this glorification of Beth-el is only a *dream*, and it may well be thought that it need not be so pretentious; but he who considers what is still before us, as remains of the Israelitic literature in that of the Judaic, cannot fail to perceive that the literary production in Judah is sober in comparison with the poetry of the Israelitic narrative. With the point that represents the glorification of Bethel, begins an entire cycle of Israelitic literature, which embraces the history of Jacob and Joseph to the end of the first Book of Moses. From that time the dreams never cease. Jacob dreams in Haran (Gen. xxxi. 11). Laban is visited in a dream, (xxxi. 24). Joseph dreams twice foreshadowings of his fate (xxxvii. 5, &c). His fellow prisoners, the butler and the baker of Pharaoh, are visited by dreams (xl. 5). Pharaoh himself dreams, and Joseph's wisdom as an interpreter of dreams influences the fate of Egypt. In the end Elohe also comes to Jacob "in the visions of the night" (Gen. xlvi. 2), in Beer-sheba, and gives him promises which claim unlimited confidence. When one comes to consider, that in the mouth of the people, a dream often is thought *much* more significant than a perception with open eyes, one would rather see in the dream in favour of Beth-el, another argument for undoubted glorification of the place. What a patriarch *dreamed* was certainly thought in Israel much more *trustworthy* than what the people could *at any time see with their own eyes.*

Nor can we fail to see, upon closer consideration, that the story of this dream had necessarily a more intense influence upon the imagination of the people than the soft, modest, and half-concealed intimations of a glorification of Jerusalem through Abraham. As a successful rebellion is much more energetic than legitimacy, so is the legend of revolution much more powerful than the legitimate one. Beth-el is not veiled like Jerusalem under " Salem," " Moriah," and " Mount of God," but it appears *openly* with all its pretensions as does Jeroboam the rebel himself. Such things always impose upon a people. *Novelty* alone could have brought Beth-el into bad credit and raised doubts. Although Beth-el was in Samuel's times already a place where one went " to Elohe," (1 Sam. x. 3) still one had not yet an idea of *such high importance.* But why should surprise prevent any one from fully acknowledging Beth-el, when the patriarch himself avowed *that he had not known it before,* and that he saw only *now* in his dream *that Jehovah dwelt there and that the door of heaven was opened there !*"

But it was not only the religious importance which had to be won for Beth-el ; but the whole of the political importance, which through David's bold deeds had glorified the kingdom of Judah, had to be annulled in the tradition of the people and to be turned through bold inventions towards the new kingdom of Jeroboam. Whatever war might accomplish was tried with undaunted energy. The war between both kingdoms raged fully twenty-four years. But war requires also *the belief of the people in a justification for war*, and to this belief the new patriarch offered plenty of material in the kingdom of Israel.

Before the establishment of the monarchy the Hebrews lived in ten or twelve cantons which governed themselves as republics. The names of these cantons are certainly *not* the names of persons. In some of them one recognises clearly the names of the gods who were worshipped there as : " Zebulon" the On of heaven, " Dan" the Judge, " Gad" the god of Fortune, Venus. It is not unlikely that Benjamin was a district where " Meni" was worshipped (Is. lxv. 11). Other names of cantons probably originated in geographical or historical reasons, which can no more be followed up. However that may be, it is absurd to allege the population of ten or twelve cantons to be the issue of as many sons of one and the same father. An idea like this can no more be believed than perhaps an assertion that an ancestress "Borussia" had a number of children, each of whom was the founder of a Prussian province.

But the justification of Jeroboam's politics required strong belief from the people, and for the sake of such a strong belief the patriarch of Beth-el was made ancestor of all the cantons. The chief object in view was naturally to claim a privilege for the canton. "Ephraim" Jeroboam's home (1 Kings xi. 26). Ephraim, which is synonymous with " Joseph" (both mean fecundity, multiplication, and characterise the canton as densely populated), had to be fully justified by the legend of Beth-el in the privilege which Jeroboam usurped. With this intention a complete cycle of legends was marked out, which might rival in system the cycle of the legends of Abraham, surpassing them far in poetical elaboration, and which, in parts, are a real masterwork of epic style, whilst polemically they are as regardless of the Judaic cycle of legend as Jeroboam was of the Davidic dynasty.

IX.

THE CONFLICT OF THE CYCLES OF LEGEND.

We proceed now to show the parallelism, the rivalry, and lastly, the cutting polemics of these legends.

The patriarch of Beth-el went direct to Mesopotamia to marry. The legend of Abraham which—as a proof of Judah's intimate relation to Mesopotamia—has a wife *fetched* thence for the son of the patriarch, is much surpassed by the new legend, which lets Jacob travel there in *propriâ personâ*. He married two wives, sisters. One of them, the elder, was imposed upon him and he hated her (Gen. xxix. 31). The other, the younger one, was the beloved, for whose sake he joyfully served as a herdsman for fourteen years. The former, the hated one, bore him sons; the latter, the beloved one, remained childless for a long time. Each of the two wives brought to the patriarch her maid, so that she might number her children as her own. In this way ten sons were born to the patriarch in Mesopotamia, each of whom received the name of one of the cantons of Palestine, and was intended to count as its ancestor. But the mission of the patriarch was not fulfilled thus. He waited patiently. At last the beloved wife also bore him a son, who received the name of Joseph, and *directly* after his birth (Gen. xxx. 25) the patriarch wished to return to the land of promise. Then, at length, he saw his mission fulfilled, because not only was he going to take home the ancestors of *all* the cantons, but also *the own son of the beloved one, the son full of promise*, who was to be subject to wonderful fates in the war with his brothers, the children of the unbeloved one and of the maids, and who was destined to wear the crown, the crown of the kingdom of "Joseph" "Ephraim" "Israel," of the kingdom which Jeroboam, the Ephraimite, had founded.

The intention of this history is clear enough. The peaceful relations of the kingdoms of Jeroboam to neighbouring Mesopotamia, could scarcely be better expressed than by the family legend, that all cantons of this kingdom, Judah included, were no more than *colonies, peopled by the children who had been born to the patriarch in that district.* Why the legend makes an exception " with Benjamin" we shall soon consider.

But such very near family ties have their dangerous points. A Mesopotamian conqueror might easily thereby have proved well-founded pretensions to these colonies sprung from his blood. For this reason the separation of the patriarch from Mesopotamia was not a light matter. Chapters xxx. and xxxi. contain a very elaborate discussion about property between Laban the representative of those countries and the patriarch, a discussion which, like every one of its kind, does not pass without serious moments of threatened conflict, but which in the end terminates with a contract of peace, the validity of which was unexceptionable.

The contract of peace was concluded as we see (Gen. xxxi. 23) at the frontier of the country, in the Mount of Gilead. There, at a place no longer to be traced, and probably remarkable for its towering rocks, the treaty was concluded at the express wish of Laban. The companions of both parties gathered stones and constructed a rocky hill. This hill " Gal" was to be "witness." Thence originated the name " Galeed," " Gilead" (גלעד). On the heights was a beacon, a watchtower, giving the motive for calling the place " Mizpah" (מצפה, מצבה), because, as Laban exclaims, Jehovah shall judge between me and thee." This hill and this Mizpah shall be witnesses that *I will not pass over this frontier to thee, and thou wilt not pass over to me in hostile intention.* Solemn vows, a meal, and a hearty leave-taking concluded the contract of peace.

We may assert, with great probability, that this legend has for its foundation a real political motive, from the time of Jeroboam. It is a matter of course that neither Egypt nor Mesopotamia could observe with indifference the growth of a bold, vigorous monarchy, out of a conglomeration of small powerless strips of land, upon a border, which formed the natural guard at the people's bridge in Suez. Although one cannot say that David's kingdom really extended from Egypt's "brook unto the Euphrates," still, it is a fact, that all through this wide territory his power made itself felt. David's glorious wars against Aram, and his treaty with Toi, king of Hamath, could not appear insignificant. In Egypt those events were considered with attention. Solomon received a daughter of Pharaoh from Egypt, as his wife, which really was no small concession to so young a kingdom, considering the pride of caste of the Egyptian dynasty. Nevertheless, Egypt was soon filled with jealousy of the Davidic kingdom. The Court received, in a friendly spirit, Hadad, a fugitive prince from Edom, who was waiting for the death of David and his general, Joab, to free his country from the yoke of the Davidic reign (1 Kings xi. 14-22). The Edomite prince found such favour in the sight of Pharaoh, that he gave him as a wife, the sister of his own wife, the queen, and allowed him to undertake, after the death of David, the war of deliverance in Edom.

Just as in Egypt, a fugitive, "Rezon," proved in Damascus a lucky adversary of Solomon, (1 Kings xi. 23,) we may also conclude with certainty, that Jeroboam, as a fugitive in Egypt, leagued himself with the Court there, against the kingdom of Judah. This alone explains that five years after Jeroboam's reign in Israel (1 Kings xiv. 25), Shishak, king of Egypt came up to Jerusalem, took away all the treasures of the temple and the palace, but left the kingdom of Israel perfectly intact. Although we must not accept the repeated statement that the war between Jeroboam and Rehoboam lasted "all their days" as an exact expression, still we cannot doubt that Shishak had been incited to this predatory invasion against Rehoboam, by the former fugitive in Egypt, then king Jeroboam in Israel.

Under such political conditions, it was quite within the reach of probability, that Jeroboam should not fail to strive for friendly opinion for his newly formed kingdom in the North East ; not, however, by means of patriarchal legends of ancient times, but by means of real diplomatic negotiations, such as had been usual in the time of David (2 Sam. viii. 10). But when a friendly treaty of this kind had been concluded, it was quite natural, that for the ingenuous belief of the people, it should be represented as a family picture of the life of Laban and the Patriarch of Bethel.

This well contrived plan, to consecrate in a popular spirit, through the Patriarch of Bethel, the peaceful relations between the newly formed kingdoms of Israel and Mesopotamia, was surpassed by the cleverness, in which the same legend made the much more intimate relation of Jeroboam to Egypt, palatable to the people.

It would have been an easy matter to give to the real son of the Patriarch and his beloved wife, the name of "Ephraim," and thus to introduce the ancestor of the canton who was to have the vocation to stand at the head of all, as a true Mesopotamian. But the intimate relation of Jeroboam to Egypt required a much more subtle plan. Joseph, the real son of the Patriarch, was to come from the Euphrates, but diplomacy was not satisfied with this title alone. It was necessary that the real son should be hated, persecuted by his brothers, and left to die ; should be saved from being murdered by a feeling of humanity in the bosom of the eldest of his brothers, Reuben, and through God's wonderful interposition, sold as a slave at the advice of Judah, the most mighty of the brothers.

Joseph, thus arrived in Egypt, rose to the posts of preserver, benefactor, and powerful minister of Egypt.

Abraham, Isaac, and Jacob. 47

Pharaoh gave him as a wife, the daughter of Potiphera, priest of On, in the temple of the Sun, Heliopolis, and he had by her, Ephraim, the ancestor of Jeroboam, the new king. He was, in truth, only a grandson of the Patriarch, but for that very reason, Jacob solemnly adopted him in Egypt as his own son (Gen. xlviii. 5). By the maternal side, however, Ephraim was related by blood, *at the same time, to Mesopotamia and Egypt*. How could he fail to be incontestably acknowledged as the crowned one, among the brothers? (Gen. xlix. 26, and Deut. xxxiii. 16).

X.

ANIMOSITY AGAINST THE JUDAIC LEGENDS.

If already a slight sketch of the Ephraimitic legend suffices to show its Jeroboamic tendency, a closer inspection of details affords a deeper view of the entire want of consideration, and of the hostility with which that legend attacks the Davidic dynasty. It needs only impartial observation to discover in the rich, much altered, and even mutilated material, the fundamental characteristics which the legend had in its original shape. By this means there are also opened to our view large portions of the side scenery, which under the present harmonious covering present themselves to us as so many dark problems. We perceive, not a *one-sided* attack proceeding from a legend only, but a *mutual* conflict of the two legends. We observe how, besides the eternal wars of the kings Jeroboam and Rehoboam, of which history contains but scanty records, religious contests also of an embittered nature were recorded and fought out in the popular tales.

First of all, let us divert our attention from the great Jeroboamic characteristics which the legend presents for Ephraim's glorification to some smaller traits which strengthen our conviction by their number rather than their weight. For this purpose we cannot consider the events in the same order as they are described in the first book of Moses, but, as the conclusion will show, our digressions for a few moments will always be with a view to compass the entire round of legends.

After the patriarch had taken leave of Laban, he forthwith sent a message of peace and friendship to Esau, who at once hastened to meet him, and demonstrated his brotherly love to such a degree, that the patriarch exclaimed that Esau's face appeared to him as though it was "the face of God," (Gen. xxxiii. 10). Before however this meeting took place, the patriarch had at night (xxxii. 24, &c.) a struggle with a real God, a matter we shall afterwards consider. At present only the one fact is of interest, that the patriarch saw there also a "face of God" face to face, so vividly indeed, that he could not help calling the place "Peniel," God's face (פני אל).

The conference with Esau having been satisfactorily concluded, the patriarch proceeded. He built a house and erected "booths" for his cattle, wherefore he called the place "Succoth." But he did not remain there. He went to Shecem and encamped before the city. There he bought part of the field where he pitched his tent from the hand of the children of Hamor, the father of Shecem for the price of a hundred kesitah, and he erected there an altar and called it "El God of Israel."

If we stop a moment to consider the latter passage in particular, there is no doubt that the word "altar," (מזבח mizbeach,) does not at all agree with the word vaiatzeb, ויצב, which informs us of the setting up. For the erection of an altar we find everywhere either ויבן vaiiben, "he built," or ויעש vaiaas, "he made," or also, ויקם vaiakam, "he erected," whilst the word ויצב vaiatzeb is only used for the erection of a pillar מצבה matzebah, which is clearly based upon the uniformity of sound and origin of both words. We have evidently only the choice of assuming either the verb or the substantive as the wrong reading, and we shall have to

Abraham, Isaac, and Jacob. 49

consider for which rectification we have to pronounce. Certainly we find in the further history of the patriarch that he also "built" an altar מזבח mizbeach, in Bethel, (xxxv. 7.) but we have already quoted the plan according to which (xxviii. 18-22.) he erected a pillar "Matzebah" in Bethel; in the same chapter xxxv. while, according to verse 7, he built the "altar" in Bethel, his wandering to Bethel is again related where he set up a Matzebah, (v. 14.) "a matzebah of stone," as is added with peculiar stress. Inquiring further, we find that the same patriarch raised up a matzebah in Gilead (Gen. xxxi. 45.), and finally that he set up another upon the tomb of Rachel (Gen. xxxv. 20). Now we are well justified in the opinion that the fact cannot be accidental, that Abraham should never set up a pillar but always build "an altar," for which he always invoked the name of "Jehovah," and that it should be a speciality of our *new* patriarch throughout, *only* to set up *pillars*, and never to invoke or exclaim "Jehovah," but always "El" or "Elohe:" he even sometimes called *the erected stone itself by that name*.

After this, one may well allow that in the passage itself (xxxiii. 20), we must also read "pillar" matzebah, instead of "altar," mizbeach, and that, in consequence, the patriarch set up in Shecem a stone, calling it "El, Elohe, Israel," "God, a God of Israel." How much this is antagonistic to Judaic worship is clearly shewn by the so-called Mosaic law, in the following words,—"Neither shalt thou set thee up any pillar, matzebah, *which Jehovah thy God hateth.*" (Deut. xvi. 22.)

The above mentioned circumstance, however, causes us to ask why a place before Shecem should be honoured in this way? But when we recollect that Abraham upon his first entry into Canaan (Gen. xii. 6, 7), came also exactly unto the place of Shecem and there built "an altar, mizbeach, to Jehovah," it is sufficiently clear that it was incumbent upon his com-

D

petitor and adversary to set up a pillar matzebah, in
that very place for "Elohe," and even to designate *the
stone itself* with the title of "El," God.

The wonderful purchase, too, for a hundred Kesitah
is nothing but a competing side-piece to Abraham's
purchase of an hereditary burial-ground. How much
a Kesitah is worth we do not know. Judging by Job
xlii. 11, we are justified in thinking it of value. A
hundred such pieces of money may be more than 400
shekels of silver, the sum paid by Abraham at the purchase at Hebron. But the competing legend is right
in representing the new patriarch as liberal. He founded
something greater than Abraham's burial-ground. The
place was to be the burial-ground of Joseph ; so the
continuation of the legend (Joshua xxiv. 32) states.
To the glory of Hebron as Abraham's burial-place,
Shecem is here opposed as the burial-place of the
crowned one among the brothers. There a Davidic,
here an Ephraimitic memorial, which might well take
up the challenge for precedence.

But will not the new patriarch, be himself buried in
Hebron ? According to the present harmonious com-
pilation of the material of the whole of the legends,
yes, but according to the originally contrived and ener-
getically worked out legend, *no*. We will show this,
when we have more closely observed the territory on
which we are now standing.

We are before Shecem, as the narrator states, the
stations of the patriarch were, "Mizpah, Mahanaim,
Succoth and Peniel." Now we have cause to remember, that those places were not, simply, as they are
represented, places of encampment, pasture-grounds,
and places where one saw *God's face*. They are places
full of historical reminiscences. Mizpah is the place
where Saul was appointed king, he whose dynasty was
overthrown by David (1 Sam. x. 17). Mahanaim is
the city where the adversaries of David, after Saul's
death, proclaimed his son Ishbosheth as king of all

Israel (2 Sam. ii. 8). Shecem is the place where, in the republican period, which was called the time of the Judges, the unfortunate attempt was made to establish a kingdom. The hero, Gideon, has left in Succoth and Peniel memorials of the severe punishment which he inflicted upon the chiefs of those towns, because they would not give him bread when he fought against the enemies of the country, Zebach and Tsalmunna (Judges viii. 10). When the hero returned, the royal crown was offered to him. One of his sons, however, Abimelech of Shecem, knew how to raise himself by lucky intrigues, and after having murdered seventy of his brothers upon a stone, founded a kingdom, which was ruined after wild energy and bloody anarchy, but not until Shecem, the birthplace of the miserable kingdom, had, by self-chosen tyrants, been ravaged by fire and sword. But the town recovered. Nay, it soon became the centre of popular life, because there, the assembly was held, which was to crown the grandson of David. There Jeroboam appeared and destroyed the Davidic monarchy. The Judaic minister of Finance, Adoram, appears to have been stoned to death in Shecem, whereupon the legitimate king fled to Jerusalem (1 Kings xii. 18). Then Jeroboam seized the sceptre, and was proclaimed king in Shecem, where he took up his residence. His first royal act was to build the fortress of Peniel, and to establish worship in Bethel.

Remembering that this was the birthplace of the life and deeds of a new patriarch, it is clear why legend cannot pass over this portion of Jeroboam's kingdom without conferring a special sanctity upon Shecem. Was it not the first residence of the king Jeroboam, just as Hebron was of David, and certainly as worthy as the latter, of a great patriarch's visit and adoration?

But Peniel also, the first fortress of Jeroboam, deserves the honour of high consideration. The patriarch named the place thus, because there he had seen God "face to face." We possess too few historical records of Jeroboam's reign, to judge why it was necessary for Jeroboam's patriarch to confer, also, upon Succoth, the honour of a visit. But the coincidence of "Mizpah, Mahanaim, Shecem and Peniel" in history and legend, is sufficient to prove that *legend makes the patriarch appear wherever history glorifies the adversaries of David, and the king Jeroboam.*

We have, however, not yet done with Shecem. We see, in legend, a whole chapter dedicated to a sanguinary romance, enacted in Shecem (Gen. xxxiv.). Is not some *Jeroboamic partisanship* concealed behind this little masterpiece?

We shall treat this question presently: but first, we must make the history a little clearer than it appears at present, and we must glance over some other matters, before we are able to throw a light upon the true intention of the romance.

A romantic adventure is very well placed here. If the patriarch of Hebron experienced the same at the Courts of Abimelech and Pharaoh, we must not grudge to his competitor an event of this nature, especially as it concerns a virgin daughter who is put to no other use in the whole of the legend. But what really is supposed to have happened there, why it was invented, and how the occurrence took place, has been entirely altered by interpolation, and can only become clear, when the partisanship for Jeroboam has been thoroughly unveiled, and all its want of consideration laid bare.

That we have in chapter xxxiv. of the first Book of Moses a mere legend is sufficiently proved by the fact, that a person of the name of "*Shecem the son of Hamor*" never existed. Hamor is the name of a patrician *who, in the time of the Judges, exercised his power in Shecem*, and therefore was called "Father of Shecem" אבי שכם. The generation itself was called (Gen. xxxiii. 19, and Joshua xxiv. 32), "the *Sons* of Hamor," or "*Men* of Hamor." (Judges ix. 28). If one imagines Hamor and Shecem to be father and son, verse 19 of chapter xxxiii. of the first Book of Moses, has no meaning. According to that, Jacob bought a piece of land* מיד חמור אבי שכם *from the children of Hamor, father of Shecem*, which might very much more simply have been expressed by *from Shecem and his Brothers, the children of Hamor.* The legend contained in chapter thirty-four is thus based upon a *misinterpretation* of the words "father of Shecem." That there is nothing historical in the legend is evident from the circumstance that according to it Hamor and Shecem, and *all males of the city*, were killed, all women and children taken away, whilst according to the historically authentic book of Judges (chap. ix. 28), the patrician family of Hamor still existed at the time of Abimelech, consequently about *five hundred years after the alleged destruction!*

In fact, the 34th chapter is originally a libel upon all the grown-up sons of the patriarch. Joseph was then a mere child and naturally took no part. Simeon and Levi were specially accused of having broken their faith and word in a most sanguinary way, against the confiding, loving and well-intentioned Shecem; for, according to the original story, the princely youth Shecem did not take Dinah and defile her by force, but "he loved the damsel," spoke kindly to her, and asked his father Hamor to give him the damsel to wife. (Gen. xxxiv. 3, 4). The last words of the second verse, which state the contrary, are a later addition and incoherent. He who can and does satisfy his desire so unreservedly, is neither loving nor modest enough to ask his father's permission.

The following verse, the fifth, has also been interpolated; in the correct original text, verse 6 excellently joins verse 4. The right text also contained only the first words of verse 7, which relates how the sons of the patriarch came out of the field and overheard

* From the children of Chamor (*who was called*) abi shecem.

what the father of Shecem said to the patriarch.
Whatever else verse 7 relates of the grief and wrath of
the sons is interpolated, a fact which is clear, not only
from its purpose, but also from the circumstance that
it spoils the flow of the tale. It is sufficient proof of
the want of genuineness of this addition, that here
"Israel" is mentioned as a people, of whom naturally
the sons of Jacob could know nothing. In verse 13
again, the latter words are interpolated quite idly, and
only for the purpose of expressing something which
gives a different character to the story. In verse 27
also, the last words, which betray their heterogeneous-
ness through disturbing the text, ought to be omitted.
And clearly the whole of the concluding verse 31
should be omitted, if one would re-establish the original narrative.

That our idea about the original text is not an arbitrary one, follows from reading the chapter, omitting all
the words denounced by us as interpolations. The
coherence of the story is more close, and the character
of Shecem gains in probability. Only a sincere lover,
not a violent voluptuary, who has already satisfied his
lust, can be thought capable of the exacted sacrifices.
The very circumstance, that in a short tale one can in
six passages omit entire sentences without disturbing
the coherence, and that on the contrary by doing so,
and without adding a single word, one adds to the
sense, is a good proof that the original text *might*
have read thus. With this *probability* we are satisfied
until we show by other proofs that the text *really* read
as we allege.

For this purpose we must introduce two other parts
of the legend, one of which is only a fragment, but
still evidently betraying its intention; the second portion has been preserved in a more elaborate shape, and
although veiled, when closely considered, the intention
is clear. This intention is: *to libel the elder brothers
of Joseph.*

Abraham, Isaac, and Jacob.

The fragment in question consists of the two verses 21 and 22 of the 35th chapter of the first Book of Moses. That these two verses belong together, is clearly shown from the designation of our patriarch as "Israel;" thus these two verses form a striking contrast to the preceding and successive parts in which, as usual, the patriarch figures as "Jacob." As we have to consider more elaborately, the origin of both names, we will only precursorily observe that the name of "Israel" is certainly intended to be the more honourable one of the patriarch, and that we must therefore regard those two verses which use that name, conspicuously enough three times, as a fragment of truly Israelitic Ephraimitic production. This fragment mentions an incestuous deed of the eldest son of Leah, Reuben, the first-born of the patriarch. "Israel" heard of this incestuous deed, perpetrated by his son and . . . here the narrative breaks off, leaving us to draw our own inferences as to the probable continuation.

The mildest conjecture is this: that there, originally, followed a passage, condemning Reuben's deed, declaring him to have forfeited his right of primogeniture, and conferring the same upon another son of the patriarch. Who that should be is beyond doubt, when, upon the adoption of the two sons of Joseph, Jacob says (Gen. xlviii. 5), "Ephraim and Manasseh, as Reuben and Simeon they shall be unto me." In the first Book of Chronicles (v. 1, 2) this transfer of *primogeniture to Ephraim is expressed, together with the motive, with most complete decision.* Here we see *Ephraim* step into *Reuben's* place, a fact quite in keeping with the Ephraimitic treating of legends.

When, however, we compare with this the first Book of Moses, chapter xlix. verses 3, 4, where the patriarch upon his death-bed remembers Reuben's deed of incest, and declares him to have forfeited his right of primogeniture, we come necessarily to the conclusion, that the passage omitted in our fragment must have run *much more severely.* How severely we cannot know.

But it is sufficient for us to gather that a truly Ephraimitic legend has devised this scandalous deed against Reuben, *for the very purpose of having him dethroned from his birthright by the patriarch.*

The second portion we must here refer to, is the entire 38th chapter of the first Book of Moses. In this, Judah, the fourth son of the patriarch, is shown in a light which is to lay bare the stain of his existence. Judah went to Adullam where lived his friend "Chirah." He married a " Canaanite," the daughter of " Shuah." His eldest son was called (עֵר) " Er." He was *displeasing* in the eyes of Jehovah, therefore Jehovah slew him. His second son was called " Onan " (אוֹנָן); he died in consequence of his *sexual sins.* The third son's name was "Shelah," and, as it is mysteriously stated after his name (*v.* 5): he was at "Cezib" when she bore him. Cezib is certainly the name of a place, and the addition may therefore signify, that the mother had named the boy Shelah, because the father Judah happened to be in Cezib at the time, absent from home. Cezib has, however, a second meaning. The prophet Micah, overflowing with " plays upon words," in order to attach political thoughts to local names, knows and makes use of this second meaning. Cezib means "deception, lie," and is used by the prophet in this sense (i. 14). Now, as Shelah, in our narrative, serves to deceive Tamar's hopes, held out by Judah, the allusion to Cezib is appropriate. However this may be, *Judah's sons are all represented as despicable.* Even Judah himself fell into bad ways and was trapped into the snares laid by his daughter-in-law Tamar, *who played the prostitute.* Thus only did Judah found a generation, from which King David is said to descend, from a son of Judah, called " Paretz" (פֶּרֶץ), meaning " breaking through," in which manner he is supposed to have behaved towards his brother at his birth.

Veiled as the libel is here, it becomes apparent, as soon as we cast a glance upon David's family. The picture which this libel draws of Judah hits *David*

Abraham, Isaac, and Jacob. 57

himself sharply. The "Canaanite"—namely, whom Judah marries— is no other than the "Hittite," the wife of "Uriah the Hittite," (murdered at David's command,) whom David himself married adulterously. (2 Sam. xi. 12.) This wife of Judah is said to have been the daughter of a man of the name of Shuah. Therefore she is a "Bath-shuah," and is thus called. (Gen. xxxviii. 12.) But Bath-shuah is also Bath-sheba herself, as one may conclude from Chronicles. (1 Chron. iii. 5.) The eldest son died, *hateful in the sight of God*, just like the first son of Bath-sheba. (2 Sam. xii. 15.) This son of Judah is alleged to have been called "Er" (ער); why? because reading it backwards (רע, *wrong*) it means "bad," "wicked." The second son is called Onan (אונן), and dies for sexual sins. He is no other than David's son "Amnon" (אמנון), who meets his death on account of his sexual sins. (2 Sam. xiii.) The Tamar of Judah's story is the same, who was dishonoured by Amnon, the daughter of David, who, in spite of her misfortune and her purity, to the entire ruin of her good name, is humiliated to a person who plays the part of a public harlot. And Shelah (שלה), who does not die,—add only to his name the letter מ, and you have שלמה, Solomon! The addition of Cezib in giving the name means certainly to convey, that behind this peaceably sounding "Solomon" there is naught but lies and frauds of his father David.

It is probable that Chirah, the friend mentioned in this libel upon Judah, was no other than Chiram, king of Tyre, and a friend of David's house. To him the part is allotted to run about with a kid and to search for the harlot, to whom his friend had pledged the royal insignia, "signet, bracelets and staff." The place where the "harlot by the wayside" is sought is called Timnath; this is a reminiscence of Samson's love-adventure at the place of that name. (Judges xiv.) "Adullam," however, where Judah stopped with his friend Chirah, is really the name of a town, but here, probably, only another writing of Adunam, עדנם, which means " seat of voluptuousness." Lastly, the point of the tale, the breaking through of Paretz, is only a counterpart to the violence which was related of Jacob's birth, in the Judaic legends, as we shall further prove.

If this story of Judah is disclosed as a bitter personal libel upon David, the source whence it sprang cannot be doubted. We have before us a Jeroboamic production full of spite and venom against Rehoboam. And where is this libel? In the history of Joseph, which is to glorify the Ephraimite. The narrator, who is about to shew us the ancestor of Jeroboam, *the pure, chaste Joseph*, in the house of Potiphar, interrupts himself at the most convenient point to shew first the reverse of the picture, the ancestor of David, in a subtly devised obscenity, where each pretended person is, as intended, *a stain upon David's house*.

That this libel has been preserved shews the great *naïveté* of the later harmonists, who accept a bitter libel like this as "history." But it gives us also an approximate idea of what might appear too harsh even for such mild censorship. From what is allowed to happen to *Judah*, we may judge what has been buried for *Reuben*.

We are certainly limited only to dark hypotheses; but the whole libel upon Judah, which hits David and his house so sharply, leads us to the conclusion that the fragment about Reuben was similarly intended. Strange as Reuben's deed sounds, it agrees perfectly with the shameful act of Absalom, David's son, which the second book of Samuel (xvi. 22) mentions. Absalom was at that time the eldest son of David, as Amnon the elder had been murdered at Absalom's command, and Daniel the second son, whom Chronicles mention (1 Chronicles iii. 1), seems to have died earlier, as all communication about him is wanting. But the eldest son, when he takes possession of his father's harem, thereby, as we see in Absalom's history, irrevocably entered upon the full inheritance, and the natural consequence would be, if he did not settle with his father, the disinheriting of the son. The legend, which made Reuben perpetrate the deed of Absalom, was, on the one hand, intended to remind one of the stain upon David's house, and, on the other, to shew the legitimacy of the degradation of Reuben, the "hated" Leah's eldest son, in favour of the descendants of the beloved Rachel.

In that manner Reuben and Judah were treated, but there existed still, not so much as cantons as "sons of Leah," two more persons, Simeon and Levi, between Reuben and Judah ; and we are completely justified in the view already expressed, that the 34th chapter of the first book of Moses did not originally read as it does now, where Simeon and Levi, as avengers of the honour of their sister, seem half justified, but that all the passages which assert the forcible violation of Dinah are later additions. The original purpose of the legend was certainly no other than to *extinguish from the memory of the inhabitants of Shecem, the residence of Jeroboam, an old reminiscence of a sanguinary annihilation of Shecem, through the son of Gideon, of Joseph's tribe, who was their chosen king* (Judges vi. 15, and ix. 45), and in its stead to insert a feigned destruction, which the *brothers* of Joseph, without the patriarch's wish or knowledge, had brought about, and that at a time *when Joseph was yet a child.*

In this history, not only Simeon and Levi are accused of a most murderous breach of faith against the confiding brotherly Shecem, but *all* the brothers who hated Joseph, are said to have taken part in the plundering of the city, and the robbing of the women and children, and all that was in the houses (Gen. xxxiv. 27—29).

The harmonist, indeed, has not only endeavoured to soften, through his additions, the deed of Simeon and Levi, but also in the supposed last admonition of the patriarch (Gen. xlix. 5-7), lets these two brothers *alone* appear answerable.

XI.

THE PATRIARCH AND BENJAMIN.

But how stands it with Benjamin the youngest of the brothers? Why does the legend not permit this alleged ancestor of the canton to be born like the others (Gen. xxxv. 24-26) in Mesopotamia? Why should Rachel, the mother of Joseph, pass at the same time for the mother of Benjamin, so that a second son of the beloved wife should exist, who might compete with the first?

The solution is easily found if we do not lose sight of the fundamental thought that our whole cycle of legends is designed to popularise the Jeroboamic kingdom, by glorifying the patriarch of Beth-el, and that for this purpose the Judaic-Davidic kingdom is humiliated without the slightest consideration, and attempts are made to deprive it of any moral influence over the people. For this purpose the work of the Jeroboamic legends enters at any price into any relation *which might be used in some way* against the kingdom of Judah. Such a handle lay geographically and politically ready in the shape of the canton of Benjamin.

Geographically the canton of Benjamin was so situated that a war between the two kingdoms must necessarily have taken place first upon that territory. The military road, where the enemy had to cross defiles, mountain passes, ravines and ridges, in order to pass through Benjamin to Jerusalem, is mentioned by the prophet Isaiah with keen brevity (Chap. x. 28—32). The possession of the canton of Benjamin therefore was a matter of vital importance for Judah. Of course the Israelitic kingdom had the same interest to acquire that territory, and as far as the wars through twenty-four years of Jeroboam's dynasty made it possible, they certainly tried to acquire it strategically. However, if one may believe the strongly coloured statements in Chronicles, Jeroboam was not very successful in war

(2 Chronicles xi). With greater industry, therefore, did the legendary material turn to his moral conquests, and thus the seed fell in Benjamin upon a soil made sensitive and susceptible through David's barbarous spirit of persecution against the generation of King Saul.

The whole kingdom of Saul is historically enveloped in a very impenetrable fog. Saul's character is dark; his age, even his reign, a problem, and still more enigmatical is the fact that he was capable of converting into a monarchy a republic, which had been so completely split up into special cantons. But what speaks for him incontestibly is the affection which the people, with the single exception of Judah, displayed towards him, and the fidelity which they manifested, even seven years after his death, to his thoroughly incapable son, Ishbosheth.

Saul was a *Benjamite*, and therefore the attachment to him and his descendants was of longest duration in the canton of Benjamin; but this sympathy extended also to the adjacent mountains of Ephraim, and it was not unfrequently called into action by the adversaries of David, when inciting little rebellions against him. The rebel Sheba, son of Bicri (2 Samuel xx.), who after the rebellion of Absalom raised the flag of insurrection in favour of Saul's heirs, is called Benjamite as well as Ephraimite (Verses 1 and 21). His home may have been in the frontier mountain where some places were situated, which at one time belonged to Benjamin, at another to Ephraim. In the mountains of Ephraim a jealousy of Judah was felt even in peaceful and quiet times, and so the sympathy of Benjamin, which had been so deeply outraged by David, could always be reckoned upon.

It is true that David's persecutions of the family of Saul, which has rightly procured him the name of "bloody man" (2 Samuel xvi. 7), had exterminated the last offspring of that dangerous family. What is related to us of the last blood-scene (2 Samuel xxi. 14) is well calculated to prove that thence any trace of a Saulic revolution was destroyed. In the will of David (1 Kings ii. 8, 9) we find an admonition to his son Solomon, not to spare the Benjamite old rebel Shimei, the son of Gera, to whom David, in a capricious moment of power, had granted a free pardon, but "*to bring his hoar head to the grave with blood.*" In fact there is no instance during Solomon's reign beyond this recommended one that another execution of Saul's partisans was needed. From the fact that the Benjamites at the time of the revolution in Shecem still sided with Judah, we must draw the conclusion that their former attempts at revolution were incited only by the direct members of Saul's family, and that after that family had been extinguished no rebellious voice could sound.

However, the strategic importance of Benjamin was such for Jeroboam, that he continually tried to fan the flame of rebellion, naturally relying upon the presumption that *Joseph and Benjamin were the real sons of the patriarch and his beloved wife Rachel, and that therefore Benjamin must undoubtedly cleave to the house of Joseph.*

In itself, this assertion was not exactly a new invention but only the working out of an already existing idea. From the moment when, after Saul's death, David split the already united kingdom by severing Judah, and the fate of Saul's descendants depended upon the attitude of the powerful canton of Ephraim, the Benjamites considered themselves *partisans of Ephraim or Joseph.* The rebel Shimei son of Gera was of the family of Saul and therefore a Benjamite (2 Samuel xvi. 5), and even after his last submission had hoped for grace, because he had been the first " of all the house of Joseph " who had come to beg David's pardon and to acknowledge him (2 Samuel xix. 20). But this idea does not as yet bear the imprint of one which produces partisan legends. The Jeroboamic struggle against Judah first brought Benjamin into the great cycle of legends of the Patriarch of Bethel—into a place *fit for the interest of the Ephraimites.* The legend runs thus (Gen. xxxv. 16). The patriarch journeyed from Bethel, the sacred place where Elohe talked to him direct, through the district of Benjamin toward " Ephrath," which is *Bethlehem* in Judah. Before he reached that city, " a little piece of ground before," his beloved wife Rachel was taken in labour. She bore a son, but his life was bought with the mother's. She dying, called him Benoni, " *son of my pains,*" but the father called him Benjamin, son of the right hand. There Rachel was buried, and the patriarch set a pillar on her grave, a " matzebah " " and *that is the pillar of Rachel's grave unto this day.*"

Looking at this statement quite apart from its Jeroboamic tendency, one can at once recognise its legendary character, as it forms again only a parallel to the legend of Abraham. As Sarah there, so Rachel here, is intended to consecrate a particular spot by her grave. But to this legend is also added, for the sake of proof, a historical memorial which has long ago challenged criticism to a severe examination of the accuracy of the legend ; and the result has so much *turned against* such accuracy that we are more even than in all other portions of this cycle of legends, referred to *partisanship* as the only motive.

In the first book of Samuel (chapter x. 2), Rachel's sepulchre is simply mentioned as a designation of the locality which Saul had to pass. According to that, the grave of Rachel was situated on the way between Ramah and Gibeah, therefore in any case, *north of* Jerusalem, whilst according to the legend in question it is alleged to have been in the *south*, ten English miles from Jerusalem, in the neighbourhood of Bethlehem. Now there would be no difficulty in accepting the sepulchre of Rachel in the north of Jerusalem near Ramah as the tomb of a woman unknown to us, but celebrated in her time. Besides that monument which was

known in Saul's time, a second one might have existed
founded by our patriarch near Bethlehem, and containing the earthly remains of the ancestress of the
Benjamites. But apart from its being a miraculous
incident that two monuments of the same name should
exist north and south of Jerusalem, there is a passage
in the prophet Jeremiah (chapter xxxi. 15.) where
"Rachel's" voice was heard in Ramah "lamenting over
her children wandering as exiles." Rachel is beyond
doubt the ancestress indicated by legend. Her voice
in "Ramah" is therefore a clear proof that the prophet
Jeremiah knew nothing of a grave of Rachel in the
neighbourhood of Bethlehem. This grave of Rachel
therefore is an invention of our legend, and we have
serious cause to look for the true motives why legend
should try to transfer the birth of Benjamin, the death
of Rachel and her tomb, into the very heart of Judah,
the neighbourhood of Bethlehem.

From all that we have proved about the partisanship
of the patriarchal legends of Bethel, the solution of
things follows naturally.

It was in the interest of the Jeroboamic policy *to
gain the canton of Benjamin at any price.* Therefore
Benjamin was preferred to all the so-called brothers of
Joseph. The longing for Benjamin is treated in a
masterly way in Joseph's history. Joseph is deeply
moved when he sees him again for the first time (Gen.
xliii. 29): "Elohe, be gracious unto thee, my son," he
exclaims, rushing from the room because his feelings
overcame him. He weeps in an adjoining room and
washes his face in order to hide the traces of his tears.
In a masterly spirit, approaching in dramatic effect the
most noble creations of art of any time, the historical
conflict between Judah and Joseph about the territory
of Benjamin is introduced in this history, (Gen. xliv.
11-34), as a family scene in Egypt. Judah is ready
to sacrifice himself and to bear slavery rather than
abandon Benjamin. Then Joseph discovers himself.

Abraham, Isaac, and Jacob. 65

He is the master, the benefactor, the provider for all, the mighty one, who can take revenge for all the malice of his brothers, but who deals good for evil.
The brothers all stand ashamed and frightened, but he falls upon Benjamin's neck and weeps, and Benjamin weeps upon the neck of his *magnanimous brother* (Gen. xlv. 15). The climax of Joseph's history however is reached in the concluding scene (l. 18-21), when all his brothers kneel down before him and exclaim " we are thy servants," and Joseph comforts them, that they thought evil against him but Elohe had turned it into good! He promises to nourish them and to provide for them, comforts them and speaks to their hearts. Benjamin alone is innocent and pure, and must naturally ·cleave more completely to his magnanimous brother in true love. But what is behind all these scenes, wrought out as they are with such beauty and masterly art? Nothing but the plan *to gain, through the territory of Benjamin, an entrance into the very heart of Judah.*

The monument of their common mother in Bethlehem was to be liberated. Benjamin had to recognise, that there, at the place of his birth, he had to reclaim for himself a dear memorial of his beloved mother from the usurpation of Judah. And more than the burial ground of the common *mother* had to be conquered, more still, *it was necessary to conquer also the tomb of the patriarch himself.* Of the patriarch? Certainly this sounds strange, if one accepts as matter of faith the text of the story as it has been worked out by the harmonist in chapters xlvii. 1 as the original. Luckily for a closer examination, the harmonist, evidently moved by the beauty of the original before him, has only slightly accommodated these chapters to his idea, by displacing, interpolating, and omitting: anyhow he has preserved enough of the Ephraimitic spirit of the original to enable us to re-establish it in the main. Then it sounds of course quite differently.

The passages which we have to examine begin with

E

verse 29 of the 47th chapter, and end with verse 13 of the 50th chapter of the first book of Moses. The material for this narrative is, in language and contents, so uncommonly rich, that the scientific critic has here an extraordinary scope for exploration. We, however, influenced chiefly by our task, intend simply to concentrate our attention upon this point, that an Ephraimitic idea permeates the intermingled text.

Truly Ephraimitic is every part where the name of the patriarch "Israel" pervades the whole story. Where it alternates with the name of "Jacob," the text is, to say the least, suspicious. Doubtlessly Ephraimitic is the text in every passage which represents the son of Joseph, Ephraim, as much preferred by the patriarch: doubtful, at least, is the text where the sons of Joseph are represented as equal but not *superior* to the actual sons of the patriarch. Ephraimitic is the text when it shows Joseph in intimate relations with the patriarch, doubtful when the text introduces Joseph *in the midst of his brothers*. Ephraimitic is the text when it specially mentions *Rachel;* doubtful, at the least, *when it mentions Leah and is silent about Rachel.*

When we examine the text again upon these assumptions, we find that two facts are stated in two different versions, which we are still able to distinguish clearly from each other.

One of the facts is, that Israel discusses directly with Joseph (chapter xlvii. 29-31), where he wishes to be buried, and makes him swear that he will do as his father bids. In this discussion, it remains throughout doubtful *where* he is to be buried, it certainly says (ושכבתי עם אבותי) "when I lay me down with my fathers," and afterwards "bury me in their burying place" (וקברתני בקברתם) from which it might follow that he meant the tomb of his "fathers." But the expression, "when I lay me down with my fathers," is only a metaphor for *death*, by no means implying reference to particular ancestors. Anyhow, doubt may

Abraham, Isaac, and Jacob. 67

still be entertained as to where the wished for grave was to be. But besides this particular discussion with Joseph *alone*, there exists a second portion (chapter xlix. 29-32) where the same subject is discussed *with all the sons*, and where the burial place is most accurately indicated, *as if it were important to avoid a misunderstanding under any circumstances.*

After the death of the patriarch it was necessary to execute his will. Joseph sent a communication to Pharaoh, begging leave to travel, in which he says (chapter l. 5) "my father made me swear, saying : behold I die ! in my grave *which I have digged for me in the land of Canaan*, there shalt thou bury me." Where he had prepared such a grave is not said. But the text continues that the sons all did as their father had bidden them to do ; and again, it is related with painful precision (verse 13) that they buried him in the cave of the field of Macpelah, and the buyer "Abraham," and the seller "Ephron," and the place are cited so accurately, and with such stress, as if, after all the detailed descriptions in four complete verses (Gen. xlix. 29-32) it was necessary at any cost, *that any other idea about the grave of this patriarch should be emphatically averted.*

What different idea then could arise ? Wherefore all these details about a place which apparently nobody had doubted ? For the purpose of elucidating these questions, we must look at two other portions of these chapters, which also refer to one and the same subject, but with decided variations.

The patriarch adopts Joseph's sons (chapter xlviii. 1-6). He is called "Jacob" in that passage. He puts Joseph's sons upon an equality with his own two eldest sons. Ephraim and Manasseh shall be to me as Reuben and Simeon. Then without any motive, and referring to neither what had preceded, nor to what follows, comes a verse which speaks of Rachel's death, and of her grave in "Ephrath, which is Bethlehem." And now follows from verse 8 to the end of the chapter, a wonderfully drawn picture of the blessings which the patriarch of the name of "Israel" bestows upon the sons of Joseph, not thinking at all of his other sons, but blessing most Ephraim; to whom he specially says, verse 20, ישראל יברך בך with, in or by "*thee*, shall Israel bless." In this sentence which is elucidated, Israel means the *people* of "Israel," *not yet existing* at the time of the patriarch.

Comparing the two portions, the adoption of the two sons of Joseph (verses 1-6), and the high preference for Ephraim (verses 8-20), one does not fail to remark that the latter part is entirely Ephraimitic, while the preceding part suggests a *mitigation* of the same fact, a sort of balance, by which Ephraim's importance is not denied, but still, according to rank, is only placed *equal* with Reuben's and not by any means at the head of all others.

If it be correct that here one and the same scene is before us, in two portions of different significance, which compared with each other certainly do not agree, and if we must accept the first portion as interpolated, because in the second (verses 8-9), the patriarch does not even know *who these two children are whom he is just said to have adopted*, then we must consider, where the lost seventh verse ought to be put which stands between the two portions, and is not to be brought into any natural relation with one or the other.

Certainly there is ample ground for asserting that this seventh verse, which refers to the tomb of "Rachel," belongs entirely to the conversation with Joseph, as lower down (chapter xlix. 31) the remembrance of "Leah" and her grave belong to the conversation of the patriarch with the other sons.

In other words, there exist two versions of where the patriarch wished to be buried. According to the one, he had only discussed the matter with *Joseph;* according to the other, he had communicated *to all his sons*

Abraham, Isaac, and Jacob. 69

his wishes in that respect. According to the one version, he had indicated to Joseph the grave, אשר כריתי לי, as that "which he digged himself" (chapter l. 5); according to the other, he had indicated it to his sons, with uncommon elaboration and precision, with all the details of main and surrounding circumstances, which we find in the verses 29-32 of chapter xlix.

Here we have exactly the same thing as before, with the glorification of Ephraim; first, a truly Ephraimitic description of the grave, and secondly, an amelioration devised by the harmonist, and treated with particular care and accuracy, in order to remove the trenchant difference of the Ephraimitic legend. And withal, the harmonist has only moved the 7th verse, which betrays the original text, from its correct place, and has only altered one word, so that he offers the opportunity of re-establishing the original text.

Doing this, and replacing the text, it would read thus :—* ושכבתי עם אבותי ונשאתני ממצרים וקברתני בקברי כי אני בבאי מפדן מתה עלי רחל בארץ (Gen. xlvii. 30.) כנען בדרך בעוד כברת ארץ לבא אפרתה ואקברה שם בדרך אפרת הוא בית לחם (Gen. xlviii. 7.) ויאמר אנכי אעשה כדברך. (Gen. xlvii. 30.)

In the translation, the correct text, by transferring the seventh verse from chapter 48 to its right place, would run thus: "When I lay me down with my fathers, thou shalt carry me out of Egypt and bury me in my grave: for when I came from Padan (Mesopotamia) Rachel died on the road, in the land of Canaan, when there was yet but a little way to come unto Ephrath. And I buried her there on the way to Ephrath, which is Bethlehem." And he (Joseph) said, I will do as thou hast said.

Where the patriarch wished to be buried is no more doubtful after this; and all this coincides exactly with Joseph's alleged communication to Pharaoh (chapter

* Possibly there may have followed the words אשר כריתי לי. (Gen. l. 5.) which I digged for myself.

l. 5), that he would bury his father *in the grave which he had digged for himself.*

If now the accuracy of this text be proved, it cannot be a matter of doubt that this, as well as the whole legend of a grave of Rachel, the mother of Joseph and Benjamin, is nothing more than an attempt of the Ephraimite Jeroboam, to attract the Benjamites to his side in his wars against Rehoboam.

As " Abraham and Sarah in Hebron," so " Israel and Rachel" were to have a common grave near Bethlehem. To acquire this grave from Judah was to be the task of Joseph's sons, and especially of Benjamin, who was the dying Rachel's son of sorrow, and who could never be forgetful of the noble Joseph's brotherly love.

XII.

MUTUAL ELUCIDATION OF LEGEND AND HISTORY.

He who after what has preceded has arrived with us at the conviction that behind the patriarchs of Hebron and of Beth-el stand historical personalities veiled by the nimbus of legend; and that the apparently simple idyllic events of the family lives of those patriarchs, are only the ingenious reflections of the great events of their time, will have no objection to follow our attempts to draw from both causes the eventual solutions of mutual elucidation, *i.e.*, of supplementing history by means of legend, and of making legend more intelligible by means of history.

We propose to limit ourselves in that task to one fixed point, namely, to the question why the legend of the patriarch of Beth-el, in relation to neighbouring nations, deviates so essentially from the legends of the patriarch of Hebron?

We have already seen how the heroes of both legends maintain with careful consideration friendly relations to the great neighbouring states of Mesopotamia and Egypt. The Hebron legend represents in a mild mod-

Abraham, Isaac, and Jacob. 71

erate form dignified legitimacy; the Beth-el legend in an exaggerated degree, unscrupulous usurpation. Does not the Beth-el legend for the purpose of glorifying the intimacy of Jeroboam with Egypt, go so far as to bring the patriarch himself into a personal audience with Pharaoh, where the patriarch, *in coming and in going bestows "his blessing"* upon Pharaoh. The more surprising is it that the two cycles of legends differ almost purposely in their relations towards small neighbouring nations. The legend of Abraham seeks, partly through histories of descent, partly through treaties of peace, to keep up friendly intercourse with the Philistines, with Ammon and Moab, and the Ishmaelites; whilst the Beth-el legend passes these tribes and nations in entire silence. On the other hand, the Hebron legend throws Edom completely out of sight, whilst the Beth-el legend dedicates elaborate scenes to this relation, and shows the patriarch as the peace-seeking brother of Esau (Gen. xxxii. and xxxiii).

The solution of these facts can only be given by history, of which legend is the reflection. In those legends is shown the reflection of the terms on which on one side, the Davidic dynasty, on the other side the Jeroboamic usurpation stood, and were obliged to stand with neighbouring nations.

David was a warrior who, sword in hand, conquered the small surrounding nations, and who, during a state of war, repressed any opposition by prodigious cruelty (2 Sam. viii). But when the bloodshed was over he tried to win their sympathies where they could be won. In Ammon, Moab, and in the land of the Philistines this course succeeded for a long time. The warlike expeditions of the Philistines ceased. The Moabites appear to have been obliged, through the fortress Peniel having been built by Jeroboam at the frontier river, to join the kingdom of Israel, and they only recovered courage a century later under their king Mesha to strike for independence (2 Kings iii). It was almost as long before

Ammon ventured to rise against the kingdom of Judah (2 Chron. xx), and this being so, the Hebron legend stands also on friendly terms with those subjected nations, and through blood alliances as well as through treaties of peace, manages to keep up a long connection with the hero of the Judaic legends, Abraham.

The case is different with Edom, and partly also with Damascus. Both were subdued by David, but their resistance was not so soon broken. Military stations had to be erected in both kingdoms (2 Sam. viii. 6, 14). Especially in Edom, Joab the captain of David, initiated bloodshed which lasted full six months (1 Kings xi. 16), "until he had cut off every male in Edom." Therefore we hear also, very soon after David's death, of an opposition in Damascus, organised by Rezon, who caused many difficulties to Solomon (1 Kings xi. 23). From Edom, however, a young prince, "Hadad," fled to Egypt, met there, as we have already mentioned, with a friendly reception, married the sister of the Queen of Egypt, and after David's death returned to his country to liberate it (1 Kings xi. 14-22).

As we already know, Egypt was also the refuge of Jeroboam when he was obliged to leave his country after his conspiracy with Ahijah, the Shilonite, had been discovered. We have already shown the high probability of the intimacy of Jeroboam with the Egyptian court. Unprejudiced statement (1 Kings xi. 40) seems to put it beyond any doubt. The legend which makes the patriarch of Beth-el bless Pharaoh bears the seal of veracity upon it. This intimate friend, as we are already aware, soon after Jeroboam's fortunate usurpation, invaded Jerusalem and spoliated it thoroughly.

Is it, after all this, imaginable that Jeroboam should have stood in no relation to Hadad of Edom?

Hadad was certainly older than Jeroboam. At the time of David's death he was already married, and at Solomon's death he may have been sixty years old,

Abraham, Isaac, and Jacob. 73

while Jeroboam, who wore the royal crown of Israel for another twenty-two years, could only have reached the prime of manhood at Solomon's death. We must also believe, according to present historical records, that the two enemies of David's dynasty did not live contemporaneously in Egypt. The presumption, however, is on the surface, that Jeroboam did not forego gaining for himself so decided an enemy of David's house as Hadad was, and to raise hopes in him for the throne of Edom, should he be his ally.

Of this, even History itself gives *no* solution. But if we only consider clearly what sort of historical personage is concealed behind the patriarch of Beth-el, and when we find a long account *of an embassy with presents, which the patriarch sent to Edom, to his brother Esau, that this brother comes to meet him, and that the patriarch upon beholding the Edomite, expresses his assurance of having seen a face of Elohe, a face of God*—we may then well assert, that Legend, in the harmless garb of a family scene, has preserved a part of History, and that the meeting with the patriarch is only a *legendary reflexion of the historical fact of a meeting between Jeroboam and Hadad*.

Having allowed ourselves in this way to supplement History by Legend, we may also be permitted to elucidate a dark part of legend by a historical statement.

In the story of the patriarch (Gen. xxxii. 25) a scene is pictured, in which at "Peniel," a God wrestled with the patriarch the whole night, until day-break. The God could not prevail against the patriarch; on the contrary, the patriarch held him tight and would not let him go, until he got his blessing. This blessing consisted in the alteration of his name into "Israel," which means: "Champion of God" or rather "Conqueror of God." But the God had left a mark of his strength upon the patriarch, he had touched the hollow of his thigh and put it out of joint in the struggle. And when the sun rose upon Peniel, the *patriarch limped upon his thigh*.

We pass over the curious remark which verse thirty-second makes upon this strange narrative as a subject not within our enquiry.

We, therefore, purpose only to refer to the legend, which evidently endeavours to justify the name of Israel "Champion of God," and we will see, in how far that legend might be based upon historical ground.

The legend of a struggle with a God, does not belong to the curiosities of antiquity. He who dies suddenly has been struck by God, he who suddenly becomes lame has been afflicted by the same fate in a mitigated form, he who sustained an attack of the kind, and came off with only a slightly injured limb could boast of having conquered God, and could consider the conquest as an honour.

As we know now what kind of historical personage is concealed behind the patriarch of Beth-el, we may be bold enough to seek a solution of this "wrestling with God," and the fact that it is easily found is certainly not uninteresting.

In chapter xiii. of the first book of Kings the following story is related at some length:

A man of God came out of Judah, by the word of Jehovah, to Beth-el, just as Jeroboam stood by the altar to burn incense. Then the man prophesied, in an address to the altar, that a son would be born to the house of David who would slaughter all the priests who burned incense upon that altar, and, as a sign, the altar should be rent, and the ashes that were upon it should be dispersed. When Jeroboam heard this he put forth his hand, exclaiming, Arrest him! but his hand remained numb, and he could not draw it in again towards himself, and the altar was rent, and the ashes were strewn about. Then the king begged of the man of God to entreat Jehovah to restore motion to his hand. The man of God did so, and the hand recovered.

The further very strange adventures of this man of

Abraham, Isaac, and Jacob. 75

God are elaborately stated at the place mentioned. As they do not concern our subject, we only gather from the miraculous description this much, that on a certain occasion, perhaps at the building of an altar or the erection of a pillar, or perhaps at the building of the fortress of Peniel, a stone splintered and hurt the king Jeroboam, who happened to be present, upon his hand or foot, or upon both limbs, so that he could not move his hand, and was lame.

An event like that was certainly sufficient to be regarded by pious men of Judaic spirit—and their number in Israel was great—as a wonderful sign that *God had struck the sinner.* Jeroboam's partisans have given the opposite interpretation, and pronounced him to be a true "Israel" whom God could not conquer, but only slightly injure, a fact which redounded to the honour of the champion. That this, reflected in the patriarchal legend, sounds somewhat differently, is easily understood in a time where the historical material was used for legendary garb.

XIII.
THE NAMES OF "ISRAEL" AND "JACOB."

We arrive at length at the questions, under which name the patriarch of Beth-el may have been originally introduced, and how it stands about the so-called alteration of name which, in the present text of the narrative, is presented under two different versions? (Gen. xxxii. 28; xxxv. 10.)

"Jacob" signifies, as already remarked, literally, "holder by the heel," which means somebody who trips up his neighbour. But it means also "impostor," and is so thoroughly adopted in that sense in the Hebrew language, that not only personal deeds of *cunning* are designated by the word בעקבה (2 Kings x. 19), but it is also used to picture the general decadence of moral condition. The prophet Jeremiah (chap.

ix. 1-5), describing the moral abyss of his time, where lies, treason, deceit, and perfidy held sway, expresses it with the words, כי כל אח עקוב יעקב, that brother will deceive brother. Even the narrator of the patriarchal story causes Esau to exclaim, as already mentioned, "It is well that he be called *Jacob*, for he hath supplanted me these two times." (Gen. xxvii. 36.)

If the fact be surprising that this insulting word should be given as a name for a child, it is the more so when that name is not at all usual and does not recur. It is, of course, most astonishing when such a name is given to a *patriarch*, but most of all, it is surprising when, amongst the stories which are told of this patriarch, many occur which *evidently justify the appellation*. From this fact alone we must conclude that there are particular circumstances in connection with this name, and that the designation "Israel," with its most honourable signification, is a counterpoise to the reproach of the other.

But whence is the name of Israel derived?

As a proper name, it nowhere recurs. It is the name of a people, but also not the proper one—so to say, *the nationally privileged one*—because that sounds unconditionally in contradistinction to *other* nations, *Ebrim* or Hebrews. Israel is only the name of honour by which their own poets and thinkers chose to call the peoples of separate cantons in their *entirety*. Later poets attempted to introduce the still more ethical name of "Jeshurun," the just ones, but they were not able to deprive the name of Israel of its general value. The oldest designation of the people by the name of "Israel" is certainly in the very old song of Deborah. (Judges v.) But the name of Israel culminated to its true value only upon the establishment of the *Jeroboamic kingdom*, which thereafter was simply designated as the *kingdom of Israel*, in opposition to a second *kingdom of Judah*.

When we inquire into the origin of this name, and want to keep aloof from all legendary pictures, we must

Abraham, Isaac, and Jacob. 77

look for it in the country bearing the name of "Jezreel," יזרעאל (Izreel), a country which was of such importance in the history of the people that we cannot be astonished if they all gradually derived their name from it. In that country existed an old town of the same name. It is not improbable that the "God of Fecundity," יזרע־אל, was worshipped there, and that the town and country being widely celebrated for fecundity, received their name from him. The inhabitants of that table-land took their collective name of "Joseph," "Ephraim," from that "multiplication" and "fecundity." "Jezreel, Joseph, and Ephraim," are in that sense synonymous.

The country of Jezreel comprised a piece of land which formed the largest plain in the otherwise very mountainous country, for which reason also that table-land was the scene of the most important wars of the people which lived in their remembrance for centuries. Upon the plain of Jezreel was fought the battle of Tabor against Sisera which is glorified and immortalized in the song of Deborah (Judges v). The same place was the scene of Gideon's deeds whose "day of Midian" lived for centuries as a day of most glorious remembrance. (Judges vi. 33, and Isaiah ix. 3, and x. 26). There also was fought the unfortunate battle of Gilboa, where Saul and Jonathan fell (1 Samuel xxxi. 1). We find that at a later date, upon this plain were fought battles which always decidedly influenced the fate of the whole land (1 Kings xx. 26, and 2 Kings xxiii. 29). Therefore the population of that table-land felt itself politically supreme, and with the canton of Ephraim at its head, always stood up in jealousy and war against Judah as soon as that nation claimed supremacy.

Under these circumstances it needs no further explanation that the name of the land "Jezreel" passed over in old times to the entire people whose fate was decided in that valley. At first the people may have been called יזרעאלים (with a soft z) Isreelim. But the

Ephraimites whose tongue, as we know, sharpened all hissing sounds and pronounced "Shiboleth" as "Sibboleth," (Judges xii. 6), may also have altered "Izreel" into "Israel." The name of Israel would in that way have a very natural origin.

The canton of Ephraim, situated in that valley of Jezreel also turned to its own advantage the spirit against any privilege of Judah. After the death of Saul, Ephraim and Jezreel were the points of opposition against David. The son of Saul, Ishbosheth, was acknowledged there and proclaimed king over *Benjamin* (2 Sam. ii. 9). The town of Jezreel also became later the residence of the king of Israel (1 Kings xviii. 45). The town of Jezreel and the plain of Jezreel are, as we see, so much interwoven with the fate of the people that we cannot think it strange that Jeroboam who made himself *king of Israel* should also have adopted for his patriarch this universal name of the tribes, and let him appear under the denomination of "*Israel.*"

But just as natural is it that the defending patron of the rebel was called in the kingdom of Judah a "*deceiver*" or an "*impostor*" a "Jacob." The alliance of Jeroboam with the prophet Ahijah, with Shishak of Egypt, with Rezon of Aram, and with Hadad of Edom; the bitter calumnies against Reuben, against Simeon and Levi, the libel upon Judah, the part taken by the rebel in the assembly at Shecem, the agitation in Benjamin—all this could not be regarded in Judah other than as a web of high treason, of lies and frauds and deceit intended to ruin the house of David. The malignant legends were reciprocated by malignant descriptions of the patriarch. One professed to know how *already at his birth he had been a supplanter* and therefore received from his parents the name of Jacob. In face of the intrigues of Jeroboam who tried to persuade Hadad to revolt against Judah, one could readily allow that Jacob was *the brother of Esau,* but a brother who deceived his brother and only made use of him to ruin him.

Abraham, Isaac, and Jacob. 79

Even now, when the harsh differences of the legends have long been smoothed over and reconciled by harmonists, by means of omissions, interpolations, and alterations, we are well able to discern how the Judaic hostility to Ephraimitic legends was more and more nourished by mere libels. Even now we can quote passages of the so-called history of the life of Jacob and Esau which have been added to the already existing slanders in order to heap insult upon insult on "Jacob's" name.

In Gen. xxv. 19, &c., the birth of Esau is related. That their parents were Isaac and Rebekah is a harmonistic supposition of later date, when it was required at any cost *to mould all the patriarchs into one family history*.

In the narrative of the birth of the twins, Esau is so depicted as to supply numerous motives why he should become the ancestor of *Edom* upon the mount of *Seir*. Edom, we mean the country of the name, consisted mostly of red earth and iron-oxide rocks; as Edom denotes "red colour," the name also suited the outward appearance of the country. The mountain also was called "Seir," which means "hairy," and denoted either the stunted and bristly vegetation, or the inhabitants who were thought to be wild and covered with hair. Esau is described as being born "red" in colour and "all over his skin like a hairy garment or cloak ;" such description evidently furnishing the motives for the name of the land : Edom, "Seir," the ancestor of which he was intended to be.

Directly after, in verse 29, &c., is related the notorious sale of his birthright for a meal of lentils. There we read: Esau said to Jacob, "Let me swallow down, I pray thee, some of that yonder red pottage, for I am faint," and it is added : therefore was his name called Edom (a red one). Considering that in the 25th verse, the name of Edom for Esau is already fully explained, it is impossible to believe that the story of his birth, and

that of the sale of his birthright, can be one and the
same, and have originated from one and the same
author. As the first story representing Jacob as trip-
ping up his brother has the purpose of slandering the
patriarch; and as the second story, although the
harmonist probably smoothed it by describing Esau as
rough, implies still more trenchant derision of Jacob,
we see clearly enough, how the legends against the
patriarch grew by degrees, and outvied each other in
degrading the patriarch.

We can call attention to the insertion of another
libel, more bitter still, in the midst of a quite innocent
text.

Verse 32 of Gen. xxvi. begins with the word ויהי
"and it came to pass," which words are generally the
beginning of a long narrative; but in the following
verse the narrative breaks off suddenly and a new
narrative begins with the word ויהי "and it came to
pass" (Ch. xxvii. 1). This new narrative contains
down to the last verse (46) the infamous story of how
Jacob lied to his old blind father, how he cheated his
brother out of his father's blessing, and how, in consequence, he was obliged to fly, to avoid Esau's first
anger.

But the whole of that slandering story does not at all
coincide with what the following chapter (xxviii.) relates.
According to the latter, Jacob did *not* fly, was *not* dis-
missed by his father in anger, and had evidently
nothing at all to fear from Esau. That chapter, in
fact, is no other than an exaggerated imitation of the
Abrahamic legend. As Abraham (Gen. xxiv.) wished
there, so did the father of Jacob wish here, that the
son should not marry a "Canaanite," and instead of
sending a servant on the errand of wooing, Isaac sends
Jacob himself to Mesopotamia. *There is no trace of a
conflict with Esau, or of a flight from him.* On the
contrary, Esau followed *the good example* of Jacob, to
whom he in nowise grudged the farewell blessing, and

Abraham, Isaac, and Jacob. 81

married an *Ishmaelite* in addition to his Canaanite wives.

On closer examination of the text, we observe whence these contradictions originate. The original text had literally begun with the ויהי of verse 34 of chapter xxvi.; thereupon followed verse 35, and then in the closest union the 46th verse of chapter xxvii., upon which chapter xxviii. continues the story logically, and concludes with verse 9. This original story is certainly Ephraimitic. It imitates indeed, as we observed, the legend of Abraham, and tries to surpass it; but, on the whole, it is otherwise uncaptious. But the Judaic indignation could not allow "Jacob" to pass straight on, with his father's blessing. Therefore that bitter libel was devised, partly to paint the patriarch as black as possible, partly to show the Edomites what they had to think of the brotherly love of the Ephraimites.

And as a matter of fact, Jeroboam's intrigues had no great influence upon Edom. Edom remained with Judah and did not join the kingdom of Israel. It is not impossible, that the libellous legends against Jacob, and his behaviour therein depicted, towards the honest straightforward Esau, contributed much to Edom's staying with the kingdom of Judah.

Somewhat darker and more veiled are the passages which concern Jacob's relations with Laban. The text has been so much intermixed and elaborated by the harmonist, that the Ephraimitic original, and the Judaic libel, can only be disentangled with the utmost difficulty. We must be satisfied with the general characteristic that Jacob remains nowhere unsullied. Whether Laban outcheated him, or he outcheated Laban, is, in the present condition of the text, a question difficult to decide. But as a sign of the most bitter hostility, we must not fail to mention, how the so-called ancestresses are drawn into this scandal. In opposition to the Ephraimitic slander of *Leah* who is designated as "the hated one," (Gen. xxix. 31), the

F

Judaic pamphletist casts a stain upon *Rachel*, letting her *steal* the images of her father " Teraphim" (Gen. xxxi. 19), and hide them slily and successfully.

Another point is enveloped also in mysterious darkness, which it is no easy task now to penetrate. Jacob and Esau separated; the latter removed to Edom, the former remained in Canaan. The reason of this separation is so represented in chapter xxxvi. verses 6-8, as to make it obvious how the Ephraimitic legend, in the most clumsy way copied a Judaic Abrahamic one. As Abraham (Gen. xiii. 5-12) separated himself from Lot, because the number of the cattle was too large for one district, such is said also to have been the case with Jacob and Esau. The 6th verse of chapter xiii. is almost literally *copied* in the 7th verse of chapter xxxvi. But so affectionate a parting is not at all to the mind of the Judaic interpolator. Flight, hostility, deadly hatred, fear, presents, and, finally, sly subterfuge, (Gen. xxxiii. 13-14) must be brought in aid. Jacob even promised that he would follow " his lord" Esau slowly "*until he should come to him unto Seir,*" which, of course, *never* happened.

Comparing, now, the conflict of the legends with each other, it is of interest to observe that their heroes are opposed to each other, almost as faithfully, as the historical personages who peep through the veil of legend. We might be induced to say that Abraham stands to Jacob as David to Jeroboam, as legitimacy to usurpation, as simplicity to intrigue. It really seems as though the times, which govern men, imprint themselves upon their imagination. They invent what they experience. They imagine they are painting the pictures of the past, and they create forms which betray their own present to posterity.

XIV.

THE HARMONIST AND HARMONIZATION.

We have tried to ascertain the manner and times of the origin of the patriarchal legends, and we must now proceed to the much more difficult attempt of sketching the history of the development of the legends, and of following them up, at least in a general way, to the shape in which they are now before us. The conflict of legends lasted, in all probability, no longer than the interest of their producers in the continuation of such conflict. Now the epoch of the Ephraimites, the reign of Jeroboam, lasted only twenty-four years. After Jeroboam had reigned for twenty-two years, his son Nadab became king: but in the second year of his reign, he was murdered by one of his captains, Baasha, who then seized the reins of government in the kingdom of Israel and exterminated the whole house of Jeroboam (1 Kings xv. 25-34). Baasha was *no* Ephraimite, but of the canton of Issachar. He continued the wars against the kingdom of Judah, but an alliance of Judah with Aram, forced him to give up, or at least to interrupt the war. Baasha reigned thirty-four years, when his son Elah began to reign, and he, in his turn, was murdered by a captain of his, Zimri, who wanted to govern. But the captain Omri, who led the people in a war against the Philistines, dethroned Zimri and ascended the throne. Omri reigned twelve years, and was succeeded by his son Ahab, whose reign lasted twenty-two years. During the reign of the latter, an alliance was formed between Israel and Judah, which lasted some time, and so materially altered the relations of the two kingdoms towards each other, from what they had been under the reign of Jeroboam, that one may well say, the specific Ephraimitic character of the kingdom of Israel disappeared with Jeroboam its founder, although poets and prophets still designated the kingdom by the name of "*Ephraim.*" Comparing Jeroboam with all his successors on the throne of Israel, we cannot help ascribing to him a high importance. It certainly must redound to his credit, that he was, at least, endeavouring to lean his rebellion on the sympathies of the people, and to *legalize* his reign in a national spirit by traditions and legends.

He was an Ephraimite, and it cannot be denied that the canton of Ephraim had full claim to direct the nation. It is true that the whole structure which he created, and the elaboration of which he favoured, had been built up in his personal interest; still it was based upon a national idea of Ephraim's sacredness, conferred upon it by a patriarch. His religious institutions were arranged after the Egyptian type. He set up golden calves in *Beth-el* and *Dan*, but such idols were neither strange nor unknown to Israel. The legends which were circulated in his time had, although fabricated, a moral and national tendency. He did not by any means despise tradition, on the contrary, he wanted to rival and surpass the legend of Abraham. He had used the necessities of the country as an excuse for his personal ambition to obtain power: but he sought to support his power by ideal formations in the national spirit. His patriarch "Israel" may have been ever so much disfigured by the stories of "Jacob," yet there is about him a characteristic, pious spirit, which sparkles through all his deformities. But in poetic value the sound of Israel's legends far surpass the legends of Abraham. The pictures of Joseph, of Benjamin, and of Rachel, are and must remain masterworks of art, and preserve poetically the type of immortal creations, which mere *tyrants* never had the mind or spirit to produce or to advance.

Of Jeroboam's successors, none but Ahab, stands on a higher footing than that of a military usurper who, supported by the army, seized upon power. Not one is designated "*Ephraimite.*" The origin, even of most of them is unknown. In Ahab, indeed, a more important monarch appears again in Israel. But neither in politics nor in intellect did he pursue the path which Jeroboam had smoothed for him. He sought and made a political alliance with Judah, and induced by his wife, the daughter of a Phœnician king, he raised the worship of Baal, to be the official worship, thus *offering no points of affinity with the traditions of the Ephraimite Jeroboam.*

There was, however, another revolution after Ahab and his son. A captain, "Jehu," was incited by the Jehovistic prophet "Elisha" to seize power. He murdered the king, exterminated the whole house of Ahab, destroyed the temple of Baal, and murdered its priests and followers. Of this Jehu we are told (2 Kings x. 29) that he did not depart from the sin of Jeroboam, and did not destroy the golden calves in Bethel and Dan. From this one might conclude that Jehu was also in spirit a successor of Jeroboam; but, besides there being no further trace of that fact, and not even an intimation of Jehu having been an Ephraimite, the political discussion in the kingdom of Israel now appeared so marked, that all the provinces beyond the Jordan were snatched away by Aram. Consequently all probability speaks against a spiritual flight having taken place in the kingdom of Israel.

The dynasty of Jehu, it is true, counted one other fortunate monarch, who reigned for forty-one years, and who was a successful warrior, but even he did not impede the fall of the Israelitic kingdom. His son again was removed by murder, and the murderer again was hurled from the throne by another murderer. Then Assyria appeared on the scene of our events, with its invasions of conquest, and brought about the complete ruin of the kingdom of Israel.

We quote all these well-known facts for the simple purpose of showing that in the two and a-half centuries of the existence of the kingdom of Israel (from 978-720), no other epoch than the Jeroboamic one shines forth as a period of glorification for Ephraim.

If it is undeniable, that the whole cycle of legends about the patriarch of Bethel aimed at a glorification of Ephraim, and if our proofs be sufficient to show that this did not succeed without continual wars, we must logically conclude *that with the extermination of the Ephraimitic dynasty* (about the year 950 before our usual chronology) *the conflict of the legends with each other was extinguished also. Then the epoch commenced, when in pious minds the conflicting legends gradually intermingled, and their origin faded, until the time arose when the whole material was worked up into a heroically pre-historic account of the whole nation.*

The question, whether, in such remote antiquity, the legends had been reduced to writing, we must decidedly answer in the affirmative, after having conscientiously examined those which remain, and which have not been interpolated by the harmonist. They possess already, in the song of Deborah, (Judges v.) a literary production, the original text of which was doubtless devised very soon after the conquest of Siserah (1330 before our chronology), and was preserved, not only verbally, but in writing. We must not omit to consider, that in respect of literature, Palestine stood upon a different footing to contemporary flourishing states. In great monarchies, where the dynasty is the centre of all interests, the instinct of perpetuation, is satisfied by *magnificent buildings, palaces, temples, pictures, and inscriptions.*

But in republican nations, where no dynasties absorb the common interest, but where rulers and judges, chosen for a time, hold the reins of government, *aristocracy of mind* gains an ascendancy which tries to immortalise its whole thoughts and aspirations in song and speech, and in written records. Therefore the fact must not surprise us that neither mighty Egypt nor Assyria, but the small Palestine, handed down an old literature to posterity. There, too, lite-

Abraham, Isaac, and Jacob. 87

rary production was not disturbed by a rising kingdom, but on the contrary was *used as a support, and therefore progressed.*

If we recognise, now, in the Abrahamic legends, the preliminary pictures of the Davidic kingdom, there is no reason to doubt that, in addition to verbal narrative, those legends were reduced to writing in the cultivated places of Hebron and Jerusalem. The literary fancies of Solomon certainly only tended to encourage this production.

Now, if it was Jeroboam's plan to surpass David, it is most probable that he provided for Bethel written documents of the legends. Many a comparison between the Abrahamic and the Israelitic legends shows that favourite turns and figures of speech of the one were used for the other. In illustration, the curious passage from the Abrahamic cycle שים נא ידך תחת ירכי "Put thy hand under my thigh" (Gen. xxiv. 2) is accepted literally, in the legend of Israel (Gen. xlvii. 29), whilst in the whole of the Hebrew literature there is neither a repetition nor any trace of explanation of this form of speech. If we do not adopt the orthodox loophole, that that form of speech was used by the *real* Abraham, and as chance would have it, by his grandson, the *real* Jacob, nothing remains but the supposition that it occurred in the composition of the Abrahamic legend, and *that it was copied in Bethel as a classical, patriarchal turn of speech.* We have also already mentioned that in the legend of Israel (Gen. xxxvi. 7) a whole verse from the legend of Abraham (Gen. xiii. 6) is almost *literally copied,* from which it follows that *written records of both legends existed.*

It is perfectly impossible to believe that the already characterized libel upon David and his family was not written, because all the disfigurements of names produce an effect only when written, whilst verbally, (as for instance שלה for שלמה, and ער and רע) they are entirely lost. One important fact speaks above everything in favour of the reduction of the legends to writing, namely, that we are even now in a position to pick out entire portions of the legends in their almost completely uncorrected shape, as for instance, the whole of chapter xliii., where, in contrast to the preceding chapter, the name of "Jacob" does not once occur, but the name *only* of "Israel" is used ; and lastly, the passage in which Ephraim, although the younger brother, is preferred to Manasseh the elder (Gen. xlviii. 8-22). In the 15th and 16th verses, only the few words which mention Abraham and Isaac are interpolated, but, otherwise, the original text stands forth so clearly that one cannot imagine it otherwise than as having been transmitted in a written form.

The Jeroboamic genuineness of this portion cannot well be doubted, from the fact that it is a characteristic of all usurpers, *to prefer the after-born to the first-born;* and as a proof of the genuineness comes the as completely preserved parallel passage of the harmonist (Gen. xlviii. 4-6) which we have already considered.

The reduction of the legends to writing being put now beyond doubt, we may well suppose that with the destruction of the Ephraimitic house, with the extermination of the whole family of Jeroboam, not only the mutual conflict, but also the production of the legends ceased. The thirty-eight years of bloodshed which followed the extermination of the house of Jeroboam was little conducive to literary production. At that time also the rotation of *old* circumstances returned. *Shecem*, the residence of Jeroboam, was abandoned, and in its stead *Thirzah* and at a later time *Samaria* were chosen by the new ruler. Unhappy wars and all the new regicides disturbed the course of legendary imagination, and curbed zeal for or against them. A new monarch "Ahab" appeared, who *gave up* the Ephraimitic war against the kingdom of Judah, and who supplanted the *worship at Bethel* by the *worship of Baal.* With this, political conflict also entirely

Abraham, Isaac, and Jacob. 89

abated. But religious zeal advanced in the temples of Baal, and their priests presented for persecution *a new object of hatred*, which had no relation whatever to the foregone conflict of the legends. The prophet Elijah was so filled with hatred against the worship of Baal, *that he had no words of wrath left for Bethel.*

The era of harmonizing was evidently advancing in that direction.

XV.
ELIJAH AND HARMONIZATION.

Is the prophet Elijah the harmonist? We do not answer the question in the affirmative. We possess no personal writings of Elijah which guarantee his language. The narrator of his life and deeds, the author of the Books of the Kings, lived much too late to be able to give us authentic statements, and is too fond of miracles to be historically trustworthy. Still we must not leave untouched the little in the history of Elijah which might indicate him as the harmonist. In (chapter xviii. 31) of the First Book of the Kings, we are told that Elijah took twelve stones for the purpose of building an altar, *according to the number of the tribes of the sons of Jacob, unto whom the word of the Lord came, saying, " Israel shall be thy name."* Thus we find here, completely expressed by a historical person, belief in a Jacob, who, at Jehovah's bidding, was to be called "Israel." However, these are only words of the *narrator*, to which we need not attach any value. But in verse 36 of the same chapter, words of Elijah himself are reported. If we may give full belief to them, we have before us the most perfect harmonist, because the words run thus: "Jehovah, God of Abraham, Isaac, and Israel, let it be known this day that thou art God in Israel, and that I am thy servant," and so forth. Had these words been historically authenticated, we should not only have

Abraham and Israel, or Jacob already harmonized, but also Isaac would have been joined as an intermediate link. A suggestion for this latter possibility, lies in the circumstance that Elijah upon his travels visited Beersheba (1 Kings xix. 3) and therefore, might have heard some mention of the patriarch Isaac, who had been thrust into the background. Even had he made this journey at a later period, it is still possible, even probable, that Beersheba and its patriarch would not have been unknown to him. However, all these data are and must remain much too unsafe, to be critically valuable. On the contrary, there are strong presumptions for the fact that as the legend of Isaac had been entirely out of the conflict of legends, it did not enter into the harmonizing work for a long time, and that this intermediate link between the chief patriarchs was only at a later time, accepted in its order for the purpose of entirely completing the family history.

First of all the orthography in the alleged speech of Elijah is suspicious. The older authors do not know a Itzchak יצחק but a Ischak ישחק. Even the later Jeremiah (chapter xxxiii. 26), and the Psalms (Psalm cv. 9), call him Ischak. The prophet Amos, the only one who knew anything of the worship in Beersheba, speaks likewise only of the "heights of Ischak" and the "house of Ischak." Only the very late books of the Chronicles (1 Chron. xvi. 16), quote Psalm cv. and write Itzchak instead. Anyhow the name in the mouth of the prophet Elijah must be incorrect. But even if one could look over that fact, the astonishing circumstance remains, that the prophet Micah only knows *Abraham and Jacob* as fathers "of the days of old," and does not mention an "Isaac" (at the very end of Micah). Even the very late "second Isaiah" (chapter lxiii. 16), in his surprising expression about Abraham and Israel does not mention Isaac. Another circumstance is added, which makes it probable that in the beginning of the harmonization, Abraham was made the *father* of Jacob.

Abraham, Isaac, and Jacob. 91

In the narrative of the dream of Jacob in Bethel, we read (Gen. xxviii. 13). And behold Jehovah stood above it and said, "I am Jehovah, God of Abraham thy *father*." Certainly the words, "and the God of Isaac," are added, but that does not alter the fact that Abraham is designated as Jacob's father. The same version is twice repeated in chapter xxxi. There we read : " Except the God of my *father*, the God of Abraham had been with me." Verse 42 again follows Isaac's name even associated with "Pachad." Laban likewise expresses himself (verse 53), as if Abraham were the *father* of Jacob, and again directly afterwards the "Pachad" of Isaac is quoted.

These passages, together with the words of the prophet Micah, must really make us think that originally the harmonization was only intended to reconcile the legends of *Abraham and Jacob*. As a fact *only those two* were seriously conflicting. The legend of Isaac with its modest pretension to local authority in Beersheba, could not be an object of contest when *universal value* and the great struggles between the kingdoms of Judah and Israel were concerned.

When we consider all these points which, though not strictly proof, are still most worthy of regard, we believe we are in a condition to affirm that " harmonizing" *was very slowly advanced*. It may have begun after the ruin of the Ephraimitic generation of Jeroboam. It advanced when with Ahab's reign an alliance was concluded between Judah and Israel. But the *rounding off* of the legends with all the *intermediate links* completing the family picture, was most likely a work of later date ; a literary work which probably was begun when the kingdom of Israel had been already ruined, and when the general national grief had reconciled to all minds the conflicting points of legendary materials.

ⵏ The task of following harmonization in all its phases, belongs so entirely to the *criticism of the text*, that it must be left to a special and elaborate enquiry. The bible-text, already an object of the most careful criticism through the Elohistic and Jehovistic separation of originals, will require, by reason of our indicating the *Ephraimitic and Judaic* formation of the legends a particularly exact analysis. To establish harmony between the three patriarchs as it is now before us, was also no easy or quickly executed task. It was specially necessary to make *geographical leaps* without being able to account for them from natural motives. As they were unable to send out the locally fixed Isaac, it was necessary that Abraham should undertake a journey to the south (Gen. xx. 1), for which all natural reasons are wanting. Again, as they wished to give full importance to the grave in Hebron it was necessary not only to presuppose silently the return of Abraham to the place, but also, contrary to all preceding statements, to affirm that *Isaac* also lived in Hebron (Gen. xxxv. 27). The patriarch Jacob was bound, according to the harmonist, to begin his migration from Beersheba his birthplace, and return on account of the *harmony* to *Hebron* after all his wanderings in the kingdom of Israel, where he played the chief part, though it is inconceivable how any one residing in Hebron should allow his cattle to go to pasture near Shecem, a distance of more than a hundred English miles. Finally, the harmonist, who cannot entirely drop Beersheba, makes Jacob take up his station there when he travelled to Egypt. There also he had another revelation of Elohe (Gen. xlvi. 1-4), with which he was so often favoured in the kingdom of *Israel*, while during the alleged sojourn of Jacob in the kingdom of *Judah, which lasted at least fifteen years, Elohe never appeared to the patriarch*.

To follow the harmonization in all its phases, is indeed a very interesting work, which must be separately undertaken. We must content ourselves, therefore, in this preliminary examination with a superficial survey of harmonistic views, as they are shown in the writings *of the most liberally minded of the Hebrew nation,* the *prophets*, because those are and must remain the chief intellectual source to which one can most successfully turn for *light and truth*.

Among the Judaic prophets the most sublime Isaiah stands completely free from all traditional hypothesis. It is true that he speaks of a " house of Jacob," but he means only the *nation*, not the descendants of a certain *person*. He speaks of a " house of Judah," but by no word betrays a belief in the legends already in full circulation in his time, about a person of the name of Judah. Of an Abraham or an Isaac he makes no mention. We refer, of course, to the old Isaiah, not to the so-called second Isaiah, as he abstains altogether from any traditional views, and speaks neither of a Moses nor of any other person belonging to the cycle of the legends of the nation.

All this does not yet prove that the prophet was a partisan enemy of traditions, but only that with the rich power of his thoughts and language he needed not the support of old legendary forms, and that from the depth of his soul he was creative enough to dispense with the traditional auxiliaries of rhetoric.

Nevertheless, considering that he, in common with all other prophets, who, like him, condemned the Egyptian politics of the Judaic courts, severely inveighed against the faithlessness of Egypt, we are surprised to find that *there is no allusion whatever to the history of Joseph, and to the great benefit which he is said to have conferred upon the kingdom*. If the prophets had looked upon that story as more than a flattering popular legend of the *Ephraimites*, it would be incredible that there should be no allusion to it. We have mentioned all that bears upon our subject, from the *older prophet Amos* and the prophet Micah, *Isaiah's* contemporary. Amos knew no Abraham and no Jacob, and was only aware of a worship upon the " heights of Ischak," and of a " house of Ischak," whilst Micah, who abounds with old traditions, and who knew

Moses, Aaron, Miriam, Balak, and Balaam, speaks only of *Abraham* and *Jacob*, but not of *Isaac*. He draws, in his speeches, which are directed against the demoralization of the kingdoms of Judah and of Israel, a very marked distinction between "Jacob and Judah." Jacob is with him "Samaria," the capital of *Israel*, whilst by *Judah* he understands the capital "*Jerusalem.*" (Micah i. 5.) But he still regards the *unity of the nation* as the ideal of a better future, and this is represented to his mind, as to Isaiah's, as a time "when the mountain of the house of Jehovah shall be established in the top of the mountains" (Micah iv. 1, and Isaiah ii. 2), so that the centre of the happy times would *again be Jerusalem*.

More productive than this survey is an examination of the words of the prophet *Hosea*. He shews, not only a *knowledge* of the *Ephraimitic material of legends*, but also evident traces of *harmonistic tendency*. The prophet himself was most probably an *Ephraimite*. In support of such a view, we may at least quote his unbounded love for "Israel" and "Ephraim," and the touching lamentation over apostasy, and the punishment which it should incur. The whole chapter xi. is a proof of this love and pain, and balances all reasons which might denote a *Judaic* descent of the prophet.

For our subject, however, chapter xii. is of importance. In that chapter a considerable portion of the legends of Jacob is reflected, and undoubtedly the prophet was acquainted with those legends, though, perhaps, in a sense which does not altogether agree with the materials which the legends of Bethel place before us. He speaks of Jacob (chapter xii. 4, 5), "*He took his brother by the heel in the womb, and by his strength he had power with God: he had power over the angel and prevailed, so that he wept and made supplication unto him: he would find him in Bethel, and there he will speak to us.*"

Dark as the meaning of these verses may be, they

shew beyond doubt that the Ephraimitic legends were in the mind of the prophet. Verse 13 also of the same chapter bears the type of those legends: "*And Jacob fled into the country of Aram, and Israel served for a wife and for a wife he kept sheep.*" But as an Ephraimite himself, and in his love for Ephraim, led on to the most tender and painful utterances, *the prophet feels no more of the old conflict of the legends.*

He already carries within himself the ideal of the harmony, and recognizing the fall of Ephraim, perceives a last ray of hope in *the alliance with Judah.* He sees in the fall of Israel (chapter iii. 4, 5), the fall of king and prince, of sacrifice and statue, of Ephod and Teraphim, the ruin of government and worship, of state and church.

But afterwards he hopes "that *the children of Israel shall return and seek Jehovah their God and David their king, and fearing shall hasten to Jehovah and to his goodness in the latter days.*"

From the noble Ephraimite there shines forth the *harmony*, which is the basis of the later harmonisation of the *old conflicting legends*. Ephraim did not return. Fate overtook it not long after Hosea's time. When Jeroboam, the Ephraimite, tore asunder the Davidic kingdom, he also destroyed the possibility of the existence of that intermediate realm between two great ones. *The legends of Laban and the eternal peace at the separating mountain of Gilead* (Gen. xxxi. 52) did not prevent Assyria invading the country and destroying the kingdom of Israel. The kingdom of Judah was heir to the kingdom of Israel, and thus adopted also *legends and traditions of Ephraimitic origin.* But it inherited also the *grief of ruin and the emblem of an equal fate.*

For more than a century the kingdom of Judah preserved its ever threatened existence. Its last prophet, the grief-stricken prophet Jeremiah, who saw the "misery of his people," derived the last consolation of all dying nations from the deceiving fount of a future reconstitution. " Return will the people, return Jehovah," " return history—and *renewed will be the days of old.*"

Therefore the *old time* radiated before his eye, as brilliantly *as the future does in the light of hope.* Not Judah alone, but also "Israel, Ephraim," are included in the bright dream of restoration. *Every remembrance of Ephraim's destructive influence upon the Davidic kingdom now fades.* The prophet sees the return of the banished ones (Jeremiah xxxi. 8-20). He lets Jehovah say, "Behold I will bring them from the north country, they shall come with weeping, and with supplications will I lead them! I will cause them to walk by the rivers of waters, in a straight way, wherein they shall not stumble, for *I am a father to Israel, and Ephraim is my first-born.* Then shall the virgin rejoice in the dance, both young men and old together : for I will turn their mourning into joy and will comfort them and make them rejoice from their sorrow. Jehovah hearkens to "the voice of the weeping *Rachel* in Ramah," the mother of *Ephraim*, "bewailing her children who have been banished." He hearkens to the lamentations of the mother and comforts her. "Refrain thy voice from weeping, and thine eyes from tears. I have surely heard Ephraim bemoaning himself thus. *Is not Ephraim my dear son, is he not a dear son unto me (or a child that I dandle). For the more I speak of him, do I earnestly remember him again; therefore are my inward parts moved for him; I will surely have mercy upon him, saith Jehovah.*"

The harmony *between Judah and Ephraim is here, already, so entirely completed,* that the conflicts of the legends have no more echo in the soul of the prophet. Therefore he vows in the name of Jehovah (Jeremiah xxxiii. 25, 26) " by the covenant of day and night, and the eternal ordinances of heaven and earth," that he will not despise the seed of Jacob and of David, that he will create rulers from amongst them for the returning children of *Abraham, Isaac,* and *Jacob.*

Jeremiah, the *last* prophet in the falling Judah, *is the first who introduces the three ancestors in this combination and in this order.*

XVI.

CONCLUSION.

The legends of a nation are not its history, but they often reflect in their wonderful images that which history in forgotten centuries has impressed upon the human soul. In the light conflict of the legends harsh struggles of past generations are hidden. But as on the field of battle, the strife having abated, the earth rises fresh over conquerors and conquered alike, and covers all the combatants under one hill, so poetry wreathes for friend and foe the common garland of piety, and from the sight of later times covers with its harmonising veil the discordant struggles of the past.

HELL.

PUBLISHED BY THOMAS SCOTT,
11 THE TERRACE, FARQUHAR ROAD, UPPER NORWOOD,
LONDON, S.E.

Price Threepence.

LONDON:
PRINTED BY C. W. REYNELL, LITTLE PULTENEY STREET,
HAYMARKET, W.

INTRODUCTION.

"Dieu condamne aux enfers la plupart des hommes.

"L'enfer est bon et aimable comme une partie très-considérable du palais de Dieu. Il venge tous les mépris et toutes les injures de Dieu, en quoi il lui rend un très-grand service qui fait que quiconque aime Dieu sincèrement doit aussi aimer l'enfer sous ce point de vue."—*Théologie Affective*, BAIL.

The work from which the above extract is taken is long and interesting.

Founded upon the teaching of S. Thomas Aquinas, it imparts, in five closely-printed volumes, a considerable amount of information, conveyed in lucid and forcible language, of which the above quotation is a favourable specimen. Bail thinks Hell good and amiable. Those who love God sincerely ought, in his opinion, to love Hell too, because in that large portion of *God's palace* he is avenged of his adversaries.

Some people may envy Bail the inward and spiritual light which enabled him to discern the beauty of damnation. Others may drift away from Hell to Calvary, and wonder of what use the Atonement was, if, as Bail assures us, God condemns the greater part of mankind to Hell, and places himself under an obligation to the Devil. But one and all may like to know where Hell is and what sort of an existence its inmates lead.

Availing ourselves, therefore, of the information afforded us by a contemporary writer, who views Hell from a very practical point of view, we will take a brief survey of the place which " Eternal justice had prepared for those rebellious."

HELL.

AN inexpensive but unusually comprehensive little work has long been before the public, but has not hitherto received the attention it deserves, though a striking quotation from it has found its way into Lecky's interesting pages.

The book costs only a penny, and may be bought of Duffy in the Row, or of any other Roman Catholic bookseller. It is drawn up for the use of Roman Catholic children, but it cannot fail to interest and edify adults of all denominations. It is written by the Rev. Father Furniss—a name in curious harmony with its title, 'The Sight of Hell.' Published like all Roman Catholic works *permissu superiorum*, it has the sanction and probably the approval of Cardinal Manning. It is a work of considerable merit, the result not merely of minute research, but of deep conviction, and it needs but a few good illustrations by the hand of some God-fearing artist to take its rank as the best Guide to Hell before the public. Swedenborg has written at greater length upon the fertile theme, but his work is too mystic for the general reader; that of Father Furniss is adapted to every capacity—it is a simple and soul-stirring production. There is only one point about which the writer seems in any uncertainty, and that is the exact *locality* of Hell; however, he thinks it likely to be " in the middle of the earth just four thousand miles off." Bail, on the contrary, seems to consider it a part of Heaven, and S. John, in the unintelligible work attributed to him, favours the supposition by telling us that the smoke of Hell penetrates into the region of bliss, an arrangement quite irreconcilable with mundane notions of comfort.

All Christians are supposed to know—and all Roman Catholic children are very distinctly taught, that Hell was created for Lucifer the Seraph, and about a third of the inhabitants of Heaven, who, for one sin of thought, and without one minute's time for repentance, were suddenly thrust into the new wing of what Bail is not afraid to call "God's palace," and which Father Furniss has described in such glowing language. He tells us that "millions on millions" are in Hell, and that so long ago as the time of S. Teresa, it was inconveniently crowded, for, during the visit of that great Saint to those great sinners, she found it "impossible to sit or lie down, for there was no room." From each inmate is emitted an odour of such a nature that if but one body were removed and placed among us, "in that same moment every living creature on the earth would die," and Father Furniss is of opinion that the bad smell is increasing. An incessant and appalling noise prevails there; the poor prisoners "hiss, howl, wail, shriek, groan, and yell;" but there is a worse still, for above all you hear "the roaring of the thunders of God's anger;" of course a good and an amiable anger by no means at variance with "His tender mercies which are over all His works," and of which the eternal torture of the damned is an eloquent proof.

How long the angelic host had undisturbed possession of Hell we are not informed. Countless ages may have elapsed ere the monotony was broken by the entrance of the first ill-fated human being whose

Hell.

name and crime are nowhere recorded. In the celebrated ' Catéchisme de Persévérance,' the Church teaches that, with the exception of *beauty*, "les mauvais anges n'ont rien perdu de leurs dons naturels," we may therefore venture to assume that until the mundane multitude began to pour in daily, the social condition of Hell was endurable; for Lucifer was one of the highest order of angels, called Seraphim, when that horrible thought was put into his angelic mind and caused the instantaneous damnation of a third of Heaven. Who put the sinful thought into the seraphic mind has never transpired.

At that time Lucifer was handsome—now he is hideous. S. Francis saw him. He was sitting upon a great beam which passes right through Hell. He is so tall that his hands can be chained to the roof and his feet to the floor. Horns smoking like chimnies come out of his head. His breath is fœtid and fiery. His eyes are full of pride, anger, rage, spite, blood, fire, and cruelty. Who made him so? This is the description given of the Devil by a great Saint.

People have become so familiar with the word Devil, that one would suppose it occurred very frequently in the Bible; however, it is not to be found at all in the Old Testament. As synonymous with idols we see it four times in the plural number, but of Satan we hear nothing until we come to the book of Chronicles. Brought forward by theologians of all persuasions, with what some might consider unnecessary and injudicious prominence, we are sometimes forced to consider him and his melancholy mission, especially when such a book as the one we are engaged upon falls into our hands.

Animated, doubtless by an excellent motive, Father

Furniss has produced a work of questionable utility, more calculated, some might think, to promote convulsions than conversion. We will give two extracts.

The children alluded to, have been previously cursed in the following words, taken from 'The Terrible Judgment,' by the same author :—

"The curse of God the Father Almighty is upon you; I am God the Son, my curse is upon you; the curse of the Holy Ghost who sanctified you is upon you; the curse of every creature is upon you."

"THE RED-HOT OVEN.

"'Thou shalt make him as an oven of fire in the time of thy anger'—Psalm xx. You are going to see again the child about which you read in the 'Terrible Judgment' that it was condemned to Hell! See! it is a pitiful sight. The little child is in this red-hot oven. Hear how it screams to come out. See how it turns and twists itself about in the fire. It beats its head against the roof of the oven. It stamps its little feet on the floor of the oven. You can see on the face of this little child what you see on the faces of all in Hell—*despair*, desperate and horrible! The same law which is for others is also for children. If children knowingly and willingly break God's commandments they must be punished like others. This child committed very bad mortal sins knowing that Hell would be the punishment. God was very good to this child. Very likely God saw that this child would get worse and worse and never repent, and so it would have to be punished much more in Hell. So God, *in his mercy*, called it out of the world in its early childhood."

Thus ends the story of the red-hot oven which a

Hell.

merciful father prepared for his little child, and into which he thrust her because he was so fond of her!

We will give one more extract from Father Furniss :—

"What are they doing?

"Perhaps at this moment—seven o'clock in the evening—a child is just going into Hell. To-morrow evening at seven o'clock go and knock at the gates of Hell and ask what the child is doing. The devils will go and look. Then they will come back again and say, *the child is burning*. Go in a week and ask what the child is doing; you will get the same answer, *it is burning!* Go in a year and ask, the same answer comes, *it is burning!* Go in a million of years and ask the same question, the answer is just the same, *it is burning!* So if you go for ever and ever you will always get the same answer, *it is burning in the fire.*"

Longer and equally horrible passages might be chosen, but enough has been quoted to show with what wholesome and inviting food the lambs of the Roman Catholic fold are fed, those lambs of whom the mild Son of Man is reported to have said :—" It is not the will of my father that one of these little ones should perish."

Sincere anxiety for the salvation of souls has, we doubt not, urged Father Furniss to condense into a very small compass a collection of horrors from which adults turn away with dismay, wondering that the " superiors " by whose permission the infernal little book is printed and circulated, sanction anything so ill-calculated to impress the golden rule upon the infant mind and so utterly at variance with the injunction attributed to Jesus, "If thine enemy hunger feed him, and if he thirst give him drink."

Fortunately for the interests of what is called religion, no little children and very few adults "meditate upon these things." Those who *do*, neither fear the Hell nor covet the Heaven of theology. It is the generally received opinion among the Fathers that Adam had been created but a few hours when Lucifer succeeded in procuring his ignominious dismissal from Paradise; but we have never heard how soon after his creation Lucifer himself was exposed to the malevolent and fatal influence of some occult agent who, like the Satan of the book of Job, was suffered to present himself "before the Lord" and to achieve the instantaneous transformation of angels into devils.

Accustomed from our childhood to hear much and often about the Fall of man, the depravity of our nature, our proneness to sin, innate tendency to evil thoughts, etc., but wholly unaccustomed to "meditate upon these things," we sometimes lose sight of the still more startling and indigestible doctrine of the Fall of the Seraphim, the imperfection of *their* nature, *their* proneness to evil thoughts, and their consequent liability to be precipitated into Hell. How are we to know that evil thoughts are now banished from that haven of rest where once they wrought such disastrous and abiding consequences? Those who are aspiring to that "better land," where "the ways are ways of pleasantness and all the paths peace," may rejoice that religion and theology are not synonymous—that it is possible to love God sincerely without loving Hell too, and that they can train up their children in the way they should go, without having recourse to Father Furniss's method of salvation by fear—a method singularly at variance with the teaching of One who is reported to have said, "Whoso shall offend one of these little ones which believe in me, it were better for him that a millstone were hanged about his neck, and that he were drowned in the depths of the sea." However, perhaps "the end justifies the means;" in which case 'The Sight of Hell' will contribute *ad majorem Dei gloriam*.

THE
MYTHICAL ELEMENT
IN
CHRISTIANITY.

BY

ED. VANSITTART NEALE, M.R.I.

PUBLISHED BY THOMAS SCOTT,
MOUNT PLEASANT, RAMSGATE.

—

Price One Shilling.

LONDON:
PRINTED BY C. W. REYNELL, LITTLE PULTENEY STREET,
HAYMARKET, W.

THE MYTHICAL ELEMENT
IN
CHRISTIANITY.

———◆———

THE importance attached by the teachers or defenders of Christianity to the historical character of the preternatural incidents asserted to have attended the birth of Jesus, to have illustrated his life, and to have accompanied its close, has, not unnaturally, led to a reaction, liable to be as prejudicial to a sound judgment about the origin of the Christian religion on the one side, as an uncritical reliance upon the absolute truth of all that is recorded in the New Testament has been on the other side. An unreasoning belief is in some danger of giving place to an unreasoning distrust. The inconsistencies and contradictions, of which so large a crop becomes apparent in the gospels, when surveyed by the eyes of an uncompromising critic, as the author of 'The English Life of Jesus,' forming part of this series, has demonstrated, combined with the very scanty notices of Christianity to be found in any but professedly Christian writers, during the first hundred and fifty years after the birth of Jesus, have given rise to the opinion, expressed by the writer of another tract comprised in the series, that Jesus was not really an historical person at all ; " that neither the twelve Apostles nor their divine Master ever existed." [a]

[a] 'The Twelve Apostles,' p. 28.

4 The Mythical Element in Christianity.

It may appear, probably, a sufficient reply to such a conclusion, to observe that it is not shared by any of the great critics whose labours in the investigation of the New Testament have led to that change in men's judgments as to its historical character, which seems to be now growing up into the recognised critical opinion.   Strauss, Bauer, Renan, the author of 'The English Life of Jesus,' for instance, one and all write with the obvious conviction that, in dealing with the life of Jesus, they are dealing with the life not only of a real man, but a man of a most remarkable character.[b] But, in the interest of historical truth, it is desirable to examine thoroughly the grounds for any judgment on an important question, put forth, with apparent conviction, by any writer who possesses sufficient knowledge of the subject discussed to entitle his judgment to respect, however much that judgment may run counter to received opinion. This is desirable, *first*, because the progress of critical inquiry in historical matters has involved a continuous destruction of received opinions, and the substitution for them of others which, when first announced, were considered absurd; *secondly*, because history, not admitting of verification by immediate observation, is peculiarly exposed to that paralysis of doubt which hangs over the intellect, hampering instead of stimulating its energies, and substituting the sickly feebleness of sceptical questionings in place of the vigorous health of scientific research.[c]

[b] See ' English Life of Jesus,' p. 344, for a summary of the conclusions to which this able and fearless critic comes about him.

[c] Thus, in Mr Lumisden Strange's ' Is the Bible the Word of God?' the hypothesis of the mythical origin of Christianity *peeps in*, as a theory which he neither accepts nor rejects, but which serves to aid the conclusions to which he comes about Christianity, by the mysterious uncertainty thrown over its origin. See pp. 351, 352, 374—381.

The Mythical Element in Christianity. 5

I propose, therefore, to subject to a critical examination the reasons adduced in support of the hypothesis that Jesus Christ is a mythical personage, who never had any existence, except in the imaginations of his disciples.

The way in which this mythical belief arose is supposed to have been somewhat as follows:[d] "The siege of Jerusalem kindled into a flame the enthusiastic spirit of trust in Divine aid inherent in the Jewish race. There were, says Josephus, a great number of prophets who denounced to the people that they should wait for deliverance from Heaven.[e] True, the Pharisaic historian can see in these men only persons suborned by the leaders of the Zealots—'the Tyrants,' as he calls them—John and Simon; but we may read the tale of that age better by the light of the ages preceding it. As from the depths of the captivity at Babylon there came forth the glowing hopes of triumphant deliverance which inspire the last twenty-seven chapters of our Book of Isaiah; as the sufferings and struggles under Antiochus Epiphanes produced the conception of the 'Son of Man' revealed in the clouds, to whom was given dominion, and glory, and a kingdom, that all people, nations, and languages should serve him, an everlasting dominion, which should not pass away, and 'a kingdom which should not be destroyed;'[f] so the fall of Jerusalem produced a reaction of hope and trust, which gave a new and unexpectedly fruitful development to the idea of the Messiah. To some deep prophetic spirit, meditating on the mysterious

---

[d] See 'The Twelve Apostles,' p. 16. I have taken the liberty of filling up the very scanty delineation of the supposed growth of the myth, given in that tract, with some details which seem to me to throw over it an air of plausibility, but for which the author of the above-named publication is not responsible.
[e] 'Jewish War,' vi. 5.
[f] Dan. vii. 14.

questions, why Jehovah had given over his ancient people to be trodden down of the Gentiles? why no deliverer had appeared from Heaven to save them in their sore need? light came with the notion—it is for our sins; because the Messiah *has* come, and we, that is, our rulers, have not recognised him: he has come, as the great prophet of the captivity foretold, as 'one despised and rejected of men,' 'a man of sorrows and acquainted with grief,' one 'taken from prison and from judgment,' and 'cut off out of the land of the living;' because 'for the transgressions of his people was he stricken;'[g] but yet one whom God has exalted to his throne in heaven to sit on his right hand till the time should arrive when his people, 'purified as by a refiner's fire,' 'purged as gold and silver,' should 'offer to Jehovah an offering of righteousness,'[h] and who, then, shall 'suddenly be revealed' to take vengeance on his enemies, and establish that unending kingdom which the ancient prophets have foretold."

"But *when* had this unrecognised Messiah appeared? An answer was supplied by the same prophetic voice. Had not Malachi foretold that Jehovah would send Elijah the prophet before 'that great and dreadful *day, which should burn up all that do wickedly,*' to 'turn the hearts of the fathers to the children, and the hearts of the children to their fathers?' and was it not the fact that, about forty years before the taking of Jerusalem, one had appeared 'in the spirit and power of Elijah,' preaching repentance as the preparation for a greater who should come after him? Was there not also a tradition that, not long after the death of John the Baptist, Pontius Pilate, the Roman governor, had put to death a native of Galilee, one accused by the High priest and rulers

[g] I . liii. 3--8.   [h] Mal. iii. 3 ; iv. 5. 6.

The Mythical Element in Christianity. 7

of that day of blasphemy and sedition, whom Pilate had crucified along with others, 'malefactors,' in whom it might well be that the prophecy of the innocent sufferer, who 'should make his grave with the wicked' had found its accomplishment? Thus, on the slenderest possible foundation of actual fact, may it have become possible for the Jewish imagination to launch the Messianic idea under a novel aspect, postponing to an indefinite, though not very remote future, its expectant glories, and supplementing them by the conception of an earthly life suited to one who, for our sakes, had borne our sins and tasted of our sorrows?[1] Opposed from the first to the formal spirit of the Pharisaical party, the Scribes and Lawyers of the New Testament, which had become dominant again when the ardent hopes of supernatural victory, that led to the obstinate resistance of Jerusalem, had been crushed by its fall; drawing its inspirations from the free air of ancient prophecy, rather than from the more modern 'Book of the Law,' from Isaiah and Jeremiah rather than from Ezra; the new faith, while it attracted within its influence many of the noblest and purest spirits produced in that age by the Jewish people, still met with a cold reception from the mass of the nation. But it rapidly spread among the Gentile proselytes; and soon shaking itself free from the fetter of circumcision, was able to recruit its ranks from all the varied populations comprised in the Roman em-

[1] The author of 'The Twelve Apostles' (p. 16) calls this notion an "inversion" of the popular belief, and alleges that other cases of similar "inversions" may be produced, though he does not cite any instance. But to make the Christian conception of the Messiah into an inversion of the Jewish, it would be necessary to show that the Jews believed in a Messiah who should suffer after having triumphed, a notion which might have been inverted into that of a Messiah who should triumph after having suffered; while, in fact, the notion of a suffering Messiah appears to have been quite foreign to Jewish expectations till it was introduced by the Christian teaching.

pire, and thus swell its numbers to a large body; while yet it retained, from the fervour of its original members, in the general spirit of its doctrines, and the character of the supernatural details with which the imagination of the disciples gradually clothed the supposed life of their master, the flavour of Jewish thought and the traces of Jewish beliefs. Thus grew up the myth of Jesus Christ embodied in those four gospels, themselves only a part of a far more extensive evangelic literature once widely diffused in the Christian Church, to which the subsequent course of ecclesiastical history has given such a wide and lasting influence over Europe and the countries conquered or colonised by European energy."

If we regard this hypothesis only in itself, without troubling ourselves as to its power of accounting for the positive statements relating to the rise of Christianity which have survived the waste of time, I think it must be admitted that the mythical theory of its origin presented above is not encumbered by any inherent impossibility; that stranger things have undoubtedly happened in the religious history of mankind than the growth of such a belief, deriving its nourishment, like some orchidaceous plants, only from the atmosphere in which its seeds germinated, and supporting itself on the accidental props of surrounding circumstances, without requiring to strike its roots into the solid ground of facts. And, if we are disposed to found our judgments as to the origin of Christianity *only* on arguments of internal probability, and test them *only* by the historical evidence for the *details* of the narratives relating to it, we may be ready to acquiesce in the canon proposed by the author whose hypothesis we are examining, that, " if a hero be known chiefly as the performer of supernatural exploits, both hero

The Mythical Element in Christianity. 9

and exploit are mythical."[j] But to those who value attested facts more highly than their own imaginations of possibilities, general canons of this nature are unsatisfactory. Let us see, then, if we cannot find some other test of more scientific precision than imaginary possibility to which to subject this hypothesis. It is not difficult to find one. The hypothesis of the mythical origin of Christianity above stated is founded on the revolution in the expectations as to the coming of the Messiah, supposed to have been produced in the minds of some pious enthusiastic Jews by the destruction of Jerusalem. If by good historical evidence we can trace the conceptions which associate the Messianic character with Jesus, called the Christ, to a time anterior to the siege of Jerusalem, this mythical theory must fall of itself; and for that purpose the use of the name Christian is sufficient. For Christ is the Greek equivalent of the Hebrew Messiah; "the anointed one;" the "Son whose throne is for ever, and the sceptre of whose kingdom is the sceptre of righteousness; who had loved righteousness and hated iniquity, wherefore God had anointed him with the oil of gladness above his fellows,"[k] King and High Priest for ever;[l] and the sense of the termination *anus*, in *Christianus*, is " belonging to Christ." So that, even if we could not find any direct proof of the title Christ having been applied to Jesus of Nazareth prior to the siege of Jerusalem, but have proofs of the use of the name Christian before that date, this would suffice to show that Christianity did not arise out of such a myth as has been above stated; unless it could be demonstrated that the name was then applied to persons who held tenets quite distinct from those subsequently associated with it.

Before entering upon this investigation, however,

[j] 'Twelve Apostles,' 32.   [k] Ps. xlv. 6, 7.   [l] Heb. i. 8, 9; ii. 5.

10 *The Mythical Element in Christianity.*

it will be well to consider another form of mythical hypothesis about the origin of Christianity, not admitting of being subjected to this chronological test, namely, the theory which traces the name Christian to a confusion between *Christus* and *Chrēstos*, the Greek word for "good," and supposes that "Christians" may have originally meant only "the good men," the followers of one who was imagined to have been supremely "good;" an appellation afterwards exchanged for "Christus," or "the anointed one," when this body had come, by some process not distinctly explained, to identify their supposed founder with the Messiah. This idea is suggested by the Rev. Robert Taylor in his 'Diegesis; or, Discovery of the Origin and Early History of Christianity,' who, in support of it, makes the following statement:[m] "Justin Martyr, in his account of the name (Christian), which he gives in his apology to Antoninus Pius, thus takes away *all possible* reference to the name of Christ as the founder of a sect. *Christianoi einai kategoroumetha, To de chrēston miseisthai ou dikaion—chrēstotatoi huparchomen.*[n] Theophilus of Antioch,[o] after a long string of puns upon *christus* and *chrēstus*, thinks that *christus*, not *chrēstus*, should be the word, because of the sublime significance of *christus*, which signifies the sweet, the agreeable, the most useful, and never-to-be-laughed-at article, *pomatum.* "What use of a ship," he argues, "unless it be *smeared*? What tower or palace would be good or useful unless it were greased? What man comes into life or enters into a conflict without being anointed? What piece of work would be considered finished unless it were oiled? The air itself, and

[m] Pp. 399-400.
[n] We are accused of being Christians, but it is not just to hate that which is good. We are very good.
[o] A.D. 171.

The Mythical Element in Christianity. 11

every creature under heaven, is, as it were, anointed with light and spirit. Undoubtedly we are called Christians for this reason and no other, because we are anointed with the oil of God."ᵖ

"Tertullian,ᑫ Clemens Alexandrinus,ʳ and St Jeromeˢ *abound* in the same strain. *Everywhere* we meet with puns and conundrums on the name; *nowhere with the vestige* of the real existence of a person, to whom the name was distinctively appropriated."

Mr Taylor appears to have entertained very peculiar notions as to the meaning of verbs of number. The "abounding" of which he speaks consists in the existence in the writers from whom he quotes of the passages cited, and *no others*, so far as I can discover, containing any allusion to the possible derivation of Christian from Chrēstus : while his "absence of any vestige of the real existence of a person to whom the name (Christus) was distinctively appropriated" concerns writers, from quotations in whose works the story in the Gospels might be almost, if not entirely, reconstructed, if the Gospels were lost. But, besides this, the passages cited, when examined, do not support the position that the writers of them had any doubt as to the true origin of the name Christian. It is very questionable whether Justin Martyr, in the passage quoted by Mr Taylor, refers at all to an identification of *Christus* with *Chrēstus*, though Mr Taylor, by *inverting* the order

---

ᵖ *Toigaroun gar toutou eneken kaloumetha christianoi, hoti chriometha elaion Theou.*

ᑫ Cum perperam Chrestianus pronuntiatur (puta christianus), de suavitate, vel benignitate compositum nomen est.—*Apology.*

ʳ *Strommata. Autika de eis Christon pepisteukotes chrēstoi te eisi kai legontai.*

ˢ In Gal. v. 22: Quum apud Græcos *chrēstētes* utrumque sonat, virtus est lenis, blanda tranquilla, et omnium bonorum censors.

of Justin's sentences, and *leaving out* the connecting passages, gives his words this appearance. Justin's argument, which is too long to quote fully, is, that we (Christians) are very good men (*chrēstotatoi*); therefore, we ought not to be condemned simply on account of our name, because we are called Christians, for it is not just to hate that which is good. He does not say, as Mr. Taylor insinuates, our *name shows* that we are good men; he directly asserts the fact of this goodness. And that he did not himself derive the name Christian from *chrēstos* is placed beyond a doubt by two other passages in his *Apology*, the first of which says, " Our Master, the Son of God, the Father and Ruler of all things, is Jesus Christ, *from whom also we come to be named Christians;*"[t] while the second states that the true Son of God . . . . is called Christ, because God had anointed and set in order all things by Him.[u] Theophilus, in the passage referred to by Mr Taylor, is arguing that his correspondent Autolycus "did not know what he was saying, in laughing at him for calling himself a Christian."[v] A proposition which he proceeds to prove, by dwelling on the common practice and admitted usefulness of the act of anointing, to show the excellent qualities implied in the Christian name; an argument in which we, who are not accustomed to anoint ourselves or our houses, &c., may see as little force as those who never wash themselves might see in the praise of water as a source of cleanliness; but which is very far from showing any doubt in the mind of Theophilus about the derivation of the name Christian from the verb *chriō*, to anoint. The quotation from Tertullian,

[t] 1 Apol. 12.
[u] *Christos men kata to kechristhai, kai kosmēsai ta panta di hautou tou Theou legetai.*—2 Apol. 6.
[v] *Peri de sou katagelan me, kalounta me Christianon, ouk oidas ho legeis.*—Ad. Aut. i. 1.

made by Mr Taylor, is garbled. The complete passage reads thus : " The interpretation of Christianus is rarely derived [by you] from anointing. For since it is very badly pronounced by you *Chrestianus*, for you have no accurate knowledge even of the name, it is compounded from suavity, or benignity."[w] So that Tertullian, instead of intimating any doubt in his own mind of the origin of the name, as Mr Taylor suggests, adduces the use of the name *Chrestianus* in proof of the *gross ignorance* of his contemporaries about the true origin of *Christianus*; but says, if you *will* make this mistaken substitution of *e* for *i*, then you must derive the name from goodness. The passage quoted from Jerome has nothing at all to do with the origin of the name Christian; but is simply an explanation of the meaning of *chrēstotēs* in the passage in Galatians, which, he says, is the Greek equivalent of either suavity or benignity.[x] Lastly, the passage cited from Clemens Alexandrinus [y] is part of a metaphysical argument, based upon a statement of Plato, " that the knowledge of a true king is a kingly knowledge, and he who has acquired it, whether he is a king or a private person, would always, according to the true method, be rightly addressed as a king;" whence, continues Clemens, " those who have believed in Christ are, and are to be addressed as good, since they are cared for as kings by the true king. For as the wise are wise by wisdom, and the legal legal by law, so those who belong to Christ the king

[w] Apol. c. 3. Christianus raro quantum interpretatio est de unctione deducta. Nam et cum perperam Chrestianus pronuntiatur, a vobis, nam nec nominis certa est notitia vobis, de suavitate vel benignitate compositum est.
[x] Benignitas autem sive suavitas, quum apud Græcos *chrēstotes* utrumque sonat, virtus est lenis, &c. Mr Taylor's scholarship appears to have stopped short of teaching him that *utrumque sonat* means has either *sense*, and has no reference to the *sound* of chrēstotes.
[y] Strom. ii. c. 418.

are kings, and those who are of Christ are Christians" Whatever we may think of the argument, its conclusion both shows that, in the idea of Clemens, it rested on the office of Christ as " anointed " king, and supplies in itself a clear " vestige of a person to whom the name Christ was distinctively appropriated," which Mr Taylor finds so difficult of discovery in the writers cited by him.

The hypothesis that Christian may have grown up by the transformation of *chrēstos*, is thus left destitute of any support from ancient authority. But, besides this, it is exposed to a grave objection of a linguistic character. *Anos* is a termination very little used by Greek writers, and when it is employed, this is in the sense of the possessor of a quality, which the primitive expresses; as *peukedanos* from *peukē*, having bitterness; *rigedanos* from *rigos*, having cold.[z] But there is no Greek primitive expressing goodness, from which *Chrēstianos* could be derived. The primitive is *chrēstotēs*, and the name, therefore, if formed from this source, would have been not *Chrēstianos*, but *Chrēstotētanos*. On the other hand, *anus* is a very common Latin termination, in the sense of belonging to a distinct place or person, as Montanus, Fontanus, Romanus, Albanus, Spartanus, Tullianus, Catonianus, Sullanus;[a] the sense in which Christianus is commonly employed. Whence F. C. Bauer has expressed the opinion that the name probably arose at Rome, notwithstanding the statement in the Acts,[b] "that the disciples were first called Christians in Antioch." And, at all events, if it was first used in Antioch, this was most likely done by Italians, or in order to make the name intelligible to Roman ears.

[z] Matthiæ Greek Gram I. Adjectives III.
[a] Zumpt. Lat. Gram. 181, sec. lix.
[b] xi. 26. Kirchengeschichte der drei erster Jahrhunderte, i. 432.

The Mythical Element in Christianity. 15

Now *Chrēstos* or *Chrestus* is by no means uncommon as an ancient name among Greeks and Romans. Appian mentions a Socrates Chrēstos, whom Mithridates made King of Pontus; Aurelius Victor speaks of a *Chrestus* as engaged in a conspiracy to kill Hannibal; Martial has two epigrams on a "*Chrestus,*" and one on a *Chrestillus*.[c] *Chrēstē* occurs in an ancient epitaph; Fulgentius mentions a *Manlius Chrestus*, who wrote a book on Hymns to the Gods; and Ausonius has an epigram [d] on two brothers, *Chrēstos* and *Akindunos*, of whom he says that, if Akindunos would make a present of the *a* in his name to Chrēstos, the names would answer better to their characters; for Chrēstos would become *Achrēstos*—*i.e.*, useless, and *Akindunos* Kindunos—*i.e.*, dangerous.[e] And Mr Fynes Clinton, in his 'Fasti Romani,' mentions three other persons named *Chrestus*, one contemporary with the sophist Adrian, A.D. 171; another put to death by Ulpian, A.D. 228; and a third, a grammarian, living A.D. 359. It cannot therefore be at all surprising that the non-Christian population of the Roman empire, in the first Christian centuries, should have supposed the name of the founder of the new religion to be Chrestus, and have called his disciples Chrestiani, without intentional reference to any good qualities ascribed to them; for which, indeed, we know that they were very far from disposed to give them credit.

This phase of the mythical hypothesis, where Christ is presented as an ideal concentration of the goodness manifested by his alleged followers, being thus shown to be untenable, there remains for examination only the other phase, which, resting

[c] vi. 54, ix. 25, vi. 9.
[d] xxxix.
[e] See note on Tertullian Apol. c. 3, in Migny's Edition of the Fathers.

on a supposed modification of the idea of the Messiah consequent on the destruction of Jerusalem, admits of a chronological test, in the inquiry whether there is satisfactory evidence of the use of the name Christian before that event. Now we have, in the works of two eminent Roman historians, Tacitus and Suetonius, who lived in the latter half of the first and the commencement of the second Christian century, distinct evidence of the use of this name five years before the siege of Jerusalem, and its connection with a person called Christus, who is stated to have lived about thirty-five years previously. The passage in Tacitus has often been quoted, but from its importance to the present argument I repeat it here, in the words of Gibbon's translation. Tacitus, after narrating the conflagration of Rome, the suspicions which attached to the Emperor Nero of having ordered the city to be set on fire, and the steps he had taken to avert this charge by religious ceremonies intended to appease the anger of the deities to whom he ascribed the calamity, states "that, to divert a suspicion which the power of despotism was unable to suppress, the emperor resolved to substitute in his place fictitious criminals. With this view he inflicted the most exquisite tortures on those men, who, under the vulgar appellation of Christians, were already branded with deserved infamy. They derived their name and origin from Christ, who in the reign of Tiberius had suffered death by the sentence of the procurator, Pontius Pilate. For a while this dire superstition was checked; but it again burst forth, and not only spread itself over Judæa, the first seat of this mischievous sect, but was even introduced into Rome, the common asylum which receives and protects whatever is impure, whatever is atrocious. The confessions of those who were seized discovered a great

The Mythical Element in Christianity. 17

number of their accomplices, who were all convicted, not so much for the crime of setting fire to the city as for their hatred of the human kind. They died in torments, and their torments were embittered by insult and derision. Some were nailed on crosses; others sewn up in the skins of wild beasts, and exposed to the fury of dogs; others again, smeared over with combustible materials, were used as torches to illuminate the darkness of the night. The gardens of Nero were destined for the melancholy spectacle, which was accompanied by a horse race, and honoured by the presence of the emperor, who mingled with the populace in the dress and attitude of a charioteer. The guilt of the (Christians)[f] deserved indeed the most exemplary punishment, but the public abhorrence was changed into commiseration, from the opinion that these unhappy wretches were sacrificed, not so much to the public welfare, as to the cruelty of a jealous tyrant."[g]

With this passage must be put in apposition the following account of Nero's measures in Suetonius.[h] " Many things were censured and repressed, and that severely, and some ordered. A limit was set to expenditure. Public suppers with gratuitous doles of food were established. It was provided that nothing cooked but pulse or pot-herbs should come into the cooks' shops, while previously all kinds of victuals were exposed there. *The Christians, a class of men who hold a new and mischievous superstition, were subjected to capital punishment.* The four-horse chariot games, in which, by an inveterate license, cheating and robbery were sanctioned, with a right of going everywhere, were forbidden; the troops of pantomimics were banished with the pantomimes."

Now, unless it can be shown, either that these pas-

[f] The name is not repeated in the original.
[g] Tac. Ann. xv. 44, Gibbon c. xvi.   [h] Vit. Ner., c. 16.

sages have been interpolated into the writings of Tacitus and Suetonius, or that those authors applied to the year 65 A.D. names not known till a later time, and confused the persons whom Nero put to death, on the charge of having set fire to Rome, with the body known as Christians at a later epoch, they completely upset the mythological hypothesis now under our consideration, by proving that the Christian name was in use and connected with a Christ who had suffered at a date anterior by several years to the time when, according to this hypothesis, the idea of such a Christ first arose. The author of 'The Twelve Apostles' shows too much acquaintance with classical literature to allow of our supposing that he was not aware of these passages in Tacitus and Suetonius, and too much logical power to allow of our supposing that he did not see how fatal they are to his hypothesis, unless they can be got rid of in one or the other of the modes indicated above. Unfortunately, he does not tell us which of these alternatives he adopts, but prefers to ignore the positive testimony of Tacitus and Suetonius to the existence of Christians in the reign of Nero altogether, and to rely for his external proof of the unhistorical character of Jesus upon certain negative evidences, to which I shall fully advert subsequently. I am therefore driven, in dealing with these passages, to refer to the observations of other writers, who have discussed them from a point of view opposed to Christianity—such as Mr Taylor, in the work already cited; Mr Robert Cooper, in his 'Infidel's Text Book;' and Mr Lumisden Strange, in his 'The Bible: is it the Word of God?;' especially Mr Taylor, who seems to have been a man of considerable, though not very profound learning, and to whom his successors appear to have been indebted for most of their arguments on the subject before us.

The Mythical Element in Christianity. 19

Of the alternatives above stated Mr Taylor adopts the first decidedly, in regard to Tacitus, and hints at rather than contends for the second, in regard to Suetonius. He adduces various reasons for supposing the passage in Tacitus to be a forgery, which I produce here, in a somewhat condensed shape, with my replies to them.[i]

1. The passage is not quoted by Tertullian, though he had read and *largely quotes* the works of Tacitus, and in his Apology is so hot upon it, that his missing it is almost miraculous.

Reply. Tertullian quotes Tacitus twice only, and both times the same passage—namely, an absurd account given by him of the origin of the Jews, and of their worshipping a deity with an ass's head.[j] But he does assert the existence of statements in the Roman historians, implying that Nero persecuted the Christians at Rome, which is what Tacitus and Suetonius state.[k]

2. Tertullian has spoken of Tacitus in a way that it is absolutely impossible he could have spoken of him, if his writings had contained such a passage.

Reply. He calls him "the most loquacious of the great liars,"[l] an epithet agreeing well with the more detailed abuse of the Christians to be found in Tacitus, than in Suetonius.

3. The passage is not quoted by Clemens Alexandrinus, who sets himself entirely to the task of adducing and bringing together admissions and recognitions which Pagan authors had made of the existence of Christ and Christianity.

Reply. Clemens applies himself to collect passages

---

[i] Diegesis, p. 394—396. [j] Apol. c. 16, In. Nat. c. 11.
[k] Consulite commentarios vestros, in illis reperietis Neronem primum, in hanc sectam tum maxime Romæ orientem, Cæsariano gladio fervisse.—Apol. 5.
[l] Mendaciorum loquacissimus.—Apol. c. 16, In. Nat. c. 11.

from heathen writers anterior to Christ, which might be regarded as an unconscious anticipation of his character and acts. To deal with historical notices of Christ and Christianity was entirely beside the object of his work.

4. The passage has not been stumbled upon by the laborious, all-seeking Eusebius, who could by no possibility have missed it, and whom it would have saved the labour of forging the testimony of Josephus, adducing the correspondence of Christ and Abgarus, and the Sibylline Verses, or forging a revelation from Apollo in attestation of Christ's conception.

Reply. The object of Eusebius in citing the statements referred to by Mr Taylor, of which I by no means defend the authenticity, though I do not know what proof Mr Taylor could furnish that Eusebius himself forged them, was not to establish the fact of the existence of Jesus, or that of a body of Christians before the siege of Jerusalem,—facts that probably no one in the fourth century dreamt of disputing,—but to adduce testimony favourable to the Christian beliefs about Jesus, or to the character of Christians ; and, as the passage of Tacitus was quite useless for this purpose, Eusebius had no motive for referring to it.

5. There is no vestige of the existence of the passage before the fifteenth century.

Reply. It is clearly referred to by Sulpicius Severus at the close of the fourth century, though without naming Tacitus, in a passage which is as follows : [m] " Nor could Nero in any way prevent the supposition that the fire had been ordered. Therefore he turned the reproach upon the Christians, and perpetrated the most cruel tortures on innocent persons—inventing new modes of death, that they should be sewn up in the skins of wild beasts, and torn to pieces by dogs.

[m] Sacr. Hist. 2, c. 29.

The Mythical Element in Christianity. 21

Many were nailed to crosses, or roasted in the flames. More were reserved to be burnt instead of lamps at night, when the day had waned."[n]

6. It rests on the fidelity of a single individual, who had the ability, opportunity, and the strongest possible inducement of interest, to introduce the interpolation.

Reply. To what the last words allude I cannot imagine, but the statement generally rests upon a blunder of Mr Taylor, who supposed that there were no MSS. of Tacitus in existence, but such as were copied from a printed edition published by Johannes de Spire at Venice in 1468,[o] of which he seems to have imagined that the original had disappeared. But in fact there are, in the Medicean library at Florence, two ancient MSS. of Tacitus, both containing this passage. The *first* mentioned in letters of Poggio of the 21st Oct., 1427, and the 3rd June, 1428, is stated to have been written in the eleventh century by order of Desiderius, abbot of the monastery of Casino, and to have come into the possession of the Medici from the convent of St Mark at Florence. From it numerous copies are said to have been made in the twelfth century, by which the works of Tacitus

---

[n] The following phrases in Sulpicius agree too closely with the very peculiar phraseology of Tacitus to allow of the resemblance being accidental:

Sed non ope humanâ decedebat infamia, quin jussum incendium crederetur.—*Tacitus.*

Neque ullâ re Nero efficiebat, quin ab eo jussum incendium putaretur.—*Sulp. Sev.*

Et pereuntibus addita ludibria, ut ferarum tergis contexti laniatu canum interirent.—*Tacitus.*

Quin novæ mortes excogitatatæ, ut ferarum tergis contexti, laniatu canum interirent.—*Sulp. Sev.*

Aut crucibus affixi, aut flammandi ; atque ubi defecisset dies in usum nocturni luminis urerentur.—*Tacitus.*

Multi crucibus affixi, aut flammis usti. Plerique ad id reservati, ut cum defecisset dies, in usum nocturni luminis urerentur.— *Sulp. Sev.*

[o] Diegesis, 394.

were spread through Italy, France, Britain, Germany, and Spain; and from one of these copies Johannes de Spire's edition appears to have been printed. The *second* MS. seems also to date from the eleventh century; and contains a statement relating to the works of Apuleius, written on the same set of skins, showing that the original, of which the present MS. is a copy, was made towards the close of the fourth century.[p]

7. The passage, though unquestionably the work of a master, and entitled to be pronounced a *chef d'œuvre* of the sort, betrays a *penchant* for that delight in descriptions of bloody horrors, as peculiarly characteristic of the Christian disposition as it was abhorrent to the mild and gentle mind and highly-cultivated tastes of Tacitus. It has a character of exaggeration, and trenches on the laws of natural probability. It is indeed not conceivable that Nero should have been so hardened in cruelty, and wanton in wickedness, as this passage would represent him.

Reply. The most startling atrocity, the burning men alive in dresses of combustible materials as living torches, is well attested by Juvenal,[q] Seneca,[r] Martial,[s] and Tertullian.[t]

[p] See Preface by F. Ritter to edition of Tacitus of 1848, p. 45—50.

[q] vii. 235. Ausi quod liceat tunicâ punire molestâ. Daring what may be punished by a vest of pain. The old scholiast describes this " tunica molesta " as " ex chartâ facta, pice illitâ in quâ ignibus pœnæ addicti ardere solebant "—made of paper smeared with pitch, in which those sentenced to punishment by fire were wont to burn. Ib. i. 155. Tædâ lucebis an illâ quâ stantes ardent qui fixo gutture fumant. You will shine by that torch with which those glow who smoke while standing with the neck fixed. Scholiast, Nero clothed malefactors with pitch and papyrus, and ordered them to be brought to a fire that they might burn.

[r] Epist. ii. ad Lucill. Cogita hoc loco carcerem, et circus, et equuleos, et ancum, et illam tunicam alimentis ignium et illisam et textam. Here think of the prison, and the circus, and the horses, and the hook [instruments of torture], and that tunic smeared with and woven of the food of fire. These lines appear

The Mythical Element in Christianity. 23

8. Such good and innocent people as the first Christians must be supposed to be could not have provoked so great a degree of hostility. They must have sufficiently endeared themselves to their fellow citizens to prevent the possibility of their being so treated.

Reply. The whole character of the Christian apologies shows that, from whatever cause, the first Christians did call forth great hatred from certain classes, as they called forth contemptuous disdain from other classes.

9. So just a man as Tacitus unquestionably was could not have spoken of the professors of a purer religion than the world had ever seen as justly criminal, and deserving exemplary punishment.

Reply. It does not appear that Tacitus ever examined into the tenets of the Christian religion. The charge of "hatred of mankind,"[u] which is his only definite accusation, is very intelligible, if we bear in mind the anticipation of the speedy coming of Christ to judge all men, which we know, from St Paul's epistles, that the Christians of that age generally entertained, and the consequences attached by Christian belief to that judgment.

10. The account is inconsistent with the 1st

---

to have been written while the atrocities were fresh in Seneca's memory, shortly before his own death, which took place the year following the burning of Rome.

[s] X. 25, 5. Nam quum dicatur, Tunicâ presente molestâ, Ure manum, plus est dicere non facio. For when in presence of a vest of pain the order is given, "Burn your hand," it is more courageous to say, "I won't do it;" because this might lead to the burning of your body.

[t] Apol. § 50. Licet nunc sarmenticios et semiustos appelletis, quasi ad stipitem dimidio axis revincti sarmentorum ambitu exceriamur. Though now you call us faggot men and half-axis men, as if being bound to the stake by half our axis we were scorched by the encircling faggots.

[u] Odium generis humani.

Epistle of St Peter,[v] where Nero is spoken of as the minister of God for good, and the Christians are assured that, so long as they are followers of that which is good, no one would harm them.

Reply. There is no necessary contradiction between the two accounts, even if the Epistle was written in the age traditionally assigned to it. Nero, according to Tacitus and Suetonius, in the beginning of his reign, gave a promise of good government, to which the Epistle may refer, supposing such passages as ii. 12, iii. 13, and iv. 14 do not point to a period of persecution and trial of the Christians, as has often been contended, rather than to one of tranquillity. And if it were written during the reign of Nero, no other evidence would be required for overthrowing the hypothesis which would make the origin of Christianity be subsequent to the siege of Jerusalem. But the Tübingen school of critics allege strong grounds for placing the date of the Epistle in the time of Trajan.[w]

11. It is inconsistent with the statements of Melito, Bishop of Sardis, who expressly states that the Christians up to his time—the third century—had never been the victims of persecution; and that it was in the provinces lying beyond the boundaries of the Roman empire, and not in Judæa, that Christianity originated.

Reply. Melito lived not in the third, but in the second century. He dedicated an epistle to Marcus Antoninus in defence of the Christians, which Eusebius in his Chronicon places in A.D. 170, and which cannot be later than the accession of Commodus, A.D. 180; and he expressly mentions Nero and Domitian "as having been inclined, through the persuasion of certain envious and malicious persons,

---

[v] iii. 13.   [w] Schwegler Nach Apost. Zeitalter, ii., 11—17.

to bring our doctrine into hatred ; but your godly ancestors," he continues (Trajan and Hadrian) " corrected their blind ignorance, and rebuked oftentimes by their epistles the rash enterprises of those who were ill-affected towards us."[x] Melito does not mention Judæa at all, but says only that " our philosophy first flourished among the Barbarians, and from thence having spread over thy people, under the illustrious reign of Augustus, thy predecessor, it has been an eternal benefit to thy kingdom." The use of barbarian in this passage is agreeable to the Greek practice in speaking of every nation who were not Greeks. Instances abound; I cite two only. Plutarch says of his own contemporaries, "The people have no need of statesmen for procuring peace, since all war, whether with Greeks or Barbarians, is taken away and banished for ever."[y] So Philo[z] speaks of " Caius, after the death of Tiberius Cæsar, taking the command of all the earth, and sea, the Barbarian races with the Hellenes, and the Hellenes with the Barbarians." Melito probably meant simply that the Christian faith, having originated in Judæa, had thence spread to Greece and Italy.

12. Tacitus, in no other part of his writings, makes any allusion to Christ or Christianity.

Reply. This silence is quite consistent with the tone of the passage under consideration, which shows a contemptuous indifference to Christian ideas as a religion. Tacitus noticed Christianity only when it came into collision with a political question.

In reviewing generally Mr Taylor's objections to this passage in Tacitus, we see that whatever strength they possess apart from his confident assertions depends on his supposition, *first*, that no allu-

[x] See Euseb. ii., H. E. 26.   [y] ' Political Precepts,' § 32.
[z] De Virtutibus, ii. 546. Mangey's edition.

sion to the passage can be discovered before the
fifteenth century ; *secondly,* that there then existed a
writer who had the opportunity, the disposition, and
the ability to compose an account of the persecution
of the Christians under Nero, in what Gibbon calls
" the inimitable style of Tacitus," and thus palm off a
forgery on the literary world. Nothing in the context causes any suspicion that the passage has been
interpolated. On the contrary, although it is
possible to strike out the sentences in Tacitus relating
to the persecution of the Christians by Nero without
making a gap in his narrative, his story is more consistent with itself if they are retained; because the
next paragraph begins with a statement implying the
lapse of some considerable time since the conflagration, which the account of the proceedings against
the Christians fills up.[a] And when we find that the
passage is quoted by a writer of the fourth century
instead of having been unnoticed till the fifteenth;
that MSS. containing it were widely circulated
throughout Europe two or three centuries before the
date of the supposed forgery; and that one ancient
MS. where it occurs has internal evidence of having
been copied from an original writer in the fourth
century, I can discover no reason for accepting Mr
Taylor's hypothesis as having even a shade of probability. The genuineness of the passage of Tacitus
must, I think, be considered as established, and
becomes a strong proof that, five years before the
siege of Jerusalem under Titus, there were at Rome
a considerable body[b] of persons commonly called
Christians, who traced their origin to a *Christus* put
to death by the procurator Pontius Pilate, in the
reign of Tiberius.

[a] Interea, conferendis pecuniis pervastata Italia, provinciæ
eversæ, sociique populi.
[b] " Multitudo ingens," says Tacitus.

The Mythical Element in Christianity. 27

The existence of a body of persons thus named in Rome at this time is confirmed by the passage already cited from Suetonius, on which Mr Taylor remarks only "that he hopes the Christians will not be offended, if he hopes that it may not apply to them," certainly a very feeble form of critical objection. No doubt Mr Taylor felt the absurdity of supposing that any Christian would have introduced a description of his co-religionists as men who " held a new and mischievous superstition " into Suetonius, between two passages relating the one to cooks' shops and the other to horse races; and so endeavoured to ride out of the difficulty, that the passage proves the existence in Rome under Nero of a body of Christians considerable enough to have become the subject of penal enactments, by a miserable joke. But the way in which Suetonius introduces this notice, and the way in which Tacitus refers to the death of Christ by order of Pontius Pilate, not as to a rumour but as to an ascertained fact, raises a question of considerable interest, namely, whether those acts of Pilate[c] referred to by Justin Martyr and Tertullian did not really exist, and form a solid foundation upon which the unscrupulous piety of Christian writers in later times reared that fabric of forgeries preserved to us under the name of the Gospel of Nicodemus,[d] and thus have brought into question the existence of any official documents relating to the history of Jesus? In the time of the first Roman Emperors, says Dr Lardner,[e] " there were acts of the Senate, acts of the city, or people of Rome,

[c] Tōn epi Pontiou Pilatou genomenōn actōn. Justin Martyr, I. Apol., p. 76, 84. Paris 1686. 63, 82 Bened. Ea omnia super Christo Pilatus et ipse jam pro sua conscientia Christianus retulit. Tertullian, Apol. 23.
[d] Fabricius Codex, Apocryph. N. T., i. 214.
[e] ' Heathen Testimonies,' c. ii., from which the following statement is condensed.

acts of other cities, and acts of the governors of provinces. Of all these we can discern clear proofs in ancient writers of the best credit." Thus Julius Cæsar ordered that the acts of the Senate as well as daily acts of the people should be published.[f] Augustus forbid the publication of those of the Senate.[g] Tacitus mentions a senator appointed by Tiberius to draw up these acts.[h] Elsewhere we find them referred to as containing speeches from which the oratorical talent of Pompey and Crassus might be appreciated.[i] The acts of the people appear to have been journals containing accounts of public trials and affairs, punishments, assemblies, buildings, births, deaths, marriages, divorces, &c.[j] They were kept at other places besides Rome, as, e.g., at Antium, whence Suetonius learned the day and place of birth of Caligula, and which he refers to as official documents.[k] And Philo speaks of acts or memoirs of Alexandria[l] being sent to Caligula, "which he read with more eagerness and satisfaction than anything else." That there should have been similar acts or reports of remarkable occurrences sent up from the governors of the provinces to Rome is therefore in itself probable, and would explain in a satisfactory manner the positive statement as to the death of Christ by order of Pontius Pilate made by Tacitus; though Dr Lardner does not cite, nor have I been able to discover, any reference to such acts by Roman historians. But it seems improbable that either Justin Martyr or Tertullian would have appealed to records of this nature, in writings addressed to the

[f] Suet. Vit. J. C., c. 20.
[g] Suet. Vit. Aug., c. 36.
[h] Ann. i. 5.
[i] Tac. Dial. de Oratore, 37.
[j] See instances in Lipsius Excursus on Tac. Ann. v. 4.
[k] Vit. Cal., c. 8; Vit. Tib., c. 5.
[l] *Hupomnētikais ephēmerisin.* De Leg. ad Caium, 1016 A. Mangey.

The Mythical Element in Christianity. 29

Emperor and Senate of Rome, as apologies for their religion, if it were not generally known that such records existed. So that the reference is in itself a pretty good evidence of the fact.[m] And at all events, the acts of the people of Rome must have contained full details of events so sensational as the conflagration of the city, and the steps taken by Nero to throw off suspicion from himself upon the Christians, which would supply Tacitus with official information of the name ascribed to the victims of imperial cruelty and cunning; as they probably furnished to Suetonius the materials for his summary of Nero's police regulations. Now this is all that is required to take the statement of the existence of bodies of Christians at that time in Rome entirely out of the domain of legend and myth.

To the positive evidence of the existence of Christianity as a religious belief before the date of the siege of Jerusalem, furnished by these passages in Tacitus and Suetonius, must be added, as a strong confirmatory proof, the statement of Pliny the younger, in his often cited letter to the Emperor Trajan, written probably in A.D. 107 or 108.[n] In this letter he speaks not only of the great numbers of "persons of all ages, of every rank and of both sexes," who were in danger of suffering as Christians, but of "some who declared that they had ceased to be Christians twenty years before." Surely it is far more likely that such a spread of the new faith to a point so distant from Jerusalem as Bithynia, repre-

[m] The statements of Tertullian, however, make it nearly certain, and those of Justin Martyr at least probable, that the documents to which they referred were not copies of offici·l records, but accounts similar to those circulated among the Christians in later days as the acts of Pilate, in opposition to which Eusebius states that acts derogatory to Christ were forged by the heathen in the persecution of Maximin., E. H. i. 9, and ix. 5.
[n] Lardner, 'Heathen Test.' c. v.

sents the results of a propaganda continued for three-quarters of a century, rather than that a period of about thirty-five years should have sufficed for the incubation and production of the supposed myth—its acceptance among a certain class of Jews, its diffusion among their Gentile converts, and the attainment of a following so considerable as that described by Pliny, in a province remote from Judæa?

But here again recourse has been had to the weapon which we have found used against the testimony of Tacitus—suspicion of *forgery*. The learned Dr J. S. Semler entertained doubts as to the genuineness of this letter, and his doubts are paraded, as if they were unquestioned certainties, by Mr R. Cooper, who expands them into a statement " that *the German literati* have long been of opinion that this letter is a forgery."° As the main ground for this conclusion, he adduces the objections, "that the letter is found in one MS. only of Pliny's letters, and not in the others," and that Pliny states that the Christians used to meet before daylight and sing a hymn to Christ as to a God; whereas, says Mr Cooper, "the belief in the Divinity of Christ was not established till the Council of Nice, in A.D. 325"; whence Mr Cooper suggests that the letter was forged during the century intervening between Pliny and Tertullian, A.D. 216, by whom it is quoted. How the forger came to introduce a form of address to Christ, which, according to Mr Cooper, did not come into use till a century after Tertullian's death, he does not condescend to explain. But, in fact, Tertullian's quotation, while it proves the existence both of the

---

° See 'Infidel's Text Book,' or Lectures on the Bible, London, 1846, pp. 56, 57. Mr Cooper cites Semler's Neue Versuche die Kirchen Historie der ersten Jahrhunderten aufzuklaren, 1788, pp. 117—226,—a work of which I have not been able to obtain a sight.

letter ascribed to Pliny, and the reply ascribed to
Trajan, at the time when his apology was written,
does create some suspicion that the particular expression to which Mr Cooper objects may have been introduced at a later date, for he makes Pliny say that
the Christians sang a hymn to Christ *and* God,
instead of to Christ *as* to God ; which is the reading
of our present copies of Pliny.[p] So that, to say
nothing of the obvious answer to this objection,
that Pliny, who does not profess to report the
exact words used by any Christian, and, in this
letter, speaks of having required those who were
charged before him " to repeat after him an invocation
to the gods, and make offerings of wine and incense
to the statue of *Trajan*, which, for that purpose, he
had ordered to be brought out with those of the
deities," may have somewhat misapprehended the
nature of the addresses made by the Bithynians to
Christ, the objection vanishes before the same kind
of doubt to which it owes its existence. The *other*
objection, that the letter is not to be found in some
of the best MSS. of Pliny's letters, states a fact, but
omits to state that the omission is not confined to
this particular letter, but extends to the *whole correspondence* between Pliny and Trajan, which forms the
10th book of his letters, and apparently was not published till some considerable time after Pliny's death,
while the bulk of his other letters were collected and
published during his life, or immediately after his
decease, whence these letters were not found in
many copies of his works.[q]

As for the *German literati*, they are so far from

---

[p] Christo *et* deo, instead of Christo *quasi* deo. This is stated to
be the reading of the best MSS. of Tertullian. Others have *ut*
deo. Eusebius renders the phrase *dikēn theō*, which seems to show
that he read ' quasi' in Pliny.

[q] See Preface to Titze's Edition of ' Pliny,' Leipsic, 1823.

having "generally concluded this letter to be a forgery," as Mr Cooper asserts, that edition after edition of Pliny's letters has been published in Germany, since Semler's work appeared, in which this letter is treated as genuine. Its genuineness is ably defended by a recent editor, Moritz Döring,[r] who observes, as appears to me with perfect justice, "that it is difficult to see what object could be gained by forging it. An enemy of Christianity would have shown his desire for persecution more openly. A secret Christian could not have hoped to stop it by such means;" that is to say, by suggesting the adoption of a mixture of leniency and severity, involving death to those who refused to recant,[s] with the statement that, by the adoption of this course, coupled with free pardon to such as would worship the Roman deities, "the temples, which had been almost forsaken, were beginning to be more frequented, and the sacred solemnities, after a long intermission, to be revived;" and "that victims were everywhere bought up, whereas, before, there were few purchasers." How too can we suppose that any Christian would have been contented to ascribe the conduct of martyrs, who "resisted even unto death," only to "contumacy and inflexible obstinacy;"[t] or would not have insinuated some words of pity, if not of praise, for the two deaconesses, whom Pliny put to the torture, instead of simply stating that he "discovered nothing but a bad and extravagant superstition."[u] On the other hand, can we imagine that an enemy to Christianity would make Trajan direct, as he does in his reply to Pliny, that the Christians

[r] In an Edition published at Freyberg, 1843.
[s] Confitentes, iterum ac tertio interrogavi, supplicium minatus: perseverantes *duci* jussi.
[t] Pertinaciam, et inflexibilem obstinationem.
[u] Superstitionem pravam et immodicam.

The Mythical Element in Christianity. 33

were not to be sought for, and were in all cases to be pardoned "on supplicating our gods," without even insisting " on their reviling Christ," though this is suggested in Pliny's letter, and absolutely prohibit the reception of anonymous accusations, as "a very bad precedent and unworthy of his age." But the tone of the letters is just what might be reasonably expected from what else we know of Pliny and Trajan. Trajan expresses his hatred of the system of spies. Pliny institutes careful inquiries, and does not conceal from the emperor what is favourable to the Christians; that they pledged themselves solemnly, "not to the commission of any crime, but not to be guilty of theft, or robbery, or adultery, never to falsify their word, or refuse to give up property entrusted to them;" but he judges their refusal to sacrifice to the gods to be a criminal obstinacy, and their belief to be a contemptible superstition, and dislikes particularly the secrecy of their meetings, and their forming a separate society, to which others of his letters show that Trajan was particularly adverse. Add that the style and language of these letters agrees perfectly with those of the other letters of Pliny and Trajan, a point by no means unimportant, when we remember that this style is far from easy of imitation. On the whole, then, there seems no reason for doubting what Tertullian and Eusebius assume, that the letters are genuine parts of the correspondence between Pliny and the Emperor Trajan.

The conclusion of the genuineness both of these letters and the passages from Tacitus and Suetonius previously adduced, is confirmed, I think, if we compare either of these authorities with the documents which a mistaken piety undoubtedly did forge, for the better confirmation of the Christian faith, such as the letters of Pilate to Tiberius, or the testimony to Christ interpolated into Josephus, which I select for comparison, because they are the *least* obviously absurd of these fictitious evidences.

2nd letter of Pilate.[v]

"Pilate to Tiberius Cæsar. Health!

"On Jesus Christ, of whom I gave you clear information in my last, at length, by the desire of the people, as it were against my will, and without my order, a severe punishment has been inflicted. But, by Hercules, so pious and pure a man no age has ever produced, or will produce. But a wonderful struggle of the people itself, and concurrence of all the scribes and rulers existed, as their own prophets and our sybils had forewarned, to crucify this ambassador of the truth; signs in nature, which in the judgment of philosophers threatened destruction to the universe, appearing while he was hanging. His disciples thrive, not belying their master by their words, and the continency of their lives—yea, being in his name great doers of good. If I had not dreaded a sedition of the people, who were all but boiling over, perhaps this man would still live. But being rather driven by my regard for your dignity, than led by my own will, I did not oppose with my full strength that this pure blood, innocent of any charge, should by the malignity of the men, unjustly, on their clamour, as the documents explain, suffer death, and be exposed to the winds."

Extract from Josephus: [w]

"At that time lived Jesus, a wise man, if he may be called a man; for he performed many wonderful works. He was the teacher of such men as received the truth with pleasure. He drew over to himself many Jews and Gentiles. This was the Christ. And when Pilate, at the instigation of the chief men

[v] Acta Pilati, Fab. Cod. Apocryph. N. T. I., 244. The poverty of the Latin style is necessarily concealed in the translation.
[w] Ant. xviii. 3, 3.

The Mythical Element in Christianity. 35

among us, had condemned him to the cross, they who beforehand had conceived a love for him did not cease to adhere to him., For, on the third day, he appeared to them again alive, the divine prophets having foretold these and many wonderful things respecting him; and the sect of Christians, so called from him, subsists to this day."

The contrast between the tone of such passages, and those adduced above from Tacitus, Suetonius, and Pliny, is apparent; and shows, what it is reasonable to expect that, when the Christian imagination invented testimonies, it neither made these imaginary witnesses abuse the Christian religion, nor contented itself with making them attest what no one at the time disputed—namely, the existence of a body of Christians before the middle of the first century; but applied itself to meet the matters really contested, which was, not whether Jesus had lived at the time when they asserted that he did live, but whether his life and acts had been such as they represented.

Now, in opposition to this direct evidence of the existence of Christianity before the siege of Jerusalem, borne by the concurrent testimony of two eminent writers, who were not Christians, and confirmed incidentally by the official correspondence of a third, what is adduced? Simply a list of other non-Christian writers living in that age, who make no mention of Christianity.

The author of 'The Twelve Apostles' enumerates the following alleged contemporary writers, whose silence on this subject, he says, "is most remarkable"[1]:—

[1] Mr Cooper, in his 'Infidel's Text-Book,' pp. 50, 51, gives a much longer list, to which Mr I. L. Strange refers in his 'The Bible; is it the Word of God?' p. 351, of writers who have said nothing about Christians, including several, though not all, of those mentioned above. The list is not remarkable for the classical knowledge of names displayed in it; and as it includes several writers who lived

36　The Mythical Element in Christianity.

	A.D.
Josephus, born	37
Philo, the Jew, died about	42
Plutarch, flourished	80
Pamphilus, the Grammarian, flourished	30
Memnon, ,, ,,	50
Epictetus, the Philosopher, ,,	90
Lesbonax, the Sophist, ,,	10
Pliny the elder, died	77
Seneca, the Philosopher, died	65
Curtius, the Historian, flourished	69
Pomponius Mela, the Geographer, flourished	45
Velleius [y] Paterculus, the Historian ,,	30
Valerius Maximus ,, ,, ,,	26

Exception may be taken to the dates assigned to some of these authors. The age of *Pamphilus* is doubtful. On the one hand he is called *Aristarcheios*, of which the natural meaning is a pupil of Aristarchus, who lived 130 B.C. On the other hand, he is said to have quoted Apion, who was alive in A.D. 41. Mr Fynes Clinton attaches most weight to the last statement in fixing the date of Pamphilus, and adduces another case to show that *Aristarcheios* may mean only, of the school of Aristarchus.[z] But, as we do not possess the alleged quotation from Apion, it is possible that the statement may be a mistake, or

---

in the second century, when, even according to the mythical theory, the name Christian was known, their silence tends to destroy the weight of any argument drawn from the silence of those who lived in the first century, by showing that this silence may have proceeded from other reasons than the one of the name being unknown at the time. (See p. 65). The remarks made below, on the improbability of the writers referred to by the author of 'The Twelve Apostles' mentioning Christianity, apply to the other writers mentioned by Mr Cooper, as I have ascertained by individual examination of them. I have not gone more fully into these cases here, to avoid making this tract tediously long.

[y] Misprinted Valerius.
[z] Fasti Hell., iii. 584 ; C. N. 228.

The Mythical Element in Christianity. 37

refer to some other Apion than the noted grammarian, and that *Aristarcheios* should be taken in its ordinary meaning, which would make Pamphilus anterior to the Christian era.

The age of *Memnon* is also very uncertain; our only acquaintance with him being derived from fragments of his works preserved by Photius. Voss places him in the time of Augustus; while Orellius, in the preface to an edition of his works, published in 1816, contends that he could not have written before the time of Hadrian, or even of the Antonines.

Again, the date of *Quintus Curtius* has been placed by different editors of his works at various periods between the time of Cicero and that of the Emperor Theodosius; the epoch which seems the most probable being that of the Emperor Constantine.[a] As to the Sophist, *Lesbonax*, since the only writings of his which have come down to us are two orations supposed to have been delivered during the Corinthian war, B.C. 413, it is difficult to see why his silence about Christianity should be considered remarkable.

In the case of the other writers, the question arises, what probability is there that they would notice such a fact as Christianity probably was up to the close of the first century? If we assume the historical truth of all the prodigies recorded in the N. T., the case would, no doubt, be very different from what I take it to be. Gibbon, for instance, is, I think, quite justified in arguing that Pliny the elder could hardly have failed to notice the darkness which is said to have overspread all Palestine for several hours during the Crucifixion, in his careful examination of all known instances of failure of the sun's light, if such a darkness had actually occurred. But suppose these marvels to have been simply the

[a] See Dissertations in Valpy's Delphin Ed. 1826, i., p. 32.

colouring given by the belief of the Christian community in the superhuman character of Christ to the events of his life: suppose that the Christians, until after the siege of Jerusalem, were commonly regarded as a Jewish sect,[b] distinguished from other sects only because "after a way which these called heresy, so worshipped they the God of their fathers;"[c] differing from them only "on certain questions touching their own superstitions, and one Jesus, which was dead, whom [the Christians] affirmed to be alive,"[d] there would be no reason for expecting to find notices of Christianity by any writers other than Christian, unless it can be shown that these writers bestowed much attention upon the Jewish sects and their opinions generally. Now, so far is this from being the case, that of the writers mentioned above, the only ones not Jews who notice the Jews at all are Memnon, Plutarch, Epictetus, Pliny the elder, Seneca, and Pomponius Mela,[e] and the notice which they take of the Jews is very slight. *Memnon* states only that they were subject to Antiochus, the King of Syria, whom the Romans defeated.[f] *Plutarch's* notice is confined to the questions, suggested as topics for after-dinner conversation, whether the Jews abstained from swine's flesh because they worshipped that animal, or because they had an antipathy to it; and whether Adonis, which he seems to have supposed to be the name of the God of the Jews, is not the same as Bacchus.[g] *Epictetus*, in blam-

[b] "Thou seest, brother, how many thousands of Jews there are who believe, and they are *all zealots of the law.*" Acts xxi. 20.
[c] Acts xxiv. 14.
[d] Acts xxv. 19.
[e] I must except Pamphilus, whose works I have not been able to obtain, of whom, therefore, I cannot say whether he mentions the Jews or not.
[f] Ch. 25, 26.
[g] Sympos. iv., Ques. 5 and 6. How unsafe is it to argue from the silence of ancient writers, as to remarkable persons in or near

The Mythical Element in Christianity. 39

ing those who assume the profession of philosophy without acting up to it, says, "Why should you pretend to be a Greek when you are a Jew? Do you not perceive on what terms a man is called a Jew, a Syrian, an Egyptian? When we see a man inconstant to his principles we say he is not a Jew, but when he has the temper of a man dipped and professed, then he is, indeed, and is called, a Jew. Even so, we are counterfeits—Jews in name, but in reality something else."[h] Again, when discoursing of intrepidity, he says, "It is possible that a man may arrive at this temper and become indifferent to those things [dangers] from madness, or from habit, as the Galileans."[i] Both passages have been supposed, and it seems not unlikely, do refer to the Christians; they are all that Epictetus says about the Jews. *Pliny* the elder gives a short account of the geographical position of Judæa and its natural productions, and relates that there is a river in it which dries up every Sabbath day; but of the religious beliefs of the nation he says only that they were remarkable for their contempt of the Deities,[j] and that they practised a magical art, taught them by Moses and Jochabela many thousand years after Zoroaster, whom Eudoxus states to have lived 6000 years before Plato.[k] *Seneca* twice alludes to the Jewish Sabbath, once in a fragment of his dialogue on "Superstition," preserved by St Augustine, where he

to their own day, to their non-existence, appears from the fact that Plutarch never mentions Persius, Juvenal, Lucan, Seneca, Quintilian, Martial, Tacitus, Suetonius, or either Pliny, with all of whom he was contemporary either in his youth or his old age. Nor is he mentioned by any Roman writer. Yet he had lived for some years in Rome and given popular lectures there. Emerson, Preface to translation of Plutarch's Morals, ix.
[h] Book ii. 9, Upton's translation.
[i] Book iv. 7, Ib.
[j] Gens contumeliâ numinum insignis. Hist. Nat. xiii. 4.
[k] Ib. xxx. 1.

accuses the Jews of "thus causing a useless waste of the seventh part of their time ;" and a second time, in one of his letters,[1] in which he speaks of a "prohibition to light candles on the Sabbaths ;" and this is the only notice which he takes of them. Lastly, *Pomponius Mela* simply mentions that Judæa is a district of Syria. Why should we expect that authors who take so little notice of the ancient faith of the Jewish people, who in the first Christian century had spread so widely over the Roman empire, should specially busy themselves about a recent offshoot of that faith rejected by the body of the Jewish nation, then slowly diffusing itself, principally among the poorer classes, slaves, and freed-men, and women probably more than men,[m] in the great cities of the empire ; and numbering, at the outside, not more than a few thousand adherents in any one of those cities.[n]

[1] Ep. 95.
[m] 'Ye see, brethren, your calling. God hath chosen the foolish things of the world, and base things, and things which are despised.' 1 Cor. i. 25—28.
[n] Gibbon, after a careful consideration of all the numerical data which he could find, concludes, " that the most favourable calculations will not permit us to imagine that more than a twentieth part of the subjects of the empire had enlisted under the banner of the Cross before the important conversion of Constantine," C. xv., near end; an estimate not contested by his modern editors. He remarks also that *ingens multitudo*, the expression used by Tacitus of the Christians under Nero, is the same as that used by Livy of the Bacchanals, *multitudinem ingentem alterum jam prope populum esse*. Yet the whole number was found to be 7,000. Liv. 39, ch. 14—17. Of the ancient writers whom I have examined, *Strabo* gives the fairest and fullest account of the Jewish religion. Yet even he dwells almost exclusively on the prohibition against making any image of the Deity, which seems to have made a deep impression on him as profoundly reasonable, and which he ascribes to Moses, from the purity of whose teachings he conceives that his followers had degenerated into superstitious practices. Obviously, he had not at all studied their religious history. Geog. xvi. 2, secs. 34—36. *Cicero*, his contemporary, though he lived in the age when the Romans first became acquainted with the Jews from the capture of Jerusalem by Pompey, takes no notice whatever of them.

The Mythical Element in Christianity. 41

Among the list of writers enumerated by the author of 'The Twelve Apostles' there are really two only whose silence respecting Christianity can be reasonably a subject of surprise, because, undoubtedly, both of them were familiar with Jewish thought, and paid great attention to the religious beliefs of their nation—*Philo* and *Josephus*. But Philo was of a generation earlier than Jesus. He calls himself old, that is, probably, over 70, in A.D. 40, on the occasion of his mission to Rome.º His works, which principally consist in a series of commentaries on the Pentateuch, must have been written before that date, with the exception of the account of his embassy to Rome placed at the end of them; since he was selected for this office, in spite of his advanced years, in consequence of the influence which his learning and reputation was considered to give him. It is true that in this narrative p he gives "an account of the state of the Jews and their afflictions under Augustus, Tiberius, and Caligula," as Mr Cooper states; but this account is so far from entering into the particulars of their religious opinions, that it does not even mention the divisions of Pharisees and Sadducees, of which we learn nothing from Philo; though he has devoted a separate treatise to the Essenes, from his admiration of the contemplative life, withdrawn from all worldly distractions, which they led. The silence of Philo on the existence of a sect of Christians among the Jews cannot, under these circumstances, be considered of any weight as an argument against its existence, whatever may be the weight due to it, when adduced, as is done by Mr Cooper, to prove "that the pretensions of the Christians to the *divine* influence of their master

º See Preface to Mangey's Edition of his works.
p Satirically called 'Of Virtues.'

are perfectly gratuitous;"[q] a matter with which I am not now dealing.

Josephus comes under another category. But the allegation that he "does not make the slightest mention of Jesus Christ"[r] can be established only if it can be shown not only that the passage quoted above is interpolated into his works, of which there appears to be no reasonable doubt,[s] but also that the short incidental notice of Jesus, contained in his account of the death of James, by order of the High Priest Ananus, is an interpolation. Now this is a much more doubtful question. The passage is as follows: "Ananus, thinking that he had met with a fitting opportunity, seeing that Festus was dead and Albinus was still on his journey, convened a Sanhedrim of judges, and having brought before it the brother of Jesus, who is called Christ, named James, and some others, accused them of having broken the law, and gave them over to be stoned."[t]

This passage was known to Photius, whose silence as to the passage in Ant. xviii. is one strong argument against it.[u] It is quoted by Eusebius, and by Jerome, though inaccurately, and it appears probable that it is referred to by Origen.[v] Objection has

[q] 'Infidel's Text Book,' p. 51.
[r] Ib. p. 54, 'Twelve Apostles,' p. 10.
[s] See Lardner's discussion of this passage in his 'Jewish Testimonies and Credibility of the Gospel.'
[t] Ant. xx. 9. 1.
[u] Lardner's Jewish Test. v. 3.
[v] Origen says "that Josephus, who wrote the 'Jewish Antiquities' in twenty books, being desirous to assign the cause why the Jews suffered such things, that even their temple was demolished to its foundations, says that these things had happened because of the anger of God against them for what they had done to James, the brother of Jesus, called Christ." In Matt., sec. 17. Again, in his work against Celsus, i. c. 37, he states "Josephus says that these things befel the Jews in vindication of James, called The Just, who was the brother of Jesus, called Christ; inasmuch as they killed him who was a most righteous man." And afterwards, in

The Mythical Element in Christianity. 43

been taken to the genuineness, on the ground—*first*, that it implies some longer account of Jesus, of which none is given in Josephus except the passage allowed to be interpolated. *Secondly*, that the absence of a reference to Christ in any other passage of Josephus than this one, shows a settled intention on his part not to notice him, which is inconsistent with the notice here. But neither of these objections appears to me of much force. Josephus may have designedly abstained from any notice of Christ, or Christianity as a religious belief, and yet have mentioned the title commonly given to Jesus, as a means of identifying the James whom he names as condemned to death; and if he introduced the title *only* for this purpose, and his object was sufficiently attained by its introduction, he would have no reason for giving any further account of Jesus, whom we know that he did not acknowledge to be the true Messiah. The fact that the passage is quoted by Photius, who does not notice the account in Ant. xviii., proves that, at all events, the two passages are independent of each other. On the other hand, if any part of the passage is struck out, the whole must go, including the notice of James, and the sentence must be reduced to the words, "and bringing before it some, he accused them of having broken the law." But this is an

---

' Cont. Cels.' ii, sec. 13, he says of the destruction of Jerusalem, "which, as Josephus writes, happened on account of James the Just, the brother of Jesus, called Christ; but, in truth, upon account of Jesus, *the* Christ, the Son of God." This account is not to be found in Josephus; but the expression, "the brother of Jesus, *called* Christ," is peculiar, and not likely to be used by Origen except as a quotation, as we may see from the continuation of the last passage. If he knew that Josephus had given an account of the death of James under the description of the "brother of Jesus, *called* Christ," he may have ascribed to Josephus notions as to the consequences of this crime, which he had gathered from other sources; but it seems improbable that he should have done this, if Josephus had not mentioned the death of James at all.

awkward statement. It is not likely that Josephus would have said, Ananus "brought some" before the Council without any explanation of who they were. Nor is it probable that an interpolator would have divided the sentence, inserting the words from "the brother of Jesus" to "and," before "some," and "others" after it, though the Greek would have allowed him to say, with even more elegance, "others some," instead of "some others." And if the interpolator were a Christian, as is supposed, he would probably have said, "the brother of Jesus, *the* Christ," not "the brother of Jesus, *called* Christ."[w] The gravest objection to the passage lies in its alleged inconsistency with the account of the death of James, given by Hegesippus and Clemens of Alexandria, as cited by Eusebius, who do not mention any trial of him instituted by Ananus, nor any others put to death with him, but describe him to have been "killed in a tumult near the temple, where some flung him down and threw stones at him; but his death was completed by a blow on the head with a fuller's pole."[x] Yet, surely, it is quite possible that this may have been the actual mode of the death of James, while it had been preceded by an informal judicial process such as Josephus mentions. He does not tell us on what particular transgressions of the law the accusation turned. If the other persons accused were not Christians, or were not put to death as such, the Christian tradition would probably have ignored them. The whole proceeding was irregular, according to Josephus.[y] So that it is not improbable that the attempt to execute the sentence may have

---

[w] As in Ant. xviii. 1, where we read, "He was *the* Christ."
[x] Lardner's 'Jewish Testimonies,' iv. 3.
[y] So that "Albinus wrote to Ananus in great anger, threatening to punish him for what he had done, and King Agrippa took away from him the High Priesthood." Josephus, u.s.

The Mythical Element in Christianity. 45

led to a riot, in which James was killed—some persons, perhaps, attempting to rescue him from a judgment which they considered illegal.

On the whole, then, the arguments for the genuineness of this passage appear to me to preponderate over those against it; and, if it is genuine, we have in Josephus a witness not only to the fact but to the notoriety of the ascription of the title of Christ to Jesus, at a period anterior to the siege of Jerusalem; since he uses this title as a sufficient means of identifying another person, by describing him as the "brother of Jesus, called Christ."[1] But if this conclusion is mistaken, other cases in Josephus must put us on our guard against attaching much weight to his silence. Dr Lardner has observed that, although in the preface to his 'Jewish Antiquities' 'he engages to write of things as he found them mentioned in the Sacred Books, without adding anything to them, or omitting anything from them,' yet he says nothing about the golden calf made by the people in the wilderness, nor does he once name Mount Sion or Zion, either in his 'Antiquities' or his 'Jewish War,' though there were so many occasions for it, and it is so often mentioned in the Old Testament.[a] The importance of such a caution, in dealing with Jewish authorities, is confirmed by the absence of any direct mention of Christianity in the *Mischna*, or original text of the Talmud, though this was certainly not compiled earlier than the second Christian century, and pro-

[1] Mr Cooper, in his 'Infidel's Text Book,' p. 54, omits to notice this passage, and thus leaves his readers under the impression that "there is not the slightest mention made of Jesus Christ in the works of Josephus except the passage interpolated in Ant. xviii. ;" and yet he was not ignorant of its existence, for, in an earlier work, called 'The Bible and its Evidences,' p. 81, he quotes it, and makes to it one of the objections noticed above.

[a] 'Jewish Testimonies,' iv. 4.

bably at a still later date, and though there appear to be some covert allusions to it.[b] Yet, unquestionably, this silence cannot proceed from the absence of a large body of Christians in that age.

Thus the negative testimony to which the author of 'The Twelve Apostles' attaches so much importance dwindles into insignificance when examined, and leaves unimpugned the positive testimony of Tacitus and Suetonius to the existence at Rome of a body of persons known as Christians some years before the siege of Jerusalem, confirmed by the testimony of Pliny to the extensive diffusion of the Christian faith in Bithynia between A.D. 100 and 110; evidence fatal to the mythical hypothesis advocated by this writer. Having thus a solid foundation for believing Christianity to have originated in the faith in an historical person, laid by the testimony of writers who did not share that faith, we may proceed to inquire whether this testimony is not placed beyond any reasonable doubt by the evidence of those who did share it. Mr Cooper, indeed, objects to quotations from Christian writers in support of Christian statements, that it is a *petitio principii*, proving a position by that which is denied; establishing Christian statements by Christian statements, a *modus operandi* which cannot be tolerated in an examination into their truth.[c] And an objection of this nature would have much force, if the matter to be proved were of a nature likely to be coloured by the imaginations of the narrators. To take the case of Mr Cooper himself. If a question were raised as to the learning, the fairness, the cogency of reasoning, and critical sagacity displayed by him in his 'Infidel's Text Book,' the testimony of a professed disciple of Mr Cooper to the display of these qualities in his work

[b] 'Jewish Testimonies,' v. 1. ii. 8.
[c] 'Infidel's Text Book,' p. 69.

might reasonably be looked at with suspicion. But if the question were only when or where Mr Cooper was born, or the lectures which compose that book were delivered, to whom could we turn, with so good a prospect of obtaining correct information on these matters, as to those who might be associated with him in diffusing his Gospel of Infidelity. The Mormons may be very questionable witnesses to the character of Hiram Smith or Brigham Young, but they are the best witnesses to the dates and ordinary incidents of their lives. And so the writings of the first generations of Christians must be regarded as authorities, I will not say absolutely trustworthy, for they must always be open to reasonable criticism, yet certainly entitled to great weight, on questions concerning the time when the Christian religion began. Now on this point the New Testament gives no "uncertain sound." All the Gospels agree in connecting the appearance of Jesus as a teacher with the preaching of John the Baptist, whose date is fixed by Josephus. All agree in ascribing the crucifixion of Jesus to Pontius Pilate, the period of whose government of Judæa is well ascertained. One of the evangelists had apparently taken considerable pains to fix the time when Jesus began to teach, by reference to a number of contemporary sovereigns. And though it is doubtful whether he was in all these cases well-informed, still the fact of his having made such researches shows that he was not indifferent to the duty of an historian to fix as far as possible the time when the events recorded by him happened, and, in consequence, deserves the credit generally conceded, upon such matters, to the statements of a writer who certainly was not removed by a period of more than seventy years from the time of which he writes.

It may perhaps be objected to the statements of

the Gospels, that the existence of *some one* on whom the imagination of those who first launched the Christian faith pitched, as the solid point round which their mythical conceptions could crystallize, as has been suggested in the beginning of this essay, may be admitted without allowing an historical foundation for the statement that a Messianic character was attributed to Jesus before the siege of Jerusalem; and that the Gospels, which cannot be shown to have been written before that event, may have antedated this belief, by assigning to a time forty years earlier ideas which really arose subsequently to, and in consequence of, this catastrophe. But the New Testament supplies other evidence not open to this objection—the evidence of three distinct witnesses, in The Acts of the Apostles, The Epistles of St. Paul, and The Apocalypse. Let us examine their testimony.

I am by no means disposed to take up the cudgels generally in defence of the historical character of the Acts. I admit that this work appears to have been written with the object of reconciling the Petrine and the Pauline factions, whose disputes distracted the first age of the Church, by exhibiting the two leaders acting side by side in the work of evangelisation, giving to Peter especially the "ministry of the circumcision," and to Paul that of "the uncircumcision," as if by a mutual agreement generally sanctioned by the Apostles; while it ascribes to Peter the honour of making the first important Gentile convert, and makes Paul everywhere address himself first to the Jews, and turn to the Gentiles only when rejected by them, instead of presenting himself, as his epistles would lead us to expect, in the character of an ambassador for Christ, and announcing the principle of righteousness by the "faith which Abraham had yet being uncircumcised;" a faith where the difference between

The Mythical Element in Christianity. 49

Jew and Greek vanished, and all alike were convicted of "having come short of the glory of God," and needing to be justified, "not by the works of the Law," but by that inner principle of trust and love by which they might be transformed into true children of their heavenly Father. I allow that the narrative of the first preachings of the Apostles at Jerusalem is steeped in a roseate mist of mythological wonders where the features of history disappear. But this does not alter the fact that the latter chapters of the Acts embody what appears to be the narrative of an eyewitness and companion of Paul, whose natural blending of "they" and "we" in the story testifies to the truthfulness of his accounts ;[d] while the undesigned coincidences between his statements and the letters of Paul, admirably pointed out in Paley's 'Horæ Paulinæ,' "make out," to borrow Mr Taylor's words,[e] "to the satisfaction of every fair inquirer, that neither those epistles nor that part of the Acts of the Apostles are supposititious. The hero of the one is unquestionably the epistoler of the other. Both writings are therefore genuine, to the full extent of everything they purport to be. Neither are the epistles forged, nor the history, as far as relates to Paul, other than a faithful and a fair account of a person who really existed, and acted the part ascribed to him."

I may observe, in confirmation of this conclusion, that the story of the preaching of Christianity, as we read it in this part of the Acts, is not such as might be naturally expected from the Gospels, and certainly not that which the inventor of an imaginary

[d] xvi. 6—9, "they;" 10—17, "we;" 18 to xx. 4, "he" or "they;" xx. 5, to xxi. 17, "we;" xxi. 20, to xxvi. 35, "he" or "they;" xxvi. to xxvii. 37, "we;" xxvii. 38, to xxviii. 6, "he" or "they;" xxviii. 7—16, "we."
[e] 'Diegesis,' p. 376.

history would have been likely to produce. The Acts of the Apostles profess to be a continuation of the 3rd Gospel, which ends with a solemn declaration of Christ, made to the eleven Apostles immediately before his ascension, that repentance and remission of sins should be preached in his name to all nations, beginning at Jerusalem, "and ye are the witnesses of these things."[f] And the first part of the Acts narrates a story of missionary effort, spreading from Jerusalem to the countries bordering on Judæa, in apparent accordance with this injunction. But, from the xvith chapter to the end of the book, all this is changed. There is no talk of Jerusalem as a centre of propaganda: there is no mention of "the twelve," or any one connected with them, going forth among the nations. The story of missionary activity centres in the labours of a man who was not one of the original apostles, who had been at first a bitter opponent of Christianity, and between whom and "the twelve" there is no trace of a very cordial sympathy. While the only one of the latter body who is mentioned at all, James, is described as stationary in Jerusalem. Surely no one who had begun by evolving twelve apostles out of his "moral consciousness" would have gone on to assign to them a part in the preaching of the Christian faith which he records, so insignificant as this. The fact is conceivable, for fact is often stranger than fiction. The fiction is self-destructive.

Assuming, then, that Mr Taylor's judgment upon this part of the Acts is well founded, what does it show us? What are these thirteen chapters of the Acts, but records of journies made by St Paul during a long series of years, while the city and Temple of Jerusalem were still undestroyed, for the purpose of

[f] Luke xxiv. 47, 48. The 1st and 2nd Gospels contain corresponding statements: Matt. xxviii. 20; Mark xvi. 15—20.

The Mythical Element in Christianity. 51

spreading through Asia Minor, Macedonia, and Greece the faith in Jesus as the Christ ?[g] And with this statement, the letters of Paul, whose genuineness we have seen Mr Taylor admits, and no critic of whom I know, who has studied them, has ever denied, to the Galatians, Corinthians, and Romans, are in complete agreement. From beginning to end, they are full of earnest faith in Jesus Christ, "who was made of the seed of David according to the flesh, and declared to be the son of God with power, according to the spirit of holiness, by the resurrection from the dead."[h] And of these epistles, those to the Galatians and Corinthians distinctly testify to a time anterior to the siege of Jerusalem. The Galatians describes two journies made by Paul to Jerusalem, at an interval of fourteen years.[i] The 1st Epistle to the Corinthians provides for the sending to Jerusalem money which had been collected "for the Saints ;"[j] the 2nd Epistle mentions an intended visit of Paul to Judæa.[k] They testify also to the existence of those apostles which the author of 'The Twelve Apostles' denies. The 1st Epistle to the Corinthians speaks of "the twelve,"[l] and twice mentions Peter under the name of Cephas.[m] The Epistle to the Galatians speaks of Peter by both names,[n] of James, the Lord's brother,[o] of John,[p] and Barnabas,[q] as names thoroughly well

[g] See Acts xvii. 3, 18; xviii. 5; xix. 4, 18; xx. 21, 24, 35; xxi. 13; xxv. 19; xxvi. 9, 15, 23, 28 ; xxviii. 31.
[h] Rom. i. 3, 4.
[i] i. 18 ; ii. 1.
[j] I Cor. xii. 3.
[k] II Cor. i. 66.
[l] I Cor. xv. 5.
[m] I Cor. i. 12 ; xv. 5.
[n] Peter, i. 18; ii. 7, 8, 11, 14 ; Cephas, ii. 9.
[o] i. 19; ii. 9.
[p] ii. 9.
[q] ii. 14.

E

known among the Christian community; and confirms to this extent the story in the Gospels.[r]

I pass to the third witness mentioned above, the Apocalypse, of which the general consent of the ablest critics, founded on the distinct reference to Jerusalem as still standing in chapter xi., places the date before the destruction of that city.[s] Now the Apocalypse professes to be "a revelation from Jesus Christ, which God gave unto him, to show his servants things which must shortly come to pass";[t] whom it describes as the "faithful and true witness;" "the first begotten from the dead;"[u] "whom every eye should see, and they also that pierced him;" and again, "as one like unto the Son of Man,[v] who was dead and is alive for ever, and has the keys of hell and of death;"[w] and again, as "the Lamb who has been slain," and now "is worthy to receive power, and

---

[r] The name Cephas does not occur in the Synoptics. We learn its application to Peter, positively, only from the fourth Gospel, i. 42; and, in this Gospel, it is never used again. In the passages where Peter is afterwards mentioned, he is called Simon Peter, except where the name occurs several times in the same story, when the Simon is dropped, xiii. 63; xviii. 11, 16, 17, 18, 26, 27; xx. 3, 4; xxi. 7, 17, 20, 21; and in xxi. 15, 17, where Jesus three times addresses him as Simon, son of Jonas. In the Synoptics we find Peter without the Simon, except on the occasion of his acknowledging Jesus as the Christ, Matt. xvi. 16; and his falling at Christ's feet, Luke v. 8. But he is several times mentioned as Simon only, especially in Luke. See Matt. xvi. 17; Mark i. 29, 30, 36; xiv. 37; Luke iv. 38; v, 3, 4, 5, 10; xxvi. 31; xxiv. 34.

[s] The author of "The Twelve Apostles" has apparently forgotten this reference when he asserts that the writer of the Apocalypse says *nothing* which can identify his Jesus with the Jesus of the Gospels. (Page 20). Surely he never can have imagined that the city which is described as the Holy city, containing the Temple of God, where "our Lord was *crucified*," xi. 1, 2, 8, is any other city than Jerusalem, or that the "Lord" can be any other than the "Jesus" from whom the whole book purports to proceed.

[t] i. 1. [u] i. 5.

[v] The name which Jesus commonly gives himself in the Gospels.

[w] i. 13; 18.

The Mythical Element in Christianity. 53

riches, and wisdom, and strength, and honour, and glory, and blessing;"[x] from whose wrath "the kings of the earth, and the rich men, and the chief captains, and the mighty men, and every bondman and every freeman should hide themselves in the dens and rocks of the mountains;"[y] with whom the nations should make war, and who should overcome them, "for he is Lord of lords, and King of kings;"[z] who, accordingly, afterwards rides forth in triumph, on a white horse, clothed in a vesture dipped in blood, and followed by the armies of heaven,[a] to "tread the wine-press of the fierceness and wrath of Almighty God;"[b] and who, after his final victory, appears, as the light of the New Jerusalem which had descended from heaven, and had twelve foundations, and "on them the names of the twelve Apostles of the Lamb."[c] Of these apostles the author of 'The Twelve Apostles' observes, that the writer does not mention their names, nor does he say whether they existed already, or were only to have a future existence;[d] which is no doubt literally true, though, if so, the exigencies of the fiction would seem to require that some important part in the events described in the Apocalypse as immediately imminent should be assigned to persons to whom so striking a position is attributed in their triumphant issue. But the objector overlooks the fact that the Apocalypse is fatal to his hypothesis in itself, and apart from its identification of the Jesus of whom it speaks with the Jesus of the Gospels. For this hypothesis is, that the *notion* of a Messiah who *had* suffered and *should* come in triumph, to deliver his people and establish his kingdom over the earth, arose after the destruction of Jerusalem, out of the

[x] v. 12.   [y] vi. 15.   [z] xvii. 14.
[a] xix. 11—14.   [b] xix. 16.   [c] xxi. 14.   [d] P. 20.

reaction of Messianic hopes against the blow inflicted upon them by the destruction of the Holy city; while here we have a book full of this idea from beginning to end, written while Jerusalem was still standing, and addressed to bodies of believers in such a Messiah, who form seven churches in seven of the principal cities in the Roman province of Asia; a conclusive proof that, in whatever cause the idea of a Messiah who should triumph after having suffered originated, it did not grow out of the destruction of Jerusalem.

Thus we have in the New Testament, besides the direct testimony of all four Evangelists, three independent witnesses, whose evidence indirectly, but in each case conclusively, negatives this mythical hypothesis. Let us go one step further, to the next generation of Christian writers, and take the evidence of Papias, bishop of Hieropolis, in the beginning of the second century, from whose writings we possess various passages, preserved by Eusebius. Papias, says Eusebius,[e] in the preface to his work, by no means gives us to understand that he had been an eye and ear witness of the holy apostles, but that he had received the orthodox doctrine from those who had known them. These are his words : " I have no hesitation in interweaving in my interpretation what I have learned from the presbyters, and impressed on my memory, since I am assured of their truth. For I did not attend, as the great mass are wont to do, especially to those who are only great talkers, but I directed my eyes to those who could testify to the truth. Not to those I turned who repeated by rote statements about which they knew nothing, but to those who knew the rules prescribed by the Lord himself

---

[e] 'Ecc. Hist.' iii. 39 ; *Exēgēsis tōn kuriakōn logiōn.*

The Mythical Element in Christianity. 55

for the faith. When I fell in with any one who had enjoyed the teaching of the elders, I inquired of him what they had spoken ? What, I asked, *have* Andrew, what Peter, what Philip, Thomas, James, what John, what Matthew *said ?* or what *do* the disciples of the Lord, men like Aristion and the Presbyter John, *say ?* "[f] Here we find Papias distinguishing two generations of teachers, both older than himself; the first, including the well-known names of six out of the twelve Apostles, of which he speaks as wholly passed away ; the *second*, disciples still alive, though his own seniors ; each of whom he mentions equally as real persons, from whose teachings he hoped to receive instruction. The statement is very intelligible and natural, if there had really existed in the last generation men well known as the apostles of Jesus, but very inconceivable, if the only answer which Papias could have obtained to his inquiries had been, what it must have been supposing the hypothesis under our consideration to be true, "we have never met with *any* such persons, nor know of any one who has seen them. We know only, that we have *heard them talked about*, during the last twenty or thirty years, as the apostles of a Jesus who is said to have been crucified eighty years since." Regarded as a statement really made by a writer who lived in the age of Papias, the passage becomes, on this hypothesis, absurd; while, if it were not a genuine statement of Papias, but one made up, in order to give credence to the story of there having been a body of apostles, the inventor must have been a great bungler, to make his witness testify only to what he had heard, instead of boldly putting into his mouth the assertion that he had seen and con-

---

[f] *Ti Petros* eipen., *ti Philippos*, &c., *ti legousin* Aristion, &c.

56 The Mythical Element in Christianity.

versed with apostles of the Lord, as he might easily have done, if any of these apostles had lived to old age. On the other hand, if the statement is not concocted, it furnishes one of those indirect proofs that Jesus and his Apostles are not mythical but historical persons, which are the more convincing because their evidence is undesigned.

It would be easy to heap up testimony to the same effect out of the writers who succeeded Papias. But as this testimony would carry us too far from the original sources, I abstain from going into it, and confine myself to one additional piece of evidence, the lists of names of the Christian bishops in the patriarchal sees of Alexandria, Antioch, Jerusalem, and Rome, preserved in the Chronicon of Eusebius; of which I may observe that it is not a record confined to ecclesiastical incidents, but a general chronicle of important events, from the earliest times to the age of Eusebius, containing the names of the different bishops of these great sees, introduced under their proper dates. The names and dates are as follows :

ALEXANDRIA.	A.D.	ANTIOCH.		A.D.
Annianus	65	Euodius	.	43
Asilus	85	Ignatius	.	71
Cerdon	98	Heros	.	115

JERUSALEM.		ROME.	CHRON.	H.E.
James	(No dates.)	Petrus	36	
Simeon	,,	Linus	66	·68
Justus	,,	Anacletus	79	80
Then twelve others, down		Clemens	87	92
to the time of Hadrian.		Evaristus	96	100

It will be seen that, in each of the great capitals, Alexandria, Antioch, and Rome, the list of names, excluding Peter, goes up beyond the time when, according to the mythical hypothesis, the idea

The Mythical Element in Christianity. 57

of Christianity arose. Yet the statements of Eusebius appear to have been founded in every case on documents preserved in the respective churches.[g] Some uncertainty seems to have attached to these records in the case of Rome ; where Augustine gives another list of bishops, in which Clemens precedes Anacletus instead of following him, and the dates given by Eusebius in his Ecclesiastical History slightly differ from those given in his Chronicon. But though some suspicion is thus cast on the accuracy of the lists, it is difficult to suppose that in all these great cities the Christians deliberately fabricated the names of bishops who never existed, in order to give countenance to the notion that the Christian religion began to be taught half a century earlier than was in fact the case. And the difficulty of this supposition is increased by the circumstance that neither in Antioch nor Alexandria is the first bishop one of the Apostles, to whom the inventors of an imaginary succession of bishops would have naturally attributed the foundation of the great Christian churches; they are persons, for the introduction of whose names no other reason can be given than the simple one that they did historically fill the office of bishops in the places and at the times where and when they are mentioned.

What is there to oppose to the accumulative force of these distinct lines of evidence, from writers who were not Christians and writers who were Christians, from histories, and memoirs, and letters, and prophetic anticipations, and autbiographical notices, and official lists of names, all combining to prove that Christianity arose out of the reverence felt for an historical person, Jesus of Nazareth, who was crucified by order of Pontius Pilate, but of whom his

[g] See the passages in Fynes Clinton, 'Fasti Romani,' ii. 535.

disciples believed that he had risen from the dead, and would shortly come in the clouds as the judge of all mankind. Absolutely *nothing* but that certain writers do not mention Christianity, the character of whose writings gives us no reason for expecting that they would mention it; and that, when we enter into the *details* of the stories preserved to us about Jesus, we find ourselves involved in such a mass of contradictory statements that we do not know on what to rely, beyond the broad facts stated above; and the evidence as to his character furnished by the sayings attributed to him, and the impression which he appears to have produced on those among whom he lived and worked.

It does not fall within my present object to consider this historical element, either in itself or in its bearing upon religious faith. I wish only to show what I hope to have succeeded in showing, that there is far more of unwarranted assumption and unreasoning credulity involved in the disbelief of the historical origin of Christianity out of reverence for the person of Jesus of Nazareth, than is involved in the belief that it did thus originate.

But this belief, if it be confined to that which is *historically* proveable, must take up an attitude very different from the one which the defenders of what is called Orthodox Christianity commonly assume. If Jesus of Nazareth can be proved, beyond any reasonable doubt, to have been a person, of whose actions and sayings we know enough to show that he exhibited a very remarkable phase of religious feeling, which produced among his disciples an unbounded reverence for him; whose death was attended by the remarkable incident, that it was followed by the firm belief of these disciples in his resurrection from the dead; and who appeared at an epoch in the spiritual

The Mythical Element in Christianity. 59

development of our race, which has given to this reverence and belief a most important influence on the religious history of mankind, still, here the voice of history stops. When we attempt to pass beyond these limits, into the *details* of what are generally called the evidences of the Christian religion,—the direct external proofs of supernatural action,—we find ourselves in the domain of legend and myth; and all certainty as to the supposed facts vanishes with the traditional, imaginative, and contradictory character of the testimony adduced for them. If the Catholic faith as to the person of Jesus is to continue, the grounds for it must then be taken from other sources than these details; where the opponents of the belief of the Church have, I conceive, as decisive a victory in the argument as its defenders have on the question whether the Christian faith did not arise from that reverence for the person of Jesus, and persuasion that he had risen from the dead, to which the New Testament traces it.

That a new and more radical contest concerning the claims of Christianity will be carried on upon this ground I expect; and its result will, in my judgment, not be such as is usually assumed at the present day by those who contend for the application to the New Testament of the strict rules of historical criticism. But neither can it be such as those assume who contest the legitimacy of this application. Religious faith may, and I believe will, find a secure refuge in the supersensual world of ideal truths, and the external affirmation to them given by the course of man's religious development. But this faith will no longer be able to isolate itself from the general progress of the race, or represent itself as the exclusive *sesame* of an arbitrary salvation. It must be based on trust in the Universal Father, whose

60 *The Mythical Element in Christianity.*

love embraces *all* his creatures, a trust which the revelation of His nature, made through the course of human history, may affirm, but for which it cannot be a substitute. And the feeling engendered by it towards the ancient channels of religious influence may, I conceive, be summed up in Goethe's words : [h]

> Ich wandle auf weiter, bunter Flur,
>   Urspringlicher Natur,
>   Eine heilige Quelle in welchem ich bade,
>   Ist Ueberlieferung, ist Gnade.

---

[h] Gott Gemüth und Welt, ii, 227. Edition of 1828.
  I rove o'er the broad and varied field,
    Of primitive nature;
    A sacred spring in which I bathe
    Is tradition—is grace.

JESUS

VERSUS

CHRISTIANITY.

BY

A CANTAB.

PUBLISHED BY THOMAS SCOTT,
NO. 11 THE TERRACE, FARQUHAR ROAD, UPPER NORWOOD,
LONDON, S.E.

1873.
Price Sixpence.

LONDON:
PRINTED BY C. W. REYNELL, 16 LITTLE PULTENEY STREET,
HAYMARKET, W.

JESUS *versus* CHRISTIANITY.

THE most notable feature in the present condition of theology is, indubitably, the rapid multiplication of writings designed to point the contrast between the character, real or supposed, of Jesus, and the religion which bears his name and of which he is commonly regarded as the founder. The revolt, which every day but serves to intensify, is not against Jesus as *par excellence* " the genius of righteousness," but against the dogmatic system which theologians have substituted for him. The church, it is alleged, has outdone Iscariot, in that it has committed a twofold treachery : it has accepted the murder of its founder as a sacrifice well-pleasing to the Deity, and it has repudiated his simple heart-religion for metaphysical subtleties of its own invention. Thus, not content with making itself a participator in the murder of his body, the church has dealt a fatal outrage upon his spirit.

Among the writings to which we have referred as advocating the displacement of the *régime* of dogma and belief by the substitution of one involving character and conduct, we propose to note especially 'The True History of Joshua Davidson,' reputed to be the work of a lady well known for the vigour of her thought and style; 'Literature and Dogma,' by Matthew Arnold; 'The Fair Haven,' by W. B. Owen; 'By and By,' by Edward Maitland; 'A Note of Interrogation,' by Miss Nightingale; and 'Modern Christianity a Civilised Heathenism.' All these writings, with the exception of the last, agree in rejecting as unproved, unprovable, mistaken, or pernicious, at least much of what has always been insisted upon by the church, and in accepting the general character and teaching of Jesus as the most valuable moral possession of humanity.

We except the last one for this reason, though using it to point our argument : It gives up the state of society which has grown up under the sway of dogma as utterly un-Christian in character and conduct, but it does not give up the dogma. The work of the clergyman who gained an undesirable notoriety during the Franco-German war by his mischievous brochure entitled 'Dame Europa's School,' it manifests all the confusion of thought which distinguished that production. It was scarcely to be expected that the writer who could represent England as placed at the head of the school of Europe to keep the other nations from quarrelling, and declare that "neutral is another name for coward," would escape committing absurd inconsistencies when he took to writing about modern Christianity. In a dialogue with a Hindoo resident in London, he makes the heathen discourse in this fashion :

"How can you soberly believe and eloquently preach that an overwhelming majority of your fellow-creatures will be burnt alive throughout all eternity in the flames of hell, and yet can find time or inclination at any moment of your life for any other work than the work of rescuing the souls around you from their appalling doom? How contemplate even so much as the distant possibility of being yourself tortured with agonies insupportable, for ages and ages and millions of ages more, and all the while laugh and joke, and talk of politics and business and pleasure, as if you were the happiest fellow on earth? You parsons do actually stand in imminent peril of being burnt alive for ever, or else you do not. The souls committed to your teaching, or a certain proportion of them, are destined to spend a whole eternity in torment, or else they are destined to nothing of the kind. If they are so destined, and if you, unless by precept and example you have done all in your power to save them, shall have your part in their unutterable woe, what can you do from morning to night but pray for them, and weep for them, and implore them earnestly to escape at any cost from the horrors of an unquenchable flame? Yet, in the face of your alleged persuasions that you yourself and all your flock are standing, for all you know, upon the very brink of an everlasting hell, you have deliberately chosen and cheerfully maintain a course of occupations and a position in society which no man could possibly endure for half a day who really believed himself and those dear to him to be placed in any such peril. What I say is that, if you are not leading a downright ascetic life—the life of Christ and nothing less—you waste words upon the air when you preach the punishment of eternal flames. Would you believe that my dearest friend upon earth was on trial for his life, and would very probably be hanged, if you met me somewhere at five o'clock tea, talking nonsense to some young lady? Whereas the average minister delivers his most awful message, tells his people plainly that they will be damned, knows for a certainty that they will go on sinning all the same, and, under a strong impression that several of his cherished acquaintances and kindly neighbours will be devoured by flames unquenchable, walks home to his vicarage, jokes with his wife, romps with his children, chaffs his friend, sits down comfortably to his luncheon, and thoroughly enjoys his slice of cold roast beef and his glass of bitter beer. Will any man, in his senses, believe that he means what he has just been saying in his sermon? Of course he will believe nothing of the sort; and therefore it has come to pass that England is full of intelligent laymen who doubt and disbelieve.

No; let me see Christians imitating, not a Christ whom I could fashion for myself out of heathen materials, not the pattern philosopher, not the ideal man—but a Christ who at every point is making himself an intolerable offence to the un-Christ-like, a thorn and scourge to every man who does not lie stretched at the foot of his cross! I know for certain how Christ would be treated if he were here; I can see the press deriding him, the fine lady picking her way past him in the street, the poor flocking round him as a friend, the magistrate committing him to prison. Let me see his witnesses treated thus, and I shall believe that he has sent them. But while I see them claiming the right to live as other men, glorying in the fact that they have no peculiarities, smiling politely on sin, and caressed by those who would have spat upon their Lord—so long as I see them thus, they shall teach me if they please the principles of Christ's philosophy, but they shall not dare to tell me that they are priests of a crucified Christ."

The conclusion shows that the heathen, having found such a witness as he requires, accepts the life —though whether for the sake of the life or through fear of the hell, does not appear—while the parson retains the dogma described as above, impervious to any sense of its hideous immorality, " and walks slowly and sadly home, feeling more and more dissatisfied with his own position."

In 'Joshua Davidson' we have an attempt to transfer the Jesus of the gospels, poor and untaught, but enthusiast of noble ideas, to our own day, for the purpose of showing from the inevitable failure of his life and work, either that modern society is not Christian, or that Christianity as a system will not work. The hero of the tale, a carpenter by trade, early gives up Christianity as a dogma or collection of dogmas, and falls back upon the character and

Jesus versus Christianity. 7

social teaching of Jesus as the essence of the gospel, and alone possessing any real value for us. What would Jesus be and do were he to live now? This is the question essayed to be answered in 'Joshua Davidson,' by representing him as a plain working-man, attacking alike banker and bishop, advocating indiscriminate almsgiving, fraternising with the poor and discontented, unorthodox in faith, an ultra-radical in politics, exciting the bitter hostility of the whole respectable press, denouncing shams, clutching eagerly at any Utopian extravagance that had a heart of good in it, a red republican in France, an itinerant lecturer on the rights of man in England, and finally trampled to death by conservative roughs, hounded on by dignitaries of the Established Church.

Confident that such would be the career of Jesus among us, the author is justified in asking of us, why, if we should thus regard him, do we persist in calling ourselves by his name and pretending to be his followers. Surely a question not to be left unanswered. "We ought," says the preface to the third edition, "to be brave enough in this day to dare ask ourselves how much is practicable and how much is impracticable in the creed we profess; and to renounce that which is even the most imperatively enjoined if we find that it is not wise or possible. If our religion leads us to political chimeras, let us abjure it: if it teaches us truth, let us obey it, no matter what social growths we tear up by the roots. There is no mean way for men. To slaves only should the symbols of a myth be sacred, and our very children are forbidden the weakness of knowing the right and doing the wrong. If such a man as Joshua Davidson was a mistake, then acted Christianity is to blame. In which case, what becomes of the dogma? and how can we worship a life as divine, the practical imitation of which is a moral blunder and an economic crime?"

It is thus that the author makes the very humanity of Jesus the proof of his divinity. He is *extra-human*, not in any metaphysico-theological sense, but in the intensity of the sympathy which impels him to attempt to benefit his fellows. His very failures are more divine than the successes of other men. It is thus, too, that having at the start repudiated the dogmatic system attached to his name, we are called on to re-examine his ethical and social teaching, and to avow honestly our rejection of such parts of it as do not coincide with our notions of the practicable and right. In short, the appeal is to be neither to authority nor tradition, but to our own intelligence and moral sense.

This, too, is the import of Miss Nightingale's recent utterance (in *Fraser's Magazine* for May). Rebuking the tendency of modern reformers to ignore the character of God, as necessarily underlying the phenomena which form the subject of their investigations, this 'Note of Interrogation' calls upon us to regard the moral laws which govern men's motives as the real exponents of the divine nature. While thus adopting the inductive method of Positivism, she blames the Positivists " for leaving out of consideration all the inspiring part of life," and stopping short at phenomena, instead of seeking to learn that of which phenomena are but the manifestation, and to which, therefore, they must be the index. In this view, she rejects the main points of the creeds of Roman, Protestant, and Greek alike, and utterly ignores what is called "revelation" as a guide to the nature of God, and points to the character and teaching of Christ as among the best indications to that which ought to be the prime object of search. In all this it appears clearly that by the term *God* Miss Nightingale really means a human ideal of perfection, and that she would have us perfect our ideal for the sake of the reflex influence it would exercise upon ourselves. It is by the adoption of the Christ-ideal of character, and rejection of Christian dogma, and those on the question of their intrinsic merits as estimated by her own mind and conscience, apart from tradition or authority, that Miss Nightingale justifies us in ranking her among the supporters of Jesus in the great cause of JESUS *versus* CHRISTIANITY.

'The Fair Haven' is an ironical defence of orthodoxy at the expense of the whole mass of church tenet and dogma, the character of Christ only excepted. Such, at least, is our reading of it, though critics of the *Rock* and *Record* order have accepted the book as a serious defence of Christianity, and proclaimed it as a most valuable contribution in aid of the faith. Affecting an orthodox standpoint, it bitterly reproaches all previous apologists for the lack of candour with which they have ignored or explained away insuperable difficulties, and attached undue value to coincidences real or imagined. One and all they have, the author declares, been at best but zealous "liars for God," or what to them was more than God, their own religious system. This must go on no longer. We, as Christians, having a sound cause, need not fear to let the truth be known. He proceeds accordingly to set forth that truth as he finds it in the New Testament; and, in a masterly analysis of the accounts of the resurrection, which he selects as the principal and crucial miracle, involving all other miracles, he shows how slender is the foundation on which the whole fabric of supernatural theology has been reared. Rejecting the hypothesis of hallucination by which Strauss attempts to account for the belief of the disciples in the resurrection, he shows that they had no real evidence that Jesus had died upon the cross at all. It is true that the disciples believed him dead; so that we need not charge them with fraud. That charge he reserves for the Paleys and Alfords, whose disingenuousness he scathingly exposes, using the arguments of the latter to show the absence of any proof that Jesus died either of the cross or of the spear-wound. All that the evangelists knew was that the body was deposited in the tomb apparently dead, and that at the end of some thirty hours it had disappeared. Rejecting the statement in Matthew as palpably untenable, he makes that in John the basis of the true story, this being the simplest and manifest source of the rest.

As told by our author, the whole affords an exquisite example of the natural growth of a legend. First, we have Mary Magdalene, who, finding the stone removed, investigates no further, but runs back and declares that the body has been taken away (not that it has come to life). Then we have John and Peter ascertaining for themselves, by looking in, that Jesus was no longer there, but only the linen clothes lying in two separate parts of the tomb. Then, these having taken their departure, we have the warm, impulsive Magdalene remaining behind to weep. At length, mustering courage to look into the sepulchre for herself, she sees, as she thinks, sitting at opposite ends, two angels in white, who merely ask her why she weeps. She makes no answer, but turns to the outside, where she sees Jesus himself, but so changed that she does not at first recognise him.

How from this simple and natural story of the white grave clothes, in the dark sepulchre, looking like angels to the tear-blinded eyes of a woman who was so liable to hysteria or insanity as to have had "seven devils" cast out of her, grew, step by step, the myth so freely amplified in the gospels, the reader must find in the book itself.

If he can once fully grasp the intention of the style and its affectation of the tone of indignant orthodoxy, and perceive also how utterly destructive are its "candid admissions" to the whole fabric of supernaturalism, he will enjoy a rare treat. It is not, however, for the purpose of recommending what we, at least, regard as a piece of exquisite humour that we call attention to 'The Fair Haven,' but in order to show how, while rejecting popular Christianity, we may still accept the " Christ-ideal," to use our author's phrase, and this with an enhanced sense of its beauty and use to the world.

One of the most characteristic parts of the book is that in which he argues in favour of the providential character of the gospel narratives, notwithstanding their inaccuracies. After stating that no ill effects need follow from a rejection of the immaculate conception, the miracles, the resurrection, or the ascension, because "the Christ-ideal, which, after all, is the soul and spirit of Christianity, would remain precisely where it is, while its recognition would be far more general, owing to the departure on the part of the Apologists from certain lines of defence which are irreconcilable with the ideal itself," he says :

" The old theory that God desired to test our faith, and that there would be no merit in believing if the evidence were such as to commend itself at once to our understanding, is one which need only be stated to be set aside. It is blasphemy against the goodness of God to suppose that he has thus laid, as it were, an ambuscade for man, and will only let him escape on condition of his consenting to violate one of the very most precious of God's own gifts. There is an ingenious cruelty about such conduct which it is revolting even to imagine. Indeed, the whole theory reduces our heavenly Father to a level of wisdom and goodness far below our own, and this is sufficient answer to it."

There is, however, a reason why we should be required to believe in the divinity of the Christ-ideal, and regard it as exalted beyond all human comparison;

namely, in order to exalt our sense of the paramount importance of following and obeying the life and commands of Christ. And this being so, "it is natural, also, to suppose that *whatever may have happened to the records of that life* should have been ordained with a view to the enhancing the preciousness of the ideal." Thus the very obscurity and fragmentariness of the gospel narratives have added to the value of the ideas they present, just as the mutilations of ancient sculptures serve to enhance their beauty to the imagination. Or, as "the gloom and gleam of Rembrandt, or the golden twilight of the Venetians, the losing and finding, and the infinite liberty of shadow," produce an effect infinitely beyond that which would be gained by any hardness of definition and tightness of outline. The suggestion of the beautiful lineaments to the imagination is far more effective than would be any minutely detailed portrait. "Those who relish definition, and definition only, are indeed kept away from Christianity by the present condition of the records; but even if the life of our Lord had been so definitely rendered as to find a place in their system, would it have greatly served their souls? And would it not repel hundreds and thousands of others, who find in the suggestiveness of the sketch a completeness of satisfaction which no photographic reproduction could have given?"

The fact is "people misunderstand the aim and scope of religion. Religion is only intended to guide men in those matters upon which science is silent: God illumines us by science as by a mechanical draughtsman's plan; he illumines us in the gospels as by the drawing of a great artist. We cannot build a 'Great Eastern' from the drawings of the artist, but what poetical feeling, what true spiritual emotion was ever kindled by a mechanical drawing? How cold and dead were science, unless supplemented by art and religion! Not joined with them, for the merest touch of these things impairs scientific value, which depends essentially upon accuracy, and not upon any feeling for the beautiful and loveable. In like manner the merest touch of science chills the warmth of sentiment—the spiritual life. The mechanical drawing is spoilt by being made artistic, and the work of the artist by becoming mechanical. The aim of the one is to teach men how to construct; of the other, how to feel. We ought not, therefore, to have expected scientific accuracy from the gospel records. Much less should we be required to believe that such accuracy exists." The finest picture, approached close enough, becomes but blotches and daubs of paint, each one of which, taken by itself, is absolutely untrue, yet, at proper distance, forms an impression which is quite truthful. "No combination of minute truths in a picture will give so faithful a representation of nature as a wisely-arranged tissue of untruths." Again, "all ideals gain by vagueness and lose by definition, inasmuch as more scope is left for the imagination of the beholder, who can thus fill in the missing detail according to his own spiritual needs. This is how it comes that nothing which is recent, whether animate or inanimate, can serve as an ideal unless it is adorned by more than common mystery and uncertainty. A new cathedral is necessarily very ugly. There is too much found and too little lost. Much less would an absolutely perfect Being be of the highest value as an ideal as long as he could be clearly seen, for it is impossible that he could be known as perfect by imperfect men, and his very perfections must perforce appear as blemishes to any but perfect critics. To give, therefore, an impression of perfection, to create an absolutely unsurpassable ideal, it became essential that the actual image of the original should become blurred and lost, whereon the beholder now supplies from his own imagination that which is, *to him*, more perfect than the original, though objectively it must be infinitely less so.

"It is probably to this cause that the incredulity of the Apostles during our Lord's lifetime must be assigned. The ideal was too near them, and too far above their comprehension; for it must always be remembered that the convincing power of miracles in the days of the Apostles must have been greatly weakened by the current belief in their being events of no very unusual occurrence, and in the existence both of good and evil spirits who could take possession of men and compel them to do their bidding.

"A beneficent and truly marvellous provision for the greater complexity of man's spiritual needs was thus provided by a gradual loss of detail and gain of breadth. Enough evidence was given in the first instance to secure authoritative sanction for the ideal. During the first thirty or forty years after the death of our Lord, no one could be in want of evidence, and the guilt of unbelief is, therefore, brought prominently forward. Then came the loss of detail which was necessary in order to secure the universal acceptability of the ideal. . . But there would, of course, be limits to the gain caused by decay. Time came when there would be danger of too much vagueness in the ideal, and too little distinctness in the evidences. It became necessary, therefore, to provide against this danger.

"*Precisely at that epoch the gospels made their appearance.*" Not simultaneously, and not in perfect harmony with each other, but with such divergence of aim and difference of authorship as would secure the necessary breadth of effect when the accounts were viewed together. "As the roundness of the stereoscopic image can only be attained by the combination of two distinct pictures, neither of them in perfect harmony with the other, so the highest possible conception of

Christ cannot otherwise be produced than through the discrepancies of the gospels."

Now, however, "when there is a numerous and increasing class of persons whose habits of mind unfit them for appreciating the value of vagueness, but who have each of them a soul which may be lost or saved, the evidences should be restored to something like their former sharpness." To do this it demands only "the recognition of the fact that time has made incrustations upon some parts of the evidences, and has destroyed others." Nevertheless, as "*it is not belief in the facts which constitutes the essence of Christianity*, but rather the being so impregnated with love at the contemplation of Christ that imitation becomes almost instinctive," we may probably suppose "that certain kinds of unbelief have become less hateful in the sight of God, inasmuch as they are less dangerous to the universal acceptance of our Lord as the one model for the imitation of all men."

To advocate conduct instead of belief, experience instead of tradition, and intuition instead of conventionality, and to exhibit a model for the imitation of all men, married as well as single, is at least one purpose manifest in the series of novels of which 'By and By' is announced to be the completion :—novels differing from the ordinary kind in that, while others treat of man only in relation to man, and are, therefore, merely moral, these bear reference to man in relation to the Infinite, and are, therefore, essentially religious.

It does not come within our design to treat of the surface aspect of Mr Edward Maitland's 'Historical Romance of the Future,' which represents the world as it may be when a few more centuries have passed over it, and the problems, social, political, and religious, which now trouble it, shall have found their solution, and people may, without detriment or reproach, regulate their lives in accordance with their own preferences. It is with the deeper design of the book that we have now to do, the design which reveals itself in the entire series to which, with 'The Pilgrim and the Shrine' and 'Higher Law,' it belongs. This design is *the rehabilitation of nature*, by showing its capacity for producing of itself, if only its best be allowed fair play, the highest results in religion and morals. Seeing that to rehabilitate nature is in effect to rehabilitate the author of nature, and replace both worker and work in the high place from which they have been deposed by theologians, such a design can be no other than an eminently religious one.

In the first of the series, 'The Pilgrim and the Shrine,' the wanderer in search of a faith that will stand the test and fulfil the requirements of a developed mind and conscience emerges from the wilderness of doubt, through which he has been painfully toiling, to find that the best that we can comprehend must ever be the Divine for us, and this by the very constitution of our nature, inasmuch as we can only interpret that which is without by that which is within. And he bears testimony to the value of the Bible as an agent in the development of the religious faculty by noting the subjective character of all that really appertains to religion in both the Old and New Testaments. "Constantly," he says, "is the inner ideal dwelt upon without any reference to corresponding external objects. Think you it was the law as written in the books of Moses that was a delight to the mind and a guide to the feet of the Psalmist? No, it was something that appealed much more nearly to his inmost soul, even 'the law of God in his heart.' And what else was meant by 'Christ in you the hope of glory?' The *idea* of a perfect standard is all that can be in us. The question whether it has any external personal existence in history does not affect the efficacy of the idea in raising us up towards itself. God, the Absolute, is altogether past finding out. Wherefore we elevate the best we can imagine into the Divine, and worship that:—the perfect man or perfect woman. Surely it is no matter which, since it is the character and not the person that is adored. . . Christianity is a worship of the divinest character, as exemplified in a human form. . . The very ascription to Jesus of supernatural attributes shows the incapacity of his disciples to appreciate the grandeur and simplicity of his character. . . . Here, then, is my answer to the question, 'What was the exact work of Christ?' It was to give men a law for their government, transcending any previously generally recognised. Ignoring the military ruler, the priest, and the civil magistrate, he virtually denounced physical force, spiritual terror, and legal penalties as the compelling motive for virtue. The system whereby he would make men perfect, even as their Father in heaven is perfect, was by developing the higher moral law implanted in every man's breast, and so cultivating the idea of God in the soul. The 'law of God in the heart' was no original conception of his. It had been recognised by many long before, and had raised them to the dignity of prophets, saints, and martyrs. Its sway, though incapable of gaining in intensity, is wider now than ever, till the poet of our day must be one who is deeply imbued with it; no mere surface painter like his predecessors, however renowned, but having a spiritual insight which makes him at once poet and prophet. The founding of an organised society, having various grades of ecclesiastical rank, and definite rules of faith, does not seem to me to have formed any part of Christ's idea. His plan was rather to scatter broadcast the beauty of his thought, and let it take root and spring up where it could. Recognising intensely, as he did, the all-winning loveliness of his idea, he felt that it would never lack ardent disciples to propagate it, and he left it to each age to devise such means as the varying character of the times might suggest. The 'Christian Church,' therefore, for me, consists of all who follow a Christian ideal of character, no matter whether, or in whom, they believe that ideal to have been personified."

Such is the teaching of a book that is, to the *Pall Mall Gazette*, foolishness, and to Mudie's a stumbling-block and an abomination; yet which, in spite of clerical denunciation and the expurgatorial indexes of Protestant Nonconformist circulating-librarians, has in a short space travelled to all lands where the English tongue is spoken, and perceptibly influenced the course that religious thought must henceforth take. We shall have a proof of this when we come to the last book on our list. In the meantime it seemed to us well to digress for a moment in order to denounce the obstacles which still are thrown in the way of genuine religious thought by ecclesiastic and layman, Churchman and Dissenter, alike in this "Christian" land of ours.

As the 'Pilgrim and the Shrine' exhibited the process of thinking and feeling out a religion, so its successor, 'Higher Law,' represented the natural growth of a morality. Repudiating all conventional methods, as the other repudiated theological and traditional ones, the design here is to represent the action of persons under the sole guidance of their own perceptions and feelings under circumstances of supreme temptation and difficulty.

It is by the steadfast adherence to the simple rule of unselfishness, which forbids the commission of aught that can injure or pain those whom we are bound to respect, that the sufficiency of the intuitions to constitute the higher, or rather highest, law of morality is demonstrated.

It is not necessary to the perfection of nature that all germs should reach the highest stages of growth, whether in the vegetable or in the spiritual kingdom.

The capacity to produce a single perfect result is sufficient to redeem nature from the old reproach cast upon it by theologians, "just as one magnificent blossom suffices to redeem the plant, that lives a hundred years and flowers but once, from the charge of having wasted its existence." Nay, more. "Even if the experience of all past ages of apparent aimlessness and sterility affords no plea in justification of existence, the one fact that there is room for hope in the future may well suffice to avert the sentence men are too apt to pronounce,—that all is vanity and vexation, and that the tree of humanity is fit only to be cut down, that it cumber the ground no longer."

From this point of view it is evident that at least one object of the creation of the leading character in 'By and By' is to show how an ideally perfect disposition may be produced from purely natural circumstances, and if in the present or future, why not in the past? The "Christmas Carol" of 'By and By' thus becomes for us a parallel to the "Joshua Davidson" of the book already noticed; for it is an attempt to transfer the Jesus of the gospels from Judæa to our own country, only a Jesus wealthy instead of poor, educated instead of untaught, married instead of single, having all the advantages of a civilisation more advanced than any yet attained, and with his intense religious enthusiasm kept from surpassing the limits of the practical, by science, wedlock, and work. In his liability to personify the products of his own vivid and spiritual imagination, and out of his idealisations of things terrestrial to people the skies with "angels," we see but a reproduction of one of the characteristics by which all the enthusiasts of old, to which the world owes its religions, have been distinguished. By placing such a character in his picture of the future, we understand the author to indicate his conviction that man will always, no matter how rigidly scientific his training, have a religious side to his nature, a side whereby he can rise on the wings of emotion far beyond the regions of mere Sense. Of course such an one must at some moment of his life feel himself impelled to use his wealth and freedom for his own selfish gratification (he would not otherwise be human), but resisting such promptings of his own lower nature, will fix himself upon some great and useful work. It is almost as much of course that he will in his earliest love be attracted by the character that most nearly resembles pure unsophisticated nature. But the love that is of the sexes will not contain half his nature. He will be the friend and servant of all men, and so provoke to jealousy the small, intense disposition of her to whom he has allied himself. Striving to inoculate her with a sense of the ideal, their relations will aptly typify the world-old conflict of Soul and Sense. He may suffer greatly, but if she be true and genuine, and loves him her best, so far as is in her, he will be tender and kind and endure to the end. Losing her, and after long interval wedding again, more for his child's sake than his own, he will naturally be tempted to make trial of one less unsophisticated and untrained. But mere conventionality will disgust him. Its hollow artifices and insincerity will be odious, and the ideal man will find a moral jar a fitting plea for repudiation. Should his child—his daughter—err, he will be tender and forgiving, provided her fault be prompted by love. It will ever be in his *conduct* that we shall find his faith. Recognising himself as an individualised portion of the divine whole, his intuitions are to him as the voice of God in his soul, and to fail to live up to his best would be to fall short of the duty due to his divine ancestry.

So confident is he of the divinity of his own intuitions, and so inexorable in his requirements of perfection in conduct up to the highest point of individual ability, that he fails to be at ease until he has established the character of God himself for perfect righteousness in his dealings, even with the meanest thing in his creation. We do not know whether or not the argument is new. It certainly has not been suggested by any of the theologians who have busied themselves in seeking solutions for the problem of the origin of evil. It is that all things are the product of their conditions, and that all conditions have a right to exist, so that the products have a right to exist also; and the maker of the conditions cannot in justice refuse to be satisfied with the products of conditions which he has permitted. "The poor soil and the arid sky are as much a part of the universal order as the rich garden, soft rain, and warm sunshine. It is just that one should yield a crop which the other would despise. It would be unjust were both to yield alike." Man's highest function is to amend the conditions of his own existence. Finding himself launched into the universe, he must till it and keep it and fit it to produce better and better men and women. It is by labouring in this direction that he works out his own salvation. They are poor teachers who inculcate but the patience of resignation, or look to another life to compensate the evils of this. The ideal man of the future appeals to the intuitive perceptions as the divine guides of conduct while here, and to the physical laws of nature for the means of subduing the world to man's highest needs. To his intensely sympathetic nature "good" is necessarily that which assimilates and harmonises to the greatest extent its surrounding conditions—not the *immediately* surrounding merely —that which works in truest sympathy with the rest. While that is evil which by its very selfishness arraigns the rest against it, good needs no power working from without to make it triumphant. It triumphs by winning the sympathies of all to work with it.

What Mr Maitland has done in the form of fiction Mr Matthew Arnold has done in the form of a treatise. We look upon his 'Literature and Dogma' as clinching the blow struck at the whole fabric of dogmatic theology, and crowning the effort to restore the intuitions as the sole court of appeal, not only between man and man, but between man and God. In his view the glory of the Bible consists in its exhibition of Israel as a people with a special faculty for righteousness, at least in conception. As other races have their special faculties, the Greek for sculpture, the Italian for painting, the German for abstract thought, the French for sensuous art, &c., so the genius of Israel was for the righteousness which consists in *morality touched by emotion towards something that is not ourselves, but which makes for righteousness*. And it was in Christ that the national genius of his race culminated, as genius for painting in Raphael, for science in Newton, for the drama in Shakespeare.

It was to God, not as "an intelligent First Cause and Moral Governor of the Universe," but as the *influence* from whence proceed the intuitions which constitute the basis of conscience, that the higher writers of the Old Testament appealed. And it was in Jesus, not as the "Eternal Son" of a personal father, but as the restorer of the intuitions that the disciples believed. No doubt they had *extra beliefs*, and what we should term not so much superstition as the poetry of religion, and it is very difficult to separate the husks of this from the grain of the other; but it is always the appeal to the intuitive perceptions of right that excites their enthusiasm, and thus they preach as the sole efficient cause of man's regeneration.

Entitling his work 'An Essay towards a Better

Apprehension of the Bible,' Mr Arnold maintains that it is through the lack of literary culture that the Bible has been utterly misunderstood, and that it is through such misunderstanding that difficulties and dogmas have arisen, and that conduct has come to be ranked below belief as the effective agent of all good. Of the Bible itself he says that, while it cannot possibly die, and its religion is all-important, nevertheless to restore religion as the clergy understand it, and re-inthrone the Bible as explained by our current theology, whether learned or popular, is absolutely and for ever impossible. Whatever is to stand must rest upon something which is verifiable, not unverifiable; and the assumption with which all churches and sects set out, that there is "a great Personal First Cause, the moral and intelligent Governor of the Universe, and that from him the Bible derives its authority, can never be verified."

There is, however, something that can be verified; something that, after the deposition of the magnified and non-natural man ordinarily set up by people as their God, will for ever remain as the basis and object of religious thought. This something is to be found in the Bible, not there alone, but there in a greater degree than in any other literature. It is the influence wholly divine which is not ourselves, and makes for righteousness. The instant we get beyond this in our definitions of Deity we fall into anthropomorphism and its attendant train of dogmas, Apostolic, Nicene, or Athanasian, all of which are but human metaphysics, and the product of minds untrained to distinguish between things and ideas. "Learned religion" is the pseudo-science of dogmatic theology; a separable accretion which never had any business to be attached to Christianity, never did it any good, and now does it great harm. In the Apostles' Creed we have the popular science of that day. In the Nicene Creed, the learned science. In the Athanasian Creed, the learned science, with a strong dash of violent and vindictive temper. And these three creeds, and with them the whole of our so-called orthodox theology, are founded upon words which Jesus, in all probability, never uttered, inasmuch as they are inconsistent with the essential spirit of his teaching, and are ascribed to him as spoken after his death.

Of the capacity of people at that time to compose a form of belief for us, we may judge by their ideas on cosmogony, geography, history, and physiology. We know what those ideas were, and their faculty for Bible criticism was on a par with their other faculties. To be worth anything, literary and scientific criticism require the finest heads and the most sure tact. They require, besides, that the world and the world's experience shall have come some considerable way. There must be great and wide acquaintance with the history of the human mind, knowledge of the manner in which men have thought, their way of using words and what they mean by them, delicacy of perception and quick tact, and besides all these, an appreciation of the spirit of the time. What is called orthodox theology is, then, no other than an immense misunderstanding of the Bible, due to the junction of a talent for abstruse reasoning with much literary inexperience. The Athanasian Creed is a notion-work based on a chimæra. It is the application of forms of Greek logic to a chimæra, its own notion of the Trinity, a notion un-established, not resting on observation and experience, but assumed to be given in Scripture, yet not really given there. Indeed, the very expression, *the Trinity*, jars with the whole idea and character of Bible-religion, just as does the Socinian expression, *a great personal first cause.*

What, then, is Christian faith and religion, and how are we to get at them? Jesus was above the heads of his reporters, and to distinguish what Jesus said and meant, it is necessary to investigate the spirit which prompted and is involved in the words attributed to him. This spirit is identical with that which made Israel (as expressing himself through his most highly spiritual writers) the most religious of peoples. The utterance of Malachi, *Righteousness tendeth to life*, life being salvation from moral death, was identical with the assertion of Jesus that he was *the way, the truth, and the life*, inasmuch as the Messiah's function was to *bring in everlasting righteousness*, by exhibiting it in perfection in his own conduct. Thus, the religion he taught was personal religion, which consists in the inward feeling and disposition of the individual himself, rather than in the performance of outward acts towards religion or society. The great means whereby he renewed righteousness and religion were self-examination, self-renouncement, and mildness. He succeeded in his mission by virtue of the *sweet reasonableness* which every one could recognise, particularly those unsophisticated by the metaphysics of dogmatic theology. He was thus in advance of the Old Testament, for while that and its Law said, *attend to conduct*, he said, *attend to the feelings and dispositions whence conduct proceeds*. It was thus that man came under a new dispensation, and made a new covenant with God, or *the something not ourselves which makes for righteousness*.

Thus the idea of God, as it is given in the Bible, rests, not on a metaphysical conception of the necessity of certain deductions from our ideas of cause, existence, identity, and the like; but on a moral perception of a rule of conduct, not of our own making, into which we are born, and which exists, whether we will or no; of awe at its grandeur and necessity, and of gratitude at its beneficence. This is the great original revelation made to Israel, this is his "Eternal." The whole mistake comes from regarding the language of the Bible as scientific instead of literary, that is, the language of poetry and emotion, approximative language thrown out at certain great objects of consciousness which it does not pretend to define fully.

As the Old Testament speaks about the Eternal and bears an invaluable witness to him, without ever yet adequately in words defining and expressing him, so, and even yet more, do the New Testament writers speak about Jesus and give a priceless record of him, without adequately and accurately comprehending him. They are altogether on another plane, and their mistakes are not his. It is not Jesus himself who relates his own miracles to us; who tells us of his own apparitions after death; who alleges his crucifixion and sufferings as a fulfilment of prophecy. It is that his reporters were intellectually men of their nation and time, and of its current beliefs; and the more they were so, the more certain they were to impute miracles to a wonderful and half-understood person. As is remarked in 'The Pilgrim and the Shrine,' the real miracle would have been if there were no miracles in the New Testament. The book contains all we know of a wonderful spirit, far above the heads of his reporters, still farther above the head of our popular theology, which has added its own misunderstandings of the reporters to their misunderstanding of Jesus.

The word *spirit*, made so mechanical by popular religion that it has come to mean *a person without a body*, is used by Jesus to signify *influence*. "Except a man be born of *a new influence* he cannot see the kingdom of God." Instead of proclaiming what ecclesiastics of a metaphysical turn call " the blessed truth that the God of the universe is a PERSON," Jesus uttered a warning for all time against this unprofitable jargon, by saying: "God is an *influence*, and those who would serve him must serve him not by any form of words or rites, but by inward motive and in reality."

Jesus versus Christianity. 27

The whole centre of gravity of the Christian religion, in the popular as well as in the so-called orthodox notion of it, is placed in Christ's having, by his death in satisfaction for man's sins, performed the contract originally passed in the council of the Trinity, and having thus enabled the magnified and non-natural man in heaven, who is the God of theology and of the multitude alike, to consider his justice satisfied, and to allow his mercy to go forth on all who heartily believe that Christ has paid their debt for them. But the whole structure of materialising theology, in which this conception of *the Atonement* holds the central place, drops away and disappears as the Bible comes to be better known. The true centre of gravity of the Christian religion is in the *method* and *secret* of Jesus, approximating, in their application, even closer to the " sweet reasonableness " and unerring sureness of Jesus himself. And as the method of Jesus led up to his secret, and his secret was dying to " the life in this world," and living to " the eternal life," both his method and his secret, therefore, culminated in his " perfecting on the cross."

A century has passed since it was said by Lessing, " Christianity has failed. Let us try Christ; " and the interval has not proved the utterance a fallacy. Though there never was so much so-called Christian teaching and preaching in school and church as now, the progress of civilisation has been little else than another name for progress in immorality, whether in the form of trade dishonesty, social selfishness, or any other. The reason is plain. It is not God as righteousness and Jesus as the way thereto that is inculcated, but systems of impossible metaphysics and rituals that profit nothing. The spread of intelligence is leading the masses daily more and more to reject what is good in religion, because their intelligence does not go far enough, and because their teachers insist on substituting human inventions for eternal truth. Alike within the Established Church and without, it is the teaching vain and foolish. Even politics are degraded by its influence. For, as Mr Arnold asks, "What is to be said for men, aspiring to deal with the cause of religion, who either cannot see that what the people now require is a religion of the Bible quite different from that which *any* of the churches or sects supply ; or who, seeing this, spend their energies in fiercely battling as to whether the church shall be connected with the nation in its collective and corporate character, or no ? The thing is to recast religion. If this is done, the new religion will be the national one. If it is not done, separating the nation in its collective and corporate character from religion will not do it. It is as if men's minds were much unsettled about mineralogy, and the teachers of it were at variance, and no teacher was convincing, and many people, therefore, were disposed to throw the study of mineralogy overboard altogether. What would naturally be the first business for every friend of the study ? Surely to establish on sure grounds the value of the study, and to put its claims in a new light, where they could no longer be denied. But if he acted as our Dissenters act in religion, what would he do ? Give himself heart and soul to a furious crusade against keeping the Government School of Mines ! "

This brings us to another aspect of the allegorical romance already referred to. Mr Maitland represents the church of the 'By and By' as a church at once national and undogmatic. That is, it is not only the crowning division of the educational department of the State ; but it is untrammelled by any dogma that can exclude any citizen from a share in its conduct and advantages. For none can own himself a dissenter in regard to a church whose teaching is restricted to the inculcation of righteousness, and follows Christ in the work of restoring the intuitions to their proper supremacy over convention and tradition, and maintaining them there.

Archdeacon Denison has already uttered a lament over even the remote prospect of such a "creedless and sacramentless church" finding a footing in this country. But what may not the man who can reconcile the pursuit of righteousness with reason, say of the prospect afforded now? We take the answer from 'The Fair Haven.'

"Let a man travel over England, north, south, east, and west, and in his whole journey he will hardly find a single spot from which he cannot see one or several churches. There is hardly a hamlet which is not also the centre for the celebration of our Redemption by the death and resurrection of Christ. Not one of these churches, not one of the clergy who minister therein, not one single village school in all England, but must be regarded as a fountain of error, if not of deliberate falsehood. Look where they may, they cannot escape from the signs of a vital belief in the resurrection. All these signs are signs of superstition only; it is superstition which they celebrate and would confirm; they are founded upon sheer fanaticism, or at the best upon sheer delusion; they poison the fountain-heads of moral and intellectual well-being, by teaching men to set human experience on the one side, and to refer their conduct to the supposed will of a personal anthropomorphic God who was actually once a baby—who was born of one of his own creatures—and who is now locally and corporeally in heaven, "of reasonable soul and human flesh subsisting." Such an one as we are supposing cannot even see a clergyman without saying to himself, "There goes one whose whole trade is the promotion of error; whose whole life is devoted to the upholding of the untrue."

How different it will be when the teaching in church

and school alike are built upon the axiom ascribed to them in 'By and By,' that "As in the region of Morals, the Divine Will can never conflict with the Moral law; so, in the region of Physics, the Divine Will can never conflict with the Natural law."

It must be so some day. "It is not for man to live for ever in the nursery. As in the history of an individual, so in that of a people, there is a period when larger views must prevail and greater freedom of action be accorded; when life will have many sides, and hold relations with a vast range of facts and interests, of which none can be left out of the account without detriment to all concerned. Formerly, it may be, men were able, or content, to recognise their relations with the infinite on but a single side of their nature. When a strongly marked line divided the object of their religious emotions from all other objects, when that alone was deemed divine, and all else constituted the profane or secular, there may have been excuse for their accordance of supremacy to the one class of emotions, and of inferior respect, or even contempt, to the other. But we have passed out of that stage; we know no such distinction in kind between the various classes of our emotions. They all are human, and therefore all divine. They all serve to connect us with the universe of which we are a portion, the whole of which universe must be equally divine for us, though we may rank some of its uses above others in reference to our own nature. Thus, if there is nothing that is specially sacred for us, it is because there is nothing that is really profane; but all is sacred, from the least to the greatest. And this is the lesson that the churches have yet to learn. Let us complete the Reformation by freeing our own church from its ancient limitations, which are of the nursery. Let us release our teachers from the corner in which they have so long

Jesus versus Christianity. 31

been cramped, and they will soon learn to take greater delight in exploring the many mansions which compose the whole glorious house of the universe, and unfolding in turn to their hearers whatever they can best tell, whether of science, philosophy, religion, art, or morality, not necessarily neglecting those spiritual metaphysics to which they have in great measure hitherto been restricted, and the consequence of which restriction has been but to distort them and all else from their due proportion. In the church thus reformed, all subjects that tend to edification will be fitting ones for the preacher. But whatever the subject, the method will have to be but one, always the scientific, never the dogmatic method. The appeal will be to the intellects, the hearts, and the consciences of the living, never to mere authority, living or dead. There will be no heresy, because no orthodoxy; or rather, the question of heresy as against orthodoxy will be a question of method, not of conclusions. From the pulpits of such a church no genuine student or thinker will be excluded, but will find welcome everywhere from congregations composed, not of the women only and the weaker brethren, but of men, men with brains and culture! Who knows what edifices of knowledge may be reared, what reaches of spiritual perception may be attained, upon a basis from which all the rubbish of ages has been cleared away, and where all that is useful and true in the past is built into the foundations of the future! Who can tell how nearly we may attain to the perfections of the blessed when, no longer straitened in heart and mind and spirit by a narrow sectarianism, but with the scientific and the *verifiable* everywhere substituted for the dogmatic and the incomprehensible, the veil which has so long shrouded the universe as with a thick mist shall be altogether withdrawn, when the All is revealed without stint to our gaze in such degree as each is able to bear, and

Theology no longer serves but to paint and darken the windows through which man gazes out into the infinite!

Thus reformed, amended, and enlarged, the established churches of Great Britain will be no exclusive corporations, watched with jealous eyes of less favoured sects. Nonconformity will disappear, for there will be nothing to nonconform to: Fanaticism, for there will be no Dogma; Intolerance and Bigotry, for there will be no Infallibility. Comprehensive, as all that claims to be national and human ought to be, no conditions of membership will be imposed to entitle any to a share of its benefits: but every variety of opinion will find expression and a home precisely in the degree to which it may commend itself to the general intelligence.

The bitterness of sectarian animosity thus extinguished, and no place found for dogmatic assertion or theological hatred, it will seem as if the first heaven and the first earth had passed away, and a new heaven and new earth had come, in which there was no more sea of troubles or aught to set men against each other and keep them from uniting in aid of their common welfare. Lit by the clear light of the cultivated intellect, and watered by the pure river of the developed moral sense, the State will be free to grow into a veritable city of God, where there shall be no more curse of poverty or crime, no night of intolerant stupidity, but all shall know that which is good for all, from the least to the greatest."*

"What, then, becomes of the Revelation?" asks one of the hero in 'By and By.' "My friend," is the reply, "so long as there exist God and a Soul, there will be a revelation; *but the soul must be a free one.*"

---

* 'How to Complete the Reformation.' By Edward Maitland. Thomas Scott.

THE
MYSTERY OF EVIL.

THE

MYSTERY OF EVIL.

PUBLISHED BY THOMAS SCOTT,
11 THE TERRACE, FARQUHAR ROAD, UPPER NORWOOD,
LONDON, S.E.

1875.
Price Ninepence.

LONDON:
PRINTED BY C. W. REYNELL, LITTLE PULTENEY STREET,
HAYMARKET.

THE
MYSTERY OF EVIL.

THIS subject is not one of mere sectarian or temporary interest. It touches a depth far deeper than even the differences which separate disciples of Naturalism from those who profess faith in a miraculous book revelation. The following inquiry reaches down to the " bed rock " of all intellectual and moral life, and deals with the source and development of force in the universe, with the nature of human actions, and with the true *fulcrum* which is to bear the leverage by which this still suffering and disordered world is to be raised towards perfect harmony with law, and with the highest ideal of human intelligence and happiness.

Orthodox guides are constantly warning their people against this proposed line of investigation. We are cautioned that the study of such a topic is unpractical and unprofitable—if not actually profane*— that it involves a mystery which is hopelessly inexplicable, that attempts to solve the mystery have been made over and over again by the "carnal" intellect, but always with the same unsatisfactory result—the mocking of our hopes, the answering of our questions by empty echoes, which but rebuke our presumption. This has been the favourite way of silencing the

---

* To proscribe as *profane*, studies beyond the comprehension of a particular school or sect is a very old habit. The wisest Greek philosopher maintained that Astronomy was a subject unfit for human inquiry, and that the gods took it under their own special and immediate control.

questionings, the difficulties, and the fears of "doubting believers." There can be no harm, we are told in making ourselves acquainted, as a matter of history, with how the loyal defenders of the faith have been accustomed to " hold the fort " against the " infidel," for we should ever be ready to give a reason of the hope that is in us. But to venture to reason out the point independently for oneself is to enter on a path beset with danger and leading to despair. Minds of any *stamina*, however, and especially if familiar with the wonderful disclosures which science and critical scholarship are daily making, are not likely to submit much longer to this restraint of priestly leading-strings. They will insist on the right of testing the most "mysterious" teachings of the church for themselves, undeterred alike by threats of ecclesiastical taboo in this world and of divine punishment in the next. The light of truth—formerly claimed as the sole prerogative of a pretended "sacred order"—now finds its way as freely into the poor man's cottage as into the palace of the archbishop, and will, sooner or later, compel the dullest to examine for themselves with an urgency that cannot be repressed.

If I looked upon the question under consideration as simply affording scope for curious speculation, I should be content at once to relegate it for decision to the learned hair-splitters who make it their business solemnly to adjust the distinction between "homoousion" and homo*i*ousion." But I am fully convinced that the alleged "mystery of evil" is essentially a practical question, and one upon which hangs the true theory of the universe, a right conception of man's physical and moral relations, and a just understanding of the nature of the human will and human accountability. Moreover, the vulgar notions on this subject will have to be abandoned before the many philanthropic persons whom theological superstitions have misled, are likely to unite in any effectual

The Mystery of Evil. 7

attempt at man's physical, rational, and moral elevation. With all becoming reverence for the earnest and often profound efforts of the wise and the good in past times to master the difficulties of this subject, we, in this age of riper learning and more extensive scientific acquisition, occupy a vantage ground in discussing it which was not possible to any previous generation.

"Evil", is a term having a theological origin, though it has in some measure been *adopted* in the language of common life. We usually understand by it whatever is contrary to our ideas of moral rectitude and tends to interfere with the general happiness of mankind physically, morally, and socially. It is but too easy to find endlessly varied traces of the wretchedness and wrong that seem to defy all attempts to reconcile them with the rule of infinite power, wisdom, and goodness in the universe.

What shall we say of the tribes and races that have been permitted to live many centuries in internecine strife, ignorance, filth, and pestilence, and to perish without contributing one thought worth preserving to the stock of human ideas? And still it is often around the haunts of the wandering savage or the uncultivated boor, who is incapable of appreciating the sublime, that nature puts forth her grandest feats of power and beauty. Then what shall we think of the havoc and sorrow which are the heritage of multitudes born into the world with constitutions naturally predisposing them to suffer pain or to violate the sentiments of justice and humanity, and brought up in homes that infallibly foster vice, cruelty, and crime. Nor does it relieve the difficulty to view intemperance, the sickly frame, the life-long disease, the plague and the pestilence as being, directly or remotely, penalties for the neglect of sanitary and moral laws; for reason will persist in asking, "Why, if the universe be ruled by a Being of infinite power, wisdom, and love, was not this deep turbid river of misery stemmed at the fountain?" Nay, there are forms of suffering yet more appalling and that yet more perplex and overpower us: the storm that dashes a thousand helpless vessels in pieces in spite of every expedient tried by the crews to escape an ocean grave; the earthquake that engulfs towns and cities so quickly that science and forethought are powerless to avert it; the explosion of the mine that suddenly scorches to death many an honest toiler and deprives many a family of its bread-winner. And if we turn from the fury of the unconscious elements to the conscious and troubled inward experience of human beings, the cloud of "natural ills that flesh is heir to," thickens. The tangled affairs of social and moral life is patent to us all. Why, in this century for instance, should law and order, truth and right, have so little influence upon civilised nations, to say nothing of those we deem barbarians? Look back, too, in history, and behold the long perspective of prophets and martyrs, who have sealed their loyalty to truth and righteousness with their blood, while the tyrants who slew them died without one pang of remorse. Look around and see all ages cut down, apparently at random;—in many cases the wise and vigorous, the useful, the talented, and benevolent, withering away in the morning or noontide of their days with their gifts increasing in number and activity, while the effete and the stupid, the besotted, the selfish, the useless, are spared. Knavery arrayed in purple and fine linen fares sumptuously, and at its gate honest poverty clothed in rags, desires in vain to eat of the crumbs that fall from the rich charlatan's table. Consider the millions that have innocently pined in the dungeon, or that have been worked as beasts, flogged as beasts, and sold as beasts. Consider the throng of once blooming maidens ruined by heartless human monsters. Think of nations in the first rank of civilisation, bowing at the same altar, and rising from their devotions to slay each other by weapons of fiendish ingenuity. And with the spectacle also before us of the greed of ambition, the vapourings of pride, the treachery of the false, the meanness of the little, the vices of the bad, and the frailties of the good, the moral instinct within us cannot help reiterating the question, "Is this the sort of world we should have expected under the government of a Deity clothed with the attributes of perfection? The good man—crude though his ideal be—if he had the power as he has the wish, would at once reduce this chaos to order; and does not the Theist believe in a God infinitely better than the most benevolent of men?

An eminent living physical philosopher has said: "Nature seems to take some care of the *race*, but bestows very little on *individuals*." And in brooding on the dark side of this problem, a man of literary note once exclaimed, in a private circle, "For the credit of our conception of what goodness ought to be, let us *hope* there is no God." This, too, rightly or wrongly, was the very thought put by Byron into the mouth of *Cain* in his reply to Lucifer:

>Why do I exist?
>Why art thou wretched? why are all things so?
>Even He who made us must be as the Maker
>Of things unhappy! To produce destruction
>Can surely never be the work of joy;
>And yet my sire says He's omnipotent.
>Then why is evil?—He being good?

The same thought is strongly expressed by Mrs. Browning:—

>My soul is grey
>With pouring o'er the total sum of ill.
>* * * * *
>With such a total of distracted life
>To see it down in figures on a page,
>Plain, silent, clear * * *

* * *   That's terrible
For one who is not God, and cannot right
The wrong he looks upon.*

This problem of evil has stirred deeply inquiring minds from the earliest times. In the 'Naishadha Charita' (xvii. 45), a Chārvāka, or materialistic Atheist, is represented as addressing Indra and other gods on their return to heaven from Damayantis Svayamvara, and ridiculing the orthodox Indian doctrines of the Vedas :—" If there be an omniscient and merciful God, who never speaks in vain, why does he not, by the mere expenditure of a word, satisfy the desires of us his suppliants? By causing living creatures to suffer pain, though it be the result of their own works, God would be our causeless enemy, whilst all our other enemies have some reason or other for their enmity."†

Sophocles has lines to the same effect:—" It is strange that those who are impious and descendants of wicked men should fare prosperously, while those who are good and sprung from noble men should be unfortunate. It was not meet that the gods should thus deal with mortals. Pious men ought to have obtained from the gods some manifest advantage, while the unjust should, on the contrary, have paid some evident penalty for their evil deeds, and thus no one who was wicked would have been prosperous."‡

It may be convenient at this point to glance at some of the methods that have been employed to ease or remove the contradiction between the *painful* phenomena of life and the credited rule of an all-mighty, all-wise, and all-good Father. We shall

---

* 'Aurora Leigh.'
† 'Additional Moral and Religious Passages, Metrically rendered from the Sanskrit, with exact Prose Translations "—*Scott's Series*.
‡ Quoted by Dr. Muir in the 'Additional Moral and Religious Passages.'

thus have an opportunity of detecting the fallacies which lurk under all such methods of harmonising, and which render them nugatory.

Epicurus, from a Theistic point of view, stated the case very comprehensively when, in syllogistic form, he said:—" Why is evil in the world? It is either because God is unable or unwilling to remove it. If he be unable he is not omnipotent. If he be unwilling, he is not all-good. If he be neither able nor willing, he is neither all-powerful nor all-good;"* and it is difficult to see how escape is possible from between the horns of this dilemma on the supposition that an infinite God exists.

The Manichæans believed good and evil or pleasure and pain to be rival powers in the universe. This was also virtually the Persian theory on the subject, only the latter was clothed in oriental dress.† Bolingbroke and the sceptics of his day, accounted for the phenomena referred to on an æsthetic principle—the proportion of parts in the scale of sentient being. Every animal has bodily members of varied grades of honour and importance, and all in harmonious subserviency to the general convenience of their possessor. Every picture has an arrangement of colour · producing light and shade. All harmony must consist of voices attuned from alto to bass. Every considerable dwelling must have apartments in the attic as well as on the ground floor, and of greater or less capacity. So the world is formed on a gradational plan from high intelligence, by imperceptible degrees down to life of so doubtful a

---

* The great Lord Shaftesbury, in his "Inquiry concerning Virtue," 'Characteristics,' Vol. II., page 10, puts the case thus:—" If there be supposed a designing principle, who is the cause only of good, but cannot prevent ill which happens . . . then there can be supposed, in reality, no such thing as a superior good design or mind, other than what is impotent and defective; for not to correct or totally exclude that ill . . . must proceed either from *impotency* or *ill-will.*"

† Ormuzd and Ahriman. This is also the germ of the Christian dogma of God who is "Light," and the Devil " The Prince of Darkness."

character that it is impossible to determine whether it be vegetable or animal. In the moral sphere, too, there is a ladder whose top reaches the loftiest unselfishness, and whose rounds gradually descend to the grossest forms of moral life. It is argued that the world would be tame and monotonous without these inequalities in the structure of universal life, and that it is the constant friction between beings of high and low degree which helps to give that healthful impulse to human activity that keeps the universe from stagnating; and unavoidable accidents but quicken the forethought and contrivance of men to provide against such occurrences. It will be felt, however, by the most ordinary thinker, that such a theory utterly fails to cover all the facts, and fails especially to account for the more formidable sufferings of humanity. It is but the view of an artist who lives in a one-sided and unreal region, surrounded by plenty, who simply looks out upon the world through a *coleur de rose* medium, and projects the image of his own luxurious home upon the landscape outside.

There is another theory popular with a large class of airy minds, which regards evil as a modification of good. Right and wrong, truth and falsehood proceed from the same source, and are degrees of the same thing. Lust is only a lower form of love, and what would be described as cruelty inflicted upon others is not *intended* to cause suffering *as an end*, but only occurs in some rather abrupt and unceremonious attempt being made by a person to reach some object much wished for. But the one who suffers happens to be, unconsciously perhaps, an obstacle in the way of that object being attained; and the *suffering* is occasioned simply by accident, just as we stumble against a neighbour who has the misfortune to cross our path at the moment when our attention is fixed on something we eagerly want to get at on the opposite side of the street. So much the worse for the neighbour if he sustain injury by the impact, but it is no fault of ours!

What goes by the name of meanness, according to the same theory, springs as truly from a wish to be happy in the mean nature as nobility does when manifested by a noble nature. As little harm is intended by the one nature as by the other. But it seems only necessary to state this method of meeting the difficulty in order to see its inadequacy. Even granting that the misery occasioned by men to each other were reconciled by this mode of reasoning, there is a class of troubles which are wholly beyond human agency and control that remains utterly unaccounted for; and respecting the evils which the theory professes to explain away, the question crops up afresh, why, if the government of the world be conducted by a Being of infinite power, wisdom and love, is so much distress permitted to be caused, *however casually*, by men to one another?

Perhaps the most elaborate and closely-reasoned attempt ever made to harmonise existing evil in the world with perfect wisdom, power, and goodness, in a Creator, was the celebrated "Essay on the Origin of Evil," by Archbishop King. The writer postulates, as an *axiom*, that the universe is the work of a God of infinite intelligence, power, and goodness; and he deals in precisely the same manner with the alleged existence of freedom and responsibility in human beings. The pith of the Archbishop's explanation of *moral evil* is contained in the following passage: "The less dependent on external things, the more self-sufficient any agent is, and the more it has the principles of its actions within itself, it is so much the more perfect; since, therefore, we may conceive two sorts of agents, one which does not act unless impelled and determined by external circumstances, such as vegetable bodies; the other, which have the principle of their actions within themselves, namely, free agents, and can determine themselves to action by their own natural power, it is plain that the latter are much more perfect than the former; nor can it be denied that God may create an agent with such power as this; which can exert itself into action without either the concourse of God or the determination of external causes, as long as God preserves the existence, power, and faculties, of that agent; *that evil arises from the unlawful use of man's faculties;* that more good in general arises from the donation of such a self-moving power, together with all those foreseen abuses of it, than could possibly have been produced without it."

The gist of the Archbishop's reasoning is in the words: "Evil arises from the unlawful use of men's faculties." But this is a mere begging of the question, and a shifting rather than a settlement of the difficulty; for even granting the assumption put forward, the inquiry naturally recurs: Why, in a world created and sustained by such a perfect Being as Theism recognises, was any arrangement tolerated by which men *should* exercise their faculties *unlawfully*—especially as the results are so painfully discordant with our notions of happiness? It is assumed by the Archbishop that *man* and not his maker is responsible for the moral chaos that has always characterised the condition of the race. But this is only a repetition of the now exploded theological fiction that man was created with his faculties and circumstances equally and entirely favourable to obedience; and that his departure from law was his own voluntary choice—a choice determined upon by him with a full consciousness that he *ought* to have acted differently, and that he was *free* to have done so. By the voluntary depravation of his own mind and by the force of his bad example he involved all his descendants in the moral and physical consequences of his transgression. But with the undeniable revelations of modern scientific and historical research before us such a view is too absurd to need refutation. In any case we are justified in holding that on the hypothesis of a miracle-working God, there is no tendency to disobedience, error, or vice, in mankind that might not have been easily checked in its first outbreak by an act of omnipotence. The power that is asserted to have rained manna from the skies, arrested the setting of the sun, changed water into wine, and raised the dead, might surely have been exerted in a way more worthy the dignity and goodness of an infinite God, in stopping the first outburst of moral disorder that has filled the world until now with cruel and deadly passions and overwhelmed millions of sensitive spirits in intense anguish.

By the same superficial and evasive reasoning, has this writer disposed of those calamities which cannot owe their origin, anyhow, to the will of man. He coolly tells us that "it is no objection to God's goodness or his wisdom to create such things as are necessarily attended with these evils . . . and that disagreeable sensations must be reckoned among natural evils as inevitably associated with sentient existences, which yet cannot be avoided. If anyone ask why such a law of union was established, namely, the disagreeable sensations which sentient creatures experience, let this be the answer, because *there could be no better;* for such a necessity as this follows; and considering the circumstances and conditions under which, and under which only, they could have existence, they could neither be placed in a better state, nor governed by more commodious laws." That is to say, God in his wisdom and goodness did his best to secure the general well-being of the universe and signally failed, as the physical accidents and agonies endured by innocent multitudes, prove! Yet this is a book of which a distinguished Theistic philosopher said: "If Archbishop King, in this performance, has not reconciled the inconsistencies, none else need apply themselves to the task." If the *data* of Archbishop King as regards the existence of a personal Deity, clothed with infinitely perfect physical and moral attributes, and as regards the free agency of man, had been correct, the most logical course for him would have been to have simply admitted the hopeless irreconcilableness of these data with the state of the world as we find it, and to have betaken himself to the favourite retreat of orthodoxy,—*mystery*,—and spared himself the pains of elaborating a tissue of metaphysical fallacies which only make the confusion to be worse confounded. But I reserve his data for fuller examination afterwards.

The only other theory, which I shall notice, as differing from the one to be subsequently proposed, is that of *fatalistic Deism*, which was held in the last century by a large class of European philosophers, and sought to be refuted by Butler. The following is an epitome of the argument of this school:—The existence of Deity, as infinite and uncreated, is a *necessary* fact, intuitively perceived. If God's existence be necessary, the *conditions* of his existence—physical, mental, and moral,—and the modes of its action and development, must be alike *necessary*. As the visible universe is the outcome of this necessary existence, all the forms of being contained in the universe must also be necessary, by which we are to understand that we cannot conceive the possibility of their being otherwise than they are. If so, then all the orders of existence in the universe, proceeding from the depths of his infinite nature and constantly dependent upon his support, are fated to form links in one chain of eternal and unalterable necessity, and to be precisely as they *are*. Therefore the develop-

The Mystery of Evil. 17

ment of human beings, and of every other variety of *life*, is destined to assume the particular form under which they are found to exist at any given stage of the evolution of the universe. Consequently, what, in the vocabulary of mortals, is called *freedom*, is but an illusion,—the actions and characters of rational beings of all degrees of intelligence and moral culture being included in that ceaseless development which is controlled by the same central and all-embracing principle of unexplainable *necessity*.*

It is further maintained by the same class of Deists that amidst all the apparent confusion that prevails, indications of a process of orderly developments are discernible, whether we trace the consolidation of the earth's crust, or the progressive advance of vegetable and animal forms upon it, or the gradual uplifting of the human species. This evolution, it is asserted, is either caused and directed by some controlling Intelligence, or is the result of chance, or arises from some inherent spontaneous power in the universe itself. But our conception of *chance* excludes it from the rank of a causal and regulating force, for we only understand by the term what is fortuitous, blind, undesigning, and impotent. Again, to suppose that some inherent spontaneous power in nature itself is shaping and directing universal progress would be to endow the universe with physical, rational, and moral power; in other words, to identify it with God, or to view it *as* God. Therefore, it is concluded,—these alternatives failing to satisfy the demands of logical consistency,—the only tenable view left is that the framework and development of the universe, is the work of a Deity answering to the Θεὸs of Homer, who represents the God of his conception, as being

---

* The reader will be reminded of a remarkable passage in the 'Prometheus Vinctus' of Æschylus: "Even Jove is not superior to the Fates."

the source of all *the good and evil* of life. I confess that for a time, while my own mind was passing from supernaturalism to naturalism, and while I believed that my choice in dealing with "the mystery of evil" lay alone between rival forms of Theism, this notion of God as the primal cause alike of happiness and misery was the only one which seemed co-ordinate with all the facts, and effectually to solve the mystery.

But, as will appear later in this paper, two objections ultimately arose in my mind which shook my fatalistic Deism to its foundation. The first of these was, that the God I thought myself bound to believe in fell far short of the ideal of virtue and goodness at which an average high-minded man felt himself obliged to aim, and thus I was conscious of doing violence to my better nature in holding to such a faith. The second objection was that the *intuitive* idea of Deity was found by me to be a gratuitous assumption which, with other beliefs of this description, collapsed under the unsparing analysis to which the intuitive philosophy has been subjected by the inductive philosophy—the latter being the only one which seems to me to accord with the universal principles of truth.

After the preceding statement of attempted solutions of this alleged mystery by Theistic and Deistic theories, it will probably be admitted that any method of accounting for the existence of evil based on the twofold hypothesis of an Almighty God of omniscience, wisdom, and goodness, and the doctrine of the free, self-determining action of the human will, cannot escape from the charge of mystery—or, more properly, of palpable logical contradiction. In presence of these two conceptions, evil must inevitably remain a mystery. Let them be surrendered, however, and the mystery instantly vanishes.

When a scientific analyst discovers that a hypothesis fails to cover and explain all the phenomena,

The Mystery of Evil. 19

he unhesitatingly abandons it, and there is no other alternative left to an inductive theologian—if there be such a person—when he is placed in a similar position. The *facts* in the present instance are agreed upon by all. There *is* a large proportion, if not preponderance, of what is known as *Evil* in the world; and if the idea of an infinitely wise and good personal Deity tend to embarrass instead of allaying the difficulties we have been examining, clearly the idea of an universal ruler ought, in loyalty to truth, to be removed from the category of our beliefs, let the sentimental associations be ever so hallowed and strong that have gathered round it, and the same remark applies to the allied dogma of free will in man.

As regards the first of these points, the justice of the course recommended is strengthened when we consider that the existence of such an almighty person is incapable of scientific or any other kind of proof worthy consideration. At the same time, in venturing this remark, I wish emphatically to disclaim all sympathy with positive Atheism; for a *dogmatic* negation of any vitalizing and controlling force *in* the universe, not being *itself the universe,* is almost as objectionable as the most dogmatic form of Theism. All I contend for is, that there is no ground for believing in what theologians call a *personal* God, in other words, "a magnified man" invested with certain characteristics of humanity attributed to him, these attributes being only infinitely extended. Doubtless Theists, and particularly Christian Theists, will be ready to adduce in reply their usual argument for the existence of a personal Deity derived from their *intuitions.* This, consistently enough, is also the stronghold of Christian faith in the doctrine of "a supernatural gospel," namely, "its felt adaptation to the spiritual wants of Christian believers." And the more rapidly and convincingly the evidences of science and historical criticism accumulate on the non-supernatural and non-Theistic side, they shut their eyes the closer, scream the louder against "the wickedness of Atheistic materialism," and plunge deeper into the sentimental abyss of their "intuitions." Here is a passage *à propos*, written by one of the ablest and best read leaders of the reactionary, semi-mystic, evangelical school which owes its origin (as opposed) to the "fierce light" of modern thought, against which the writer lifts a warning voice. "But whether we represent a 'new school' or a theological 'reaction' we say frankly that, in our judgment, the exigencies of the times require that Christian Churches, and especially Christian ministers, should meet the dogmas of materialism and anti-supernaturalism *with the most direct and uncompromising hostility. It is not for us to* PERMIT *men to suppose that we regard the existence of the living God as an open question*. Nor shall we make any deep impression on the minds of men *if our faith in Jesus Christ rests on grounds that are accessible to historical, scientific, or philosophical criticism*. If we are to meet modern unbelief successfully we must receive that direct revelation of Christ which will enable us to say 'we have heard him, we have seen him ourselves and know that this is indeed the Christ, the Saviour of the world!'" The great object of this school seems to be to make a religious "impression" in Evangelical fashion, and stamp out all that frustrates their doing so, proceeding from the sceptical camp. The historical truth or *error* of the thing taught seems to be of secondary consideration provided it can be made to dovetail with Evangelical intuitions. These *intense* believers deliberately tell us that it is of no use our calling their attention to discrepancies in the Gospel narratives by which these sources of Christian facts are rendered historically untrustworthy. They assure us that such criticism is idle

The Mystery of Evil. 21

and beside the mark, and they console themselves with the belief that these discrepancies are only *apparent*, and that if we could but compare the *original* documents (which, by the way, nobody has ever seen or can find the least trace of) instead of the mere *copies* of them (these pretended copies being all we possess), we should be immediately convinced !*

So in regard to the existence of a personal Deity, instead of looking at the facts as they *are*, they assure us that, if we could only know all the complications of the divine government, our difficulty in believing in *their* Deity would disappear. But those who fall back on the fitness of their conception of Deity to their intuitions as a proof of his existence, while perhaps feeling that this argument affords perfect satisfaction to themselves, place an insuperable barrier against all interchange of reasoning between themselves and those who hold opposite convictions. Any one who hides in the recesses of his intuitions, has sunk into a state of intellectual somnolency from which no argument can wake him.

There are some Theistic apologists, however, who still have unshaken faith in the argument from *design*, as establishing the existence of a beneficent designer. But the fallacy of this argument is obvious. The premises and conclusion stand thus :—" Every object which bears marks of design necessarily points to the existence of an intelligent designer. The universe is such an object, therefore *it* had an intelligent designer." But it is usually forgotten that this conclusion is arrived at by comparing the universe with an object—a watch for example, that can bear no

---

* The weak point in this *intuitional* argument is that *it proves too much*. It is the favourite proof with large sections of the adherents of Buddhism, Brahminism, Fire-worship, and Mahometanism respectively, by which these systems are all *felt* to be supernatural revelations. Therefore by proving too much *it proves nothing*.

analogy to it. It is taken for granted that the universe sustains the same relation to a personal Creator which a piece of mechanism does to a mortal contriver.

Now, it might be perfectly fair *to compare one piece of human handiwork with another*, and infer that *both* suggested the application of power and intelligence equal to their construction. But in comparing the universe—there being only *one*, and *that* one *infinite*, with articles of man's invention, which are *many* and *finite*—are we not comparing the *known* with the *unknown*, and carrying the principle of analogy into a region where it can have no place? It may be just to infer that as one work of human arrangement naturally implies skill in the maker, so another work bearing marks of human contrivance, should, in like manner, suggest to us the action of a thinking mind. But science is so far in the dark as to the mainspring of life, motion and development in the one universe that we should be totally unwarranted by the laws of thought in arguing from the origin of what is *discoverable* to the orgin of what is *undiscoverable*.* To reason, therefore, from design in the operations of man to design in the operations of nature is illogical and impossible.

One of the most remarkable signs of change, of late, in the conception of Deity, among progressive thinkers, who *still cling to the skirts of recognised religious institutions,* is the effort that has been made to reconcile an *impersonal* Power influencing and shaping the evolution of the universe with the teachings of the Bible. The line of thought in Mr. Matthew Arnold's 'Literature and Dogma' has very decidedly this leaning. Indeed, it is no exaggeration to say

---

* Axiom V., in the *Tractatus Theologico-Politicus* of Spinoza is decisive on this point. "Things that have nothing in common with each other *cannot be understood by means of each other; i.e., the conception of the one does not involve the conception of the other.*"

that this writer labours to turn the current notion of a personal God into ridicule, and even seeks to prove that, at least, the ancient Hebrews were not in sympathy with such a notion. Some will take leave to doubt whether Mr. Arnold's views of the Hebrew conception of God be not more ingenious than accurate, and whether he may not have foisted far-fetched theories of his own upon the *text* of the Bible in his zeal to make out his case. But, at any rate, we have the phenomenon of a writer cherishing devotion to the teaching of Scripture and concern for the maintenance of the national Church, and yet sapping the foundations of orthodoxy, and actually sneering at the idea of faith in a personal Deity, though professed gravely by eminent bishops—the two whose names he repeats *ad nauseam* throughout the essay.

Another recent book of essays, written with a similar purpose, but in a more reverent and philosophic spirit, is not unworthy of notice.* The author is a Nonconformist minister, and a member of the London School Board—a gentleman of marked ability and wide culture. The peculiarity of his position is that while, like the Broad Church clergy, conducting his service with a liturgy and a hymn-book, fashioned after orthodox models, he has openly renounced the dogma of the *Supernatural* in his pulpit teaching, and rejected the notion of a personal God. He has chosen to represent himself as a "Christian Pantheist,"—a term which we may be excused for deeming paradoxical—and strives throughout the volume to bring his statements into accord with certain passages in the New Testament. The essays reveal more than an average (as well as a discriminating) acquaintance with ancient and modern philosophy and theology, and with the results of modern science in relation to

---

* 'The Mystery of Matter, and other Essays.' By J. Allanson Picton, M.A. Macmillan. 1873.

the nature of the Universe. His thoughts are, now and then, diffuse, but they are always expressed with a wealth of language and sometimes with an eloquence not ordinarily met with in theological disquisitions. There are, however, as it seems to me, weak points, I had almost said occasional contradictions, in his reasoning, into which he may have been unconsciously led by his unique ecclesiastical relations, but which it is beyond the scope of the present paper to criticise at length. Nevertheless, he forcibly opposes the old error which made a distinction between *matter* and *spirit*, and he reduces the Universe, with Professor Huxley, to a *unity*, namely, SUBSTANCE, of which what have been vulgarly described as *matter* and *spirit* are simply the *phenomena*. He further boldly rejects all theories which regard Deity as *one* amidst a host of *other* beings, and while, with religious fervour, recognising the presence of an efficient though unnameable energy as vitalising and controlling all molecular forces, he seems, at the same time, to identify that unkown efficient energy with *universal substance*, and accords to it the right and title to be formally worshipped. I respectfully think he is not always clear and consistent in this part of his theme. Sometimes he refers—as Spinoza himself does—to this vitalising and all-comprehending essence as if it were invested with attributes of intelligence, wisdom, and goodness, without which attributes the writer's insistance upon the worship of universal substance as deity would be a misnomer. And yet, difficult though it be to discover homogeneity between certain parts of these essays, in one respect the author's aim throughout is unmistakeable. *He emphatically pronounces against the existence of a personal Deity.* Some of his remarks in opposition to the design argument are especially worth quoting :—

"It is demonstrable that there must be some fallacy in such an argument as that of Paley. For if it be

The Mystery of Evil.

rigorously applied, it cannot prove what Paley certainly wished to establish—the existence of an omnipotent and omniscient worker. . . . If we are to see design only when we can compliment nature on an apparent resemblance to operations of human skill; and if, the moment that resemblance ceases, we are to confess our ignorance and to refrain from carrying the analogy further, would it not be better, seeing how infinitely larger is our ignorance than our knowledge, to recognise in both bearings of the analogy an appearance only which, though for some purposes practically useful, is infinitely below the divine reality. . . . Of whatever value the analogy of human design may be, no one would think of insisting upon its *admitted imperfections* as a part of the argument; and yet, without pressing those imperfections, it is impossible to make the argument consistent. But if it be fairly carried out, what it proves is this, that an omnipotent designer, intending to produce a beautiful and perfect work, went through millions of operations, when a single fiat would have sufficed; that these operations consisted not in clearly-aimed and economical modifications of material, but in the evolution of a thousand imperfect products, amongst which some single one might form a step to the next stage, while all the rest were destroyed; and thus the living material wasted was immensely greater than that which was used; that myriads of weaklings were suffered to struggle together, as though omniscience could not decide, without experiment, which were the better worth preserving; that in each successive modification the worker preserved, as far as was possible, the form of the previous stage, until it was found to be inconsistent with life; nay, that he carefully introduced into each successive product parts which had become obsolete, useless, and even dangerous—and all not through any inevitable conditions—for omnipotence excludes them, but in pursuit of a mysterious plan, the reasons for which, as well as its nature, are acknowledged to be utterly inscrutable. Analogies which lead to such issues surely cannot be of much value for the nobler aims of religion." *

The other cause of the difficulty encountered in probing "the Mystery of Evil" is the traditional notions entertained by many, of the action of the human will. Man is represented by the orthodox as a "free agent" (I except, of course, hyper-Calvinists who now form a very small minority among Christians), and the doctrine of volitional liberty has acquired prominence in theological and philosophical discussions; not from any practical influence the doctrine can exert, one way or another, on the actual conduct of life, but simply from the accident that the question whether the will was absolutely free or determined by necessity happened to be thrown to the surface, in the fifth century, in the theological battle between the Augustinians and the Pelagians. The inquiry is itself interesting and important, but many mental philosophers from that period until recently, having a dread of the *odium theologicum*, have been desirous it should be known that they were "sound" on the subject, and have been particular in declaring themselves on the orthodox side. The strong enunciation of one view has called forth an equally vigorous statement of the opposite theory, and hence philosophers have filed off into two sharply defined parties—libertarians and necessitarians—so that the importance that has come to be attached to the free-will controversy is, in a great measure, adventitious.

The introduction of moral evil into the world, as before stated, has been ascribed by the greater number of Christians to the voluntary disobedience of the progenitor of the race. Tradition has handed down the unscientific and unhistoric story of an original man who,

---

* 'Mystery of Matter,' pp. 330, 340, 345.

The Mystery of Evil. 27

having been severely plied with temptation in order to test his virtue, voluntarily broke a certain arbitrary and positive command of his maker, and involved himself and his posterity in tendencies to wrong-doing which could only be corrected by supernatural means. But, without debating the wide question of the origin of mankind, manifestly men are so constituted and surrounded that limitations are placed as indubitably upon their volitional faculty as upon their other mental powers. So that in no libertarian sense can we be said to be free agents. The form a man's character takes is necessarily dependent on his innate predispositions and capacities—the form and size of brain and cast of temperament which he derives from his parents—and on the nature and extent of the influences under which he is trained. Some natures are constitutionally more attuned to intellectual and moral harmony than others, and when impelled by favourable influences from without, there is little merit in their moving in the line of conformity to truth and right. There are other natures that inherit less fortunate tendencies, to whom virtue must always be the result of conscious effort, and especially if they be encircled with influences unfriendly to the culture of a high and noble life. It is certain that if such persons attain any considerable degree of goodness, the end will be reached through the experience of error and folly and of the natural penalties attaching to both. As far as I can understand, the chief ground of the alarm affected by a certain class of philosophers and theologians at the idea of human actions being determined by *necessity* is the morbid and fictitious weight they have given to the doctrine of *individual responsibility*; I say *morbid* and *fictitious*, because whether a man violates the laws of nature or of society he is sooner or later made to bear more or less of his share of responsibility in enduring the natural punishment due to the offence. Had the same amount of concern been felt by society about their *collective* share of responsibility in reference to the physical, intellectual, and moral well-being of *individuals* as is felt about the influence of necessitarianism upon " men's felt sense of *individual* responsibility " the results to the community and the race would have been much more rational and beneficial. I am persuaded that the individual conduct of citizens —be they good or bad—is not affected in the slightest degree, for better or for worse, by the views they may entertain of the philosophy of the human will. This might be proved demonstratively did space permit.

The kernel of this controversy, then, lies in the inquiry, Whether the will is absolutely self-determinative, and capable of arbitrarily kicking the beam, when motives present to the mind, and tending in opposite directions, seem to be evenly balanced; or whether, in every instance, the motive, embracing a great variety of considerations in the mind itself as well as in the circumstances around it, do not infallibly determine the character of the choice that is made. If the libertarian view be the right one, no certainty can be ever predicated as to the effect upon the conduct of uniformly good or bad motives, and, consequently, the most earnest and philanthropic exertions to improve the world are, at best, disheartening. But since it can be demonstrated that the formation of human habits is governed by necessary laws, and that these laws can be ascertained and acted upon with the undoubted assurance that corresponding results may be anticipated, the labours of science and philanthropy are animated by a well-founded hope that they need not be expended in vain. What, then, is "will" but simply that faculty or power of the mind by which we are capable of *choosing ?* And an act of will is the same as an act of choice. That which uniformly determines the will is *the motive which,*

The Mystery of Evil. 29

as it stands in the view of the mind, is the strongest. The motive is that which excites or invites the mind to volition, whether that be one thing *singly* or many things *conjointly*. By *necessity*, in this connection, is meant nothing more than the philosophical certainty of the relation between given antecedents and consequents in the production of actions. Man, like every other sentient being, is necessarily actuated by a desire for happiness, according to his particular estimate of it. It would be a contradiction to suppose that he could hate happiness, or that he could desire misery for its own sake, or with a perception that *it was such*. He is placed in circumstances in which a vast variety of objects address themselves to this predominating desire, some promising to gratify it in a higher degree, some in a lower, some appealing to one part of his nature and some to another. He cannot but be attracted to those objects and those courses of conduct which his reason or his appetites, or both combined, assure him are likely to gratify his desire of happiness. The *various degrees or kinds* of real and apparent good, promised by different objects or courses of conduct, constitute the *motives* which incline him to act in pursuance of the *general* desire of happiness which is the grand impulse of his nature. Sometimes he *really* sees and sometimes he *imagines* he sees (and as regards their influence on the will they come to the same thing) greater degrees of good in some objects or proposed courses of conduct than in others; and this constitutes *preponderance* of motive, that is, a greater measure of real or apparent good at the time of any particular volition. This preponderance of motive will be as is the character of the moral agent and the circumstances of the objects, taken conjointly. This preponderance of motive will be, therefore, not only different in different individuals, but different in different individuals at different times. That which *at any particular time* is or appears to promise the greatest good, will uniformly decide the Will.* This necessarily flows from the tendency of a sentient nature to seek happiness at all, and is, indeed, only a particular application of the same general principle; inasmuch as it would imply as great a contradiction that a being capable of happiness should not take that which it *deems* will confer, all things considered, a greater degree of happiness rather than that which will confer a less, as it would be to imagine it not seeking happiness rather than the contrary, or some happiness rather than none. This *certainty* of connection between the preponderance of motive and the decisions of the will is what is meant by *necessity*, as simply implying that the cause will as certainly be followed by the appropriate effect in this instance as in any instance of the mutual connection of cause and effect whatever.†

Motive sustains a dynamical relation to will, as a cause does to an effect in *physics*. Therefore the only liberty which man possesses or *can* possess, is not the liberty of *willing as he will*—which is an idea philosophically absurd—but of *acting* as he wills, according to the laws of necessity. Otherwise he would be *independent* of cause; and, indeed, libertarians actually assert that a motive is not the cause, but only the *occasion* of choice.‡ Either human volitions are effects or they are not. If they are effects, they are consequents indissolubly associated with the antecedent causes or motives which precede them;

---

* "The greatest of two pleasures or what appears such, sways the resulting action, for it is this resulting action that alone determines which is the greatest."—Bain on the 'Emotions and the Will,' p. 447.

† This is the course of argument adopted by Edwards in his remarkable book on the WILL, and it is admirably summarised by Henry Rogers in his 'Essay on the Genius and Writings of Edwards,' prefixed to the Complete Edition of his Works, pp. xx to xxiv.

‡ For this distinction, enforced by Drs. Clarke and Price, see remarks in Bain's 'Mind and Body,' p. 76; also in 'The Refutation of Edwards,' by Tappan.

The Mystery of Evil. 31

and therefore "the liberty of indifference" is impossible.* If human volitions be *not* effects, the actions of men are independent of condition or relation, undetermined by motives or antecedents, and for that reason removed beyond the domain of that principle of necessary law which is the sole guarantee for the order and progress of the Universe.†

The elimination from this problem, therefore, of the conception of a Deity clothed with personal and moral attributes and of the notion of a self-determining will in man, liberates it from all mystery and difficulty whatsoever; for if there be no personal God the existence of *physical* evil casts no imputation upon the infinite character attributed to him. And if there be no "liberty of indifference" in man, he is exempt from the charge of being, in any sense, the originator of moral evil, as the circumstances that constitute his motives are made *for* him and not *by* him; and therefore the praise of virtue and the blame of vice and, in fact, the whole theory of conscience as held by the vulgar, are *annulled*.

What is the distinct *reality* left to us, then, after we have parted with these two inventions of fancy?

The pith of the matter may be conveniently summed up in a few simple propositions:—

---

*. Definition VII. in the 'Tractatus' of Spinoza runs thus:—"That thing is said to be free *which exists by the sole necessity of its own nature, and by itself alone is determined to action. But that is necessary or rather constrained which owes its existence to another and acts according to certain and determinate causes.*"

† The controversy on Free Will and Necessity has, within the last quarter of a century, passed from the region of mere theological wrangling into the circle of scientific studies, and has assumed to the social and moral Reformer *practical* importance. The subject now claims the attention of all who would have intelligent views of the moral condition and prospects of Humanity and who seek to work hopefully for its regeneration. It is not within the province of this Essay to particularise the various recent phases of the controversy, but those who are alive to the importance of the subject cannot fail to find intensely interesting those chapters bearing upon it in such works as Mill's 'Examination of Sir William Hamilton's Philosophy,' Bain's 'Compendium of Mental and Moral Science,' and Herbert Spencer's 'Study of Sociology.'

1. All we can know of the Universe is *phenomena*, —(including the molecular force-centres into which existing organisms are resolvable by scientific analysis) —and the fixed uniformity of the laws that regulate and control the physical and moral evolutions and developments of *universal substance;* but of *noumena* we can know nothing, and consequently any dogmatic definition—positive or negative, of a primal cause, *in* or *beyond* substance, or not in or beyond substance —is totally unsustained by facts. Therefore the systems of Theism, Deism, Pantheism, and Atheism are mere *hypotheses*, which all involve unproved assumptions. As regards the existence of any overruling power, we are in a state of *nescience*. As regards motives and actions, all we know is the uniform and necessary relation of sequence that exists between them—nothing more.

2. The universe, or, at least, the portion of it with which we have immediate acquaintance, is being slowly and gradually developed from rudimental elements, from confusion and discord to order and harmony; and this remark applies, throughout, to physical, intellectual, and moral life. Thus it follows that the generations of mankind, up to the present, having been brought upon the planet before it has reached the state of complete development and perfect equipoise of forces, are fated to suffer those physical trials which arise from storms, floods, earthquakes, droughts, blights, and other casualties, which, when the material agencies around us have attained more perfect equilibrium, may be expected to disappear. There are many more physical inconveniences experienced by the race by reason of their still necessarily limited knowledge of the operations of nature, of the laws of being, and of their true relations to the world and humanity, and by reason of the yet very imperfect stage of human culture. It is inevitable, therefore, that numerous diseases and

The Mystery of Evil. 33

sufferings should be encountered, which a broader intelligence and a clearer forethought will, in the distant future, be able to anticipate and prevent.

3. "Evil" is a word which originated with theologians, and which, from its vagueness and ambiguity, has introduced much of the mystification and error that have beclouded past investigations of the subject. In its primitive signification and as applied in theology, *evil* had a penal character assigned to it, and it derived that character from the childish tradition long believed by adherents of churches, that physical disasters, including disease and death, were the result of a trivial transgression committed by "Adam." The same cause has been adduced to account for all the moral obliquities which have brought pain and misery upon the descendants of the first man. "Sin," which denotes the moral side of evil, in the language of theology, is represented as being at once an effect and a cause of the first transgression. But with the rejection of the idea of a personal Ruler of the world, "evil" and "sin" in the sense in which they are usually understood by the orthodox, are rendered *meaningless*. Both these terms point back to a period in the intellectual and moral childhood of mankind, before the universal and uniform action of Law was dreamt of, and when human duty was held to consist only of a series of positive commands, formally proclaimed by an infinite personal governor, and constituting his "revealed will," for the direction of his creatures. And for the perpetuation of this antiquated belief down to the present we are indebted to stereotyped creeds, which clergymen and ministers of religious bodies still solemnly pledge themselves to maintain. But the light of science presents the source of duty and the nature and standard of morals, in our time, in an altered aspect. In this amended view there is nothing corresponding to the theological ideas of *evil* and *sin* in the world, at all.

What is *called* evil is simply a synonym for *imperfection* in the material or moral circumstances of humanity, or in both. The earth has not yet attained its ultimate and perfect form, and the mind of man has not yet acquired a full and practical knowledge of the working of law so as to guard successfully against collisions with the more violent and dangerous agencies of nature, and so as to use nature as a minister of good. What is known as *sin* or wrong-doing is nothing more than the result of human *ignorance*, which is but another form, again, of *imperfection*. Many acts, I am aware, are called sinful by *clerics* and their votaries, but such transgressions, though ranked by orthodox teachers as equally obnoxious to divine displeasure with acknowledged *natural* immoralities, are found when looked into to be only *ecclesiastical* sins—sins of priestly manufacture which have no place in nature and no recognition in the enlightened conscience. That this is the only true account of the matter is evident from the fact that, as men become familiar with the uniform operations of nature in their bearing on human welfare, the ills of life perceptibly diminish, and the necessity of conforming, in every sphere of existence, to natural law comes to have the force of a safe and efficient guiding impulse. No sane being ever did *wilfully* what he knew to militate against individual or social happiness as an *ulterior* end, and no one ever *continued* to practise habits having this tendency a single moment after his mind became really sensible of the character and influence of his doings. That acts mischievous and cruel are too often committed there can be no doubt; but the mischief or the cruelty is always and only *accidental* to the design the malicious person has in view. Many, it is true, persist in doing what they *profess* to know is at variance with the principles of justice, honour, and utility, and hence the *apparent* anomaly of proper knowledge and improper conduct sometimes being found united in the same person. But the anomaly is only *apparent;* for the individual *professing* to know what befits his relations to the universe and to society, and yet doing what contradicts that knowledge, deceives himself that he possesses suitable knowledge at all. *Knowledge,* in such a connection, is confounded with *notions.* A man may have a *notion* or a dim idea of what he ought to *do* or to be, in his *imagination* or his *memory,* but in this instance the notion is held by the mind as an impotent *sentiment* or a barren *tradition,* the mere semblance of actual knowledge. The *notion* of a thing is but a *theoretic or hypothetical conception,* and does not penetrate the mind and touch the springs of action. All *knowledge,* worthy to be so designated, enters into us and becomes *conviction,* modifying thought, feeling, and will. So that all the faults—so-called—committed by individuals and communities have proceeded from their *not knowiug better.* Even the crucifixion of the founder of Christianity is ascribed, in the New Testament to this cause. "I wot," says St. Peter, "that ye did it ignorantly." This point receives irresistible confirmation on every hand. The vast proportion of crimes of violence, such as wife-beating, garotte-robbery, manslaughter, and murder, are confined for the most part to one class of society—those who live beyond the pale of education and refinement, agencies by which feelings of decency and humanity are fostered. And the only cause of the difference between this social *stratum* and the one above it is that the training of the better class of people is favourable to the controlling of their passions, at least as regards the commission of crimes of that hue. The sexual vices, again, are not confined to *any* particular social grade. They are probably indulged in as great a ratio by the well-to-do as by the lower orders. But if we compare the victims of licentiousness, of whatever social grade, with the philosophic and the devout who have been taught to hold these vices in abhorrence, we here, again, find the same rule hold good. The culture of the pure-minded has been specially directed to the instructing of the mind in the bad consequences of this sort of vice, and to the habituating of the mind to the moderation and government of animal appetencies. In like manner the difference between the false ideas and practices of many at one period of their lives, and their improved ideas and practices at another, lies alone in the fact that they have come to know better.

The drift of this reasoning is plain. The ever-widening circle of knowledge, the knowledge of manifold truth in physics and morals, is the grand power by which the upward march of Humanity is to be secured. But, as has been already observed, knowledge, considered as the great curative principle, is not a mere fortuitous concourse of facts, however good and useful in themselves, thrown into the mind, any more than food is muscular strength. Our diet must first become assimilated with the tissues; and so knowledge, which strengthens, renovates, and elevates, is the concentrated essence of principles which the thoughtful mind extracts from any given collection of facts. This representation of the case is as consoling as it is true; for it reveals a "silvery lining" in the cloud of prevailing human suffering, which inspires joy and hope as we contemplate the future of the world. It is a law of nature that every common bane should carry with it a common antidote, and a careful inspection of history makes it clear that it is the tendency of each separate species of error and wrong-doing *to wear itself out*. The discovery of imperfection, usually made through enduring the painful results thereof, leads towards perfection in every department of human interests. Every dis-

The Mystery of Evil. 37

comfort, physical and moral, that vexes the lot of man, reaches a crisis; human effort is immediately braced up to grapple with the crisis, and inventive brains are excited to devise expedients for its removal. Thus have all social and political improvements been effected.

The method of viewing the problem of evil which has been adopted in the preceding pages is the only one compatible with an unruffled state of mind in presence of the defects of our race that frequently offer us such bitter provocation in daily life—bigotry, cruelty, stupidity, selfishness, ingratitude, and pride. A wise man once remarked ironically: "There are words in Scripture that afford me unspeakable consolation when I have to encounter a person who is unreasonable and unjust. 'Every creature after its kind.' If such a man attempts to over-reach or insult me; if he show treachery or unkindness; if he deceive or malign me, I look at him with pity, and my sympathy for his misfortune in inheriting a defective organisation, or in lacking efficient intellectual and moral discipline, neutralises the anger I should otherwise feel towards him." Thus the practical philosopher remains undisturbed by the turbulent passions that blind and warp the minds of the mass, who are affected chiefly by superficial effects, the causes of which they have not the patience or the capacity to discriminate.

When the principles that have been enunciated become intelligently and generally recognised, they will not fail to produce a revolution in our whole system of dealing with vice and legislating for crime. The popular way of treating offences of all kinds at present is as absurd as it would be, after the fashion of our ancestors, to carry a bay-leaf as a preventive of thunder, or to remove scrofula by hanging round the neck a baked toad in a silk bag. Social irregularities of whatever kind, in a more rational age, will no longer be visited with inflictions of corporeal pain, whether deficient nourishment, the application of the *cat*, confinement in a dismal cell, imposition of aimless grinding labour or chains. Far less will the murderous propensity to kick or beat or stab or poison a fellow-creature, be punished by so preposterous an instrument as the gallows or the guillotine. When acts of violence against society come to be viewed as the result of an imperfect nature or deficient knowledge and culture, care will be taken by the State to lay hold of the child through the influence of the school, and insist by compulsion on every citizen from tender years being taught the laws, social and legal, under which he is expected to live. And when any are found in riper years to give suspicion that the lessons of their youth are overborne by innate bad tendencies, public opinion, then enlightened as it will be by science, will, in a spirit of philosophic sympathy for the misfortune of the wrong-doer, demand his prompt separation for a time, at least, from his more fortunate neighbours, and his subjection before any extreme manifestation of his propensity accrues, to a beneficent *régime*, partly educational and partly medical, to enable him, as far as possible, to obtain the mastery over his besetting morbid tendencies, and merit a place once more, if possible, among well-conducted members of the community. The attempt, as now, to set the world right by teaching theological dogmas and by the agitations of revivalistic or ritualistic fanaticisms, or by the existing *lex talionis* of our criminal law, is mere ridiculous and wasteful tinkering. To permit a system of commerce which offers the worst temptations for the commission of fraud and fosters a heartless competition,* that often drives the honest and the weak to the wall, and then

---

* The noble-souled Robert Owen used to denounce it as "that monster, *competition;*" and by the way, it is worthy of remark, that the evident tendency of social reform now is in the very wake of the

The Mystery of Evil. 39

to treat as outcasts the victims of intemperance and poverty which this unnatural system contributes to produce, and punish them with the degradation of the jail or the workhouse, is as senseless and cruel as to sanction gins and snares in the highway and then whip men for falling into them. These social absurdities, arising from crass ignorance of the constitution of man, and of physical and moral law, cannot last for ever. They may be hallowed by prestige, pompous judicial ceremony, and Parliamentary precedent, but they belong to a transitional stage of social life which is *doomed* before the triumphs of science and philosophy. The old shallow and mischievous scheme of reformation which exhibits a jealous Deity consigning wrong-doers to eternal death and the magistrate as "a terror to evil-doers," will be superseded by a method of government in which the revolting penal code now practised by civilised nations will have no place, and in which, without exception, the reform of the offender will be the supreme consideration, while the peace and safety of society will be found to be promoted thereby. And surely such happy anticipations for the race are a satisfactory compensation for the sacrifice truth compels us to make in parting with the illusions of our intellectual childhood,—the dogmas of a personal God and a self-determining will.

The world is, indeed, racked and torn by selfishness, cruelty, ignorance, and folly. Communities and individuals have writhed under burdens of sorrow from the beginning. But manifestly the *natural tendency* of physical and moral law is not to produce

---

system of Owen which the "respectable classes" used to smile at as *Utopian*. Most intelligent men are either tacitly or openly coming round to the persuasion that "Man is the Creature of Circumstances." Mr. Owen probably inadvertently left out certain *factors*, indispensable to the success of his "New Moral World." But he has pointed out for us the only true path, and the failure of his scheme was a grand success.

these effects, but quite the contrary; and the complete happiness of the race is to be attained through the knowledge of law and yielding submission to it. But this great consummation can only be accomplished by slow degrees. A thousand years in this business is "as a watch in the night." If it should be asked, why should this training to perfect virtue and happiness be so slow and painful, and why should such slow and painful discipline be the only safe and solid basis on which the progress of humanity can be established, there is no answer except that in the nature of things it must be so. Suppose that we were living on some fair and perfect planet when the earth was in its once fluid state, and that we saw the huge animals belonging to that geological period wallowing in the mire and obscured by the dense fogs which then enveloped the half-formed world. If that had been our first introduction to the present abode of man we should probably have concluded, had we no previous experience of such a state of things elsewhere, that a world of sea and mud, with volcanoes ever and anon spouting forth their lava and steamy vapours shutting out the light, could never become fitted for human habitation. But this, nevertheless, was the elemental chaos, out of which our globe was, in the course of countless ages, evolved. So the present development of the moral world bears some analogy to the physical state of the earth in the primeval ages. It is still very gradually emerging out of its original intellectual and moral formlessness, and is yet a long way from the harmony and beauty with which humanity will, in future ages, be crowned. For any one, therefore, to judge of the tendency and goal of the universe from the seething troubles and pangs that harass the world's life now in its slow transition state, would be as rash as for the imagined spectator of the chaotic earth before man came upon it to

The Mystery of Evil. 41

suppose that it could never be built up into a habitable world. The error consists in judging the whole circle of material and moral development by the very small segment of the circle which we have an opportunity of seeing. But a retrospect of human history justifies the assurance that in nature there underlies all present contradictions and incompatibilities, a moulding principle that will eventually transmute all incongruities into palpable consistency. The very tardiness, therefore, of the process by which humanity is to attain its highest possible life may be taken as a guarantee for the permanent advance of that life when it is realised. It is not for us now living, or for immediately succeeding generations to participate in this Elysium of prophetic forecast, at least in our present state of existence; but instead of moping over our inevitable fate, and groaning over the woes of the world, it is more becoming cultured manhood to bear that fate with philosophic fortitude, make the best of it, and help our fellow-mortals to do the same. The idea of "the Colossal Man," first worked by a great German writer, and repeated in the retracted essay of Dr. Temple, looks in the direction to which these remarks point. Humanity must be viewed *as a whole*. Particular nations may decay, but *man* is destined to rise to a higher plane of being. For an indefinitely long period he is kept under the tutelage of grievous trials, which, in the wonderful economy of nature, have the effect of unfolding and invigorating his powers, that he may rise to the highest possible knowledge, and use that knowledge in correcting his faults, so that at length he may be brought into perfect accord with his own noblest moral ideal, and with the general progressive movement of the universe. Even if, for scores of thousands of years, vast continents and islands of savage or semi-barbarous people live and then perish, there is no waste. Neither is there waste anywhere in the laboratory of nature's forces. Had we seen the germs which afterwards developed into primeval forests, when these germs were just beginning to sprout in the bare rocky earth, we could not have dreamt of so mighty a use in store for them. But could we come back to the spot centuries afterwards when these tiny beeches and pines had grown into giant trees, the function of the insignificant germs would be obvious. The yearly shedding of the leaves of the trees into which they have grown has covered with mould the once barren surface in which they were planted, and supplied land suitable for the sowing of our crops. So the primeval trees in the forest of humanity, the first races, to all appearance not worth the power expended on their existence and support; these early races and tribes—so unproductive for ages—have been permitted to shed their millions of human leaves to make soil in the moral world. The barbarism that once reigned over the greater part of the earth is a pledge, in the arrangements of nature, that humanity will never, as a whole, return to barbarism again. The child cannot grow into the shrewd, cautious, enterprising man, but through the tumbles and bruises of childhood and the mistakes of passionate youth. Our measured intelligence, charity, and tolerance in the present century, has grown out of the ignorance, superstition, and intolerance of all the ages that have preceeded. The primitive races were allowed to live a life of low civilisation, and so by the picture of wretchedness they present for the warning of those who come after them, prove at once a beacon of warning and an effectual safeguard against the higher races that come after, sinking back to the same condition. The same consoling reflection applies to all the pains and discomforts which the good and the bad alike suffer in our present condition. These untoward circumstances, dark though they be, are not a mere waste of power,

The Mystery of Evil. 43

but mark an epoch in universal progress—needful, disciplinary, transitional, leading to grander issues,—to universal conformity to the standard of universal harmony. If in this unique development the interests of individuals and races,—whose lot happens to be cast in the early or intermediate periods of that development,—are not so favoured as those of mankind will be in the happier and more remote future, such a consideration is subordinate, and not to be named in comparison with the final result—the expansion, culture, and coherent use of all the faculties of humanity, the extinction of disease, want, strife, and suffering of every kind ; and if such an end is only to be gained, for a permanence, through physical and moral suffering in preceding ages of the world, the result may possibly well repay the cost. Nay, I think science justifies me in going farther. I might venture to add that the trials to which individuals and nations have ever been exposed in this life are introductory to a state of being *beyond the present*, when the island earth will be one in spirit with the invisible "summer-land," when free and pleasant communion between the embodied in the former state, and the disembodied in the latter, will be possible, when the sea of material and moral discord that now divides the one state from the other will be dried up, and when the last speck of imperfection that sullied the purity and splendour of regenerated humanity will be effaced.

In the immortal words of our Laureate :

> " O ! yet, we trust that somehow good
> Will be the final goal of ill,
> To pangs of nature, sins of will,
> Defects of doubts and taints of blood ;
>
> That nothing walks with aimless feet;
> That not one life shall be destroyed,
> Or cast as rubbish to the void,
> When *Nature makes* the pile complete.

That not a worm is cloven in vain,
That not a moth with vain desire
Is shrivelled in a fruitless fire
Or but subserves another's gain.

Behold we know not anything—
I can but trust that good shall fall
At last—far off—at last—to all,
And every winter change to spring."

ON THE EXISTENCE OF EVIL.

ON THE EXISTENCE OF EVIL.

BY THE LATE

REV. JAMES CRANBROOK,

EDINBURGH.

PUBLISHED BY THOMAS SCOTT,
NO. 11, THE TERRACE, FARQUHAR ROAD,
UPPER NORWOOD, LONDON, S.E.

Price Threepence.

ON THE EXISTENCE OF EVIL.

THE existence of evil has constituted a problem which men's speculative intellect has attempted to solve ever since speculation began. Throughout all the world there are suffering, pain and death. The young, the beautiful and the prosperous, no less than the aged, deformed and poor, are subject to them. The brightest prospects suddenly become clouded, the dearest hopes are dashed to the ground, the intensest enjoyments suddenly are turned into wormwood and gall, the most promising career ends in disaster. And it is not the immoral and irreligious alone that thus suffer; the virtuous and pious are equally the victims. The same thing happeneth to the just and the unjust.

Nor can the evil always be traced to causes which might have been avoided. It is sometimes inevitable, at all events inevitable by us. The elements of nature may combine against us—movements in society which work the general good may produce our ruin—friends may prove foes by their very friendliness. And even if we could trace all suffering to our own moral defects it would only be putting the question a step further back. Whence these moral defects? how came they into the world? how did they originate? and why are they not remedied? It is perplexing and full of mystery.

I may have something to say upon the method in which the question should be dealt with, towards the conclusion, but for the present I wish to call your attention to the way in which it was dealt with in ancient times. And it is with the oriental method I am now more concerned. Evil did not present itself to the Greeks in those same despairing colours that it appeared to the Orientals in. They lived in the enjoyment of the present, a free happy life; and nature seemed to them full of beauty and gladness. When the subject of evil came before them therefore, it came in a tempered form, and they were calmer to answer it than the Orientals were. Besides that, we know very little of Grecian thought and speculation before the scientific spirit had begun to dawn upon them. Consequently when their authentic history begins the primitive beliefs are already modified and come before us considerably toned down. Yet that they felt the existence of evil a very mysterious problem their tragedians very impressively testify. They resolved it, however, all into the operations of a dark fatality, of which there was none to give an account, and which lay beyond the control alike of gods and men.

It was in later and more corrupt times that the notion arose that evil comes from the envy of the gods —a notion however, which could only arise out of a sense of prevalent happiness. The authentic history of the Hebrews begins about the time of the Babylonian captivity, but we get some glimpses into their theological conceptions before that time. So far as their sacred books inform us, however, the subject of evil does not seem to have weighed very heavily upon their minds. The account given in Genesis of its introduction into Paradise must have originated in very primitive, that is barbarous times, and has very much the appearance of being an importation from some foreign source. None but the rudest people could have imagined that tale about the serpent's tempting Eve and the curse subsequently pronounced upon the reptile. And the account seems never to have made any very deep impression on the Hebrew mind, or to have recurred in their history until a much later period. For we can hardly take the very contradictory myth of Moses healing the children of Israel by a brazen serpent as having any reference to the one in Paradise. And yet this narrative in Genesis seems the only attempt to explain the origin of evil until the period of the prophets, if we can say an attempt was made then. But the truth is, we know so little of the Jews during the intervening period that it is difficult to say what their thoughts and speculations were. The book of Job indeed is wholly composed for the purpose of discussing this question of evil; but in the first place, it belongs to the period of the Babylonian captivity and in the second place it has been doubted whether it is Jewish in its origin at all. My own opinion is in favour of its late Chaldaic or Hebrew origin. For the introductory part which is anti-Hebraic, giving that account about Satan appearing before God and bringing evil upon Job, is no integral part of the book, and it is most noteworthy that whilst in those introductory two chapters all Job's evils are directly attributed to Satan, in the remaining forty chapters he and his doings are not once referred to as offering any solution of the mystery of evil, but the evil is directly and immediately, after the Hebrew method, referred to God.

At the time of the Jewish captivity, however, a new element was introduced into the Hebrew theology,—the doctrine of evil spirits. I do not mean to deny that they had some notions of their existence before; for they naturally arise amongst nearly all barbarous people, and it is difficult to suppose the Hebrews escaped. But during the captivity and after, the doctrine became elaborated, and henceforth formed a more and more prominent feature in their theology. It is generally said they derived these notions from the Persians. It is certain they brought them from Babylon. Amongst both Babylonians and Persians, and indeed the whole of those nations lying round about the regions of the Euphrates, these speculations concerning the source of evil occupied a very large measure of thought. Natural constitution and temperament acted on by climate, and the vicissitudes of their ever-changing fortune seem to have forced them upon them. I can here only refer to the doctrine by which the Persians attempted to solve the mystery. Evil is so mingled with the good that the only explanation seemed to them to be, that there are two creators and rulers of the world, the one evil and the other good; that these two rulers are perpetually at strife with each other; that as the one prevails good follows, as the other prevails evil follows; and this strife will go on until at last the good will prevail over the evil, and the evil spirit will be held in eternal bondage. I am not clear whether the notion of a yet higher existence than these two creators whose interference ultimately ends their strife, is of so early a date as that I am now referring to; but the probability, at all events, is that it did not belong to the original conception of the theory. Now each of these creative spirits has caused to emanate from himself other spirits through whom he carries on the government of the world, the good spirit giving existence to angels, the evil spirit giving existence to devils or demons.

Now it is clear the Hebrews could only embrace this doctrine in a modified form, and probably the Chaldaeans only held it in a modified form, since, if we may trust tradition, the doctrine of the divine unity came from them. Be that however as it may, those who held, as the Hebrews held, the strict doctrine of Monotheism, could only hold the doctrine respecting the evil spirit and his emanations in a very subordinate sense. The evil spirit must be a creation of the Supreme, and therefore if not originally good, he can at all events have no power beyond what the Supreme permits him to exercise. Only one passage in the Old and New Testaments that I recollect refers to the fall of these evil spirits from a primitively purer state; but the Jews had determined their whole history long before the canon of the New Testament closed. In First Chron. chap. xxi. ver. 1, Satan is said to have stood up against

On the Existence of Evil. 9

Israel, and provoked David to number Israel. This book of Chronicles belongs to the age after the Babylonian captivity, and strikingly illustrates the later growth of this doctrine of evil spirits; for in Second Samuel chap. xxiv. ver. 1, which is a more early composition than that of Chronicles, God himself is said to have been the instigator of David; and that is much more in accordance with the purer Hebrew idea. In the writings of the Apocrypha most of which belongs to the centuries immediately preceding the New Testament books, the doctrine of evil spirits comes out much more prominently, and you are enabled by a careful study to trace its growth with tolerable accuracy up to New Testament times.

I need not say how prominent the doctrine is made in the New Testament. Satan is invested with all but infinite powers, and all evil is traced up to his agency. The account given us of the temptation of Christ at the beginning of his ministry is one of the most extraordinary and extravagant conceptions in the world, and yet it is evident how deeply it laid hold of the Hebrew mind from the repetition of it in the three books of the evangelists. There, as you will recollect, Satan appears in person, and not only tempts Christ, but carries him sailing through the air to a pinnacle of the temple, and then whirls him away to the top of an exceeding high mountain, whence he shews him all the kingdoms of the world in an instant, the Indian, Persian, Roman, extending from the far east to the British Isles. The rationalists say, this was only a vision; but that shews, first, the rationalists will say anything to get out of a difficulty; and secondly, their ignorance of Jewish literature, which makes it plain that there would be nothing extravagant in this narrative to the Jewish mind. The Jews then could have believed more absurd things than this, if any one could have invented anything more absurd about the Devil. And therefore when the plain and evident meaning is the literal one, it is as immoral as it is unscientific to seek for any other.

In the writings ascribed to St Paul, we find the doctrine of evil spirits employed to account for nearly all evil. The chief of these spirits is the "prince of the power of the air working in the children of disobedience," "the God of this world, blinding the minds of them which believe not," and, with his hosts, he constitutes the "principalities and powers" against whom all spiritual warfare has to be maintained. All not regenerated are "the children of the devil," and "his seed remaineth in them," so that they cannot cease from sin. Here you see is a trace of the old Persian doctrine of Satan's part in the creation of the world. Wicked souls are created by the evil spirit—and have their wickedness. The notions respecting these evil spirits were taken up thus into the Christian Church and developed there with the same absurdities that we find amongst the later Jews. Some of the Rabbi contended that they were created by God with all their evil propensities, on the second day of the work of creation at the same time that hell was created. Others that their creation was on the sixth day, and that God originally intended to provide them with bodies, but that immediately on the creation of their spirits the Sabbath commenced, so that there was no time to complete this part of the work.

I must here make what may seem almost like a digression to tell you a rabbinical story about Lilith, but which also accounts for the origin of evil spirits. Modern critics have noticed a contradiction between the narrative given of the creation of woman in the first and second chapters of Genesis. In the first she appears to have been created at the same time with Adam, and in the same way. In the second she is created after him and out of his side. Now the Rabbi saw the contradiction but explained it easily. They are in fact the narratives of two distinct creations, said they. First of all God did create a woman out of the dust of the earth along with Adam. Her name was Lilith. But as soon as created, she began, like some modern ladies, to contend about her rights. Adam said, It behoves thee to be obedient; I am to rule over thee. Nay, said Lilith, we are on a perfect equality, for we were both formed out of the same earth. So neither would submit to the other. But Lilith finding she was getting the worst of it, pronounced the Shemhamphorash—*i.e.*, the forbidden name Jehovah. Instantly she was carried away through the air and became the mother of the evil spirits. God, to console Adam, afterwards created Eve out of his rib.

Amongst all barbarous people that have any idea of the supernatural at all the conception of evil spirits is found. It seems to the barbarous mind the natural counter-part of the notion of good spirits, and is as necessary to explain existent evil as that of good spirits is to explain existent good. Many of these nations pay far more attention to the worship of the evil one than they do to the worship of the good, because I presume fear is a more predominant feeling with them than trust.

But now, it is a curious and not uninstructive inquiry, how comes it to pass that so many people, apparently quite independent of each other, conceived this method of explaining the existence of evil, both physical and moral? Nay, that many people, and some of them those who are called well educated, in the present day cling to this method still? That even if we grant the existence of evil spirits, it would be no solution of the problem of evil, any thoughtful person I should think can discern. It would only remove the difficulties a step further back. For if evil spirits lead men to evil, how came they to be allowed such a power, and how came they to be evil? The Persian doctrine can be the only ultimate one in this direction, and that cuts the knot of the difficulty but does not untie it.

Now, it seems to me easy enough to account for the

method, for it arises out of the same principle as
fetishism, polytheism and all those animations of the
objects of nature which prevail in rude and barbarous
periods. The tendency of all uncultured minds is to
ascribe their own qualities to all the active powers in
nature. And hence every thing seems to them moved
by will, and is possessed of consciousness. By and
by a little culture slightly modifies this tendency.
As the natural object gives no sign of feeling, its
possession of volition begins also to be questioned.
Then comes the second, the polytheistic stage, when
the moving power, the will, and the consciousness are
supposed to reside not exactly in the natural objects
themselves but in genii or spirits belonging to them,
All nature is still instinct with life, but it is a life also
above and besides nature. It is at this period the
notion of evil spirits arises. Before, the natural object
that brought the evil was in men's apprehension the
person who did it and was blamed. Now, it is the
spirit that moves the object for the purpose of inflicting
the evil. And when once the notion of an evil spirit,
above and beyond the object in nature which brings to
one evil is conceived, every terror, every calamity
multiplies the number and increases the dread of them.
Our great poet has supplied us with the illustration of
this in the "Midsummer Night's Dream" when Puck
frightens away the mechanics of Athens by introducing
their companion with an ass's head on his shoulder.

> When they him spy,
> As wild geese that the creeping fowler eye,
> Or russet-pated choughs, many in sort,
> Rising and cawing at the gun's report,
> Sever themselves and madly sweep the sky,
> So at his sight away his fellows fly :
> And, at our stamp, here o'er and o'er one falls ;
> He murther cries, and help from Athens calls.
> *Their sense thus weak, lost with their fears thus strong,*
> *Made senseless things begin to do them wrong ;*
> For *briers and thorns* at their apparel snatch ;
> Some sleeves ; some hats ; *from yielders*
> ALL THINGS CATCH.

On the Existence of Evil.   13

Now this is precisely the principle. Fear converts the briers and thorns, catching their garments as they flee, into spirits dwelling in the bushes, overpowers their senses, and drives them headlong before unseen beings. And so before terrible calamities men became overwhelmed with fear, and construed the calamities as the work of evil spirits. It is the advance of science which has expelled these evil spirits from the domain of the physical world, and which is expelling them from the domain of the mental world. In the physical world the work is almost complete, so far as the Western nations are concerned. What was formerly considered the result of the agency of good and bad spirits, angels and demons, is now proved to be the effect of natural forces acting according to fixed and unchanging laws. Storms, plagues, earthquakes, and such like things are now reduced to the categories of science, and the demons are exorcised from them. A nation visited with pestilence, and an old woman who has lost her cow, no longer think it the work of the devil, but know it is traceable to some natural cause.

The same cannot be said with the like extent of the domain of mind. There are numbers, and some of them so-called educated people, who not only believe in the existence of evil spirits, but also that they have power over the human mind to suggest evil thoughts, and to arouse evil passions. The reason that the notion lingers so much longer in the domain of mind is quite evident. Thought and feeling have only of late been made the objects of scientific enquiry, and perceived to be subject to law. The metaphysicians here have ruled with few to dispute their sway, and whilst they have not been slow to admit the existence of law in the order of the suggestion of thought and the excitement of feeling, their dogmas concerning the freedom of the will have overridden this law, and after all made it a fitful uncertain thing. But the more rigid investigations of modern biologists having reduced thought, feeling, and will to the condition of functions of animal life, have made them as severely subject to natural law as any of the physical functions are. Thought and feeling originate in a definite order, and by a force strictly correlated with nerve force. There is no room left therefore for the play of evil spirits; and of necessity they become superannuated. But this knowledge has not yet become widely spread, and those ignorant of it are therefore left free to the play of their fancies or the indulgence of their credulity. As soon as fancy becomes chastened by knowledge they too will lay aside such creations for facts.

But now, abandoning such a method of accounting for evil, where are we? What other shall we adopt? I shall not enter into the metaphysical explanations, which are numerous. None of them can possibly satisfy the mind, for they rest on no basis of fact, and often seem nothing better than a cloud of obscure words from which one cannot draw one ray of light. It avails nothing to be told that "evil is good in making," that it is "the negation of good, and arises out of the imperfection necessarily characterizing all finite things," and that it is "the permitted means by which God raises us to a higher condition." Such phrases explain nothing. They leave the facts only more obscured. Failing therefore all methods of explanation allow me to urge upon you the only wise course left open to us. And that is to give up all quest into the mystery, and just deal with the facts as they are so as to remedy the evil. All those teleological questions about the design the creator had in this thing and in that; the questions about the reasons of this and the other, are idle and absurd. We know nothing of what lies beyond us, in regions our senses cannot penetrate. We know nothing of God's mind, designs, or aims, beyond what is actually done in nature. Let our theories therefore be ever so well constructed upon mere ideas and fancies—they remain nothing but ideas and fancies still, and these are not worth one moment's care so long as they are not tested by facts. And there would be no practical good, even supposing it were possible, in solving such a question as the origin and the reason of evil. It would not make the pressure of the evil one whit the less. It would not give us one particle of help towards removing its pressure. What we really want to know is those laws of nature by observing of which we may prevent the evil, or if it come remedy it. And that, whether we speak of physical or moral evil, we can only do by the direct and careful study of nature—nature I mean in her physical and moral aspects. And the long ages that have been wasted in speculations about demons and evil spirits, or in metaphysical fancies, are chiefly to be regretted as so much time gone which might have been devoted to the pursuit of this useful knowledge, had men but cared more for facts than fancies, and known how limited their powers are. But their absurdities and failures may teach us wisdom if we be wisely inclined. Let us give up the foolish fanciful pursuits of our fathers. Let us take the world as we find it—let us study the order of its phenomena, and the imposed conditions of human well-being and happiness. And then, although we may leave the mysteries of evil unsolved, we shall daily become more free from the evil.

THOUGHTS

ON

THE EXISTENCE OF EVIL.

BY

PROFESSOR F. W. NEWMAN.

PUBLISHED BY THOMAS SCOTT,
MOUNT PLEASANT, RAMSGATE.

Price Threepence.

My Dear Scott,
	I do not know whether you will take interest in this paper, which, in preparing to change my abode, I have routed out of a drawer. You will observe that it is dated 1841. At that time I had gone far from "the creed of the Reformers," but had not quite cut the last cords that bound me to the idea of Supernaturalism.— Yours ever, F. W. N.
	June 9th 1872.

THOUGHTS ON THE EXISTENCE OF EVIL.

IT is impossible to extend inquiry and contemplation ever so little beyond the bounds of ordinary thought, without discerning how crude and untenable is the popular conception of divine Omnipotence. The child who is informed that God is Almighty, asks in great simplicity, why then does God let any body be unhappy? We may unhesitatingly deduce, that there is a real contrariety between the divine perfections, as conceived of by the child, and the existence of any evil. With the same logical force, though with more rudeness, some have alleged that the deity ought to have made man other than he is. Nor has the highest intellect and deepest piety ever essayed even to modify and relieve the difficulty, except by suggestions drawn from the topics of Optimism. It is said, " Perhaps the allwise God sees that *it is best* so to be: he sees ends to be obtained, *which could not be obtained so well* in any other way; and which are valuable enough to deserve being bought at such a price." In different forms, this is substantially the meaning of all that the humble and pious can adduce. Whether learned or unlearned, philosophic or simple, the topic to which they refer us, is, "*Perhaps* the Allwise God saw that there was *no better way.*"

A sentiment, even conjectural, which comes to us recommended by such authority, cannot be deemed rash and profane. If it is impious, what else is more pious? Is it not the zealous effort of piety to shelter and defend its own existence? It is, and whether it be a just sentiment or not, at any rate it is devotional and humble. And yet, let us examine what it virtually means. The evil which God has either ordained or permitted is partly moral and partly physical; yet this, it is suggested, was probably seen by him to be the best means of attaining some eminently good end. Now it cannot be intended to imply that he thinks slightly of moral evil; an idea subversive of reverence for his holy character, and degrading him into one who will employ wicked means to compass his purposes. It must remain, that the argument intends to say, that inscrutable limitations exist in the divine power, which could never have been suspected until the broad facts proclaimed it; so that the deity had to submit necessarily, at least for a time, to a state of things contrary to his mind, as an essential prerequisite towards the attaining of a glorious end beyond.

A recent essayist, whose work has attracted more than usual notice, the Rev. Henry Woodward, has forced prominently forward the fact, that nearly all our reasonings concerning the *Wisdom* of God imply some limitation of his power. To a being, Omnipotent in the gross and popular sense, wisdom must be wholly useless, and in fact becomes in him an unintelligible quality. As policy is superfluous, to a conqueror who can apply overwhelming force, so is wisdom superseded by omnipotence. We admire the adaptation of lungs to air, and of air to the lungs, on the supposition that a difficult problem has been proposed,—how to free the blood from noxious particles? But if we are asked, "why might not the divine *fiat* have done it as well?" one reply alone is to be had,—that there are other objects to be gained by adhering to the general laws of matter, which objects *could not* have been so well gained by a direct exertion of divine power. If otherwise, there would be no intelligible wisdom in employing a circuitous, rather than a direct method of effecting the end. The like may be observed in every other case. Hence, wisdom and power are in one sense antagonistic qualities; the more you enlarge the sphere of the latter, the more you diminish that of the former; and every time we ascribe wisdom to the divine agent, we virtually imply some unknown limitation to his power, and deny the existence of almightiness in its vulgar sense.

To ignorant persons, who have imbibed with their devotional feelings the popular idea of omnipotence, it is apt to appear a profane thing to assert, that it is not within the power of the Almighty to recall the past; or, to construct a square which shall have the properties of a circle. But all thoughtful and philosophical minds have long been aware, that that which is self-contradictory does not lie within the sphere of power; and that it is no degradation to the Almighty that he cannot make the same thing both to be and not to be.

It being then certain, that limitations to the operations of his power may exist, and do exist, which the thoughtful of our race can discern, but of which the ignorant and unthinking are not aware; we may presume that other limitations possibly exist, which no human mind would guess at à *priori*, and which may, as yet, be concealed from all. And it has appeared, that an analysis of every argument which ascribes wisdom to the deity, manifests that there is a secret conviction in all religious minds of the *reality* of that which has been just called a presumption. Applying such principles to the creation of intelligent and free beings like man, we presently fall upon the conception, that to be able to love God, man needed to be able to hate him; if free to go right, man is free also to go wrong. At present it is enough to assert, that it is at least a plausible opinion that the two sorts of ability are inseparable. It is *not only* unproved that to create a being capable of holiness without being liable to sin, is within the sphere of divine power; but the *prima facie* aspect of the case is the reverse, tending to convince us that the very idea is as self-contradictory as that of a square circle. For when we try to analyse the notion of freedom, or indeed of holiness, we find it essentially implies a power of sin. For who would call a man honest, who had no natural power to be dishonest? or meek, who was physically unable to be angry? or humble, who could not help his humility? and so of all other moral excellences. Every one of them implies a προαίρεσις or *free choice*; and they not only could not be praised, but could not even exist; for it would not be a soul if there were no freedom. A liability to go wrong is then essentially inseparable from a capacity to go right, as much as convexity from concavity. They are little more than the same thing viewed from opposite sides. We do not praise a stone image of Xenocrates for temperance; for it cannot be gluttonous; and we do not blame a hog for gluttony or a fox for theft, for they are incapable of the virtues of temperance and of honesty.

Now if this does not wholly satisfy any one, let it be at least allowed that the opinion is not wholly imaginary or absurd, but that it has a measure of probability. That probability appears at once to be turned into practical certainty by the powerful testimony of matter of fact on the same side. We *do* find, to an amazing and appalling extent, moral disorder spread over the whole world as known to us; and the greatest difficulty is met in accounting for such a phenomenon within the realm of so beneficent and wise a ruler as we believe to superintend the earth. The fact forces on all pious contemplators the conviction, that, in some sense or other, *he could not help it*, consistently with the attaining of some paramount ends. If it is a physical difficulty which he could not overcome, that no doubt tends to degrade our conception of divine power; but if it is a metaphysical difficulty, not at all. On the contrary, our own minds are in fault for having invented an absurdity, and then proposed it as a problem for his power to effect. The latter is at once both the alternative to which the case itself points us, and that which preserves the honour of the divine attributes. It does then appear to have as much proof as have any of the received propositions of natural theology, that *to create a being capable of having a holy will, essentially implies the endowing him with a power to sin ;* and that even almighty power cannot separate the two, since the idea is self-contradictory.

If this is conceded, the first great question pressing on us is; "whether the evils resulting from the creation of man, as a being capable of holiness, are so enormous, as to outweigh all the conceivable advantages." We cannot set aside this, by imagining some metaphysical necessity to have forced the deity to the creation of mankind; without falling into a system of mere fatalism. It would make out, that he is not our voluntary creator, but is himself a kind of tool or machine in the hands of destiny; and by breaking the moral connection between the creator and his creatures, would appear to subvert all intelligent piety. Nor indeed can the intellect approve such a conception, any more than does our devotional feeling; for what can be a more unmeaning phrase, than that God should create us by necessity, and without his own choice? Forced then to regard the act as chosen deliberately and voluntarily on his part, we cannot help urgently desiring some ground to believe, that the contingent evils thence resulting are slight in comparison with the good. To suppose either that he knew they would outweigh the good, or that his foresight was defective, and that he did not know how great they would prove, would grievously impair our conception either of the goodness or of the wisdom of God.

It is useless to deny that the doctrine of eternal misery, whether as popularly understood, or as philosophically explained, spreads an impenetrable cloud over the whole divine character. It matters not whether we conceive of God as exerting a direct act of judgment, to torture in everlasting flames the vast majority of the human race; or whether the wicked are to endure countless and never-ending agonies from accusing conscience and evil passions. The two doctrines possess in common the FACT of everlasting misery and everlasting sin, in appalling and ever increasing intensity; and this, to a vast majority of the children of Adam. Even if the last point were omitted, yet if there be millions on whom this horrible lot would fall, the human heart seems incapable of conceiving how this awful evil can ever be a desirable purchase money for some greater good; but we are forced back on the inevitable persuasion, that it had been better that man had never been created. Nay, could we realize what eternal sin and eternal agony mean, perhaps we should conclude that such suffering and such moral evil to a single individual would be too great a price to pay for the everlasting blessedness and perfection of all the rest of our race. No generous mind,—or rather, no heart not harder than flint,—could desire to purchase for itself a heaven at the price of a hell to its brother; but would wish a thousand times over that not one of the family had ever come into existence. Such is the unconstrained utterance of ordinary human feeling; and if we are *not* to ascribe the like to the supreme creator, if we are to suppose his strength of mind such, that he does not flinch from bringing about the welfare of the few, by results so appalling to the many; devotion is crushed into superstition, and adoration ceases to be intelligent. No effort can be made to dispel the darkness resting on the character of the most high, if the doctrine of eternal punishment, in the philosophical and exact sense of the term *eternal*, is true.

It is, however, certain, that one who is contemplating the facts of the world with the eye of a natural theologian, will not encumber himself with this doctrine. It is, if sanctioned by Christianity, a load to be supported by the credit of "revelation;" a new diffi-

Thoughts on the Existence of Evil. 9

culty introduced, of which we know nothing from a contemplation of nature : and in this case it must be allowed, that so far from bringing us " good news," and clearing up the difficulties which distressed faith and perplexed intellect, Christ has brought us the worst news we could possibly have had, worse than the wildest misanthrope could have imagined, and has intensely aggravated all pre-existing perplexities. In short, whatever is the amount of evidence testifying to the truth of the Christian revelation, it might seem an obvious axiom that it is the duty of every good man, as it must be the impulse of every humane man, earnestly to hope that Christianity may turn out to be a fiction, rather than that this doctrine should be true : and this circumstance loads it with so enormous an improbability, as would suffice to overturn all intelligent faith in the doctrine, were it even far better supported by Scriptural evidence than it is.

Supposing then that this doctrine is set aside, let us recur to the question, whether evil (physical and moral) may not ultimately prove a sort of evanescent quantity, in comparison to the good. The first step towards this will assuredly be taken, if it is believed that *the evil is temporary, the good eternal.* Now, to this, the general spirit of the Christian Scriptures strongly testifies ; nor are there wanting special texts bearing on this result. All sin is regarded as of the nature of *corruption;* and is counted as " of this age ;" while all righteousness and goodness is regarded as both coming down from God, and as partaking of his nature, which is incorruption and eternity. To the same conclusion both conscience and philosophy point. From the very necessity of the case, inexperience appears to draw after it errors ; we make allowance for the indiscretions of youth : we should think it inhuman to wish a man to be punished to his dying day for his early offences. Moreover, the punishment which they draw after them has a very perceptible tendency to correct and improve the man. It would be unwise to desire that sin should not tend to bring after it misery; for it would be to lose a wholesome instructor: but as we must wish the punishment to be only in due measure, and to cease after it has annihilated that of which it was the chastisement, so we have the testimony of experience, that this is ordinarily the case. Man being himself finite, his sin is not infinite in its effects on others, nor on himself; and if not always remediable, yet it tends to self-exhaustion. All virtue and goodness, being self-consistent, strengthen continually with growth : but vices in every shape are opposed to one another, and though occasionally they may strengthen each other, the contrary happens far oftener. Indeed, in different men, vices are in the long run obviously and surely opposed, and wear each other out in many ways. Now the fact is (however it be explained) that man comes into this world with intellect and conscience wholly unformed, and he has to be built up into a moral and spiritual being. It would be more reasonable to expect a person to be able to swim before entering the water, than to expect a human being to learn to go right, without ever going wrong. But if in manhood we look back with a smile and without pain at the sorrows of childhood, so also do we look back without shame or remorse at the peevishness, greediness, impatience, or other follies incident to that age ; nay, nor does any sound minded man feel humbled at the faults of youth, when they are merely the necessary defects of that age, and not his own personal and peculiar transgressions—I mean, such defects as the being too sanguine and ardent, hasty and imprudent, too ready to form friendships and to trust strangers, too vehement in love and in expectation, somewhat too confident of one's own opinion. Just in proportion as any of these were a voluntary transgression, they will call for and produce humiliation, but no further. But again, whatever may have been our past sufferings, yet when at last we obtain honourable and permanent repose, the remembrance of them is rather pleasant ; and if they have brought us spiritual improvement, we

Thoughts on the Existence of Evil.

may well count them a real good. No amount then of mere outward suffering, not connected with our own sin, during this short life, need cause the slightest difficulty in our present argument. All evil is ultimately annihilated, in comparison with the good. As concerns the moral evil in which each of us may have been involved, no one can repine and justly regret, if the fire which burns in the soul from this cause is fierce and gnawing. If remorse do its work, and the man learn to go softly all his days in the bitterness of his soul; he will only the better learn that sin stingeth as a serpent and biteth as an adder. In fact, as regards the mass of mankind, perhaps no wise man would desire to have the tormenting power of remorse lessened. Nevertheless, as in the case of slight transgressions,— an unkind word—a proud thought—a selfish neglect of another—there is a soothing of the conscience, when contrition has wrought its results,—confession and restitution; so of greater offences there may be a genial repentance, quite unlike mere remorse, and where there is, some ultimate lesson may be taught both to the offender himself and to others : and though it is not to be imagined that it is better to him to have gone wrong, than to have been both wise enough and good enough to go right, yet his sin may in the end be a mere process of rising higher; just as the false notes on a violin are but a state of transition towards better play. Hence even the worst cases of guilt become reconcilable with the divine wisdom in ordaining the present scene of things : for in short, though all are transgressors, yet at the worst one portion is led on towards moral perfection and consequent happiness ; and another portion, if it does not attain this, yet at some period ceases to exist. No difficulty arises, except on the belief that the sin and misery of the latter is unsubdued and everlasting. Exclude this conception ;—believe that goodness alone is eternal; and it remains clearly intelligible, how the divine wisdom may have ordained, on the one hand, that man should gain a stable independent holy will, so as to be capable of friendship with his infinite creator; but that, on the other hand, this essentially demanded that he should be left free to sin, and consequently moral evil has abounded and abounds, but only for a time. Sin and its effects, remorse and misery, are to be abolished, and the fruit of holiness shall flourish to everlasting life.

But it will be inquired, is not this, after all, to maintain, that the holy God uses base and unholy means to work out his designs? Does it not confound our sense of moral distinctions, and make evil to be good when it tends to a good end, if the view above given is correct? This objection exerts a force that is hard to account for upon many minds; for it does not seem to have any intrinsic weight. It might seem to have been borrowed from the barbaric reasoning of King Agamemnon in Homer, or from a bye-gone Predestinarian school, whose doctrine annihilated all human agency, and imputed to the deity the acts of all men. Certainly such a doctrine makes it impossible to defend the moral character of our creator. If vice and cruelty are bad, and he is as truly responsible for their existence, as though he were the immediate agent, there is an end of reasoning. The tyrant may justify himself, by saying, that when he oppresses, he is only the tool by which God scourges men. But the first principle of all intelligent worship recognizes in ourselves a power to resist the will of God, which constitutes *sin* against him. It is in extravagant inconsistency with this first principle, to imagine that because God gives us the power to sin, therefore God ordains the sin and is responsible for it. If with reverence we may use the phrase, we may say that he *is* responsible for the *general result* of investing us with such a power. Consistently with goodness and wisdom, he must have foreseen that in the long-run this arrangement was beneficent; and consistently with justice, he must have provided that no individual should suffer disproportionately, beyond his deserts, from such an arrangement. But this may

Thoughts on the Existence of Evil.

co-exist with a steady upholding of the belief in his fixed hatred of moral evil. A wise father will give his son an allowance of pocket money, in order that he may learn to spend judiciously: and even when he sees him about to employ it foolishly, he will not check him, deeming it better that he should learn by experience, than by dictation. Without alleging that the cases are *perfectly* parallel, this suffices to put into a clear light the fact, that to make a beneficial disposal of affairs, well knowing that the parties so invested with power will partially abuse it, is quite consistent with the purest disapproval of such abuse. All that is needed to justify him who so ordains, is, a clear belief that in no other way will so good a total result be gained.

In this light we must look on the men who are generally regarded as the scourges of mankind. Who can read without shuddering the atrocities of a Timour or an Attila? Indeed, in the latter, it appears less frightful from his very savageness. We judge of him as a wild beast, rather than as a man. But Timour was a legislator and a would-be reformer. Alexander the Great was eminent for political intellect. Our question, however, is not, What are we to think of the *men?* but, How are we to vindicate the divine providence which permits their action? It does not seem to be difficult, after the above. Indeed, an Attila may be classed with earthquakes or volcanoes; fearful visitations not caused by moral evil; and no one who holds that these physical evils are consistent with divine goodness (partly as the results of good laws impressed on nature, partly, as directly remedial) will find much difficulty in believing the same of Attila. But wĕ may go further. Not only is it certain that we should injure man's nature, if we could wholly extinguish ambition; certain, that the flame which in Alexander or Napoleon burned to intense and baneful fury, is in its milder forms quite essential to man's welfare: but it is credible, that, if we did but know the alternative possibilities (which we never can know), we might find that the permanent good effected (blindly) by Alexander, by Julius Cæsar, by Napoleon, far more than out-balances their evil. We may even venture to believe, that, until mankind is otherwise more perfect, it is beneficial on the whole that men of unbridled ambition do exist, and will exist. This is God's great influence for fusing into one the separated tribes of the human race by conquest; the method by which the superior energies and talents of one nation are ultimately diffused over another : and although it produces countless miseries on the way, inasmuch as the conquerors are not *aiming* at good or concerned to use virtuous methods (and this is their sin), yet an extensive survey of human history will convince any well-judging mind, that our race would never have attained its present elevation or its present prospects of improvement, if ambition had always been thwarted before it could overflow in conquest.

It is striking to contemplate the analogy offered us in the whole field of nature, as to *the slow progress* of whatever is to be *ultimately great*. In the botanical world it has been long proverbial, that vast growths are slow; and the discoveries of geology magnificently illustrate the saying. But there is another aspect from which the same facts may be viewed. In one sense, the material universe may be called always the same. Having the same repulsions and attractions and the same material masses, only the same phenomena (it might seem) must for ever recur, did not *organic life* break in to disturb the monotony. The influx of vegetable forms introduces wonderful variety; yet each vegetable in itself is, within near limits, ever like itself; nor does any improvement in the individual, nor much in the species, take place. Moral growth is the last and most complicated of organic growths. If ferns took many thousand years to perfect themselves, it is but little to allow a hundred thousand years to man.

ON THE
DEITY OF JESUS OF NAZARETH.

AN ENQUIRY
INTO THE NATURE OF JESUS
BY AN EXAMINATION OF THE SYNOPTIC GOSPELS.

BY
THE WIFE OF A BENEFICED CLERGYMAN.
EDITED AND PREFACED BY
REV. CHARLES VOYSEY, B.A.

PUBLISHED BY THOMAS SCOTT,
NO. 11 THE TERRACE, FARQUHAR ROAD, UPPER NORWOOD,
LONDON, S.E.

1873.

LONDON:
PRINTED BY C. W. REYNELL, LITTLE PULTENEY STREET,
HAYMARKET, W.

EDITOR'S PREFACE.

THE following pages were put into my hands by a lady—the wife of a beneficed clergyman. Not wishing to compromise her husband, she has withheld her name from publication, and deserves all honour for the concession. But the fact led me to write a few words as a Preface, in which I would remind the Bishops and dignitaries of our Church that this is no uncommon case. Orthodoxy is riddled through and through with heresy. Every family has its heretic. And although but few clergymen or their wives could be found to write such an Essay as the following with equally felicitous logic and simplicity, there are many quite capable of relishing arguments so lucidly stated and so ably drawn. If most of Mr Scott's regular readers are familiar with the line of argument, there are many outside the circle whom this pamphlet may reach to whom it will be new, and whom it may powerfully affect.

The position which the person of Jesus occupies in modern Christendom is the very citadel of Christianity, and on the settlement of his claims will turn the future of the Churches.

We, who have been all our lives sceptics, are growing weary of the very name; but we must not forget that we have a great duty to perform towards those who are yet orthodox, or are clinging, like some Unitarians, to the skirts of a fading system.

When I first knew this lady, she had given up all points of disputed orthodoxy except this one of the nature of Jesus, whom she still regarded as perfect and divine. Careful and independent study of the whole question, however, led her at length to see the facts clearly—to own them to herself in spite of strong predilections the other way—and to write them down here for the benefit of others.

In the course of this change I was appealed to for an authoritative opinion. I absolutely refused to give one. I refused to be made the means of shovelling second-hand opinions into any one's mind. All I said was—"If you believe Christ to be God, stick to it: you are not obliged to believe as I do. Only make up your mind for yourself." This was no case of converting or proselytising. It was one of independent growth and natural conviction.

There are hundreds of clergymen, and clergymen's wives too, who are fast treading the same road, if they have not yet reached the same goal.

The alarmists are quite right. *Christianity is in terrible danger.* We wish we could add—*in extremis;* but when the break up of a faith has begun with its teachers, with those most interested in its being maintained, the days of that faith are numbered.

Such little works as this Essay, if well placed and well digested, will do more to open people's eyes than many a more pretentious and elaborate treatise.

CHARLES VOYSEY.

Camden House, Dulwich, S.E., March, 1873.

ON THE
DEITY OF JESUS OF NAZARETH.

"WHAT think ye of Christ, whose son is he?" Human child of human parents, or divine Son of the Almighty God? When we consider his purity, his faith in the Father, his forgiving patience, his devoted work among the offscourings of society, his brotherly love to sinners and outcasts—when our minds dwell on these alone, we all feel the marvellous fascination which has drawn millions to the feet of this "son of man," and the needle of our faith begins to tremble towards the Christian pole. If we would keep unsullied the purity of our faith in God alone, we are obliged to turn our eyes some times—however unwillingly—towards the other side of the picture and to mark the human weaknesses which remind us that he is but one of our race. His harshness to his mother, his bitterness towards some of his ópponents, the marked failure of one or two of his rare prophecies, the palpable limitation of his knowledge—little enough, indeed, when all are told,—are more than enough to show us that, however great as man, he is not the All-righteous, the All-seeing, the All-knowing, God.

No one, however, whom Christian exaggeration has not goaded into unfair detraction, or who is not blinded by theological hostility, can fail to revere portions of the character sketched out in the three synoptic gospels. I shall not dwell here on the Christ of the fourth Evangelist: we can scarcely trace in that figure the lineaments of the Jesus of Nazareth whom we have learnt to love.

I propose, in this essay, to examine the claims of Jesus to be more than the man he appeared to be during his life-time: claims—be it noted—which are put forward on his behalf by others rather than by himself. His own assertions of his divinity are to be found only in the unreliable fourth gospel, and in it they are destroyed by the sentence there put into his mouth with strange inconsistency: "If I bear witness of myself, my witness is not true."

It is evident that by his contemporaries Jesus was not regarded as God incarnate. The people in general appear to have looked upon him as a great prophet, and to have often debated among themselves whether he were their expected Messiah or not. The band of men who accepted him as their teacher were as far from worshipping him as God as were their fellow-countrymen: their prompt desertion of him when attacked by his enemies, their complete hopelessness when they saw him overcome and put to death, are sufficient proofs that though they regarded him—to quote their own words—as "a prophet mighty in word and deed," they never guessed that the teacher they followed, and the friend they lived with in the intimacy of social life, was Almighty God Himself. As has been well pointed out, if they believed their Master to be God, surely when they were attacked they would have fled to him for protection, instead of endeavouring to save themselves by deserting him: we may add that this would have been their natural instinct, since they could never have imagined beforehand that the Creator Himself could really be taken captive by His creatures and suffer death at their hands. The third class of his contemporaries, the learned Pharisees and Scribes, were as far from regarding him as divine as were the people or his disciples. They seem to have viewed the new teacher somewhat contemptuously at first, as one who unwisely persisted in expounding the highest doctrines to the many, instead

Jesus of Nazareth. 7

of—a second Hillel—adding to the stores of their own learned circle. As his influence spread and appeared to be undermining their own,—still more, when he placed himself in direct opposition, warning the people against them,—they were roused to a course of active hostility, and at length determined to save themselves by destroying him. But all through their passive contempt and direct antagonism, there is never a trace of their dreaming him to be anything more than a religious enthusiast who finally became dangerous: we never for a moment see them assuming the manifestly absurd position, of men knowingly measuring their strength against God, and endeavouring to silence and destroy their Maker. So much for the opinions of those who had the best opportunities of observing his ordinary life. A "good man," a "deceiver," a "mighty prophet," such are the recorded opinions of his contemporaries: not one is found to step forward and proclaim him to be Jehovah, the God of Israel.

One of the most trusted strongholds of Christians, in defending their Lord's Divinity, is the evidence of prophecy. They gather from the sacred books of the Jewish nation the predictions of the longed-for Messiah, and claim them as prophecies fulfilled in Jesus of Nazareth. But there is one stubborn fact which destroys the force of this argument: the Jews, to whom these writings belong, and who from tradition and national peculiarities, may reasonably be supposed to be the best exponents of their own prophets, emphatically deny that these prophecies are fulfilled in Jesus at all. Indeed, one main reason for their rejection of Jesus is precisely this, that he does not resemble in any way the predicted Messiah. There is no doubt that the Jewish nation were eagerly looking for their Deliverer when Jesus was born; these very longings produced several pseudo-Messiahs, who each gained in turn a considerable following, because each bore some resemblance to the expected Prince. Much of the popular rage which swept Jesus to his death was the re-action of disappointment after the hopes raised by the position of authority he assumed. The sudden burst of anger against one so benevolent and inoffensive can only be explained by the intense hopes excited by his regal entry into Jerusalem, and the utter destruction of those hopes by his failing to ascend the throne of David. Proclaimed as David's son, he came riding on an ass as king of Zion, and allowed himself to be welcomed as the king of Israel: there his short fulfilling of the prophecies ended, and the people, furious at his failing them, rose and clamoured for his death. Because he did *not* fulfil the ancient Jewish oracles, he died: he was too noble for the *rôle* laid down in them for the Messiah, his ideal was far other than that of a conqueror, with "garments rolled in blood." But even if, against all evidence, Jesus was one with the Messiah of the prophets, this would destroy, instead of implying, his Divine claims. For the Jews were pure monotheists; their Messiah was a prince of David's line, the favoured servant, the anointed of Jehovah, the king who should rule in His name: a Jew would shrink with horror from the blasphemy of seating Messiah on Jehovah's throne, remembering how their prophets had taught them that their God "would not give His honour to another." So that, as to prophecy, the case stands thus: If Jesus be the Messiah prophesied of in the old Jewish books, then he is not God: if he be not the Messiah, Jewish prophecy is silent as regards him altogether, and an appeal to prophecy is absolutely useless.

After the evidence of prophecy Christians generally rely on that furnished by miracles. It is remarkable that Jesus himself laid but little stress on his miracles; in fact, he refused to appeal to them as credentials of his authority, and either could not or would not work them when met with determined unbelief. We must notice also that the people, while "glorifying God, who had given such power unto *men*," were not inclined to admit his miracles as proofs of his right to claim absolute obedience: his miracles did not even invest him with such sacredness as to protect him from arrest and death. Herod, on his trial, was simply anxious to see him work a miracle, as a matter of curiosity. This stolid indifference to marvels as attestations of authority, is natural enough, when we remember that Jewish history was crowded with miracles, wrought for and against the favoured people, and also that they had been specially warned against being misled by signs and wonders. Without entering into the question whether miracles are possible, let us, for argument's sake, take them for granted, and see what they are worth as proofs of Divinity. If Jesus fed a multitude with a few loaves, so did Elisha: if he raised the dead, so did Elijah and Elisha; if he healed lepers, so did Moses and Elisha; if he opened the eyes of the blind, Elisha smote a whole army with blindness and afterward restored their sight: if he cast out devils, his contemporaries, by his own testimony, did the same. If miracles prove Deity, what miracle of Jesus can stand comparison with the divided Red Sea of Moses, the stoppage of the earth's motion by Joshua, the check of the rushing waters of the Jordan by Elijah's cloak? If we are told that these men worked by *conferred* power and Jesus by *inherent*, we can only answer that this is a gratuitous assumption and begs the whole question. The Bible records the miracles in equivalent terms: no difference is drawn between the manner of working of Elisha or Jesus; of each it is sometimes said they prayed; of each it is sometimes said they spake. Miracles indeed must not be relied on as proofs of divinity, unless believers in them are prepared to pay divine honours not to Jesus only, but also to a crowd of others, and to build a Christian Pantheon to the new found gods.

So far we have only seen the insufficiency of the usual Christian arguments to establish a doctrine so stupendous and so *primâ facie* improbable, as the incarnation of the Divine Being: this kind of negative testimony, this insufficient evidence, is not however the principal reason which compels Theists to protest against the central dogma of Christianity. The stronger proofs of the simple manhood of Jesus remain, and we now proceed to positive evidence of his not being God. I propose to draw attention to the traces of human infirmity in his noble character, to his absolute mistakes in prophecy, and to his evidently limited knowledge. In accepting as substantially true the account of Jesus given by the evangelists, we are taking his character as it appeared to his devoted followers. We have not to do with slight blemishes, inserted by envious detractors of his greatness; the history of Jesus was written when his disciples worshipped him as God, and his manhood, in their eyes, reached ideal perfection. We are then forced to believe that, in the Gospels, the life of Jesus is given at its highest, and that he was, at least, not more spotless than he appears in these records of his friends. But here again, in order not to do a gross injustice, we must put aside the fourth Gospel: to study his character "according to S. John" would need a separate essay, so different is it from that drawn by the three; and by all rules of history we should judge him by the earlier records, more especially as they corroborate each other in the main.

The first thing which jars upon an attentive reader of the Gospels is the want of affection and respect shown by Jesus to his mother. When only a child of twelve he lets his parents leave Jerusalem to return home, while he repairs alone to the temple. The fascination of the ancient city and the gorgeous temple services was doubtless almost overpowering to a thoughtful Jewish boy, more especially on his first visit: but the careless forgetfulness of his parents' anxiety must be considered as a grave childish fault, the more so as its character is darkened by the indifference shown by his answer to his mother's grieved reproof. That no high, though mistaken, sense of duty kept him in Jerusalem is evident from his return home with his parents; for had he felt that "his Father's business" detained him in Jerusalem at all, it is evident that this sense of duty would not have been satisfied by a three days' delay. But the Christian advocate would bar criticism by an appeal to the Deity of Jesus: he asks us therefore to believe, that Jesus, being God, saw with indifference his parents' anguish at discovering his absence; knew all about that three-days' agonised search (for they, ignorant of his divinity, felt the terrible anxiety as to his safety, natural to country people losing a child in a crowded city); did not, in spite of the tremendous powers at his command, take any steps to re-assure them; and, finally, met them again with no words of sympathy, only with a mysterious allusion, incomprehensible to them, to some higher claim than theirs, which, however, he promptly set aside to obey them. If God was incarnate in a boy, we may trust that example as a model of childhood: yet, are Christians prepared to set this "early piety and desire for religious instruction" before their young children as an example they are to follow? Are boys and girls of twelve to be free to absent themselves for days from their parents' guardianship under the plea that a higher business claims their attention? This episode of the childhood of Jesus should be relegated to those "gospels of the infancy" full of most unchildlike acts, which the wise discretion of Christendom has stamped with disapproval. The same want of filial reverence appears later in his life: on one occasion he was teaching, and his mother sent in, desiring to speak to him: the sole reply recorded to the message is the harsh remark: "Who is my mother?" The most practical proof that Christian morality has, on this head, outstripped the example of Jesus, is the prompt disapproval which similar conduct would meet with in the present day. By the strange warping of morality often caused by controversial exigencies, this want of filial reverence has been triumphantly pointed out by Christian divines; the indifference shown by Jesus to family ties is accepted as a proof that he was more than man! Thus, conduct which they implicitly acknowledge to be unseemly in a son to his mother, they claim as natural and right in the Son of God, to His! In the present day if a person is driven by conscience to a course painful to those who have claims on his respect, his recognised duty, as well as his natural instinct, is to try and make up by added affection and more courteous deference for the pain he is forced to inflict: above all, he would not wantonly add to that pain by public and uncalled-for disrespect.

The attitude of Jesus towards his opponents in high places was marked with unwarrantable bitterness. Here also the lofty and gentle spirit of his whole life has moulded Christian opinion in favour of a course different on this head to his own, so that abuse of an opponent is now commonly called *un*-Christian. Wearied with three years' calumny and contempt, sore at the little apparent success which rewarded his labour, full of a sad foreboding that his enemies would shortly crush him, Jesus was goaded into passionate denunciations: "Woe unto you, Scribes and Pharisees, hypocrites ... ye fools and blind ... ye make a proselyte twofold more the child of hell than yourselves ... ye serpents, ye generation of vipers, how can ye escape the damnation of hell!" Surely this is not the spirit which breathed in, "If ye love them

Jesus of Nazareth.

which love you, what thanks have ye? ... Love your enemies, bless them that curse you, pray for them that persecute you." Had he not even specially forbidden the very expression, "Thou fool!" Was not this rendering "evil for evil, railing for railing?"

It is painful to point out these blemishes: reverence for the great leaders of humanity is a duty dear to all human hearts; but when homage turns into idolatry, then men must rise up to point out faults which otherwise they would pass over in respectful silence, mindful only of the work so nobly done.

I turn then, with a sense of glad relief, to the evidence of the limited knowledge of Jesus, for here no blame attaches to him, although *one* proved mistake is fatal to belief in his Godhead. First as to prophecy: "The Son of man shall come in the glory of his Father with his angels: and then shall he reward every man according to his works. Verily I say unto you, There be some standing here which shall not taste of death till they see the Son of man coming in his kingdom." Later, he amplifies the same idea: he speaks of a coming tribulation, succeeded by his own return, and then adds the emphatic declaration: "Verily I say unto you, This generation shall not pass till all these things be done." The non-fulfilment of these prophecies is simply a question of fact: let men explain away the words now as they may, yet, if the record is true, Jesus did believe in his own speedy return, and impressed the same belief on his followers. It is plain, indeed, that he succeeded in impressing it on them, from the references to his return scattered through the epistles. The latest writings show an anxiety to remove the doubts which were disturbing the converts consequent on the non-appearance of Jesus, and the fourth Gospel omits any reference to his coming. It is worth remarking in the latter, the spiritual sense which is hinted at—either purposely or unintentionally—in the words, "The hour . . . *now* is when the dead shall hear the voice of the Son of God, they that hear shall live." These words may be the popular feeling on the advent and resurrection, forced on the Christians by the failure of their Lord's prophecies in any literal sense. He could not be mistaken, *ergo* they must spiritualise his words. The limited knowledge of Jesus is further evident from his confusing Zacharias the son of Jehoiada with Zacharias the son of Barachias: the former, a priest, was slain in the temple court, as Jesus states; but the son of Barachias was Zacharias, or Zechariah, the prophet.* He himself owned a limitation of his knowledge, when he confessed his ignorance of the day of his own return, and said it was known to the "Father only." Of the same class of sayings is his answer to the mother of James and John, that the high seats of the coming kingdom "are not mine to give." That Jesus believed in the fearful doctrine of eternal punishment is evident, in spite of the ingenious attempts to prove that the doctrine is not scriptural: that he, in common with his countrymen, ascribed many diseases to the immediate power of Satan, which we should now probably refer to natural causes, as epilepsy, mania, and the like, is also self-evident. But on such points as these it is useless to dwell, for the Christian believes them on the authority of Jesus, and the subjects, from their nature, cannot be brought to the test of ascertained facts. Of the same character are some of his sayings: his discouraging "Strive to enter in at the strait gate, *for* many," etc.; his using in defence of partiality Isaiah's awful prophecy, " that seeing they may see and not perceive," etc.; his using Scripture at one time as binding, while he, at another, depreciates it; his fondness for silencing an opponent by an ingenious retort: all these things are blameworthy to those who regard him as man, while they are

* See Appendix, page 20.

Jesus of Nazareth. 15

shielded from criticism by his divinity to those who worship him as God. Their morality is a question of opinion, and it is wasted time to dwell on them when arguing with Christians, whose moral sense is for the time held in check by their mental prostration at his feet. But the truth of the quoted prophecies, and the historical fact of the parentage of Zachariah, can be tested, and on these Jesus made palpable mistakes. The obvious corollary is, that being mistaken—as he was—his knowledge was limited, and was therefore human, not divine.

In turning to the teaching of Jesus (I still confine myself to the three Gospels), we find no support of the Christian theory. If we take his didactic teaching, we can discover no trace of his offering himself as an object of either faith or worship. His life's work, as teacher, was to speak of the Father. In the sermon on the Mount he is always striking the keynote, "your heavenly Father;" in teaching his disciples to pray, it is to "Our Father," and the Christian idea of ending a prayer "through Jesus Christ" is quite foreign to the simple filial spirit of their master. Indeed, when we think of the position Jesus holds in Christian theology, it seems strange to notice the utter absence of any suggestion of duty to himself throughout this whole code of so-called Christian morality. In strict accordance with his more formal teaching is his treatment of inquirers: when a young man comes kneeling, and, addressing him as "Good Master," asks what he shall do to inherit eternal life, the loyal heart of Jesus first rejects the homage, before he proceeds to answer the all-important question : "Why callest thou *me* good : there is none good but one, that is, God." He then directs the youth on the way to eternal life, and *he sends that young man home without one word of the doctrine on which, according to Christians, his salvation rested.* If the "Gospel" came to that man later, he would reject it on the authority of Jesus who had told him a different "way of salvation;" and if Christianity is true, the perdition of that young man's soul is owing to the defective teaching of Jesus himself. Another time, he tells a Scribe that the first commandment is that God is one, and that all a man's love is due to Him; then adding the duty of neighbourly love, he says; "There is *none other* commandment greater than these:" so that belief in Jesus, if incumbent at all, must come after love to God and man, and is not necessary, by his own testimony, to "entering into life." On Jesus himself then rests the primary responsibility of affirming that belief in him is a matter of secondary importance, at most, letting alone the fact that he never inculcated belief in his Deity as an article of faith at all. In the same spirit of frank loyalty to God, are his words on the unpardonable sin : in answer to a gross personal affront, he tells his insulters that they shall be forgiven for speaking against him, a simple son of man, but warns them of the danger of confounding the work of God's Spirit with that of Satan, "because they said" that works done by God, using Jesus as His instrument, were done by Beelzebub.

There remains yet one argument of tremendous force, which can only be appreciated by personal meditation. We find Jesus praying to God, relying on God, in his greatest need crying in agony to God for deliverance, in his last struggle, deserted by his friends, asking why God, his God, had also forsaken him. We feel how natural, how true to life, this whole account is : in our heart's reverence for that noble life, that "faithfulness unto death," we can scarcely bear to think of the insult offered to it by Christian lips: they take every beauty out of it by telling us that through all that struggle Jesus was the Eternal, the Almighty, God : it is all apparent, not real : in his temptation he could not fall : in his prayers he needed no support: in his cry that the cup might pass away he foresaw it was inevitable: in his agony of desertion and loneliness he was present everywhere with God. In all that life, then, there is no hope for man, no pledge of man's victory, no promise for humanity. This is no *man's* life at all, it is only a wonderful drama enacted on earth. What God could do is no measure of man's powers: what have we in common with this " God-man ?" This Jesus, whom we had thought our brother, is, after all, removed from us by the immeasurable distance which separates the feebleness of man from the omnipotence of God. Nothing can compensate us for such a loss as this. We had rejoiced in that many-sided nobleness, and its very blemishes were dear, because they assured us of his brotherhood to ourselves: we are given an ideal picture where we had studied a history, another Deity where we had hoped to emulate a life. Instead of the encouragement we had found, what does Christianity offer us ?—a perfect life ? But we knew before that God was perfect: an example ? it starts from a different level: a Saviour ? we cannot be safer than we are with God: an Advocate ? we need none with our Father: a Substitute to endure God's wrath for us ? we had rather trust God's justice to punish us as we deserve, and His wisdom to do what is best for us. As God, Jesus can give us nothing that we have not already in his Father and ours: as man, he gives us all the encouragement and support which we derive from every noble soul which God sends into this world, " a burning and a shining light ":

> " Through such souls alone
> God stooping shows sufficient of His light
> For us in the dark to rise by."

As God, he confuses our perceptions of God's unity, bewilders our reason with endless contradictions, and turns away from the Supreme all those emotions of

love and adoration which can only flow towards a
single object, and which are the due of our Creator
alone: as man, he gives us an example to strive after,
a beacon to steer by; he is one more leader for
humanity, one more star in our darkness. As God,
all his words would be truth, and but few would enter
into heaven, while hell would overflow with victims:
as man, we may refuse to believe such a slander on
our Father, and take all the comfort pledged to us by
that name. Thank God, then, that Jesus is only man,
human child of human parents: that we need not
dwarf our conceptions of God to fit human faculties,
or envelope the illimitable spirit in a baby's feeble
frame. But though only man, he has reached a
standard of human greatness which no other man, so
far as we know, has touched: the very height of his
character is almost a pledge of the truthfulness of
the records in the main: his life had to be lived
before its conception became possible, at that period
and among such a people. They could recognise his
greatness when it was before their eyes: they would
scarcely have imagined it for themselves, more especially that, as we have seen, he was so different from
the Jewish ideal. His code of morality stands un-
rivalled, and he was the first who taught the universal
Fatherhood of God publicly and to the common
people. Many of his loftiest precepts may be found
in the books of the Rabbis, but it is the glorious
prerogative of Jesus that he spread abroad among
the many the wise and holy maxims that had hitherto
been the sacred treasures of the few. With him none
were too degraded to be called the children of the
Father: none too simple to be worthy of the highest
teaching. By example, as well as by precept, he
taught that all men were brothers, and all the good
he had he showered at their feet. " Pure in heart,"
he saw God, and what he saw he called all to see: he
longed that all might share in his own joyous trust in

Jesus of Nazareth. 19

the Father, and seemed to be always seeking for fresh images to describe the freedom and fulness of the universal love of God. In his unwavering love of truth, but his patience with doubters—in his personal purity, but his tenderness to the fallen—in his hatred of evil, but his friendliness to the sinner—we see splendid virtues rarely met in combination. His brotherliness, his yearning to raise the degraded, his lofty piety, his unswerving morality, his perfect self-sacrifice, are his indefeasible titles to human love and reverence. Of the world's benefactors he is the chief, not only by his own life, but by the enthusiasm he has known to inspire in others: " Our plummet has not sounded his depth :" words fail to tell what humanity owes to the Prophet of Nazareth. On his example the great Christian heroes have based their lives: from the foundation laid by his teaching the world is slowly rising to a purer faith in God. We need now such a leader as he was, one who would dare to follow the Father's will as he did, casting a long-prized revelation aside when it conflicts with the higher voice of conscience. It is the teaching of Jesus that Theism gladly makes its own, purifying it from the inconsistencies which mar its perfection. It is the example of Jesus which Theists are following, though they correct that example in some points by his loftiest sayings. It is the work of Jesus which Theists are carrying on, by worshipping, as he did, the Father, and the Father alone, and by endeavouring to turn all men's love, all men's hopes, and all men's adoration, to that " God and Father of all, who is above all, and through all, and," not in Jesus only, but " *in us all.*"

APPENDIX.

"Josephus mentions a Zacharias, son of Baruch ('Wars of the Jews,' Book iv., sec. 4), who was slain under the circumstances described by Jesus. His name would be more suitable at the close of the long list of Jewish crimes, as it occurred just before the destruction of Jerusalem. But, as it took place about thirty-four years after the death of Jesus, it is clear that he could not have referred to it; therefore, if we admit that he made no mistake, we strike a serious blow at the credibility of his historian, who then puts into his mouth a remark he never uttered."

"ACCORDING TO ST JOHN."

ON THE

DEITY OF JESUS OF NAZARETH.

PART II.

A COMPARISON BETWEEN THE FOURTH GOSPEL AND
THE THREE SYNOPTICS.

BY

THE WIFE OF A BENEFICED CLERGYMAN.

EDITED AND PREFACED BY

REV. CHARLES VOYSEY, B.A.

PUBLISHED BY THOMAS SCOTT,
NO. 11 THE TERRACE, FARQUHAR ROAD, UPPER NORWOOD,
LONDON, S.E.

1873.

Price Sixpence.

LONDON:
PRINTED BY C. W. REYNELL, 16 LITTLE PULTENEY STREET,
HAYMARKET, W.

PREFACE.

THE Gospel "according to St John" has long been regarded as the bulwark of the doctrine of the Deity of Jesus; but, apart from its controversial value, many Christians have prized it as the most precious of the New Testament treasures. It is easy to see that it favours not only the Deity of Jesus, but even his supremacy as an object of religious affection; that it flatters the "believers" by giving them exclusive privileges; that it draws hard and fast the line between the elect and the rest of the doomed world who are "the children of the Devil;" that it tends to awaken a sense of considerable obligation to Jesus, and thus to make him the special object of faith and love; that, therefore, it pushes God the Father into the background, and even renders Him superfluous. The present tone of popular Christianity is the very echo of this Fourth Gospel; and hardly any offence could be offered to Christians so great as to impugn the authority, or to reject the statements, of that book which is the foundation of their dogmas and the fountain of their unction.

It is on this account that, if thoroughly false and misleading, this Gospel ought to be most vigorously assailed. This is the author of so much mischief, of all that is most disgraceful and unhumanising in the Christian religion; and, therefore, it must be hunted down.

To paraphrase the old war cry of the king of Syria, we say to all true worshippers of God, fight neither with small nor great, neither with Matthew, Mark, or Luke, save only with John. Let him have no mercy, bring into daylight all his perverse and crooked sayings, all his bitterness and bigotry, all his contradictions, all his fictitious dialogues, and let the world hear what he really has said in this mendacious record, this pseudo-biography of Christianity. Let it be seen how, in his wild endeavour to exalt Jesus into a God, he has degraded and dishonoured that really ingenuous and truthful man.

My own repugnance to St John, and nearly all he ever wrote, dates from very early days, long before I knew that he was most probably the author of the Apocalypse. Almost my first revulsion against the words of Scripture was excited by that malevolent threat which closes the book of Revelation. "If any man shall add unto these things, God shall add unto him the plagues that are written in this book." "If any man shall take away from the words of the book of this prophecy, God shall take away his part out of the book of life, and out of the holy city, and from the things which are written in this book."

I well remember, as a little boy, longing to run the risk of the consequences by tearing out this leaf from my Bible; but I stood in wholesome terror of a whipping, and piously refrained.

Preface. v

Just such repugnance and defiance I feel today towards the greater part of this Fourth Gospel, inasmuch as it is the concentrated essence of dogmatism, bigotry, and persecution. Metaphorically speaking, I did tear out some of its leaves and exposed some of its malevolence; this time braving the curses and the whipping too. The latter I duly received at the hands of the Privy Council; (but I thoroughly enjoyed my piece of work), and I have not the shadow of an apprehension from any one or all of St John's anathemas, or from those of his followers. I would rather be damned with the many than saved with the few on such terms as he offers.

The charming treatise which I have the honour of introducing to the reader in the following pages has for its chief attractions order, simplicity, and clearness. There is no time wasted over the dry bones of controversy about authorship. The writer takes for granted that the Fourth Gospel is apostolic, and, having done so for the sake of argument, shows up the *animus* of its author, thus securing a double advantage—depraving the book itself, and giving a fresh proof that "apostolic" and "infallible" are not convertible terms. The book is shown to be bad; and, if any one says, "Oh, but it was written by an apostle," we have the pleasure of replying, "all the worse for the apostle."

Still we would not forget there are some really good things in it, and these we should be the last to throw away. They are the grains of wheat—sown by whatever hand—among heaps of chaff, and will yet bear good fruit. Here is a specimen, and let the reader say, when he has read this treatise, whether it be possible to reconcile this text with the rest of the Gospel in which it is found : " The hour is come when the true worshippers shall worship the *Father* in spirit and in truth, for the Father seeketh such to worship him." The authoress herself is a standing witness of the truth of another passage from the Fourth Gospel, which is, or ought to be, the motto for these times—" *The truth shall make you free.*"

I leave her admirable *critique* in the hands of the reader, assured beforehand that every one will be more or less convinced by it that the Gospel ought to be rejected on its own demerits. Those who are "more" convinced will be very grateful; those who are "less" so will bear witness to its power by being very angry.

CHARLES VOYSEY.

Camden House, Dulwich, S.E.,
June, 1873.

A COMPARISON

BETWEEN THE

FOURTH GOSPEL AND THE THREE SYNOPTICS.

EVERY one, at least in the educated classes, knows that the authenticity of the fourth gospel has been long and widely disputed. The most careless reader is struck by the difference of tone between the simple histories ascribed to Matthew, Mark, and Luke, and the theological and philosophical treatise which bears the name of John. After following the three narratives, so simple in their structure, so natural in their style, so unadorned by rhetoric, so free from philosophic terms,—after reading these, it is with a feeling of surprise that we find ourselves plunged into the bewildering mazes of the Alexandrine philosophy, and open our fourth gospel to be told that, "In the beginning was the word, and the word was with God, and the word was God." We ask instinctively, "How did John, the fisherman of Galilee, learn these phrases of the Greek schools, and why does he mix up the simple story of his master with the philosophy of that 'world which by wisdom knew not God?'"

The general Christian tradition is as follows: The spread of "heretical" views about the person of Jesus alarmed the "orthodox" Christians, and they appealed to John, the last aged relic of the apostolic band, to write a history of Jesus which should confute their opponents, and establish the essential deity of the founder of their religion. At their repeated solicitations, John wrote the gospel which bears his name, and the doctrinal tone of it is due to its original intention,—a treatise written against Cerinthus, and designed to crush, with the authority of an apostle, the rising doubts as to the pre-existence and absolute deity of Jesus of Nazareth. So far non-Christians and Christians—including the writer of the gospel—are agreed. This fourth gospel is not —say Theists—a simple biography of Jesus written by a loving disciple as a memorial of a departed and cherished friend, but a history written with a special object and to prove a certain doctrine. "St John's gospel is a polemical treatise," echoes Dr Liddon. "These are written that ye may believe that Jesus is the Christ, the Son of God," confesses the writer himself. Now, in examining the credibility of any history, one of the first points to determine is whether the historian is perfectly unbiassed in his judgment and is therefore likely to give facts exactly as they occurred, uncoloured by views of his own. Thus we do not turn to the pages of a Roman Catholic historian to gain a fair idea of Luther or of William the Silent, or expect to find in the volumes of Clarendon a thoroughly faithful portraiture of the vices of the Stuart kings; rather, in reading the history of a partisan, do we instinctively make allowances for the recognised bias of his mind and heart. That the fourth gospel comes to us prefaced by the announcement that it is written, not to give us a history, but to prove a certain pre-determined opinion, is, then, so much doubt cast at starting on its probable accuracy; and, by the constitution of our minds, we at once guard ourselves against a too ready acquiescence in its assertions, and become anxious to test its statements by comparing them with some independent and more impartial authority.

Jesus of Nazareth. 3

The history may be most accurate, but we require proof that the writer is never seduced into slightly—perhaps unconsciously—colouring an incident so as to favour the object he has at heart. For instance, Matthew, an honest writer enough, is often betrayed into most non-natural quotation of prophecy by his anxiety to connect Jesus with the Messiah expected by his countrymen. This latent wish of his leads him to insert various quotations from the Jewish Scriptures which, severed from their context, have a verbal similarity with the events he narrates. Thus, he refers to Hosea's mention of the Exodus : " When Israel was a child then I loved him and called my son out of Egypt," and by quoting only the last six words gives this as a " prophecy " of an alleged journey of Jesus into Egypt. Such an instance as this shows us how a man may allow himself to be blinded by a pre-conceived determination to prove a certain fact, and warns us to sift carefully any history that comes to us with the announcement that it is written to prove such and such a truth.

Unfortunately we have no independent contemporary history—except a sentence of Josephus—whereby to test the accuracy of the Christian records; we are therefore forced into the somewhat unsatisfactory task of comparing them one with another, and in cases of diverging testimony we must strike the balance of probability between them.

On examining, then, these four biographies of Jesus, we find a remarkable similarity between three of them, amid many divergences of detail. Some regard them, therefore, as the condensation into writing of the oral teaching of the apostles, preserved in the various Churches they severally founded, and so, naturally, the same radically although diverse in detail. " The synoptic Gospels contain the substance of the Apostles' testimony, collected principally from their oral teaching current in the Church, partly also from written documents embodying portions of that teaching."* Others think that the gospels which we possess, and which are ascribed severally to Matthew, Mark, and Luke, are all three derived from an original gospel now lost, which was probably written in Hebrew or Aramaic, and variously translated into Greek. However this may be, the fact that such a statement as this has been put forward proves the striking similarity, the root identity, of the three " synoptical gospels " as they are called. We gather from them an idea of Jesus which is substantially the same : a figure, calm, noble, simple, generous ; pure in life, eager to draw men to that love of the Father and devotion to the Father which were his own distinguishing characteristics ; finally, a teacher of a simple and high-toned morality, perfectly unfettered by dogmatism. The effect produced by the sketch of the Fourth Evangelist is totally different. The friend of sinners has disappeared (except in the narrative of the woman taken in adultery, which is generally admitted to be an interpolation), for his whole time is occupied in arguing about his own position ; " the common people " who followed and "heard him gladly " and his enemies, the Scribes and Pharisees, are all massed together as " the Jews," with whom he is in constant collision ; his simple style of teaching—parabolic indeed, as was the custom of the East, but consisting of parables intelligible to a child—is exchanged for mystical discourses causing perpetual misunderstandings, the true meaning of which is still wrangled about by Christian theologians ; his earnest testimony to "your heavenly Father" is replaced by a constant self-assertion ; while his command "do this and ye shall live," is exchanged for " believe on me or perish." " How great is the contrast between that discourse and the Sermon on the Mount. . . . In the

* Alford.

last discourse it is His Person rather than His teaching which is especially prominent. His subject in that discourse is Himself. Certainly he preaches Himself in His relationship to His redeemed; but still He preaches above all, and in all, Himself. All radiates from Himself, all converges towards Himself . . . . in those matchless words all centres so consistently in Jesus, that it might seem that Jesus Alone is before us."* These and similar differences, both of direct teaching and of the more subtle animating spirit, I propose to examine in detail; but before entering on these it seems necessary to glance at the disputed question of the authorship of our history, and determine whether, if it prove apostolic, it *must* therefore be binding on us.

I leave to more learned pens than mine the task of criticising and drawing conclusions from the Greek or the precise dogma of the evangelist, and of weighing the conflicting testimony of mighty names. From the account contained in the English Bible of John the Apostle, I gather the following points of his character: He was warm-hearted to his friends, bitter against his enemies, filled with a fiery and unbridled zeal against theological opponents; he was ambitious, egotistical, pharisaical. I confess that I trace these characteristics through all the writings ascribed to him, and that they seem to be only softened by age in the fourth gospel. That John was a warm friend is proved by his first epistle; that he was bitter against his enemies appears in his mention of Diotrephes, " I will remember his deeds which he doeth, prating against us with malicious words;" his unbridled zeal was rebuked by his master; the same cruel spirit is intensified in his " Revelation;" his ambition is apparent in his anxiety for a chief seat in Messiah's kingdom; his egotism appears in the fearful curse he imprecates on those who alter *his* revelation; his

* Liddon.

pharisaism is marked in such a feeling as, "we know *we* are of God, and the whole world lieth in wickedness." Many of these qualities appear to me to mark the gospel which bears his name; the same restricted tenderness, the same bitterness against opponents, the same fiery zeal for "the truth," *i.e.*, a special theological dogma, are everywhere apparent. The same egotism is most noticeable, for in the other gospels John shares his master's chief regard with two others, while here he is "*the* disciple whom Jesus loved," and he is specially prominent in the closing scenes of Jesus' life as the *only* faithful follower. We should also notice the remarkable similarity of expression and tone between the fourth gospel and the first epistle of John, a similarity the more striking as the language is peculiar to the writings attributed to John. It is, however, with the utmost diffidence that I offer these suggestions, well knowing that the greatest authorities are divided on this point of authorship, and that the balance is rather against the apostolic origin of the gospel than for it. I am, however, anxious to show that, *even taking it as apostolic*, it is untrustworthy and utterly unworthy of credit. If John be the writer, we must suppose that his long residence in Ephesus had gradually obliterated his Jewish memories, so that he speaks of "the Jews" as a foreigner would. The stern Jewish monotheism would have grown feebler by contact with the subtle influence of the Alexandrine tone of thought; and he would have caught the expressions of that school from living in a city which was its second home. To use the Greek philosophy as a vehicle for Christian teaching would recommend itself to him as the easiest way of approaching minds imbued with these mystic ideas. Regarding the master of his youth through the glorifying medium of years, he gradually began to imagine him to be one of the emanations from the Supreme of which he heard so much. Accustomed to the

Jesus of Nazareth. 7

deification of Roman emperors, men of infamous lives, he must have been almost driven to claim divine honours for *his* leader. If his hearers regarded *them* as divine, what could he say to exalt *him* except that he was ever with God, nay, was himself God ? If John be the writer of this gospel, some such change as this must have passed over him, and in his old age the gradual accretions of years must have crystallised themselves into a formal Christian theology. But if we find, during our examination, that the history and the teaching of this gospel is utterly irreconcilable with the undoubtedly earlier synoptic gospels, we must then conclude that, apostolic or not, it must give place to them, and be itself rejected as a trustworthy account of the life and teaching of Jesus of Nazareth.

The first striking peculiarity of this gospel is that all the people in it talk in exactly the same style and use the same markedly peculiar phraseology. (*a*) "The Father loveth the Son and hath given all things into his hand." (*b*) "For the Father loveth the Son, and showeth him all things that Himself doeth." (*c*) "Jesus, knowing that the Father had given all things into his hand." These sentences are evidently the outcome of the same mind, and no one, unacquainted with our gospel, would guess that (*a*) was spoken by John the Baptist, (*b*) by Jesus, (*c*) by the writer of the gospel. When the Jews speak, the words still run in the same groove : "If any man be a worshipper of God, and doeth His will, him He heareth," is not said, as might be supposed, by Jesus, but by the man who was born blind. Indeed, commentators are sometimes puzzled, as in John iii., 10-21, to know where, if at all, the words of Jesus stop and are succeeded by the commentary of the narrator. In an accurate history different characters stand out in striking individuality, so that we come to recognise them as distinct personalities, and can even guess beforehand how they will probably speak and act under certain conditions. But here we have one figure in various disguises, one voice from different speakers, one mind in opposing characters. We have here no beings of flesh and blood, but airy phantoms, behind whom we see clearly the solitary preacher. For Jesus and John the Baptist are two characters as distinct as can well be imagined, yet their speeches are absolutely indistinguishable, and their thoughts run in the same groove. Jesus tells Nicodemus: "We speak that we do know and testify that we have seen, and ye receive not our witness; and no man hath ascended up to heaven, but he that came down from heaven." John says to his disciples: "He that cometh from heaven is above all, and what he hath seen and heard that he testifieth, and no man receiveth his testimony." But it is wasting time to prove so self-evident a fact: let us rather see how a Christian advocate meets an argument whose force he cannot deny. "The character and diction of our Lord's discourses entirely penetrated and assimilated the habits of thought of His beloved Apostle; so that in his first epistle he writes in the very tone and spirit of those discourses; and when reporting the sayings of his former teacher, the Baptist, he gives them, consistently with the deepest inner truth (!) of narration, the forms and cadences so familiar and habitual to himself." * It must be left to each individual to judge if a careful and accurate historian thus tampers with the words he pretends to narrate, and thus makes them accord with some mysterious inner truth; each too must decide as to the amount of reliance it is wise to place on a historian who is guided by so remarkable a rule of truth. But further, that the "character and diction" of this gospel are moulded on that of Jesus, seems a most unwarrantable assertion. Through all the recorded sayings of Jesus in the three gospels, there is no trace

*Alford.

Jesus of Nazareth. 9

of this very peculiar style, except in one case (Matt. xi., 27), a passage which comes in abruptly and unconnectedly, and stands absolutely alone in style in the three synoptics, a position which throws much doubt on its authenticity. It has been suggested that this marked difference of style arises from the different auditories addressed in the three gospels and in the fourth; on this we remark that (*a*), we intuitively recognise such discourses as that in Matt. x. as perfectly consistent with the usual style of Jesus, although this is addressed to "his own;" (*b*), in this fourth gospel the discourses addressed to "his own" and to the Jews are in exactly the same style; so that, neither in this gospel, nor in the synoptics do we find any difference—more than might be reasonably expected —between the style of the discourses addressed to the disciples and those addressed to the multitudes. But we *do* find a very marked difference between the style attributed to Jesus by the three synoptics and that put into his mouth by the fourth evangelist; this last being a style so remarkable that, if usual to Jesus, it is impossible that its traces should not appear through all his recorded speeches. From which fact we may, I think, boldly deduce the conclusion that the style in question is not that of Jesus, the simple carpenter's son, but is one caught from the dignified and stately march of the oratory of Ephesian philosophers, and is put into his mouth by the writer of his life. And this conclusion is rendered indubitable by the fact above-mentioned, that all the characters adopt this poetically and musically-rounded phraseology.

Thus our first objection against the trustworthiness of our historian is that all the persons he introduces, however different in character, speak exactly alike, and that this style, when put into the mouth of Jesus, is totally different from that attributed to him by the three synoptics. We conclude, therefore, that the style belongs wholly to the writer, and that he cannot, consequently, be trusted in his reports of speeches. The major part, by far the most important part, of this gospel is thus at once stamped as untrustworthy.

Let us next remark the partiality attributed by this gospel to Him Who has said—according to the Bible—" *all* souls are Mine." We find the doctrine of predestination, *i.e.*, of favouritism, constantly put forward. "*All that the Father giveth me* shall come to me." "No man can come to me except the Father draw him." "That of all *which He hath given me* I should lose nothing." "Ye believe not, *because* ye are not of my sheep." "Though he had done so many miracles before them, yet they believed not on him: *that the saying* of Esaias the prophet *might be fulfilled.*" "*Therefore, they could not believe because* that Esaias said, &c." "I have chosen you out of the world." "Thou hast given him power over all flesh, that he should give eternal life to *as many as Thou hast given him.*" "Those that thou gavest me I have kept and none of them is lost, but the son of perdition, *that the Scripture might be fulfilled.*" These are the most striking of the passages which teach that doctrine which has been the most prolific parent of immorality and the bringer of despair to the sinner. Frightfully immoral as it is, this doctrine is taught in all its awful hopelessness and plainness by this gospel: some "*could not* believe" because an old prophet prophesied that they should not. So, "according to St John," these unbelieving Jews were pre-ordained to eternal damnation and the abiding wrath of God. They were cast into an endless hell, which "they *could not*" avoid. We reject this gospel, secondly, for the partiality it dares to attribute to Almighty God.

We will now pass to the historical discrepancies between this gospel and the three synoptics, following the order of the former.

It tells us (ch. 1) that at the beginning of his ministry Jesus was at Bethabara, a town near the junction of the Jordan with the Dead Sea; here he gains three disciples, Andrew and another, and then Simon Peter: the next day he goes into Galilee and finds Philip and Nathanael, and on the following day —somewhat rapid travelling—he is present, with these disciples, at Cana, where he performs his first miracle, going afterwards with them to Capernaum and Jerusalem. At Jerusalem, whither he goes for "the Jews' passover," he drives out the traders from the temple and remarks, "Destroy this temple, and in three days I will raise it up:" which remark causes the first of the strange misunderstandings between Jesus and the Jews, peculiar to this gospel, simple misconceptions which Jesus never troubles himself to set right. Jesus and his disciples then go to the Jordan, baptising, whence Jesus departs into Galilee with them, because he hears that the Pharisees know he is becoming more popular than the Baptist (ch. iv. 1-3). All this happens before John is cast into prison, an occurrence which is a convenient note of time. We turn to the beginning of the ministry of Jesus as related by the three. Jesus is in the south of Palestine, but, hearing that John is cast into prison, he departs into Galilee, and resides at Capernaum. There is no mention of any ministry in Galilee and Judæa before this; on the contrary, it is only "from that time" that "Jesus *began* to preach." He is alone, without disciples, but, walking by the sea, he comes upon Peter, Andrew, James, and John, and calls them. Now if the fourth gospel is true, these men had joined him in Judæa, followed him to Galilee, south again to Jerusalem, and back to Galilee, had seen his miracles and acknowledged him as Christ, so it seems strange that they had deserted him and needed a second call, and yet more strange is it that Peter (Luke v. 1-11) was so astonished and amazed at the miracle of the fishes. The driving out of the traders from the temple is placed by the synoptics at the very end of his ministry, and the remark following it is used against him at his trial: so was probably made just before it. The next point of contact is the history of the 5,000 fed by five loaves (ch. vi.), the preceding chapter relates to a visit to Jerusalem unnoticed by the three: indeed, the histories seem written of two men, one the "prophet of Galilee" teaching in its cities, the other concentrating his energies on Jerusalem. The account of the miraculous feeding is alike in all: not so the succeeding account of the conduct of the multitude. In the fourth gospel, Jesus and the crowd fall to disputing, as usual, and he loses many disciples: among the three, Luke says nothing of the immediately following events, while Matthew and Mark tell us that the multitudes—as would be natural —crowded round him to touch even the hem of his garment. This is the same as always: in the three the crowd loves him; in the fourth it carps at and argues with him. We must again miss the sojourn of Jesus in Galilee according to the three, and his visit to Jerusalem according to the one, and pass to his entry into Jerusalem in triumph. Here we notice a most remarkable divergence: the synoptics tell us that he was going up to Jerusalem from Galilee, and, arriving on his way at Bethphage, he sent for an ass and rode thereon into Jerusalem; the fourth gospel relates that he was dwelling at Jerusalem, and leaving it, for fear of the Jews, he retired, not into Galilee, but "beyond Jordan, into the place where John at first baptised," *i.e.*, Bethabara, "and *there he abode.*" From there he went to Bethany and raised to life a putrefying corpse: this stupendous miracle is never appealed to by the earlier historians in proof of their master's greatness, though "much people of the Jews" are said to have seen Lazarus after his resurrection: this miracle is also given as the reason for the active hostility of the priests, "from that day forward." Jesus then retires to Ephraim near the wilderness, from which town he goes to Bethany, and thence in triumph to Jerusalem, being met by the people "for that they heard that he had done this miracle." The two accounts have absolutely nothing in common except the entry into Jerusalem, and the preceding events of the synoptics exclude those of the fourth gospel, as does the latter theirs. If Jesus abode in Bethabara and Ephraim, he could not have come from Galilee; if he started from Galilee, he was not abiding in the south. John xiii.-xvii stand alone, with the exception of the mention of the traitor. On the arrest of Jesus, he is led (ch. xviii. 13) to Annas, who sends him to Caiaphas, while the others send him direct to Caiaphas, but this is immaterial. He is then taken to Pilate: the Jews do not enter the judgment-hall, lest, being defiled, they could not eat the passover, a feast which, according to the synoptics, was over, Jesus and his disciples having eaten it the night before. Jesus is exposed to the people at the sixth hour (ch. xix. 14), while Mark tells us he was crucified three hours before—at the third hour—a note of time which agrees with the others, since they all relate that there was darkness from the sixth to the ninth hour, *i.e.*, there was thick darkness at the time when, "according to St John," Jesus was exposed. Here our evangelist is in hopeless conflict with the three. The accounts about the resurrection are irreconcilable in all the gospels, and mutually destructive. It remains to notice, among these discrepancies, one or two points which did not come in conveniently in the course of the narrative. During the whole of the fourth gospel, we find Jesus constantly arguing for his right to the title of Messiah. Andrew speaks of him as such (i. 41); the Samaritans acknowledge him (iv. 42); Peter owns him (vi. 69); the people call him so (vii. 26, 31, 41); Jesus claims it (viii. 24); it is the subject of a law (ix. 22); Jesus speaks of it as already claimed by him (x. 24, 25); Martha recognises it (xi. 27). We thus find that, from the very first, this title is openly claimed by Jesus, and his right to it openly canvassed by the Jews. But—in the three— the disciples acknowledge him as Christ, and he charges them to "tell *no man* that he was Jesus the Christ" (Matt. xvi. 20; Mark viii. 29, 30; Luke ix. 20, 21); and this in the same year that he blames the Jews for not owning this Messiahship, since he had told them who he was "from the beginning" (ch. viii. 24, 25); so that, if "John" was right, we fail to see the object of all the mystery about it, related by the synoptics. We mark, too, how Peter is, in their account, praised for confessing him, for flesh and blood had not revealed it to him, while in the fourth gospel, "flesh and blood," in the person of Andrew, reveal to Peter that the Christ is found; and there seems little praise due to Peter for a confession which had been made two or three years earlier by Andrew, Nathanael, John Baptist, and the Samaritans. Contradiction can scarcely be more direct. In John vii. Jesus owns that the Jews know his birthplace (28), and they state (41, 42) that he comes from Galilee, while Christ should be born at Bethlehem. Matthew and Luke distinctly say Jesus was born at Bethlehem; but here Jesus confesses the right knowledge of those who attribute his birthplace to Galilee, instead of setting their difficulty at rest by explaining that though brought up at Nazareth he was born in Bethlehem. But our writer was apparently ignorant of their accounts. We reject this gospel, thirdly, because its historical statements are in direct contradiction to the history of the synoptics.

The next point to which I wish to direct attention

Jesus of Nazareth. 15

is the relative position of faith and morals in the three synoptics and the fourth gospel. It is not too much to say that on this point their teaching is absolutely irreconcilable, and one or the other must be fatally in the wrong. Here the fourth gospel clasps hands with Paul, while the others take the side of James. The opposition may be most plainly shown by parallel columns of quotations:

"Except your righteousness exceed that of the scribes and Pharisees, ye shall *in no case* enter . . Heaven."—Matt. v. 20.

"He that *believeth on the* Son hath everlasting life."—iii. 36.

"Have we not prophesied in thy name and in thy name done many wonderful works. "Then will I profess unto them . . . Depart . . . ye that work iniquity."—Matt. vii. 22, 23.

"He that believeth on Him *is not condemned.*"—iii. 18.

"If thou wilt enter into life, keep the commandments."— Mark x. 17-21.

"He that believeth not the Son shall not see life."—iii. 36.

"Her sins, which are many, are forgiven, *for she loved much.*"—Luke vii. 47.

"If ye *believe not that I am* he, ye shall die in your sins." —viii. 24.

These few quotations, which might be indefinitely multiplied, are enough to show that, while in the three gospels *doing* is the test of religion, and no profession of discipleship is worth anything unless shown by "its fruits," in the fourth *believing* is the cardinal matter: in the three we hear absolutely nothing of faith in Jesus as requisite, but in the fourth we hear of little else: works are thrown completely into the background and salvation rests on believing—not even in God—but in Jesus. We reject this gospel, fourthly, for setting faith above works, and so contradicting the general teaching of Jesus himself.

The relative positions of the Father and Jesus are reversed by the fourth evangelist, and the teaching of Jesus on this head in the three gospels is directly contradicted. Throughout them Jesus preaches the Father only : he is always reiterating "your heavenly Father;" "that ye may be the children of your Father," is his argument for forgiving others ; " your Father is perfect," is his spur to a higher life ; " your Father knoweth," is his anodyne in anxiety; "it is the Father's good pleasure," is his certainty of coming happiness ; "*one* is your Father, which is in Heaven," is, by an even extravagant loyalty, made a reason for denying the very name to any other. But in the fourth gospel all is changed : if the Father is mentioned at all, it is only as the sender of Jesus, as *his* Witness and *his* Glorifier. All love, all devotion, all homage, is directed to Jesus and to Jesus only : even "on the Christian hypothesis the Father is eclipsed by His only begotten Son."* " All judgment " is in the hands of the Son : he has " life in himself;" " the work of God " is to believe on him ; he gives " life unto the world ; " he will " raise " us " up at the last day ; " except by eating him there is " no life ; " he is " the light of the world ; " he gives true freedom ; he is the " one shepherd : none can pluck " us out of his hand ; he will " draw all men unto " himself : he is the " Lord and Master," " the truth and the life ; " what is even asked of the Father, *he* will do ; he will come to his disciples and abide in them ; his peace and joy are their reward. Verily, we need no more : he who gives us eternal life, who raises us from the dead, who is our judge, who hears our prayers, and gives us light, freedom, and truth, He, He only, is our God ; none can do more for us than He : in Him only will we trust in life and death. So, consistently, the Son is no longer the drawer of believers to the Father, but the Father is degraded into becoming the way to the Son, and none can

* Voysey.

come to Jesus unless Almighty God draws them to him. Jesus is no longer the way into the Holiest, but the Eternal Father is made the means to an end beyond Himself.

For this fifth reason, more than for anything else, we reject this gospel with the most passionate earnestness, with the most burning indignation, as an insult to the One Father of spirits, the ultimate Object of all faith and hope and love.

And who is this who thus dethrones our heavenly Father? It is not even the Jesus whose fair moral beauty has exacted our hearty admiration. To worship *him* would be an idolatry, but to worship him—were he such as "John" describes him—would be an idolatry as degrading as it would be baseless. For let us mark the character pourtrayed in this fourth gospel. His public career begins with an undignified miracle : at a marriage, where the wine runs short, he turns water into wine, in order to supply men who have already "well drunk" (ch. ii. 10). [We may ask, in passing, what led Mary to expect a miracle, when we are told that this was the first, and she could not, therefore, know of her son's gifts.] The next important point is the conversation with Nicodemus, where we scarcely know which to marvel at most, the stolid stupidity of a "Master in Israel" misunderstanding a metaphor that must have been familiar to him, or the aggressive way in which Jesus speaks as to the non-reception of his message before he had been in public many months, and as to non-belief in his person before belief had become possible. We then come to the series of discourses related in ch. v. 10. Perfect egotism pervades them all ; in all appear the same strange misunderstandings on the part of the people, the same strange persistence in puzzling them on the part of the speaker. In one of them the people honestly wonder at his mysterious words : "How is it that he saith, I came down from heaven," and, instead of any explanation, Jesus retorts that they should not murmur, since no man *can* come to him unless the Father draw him; so that, when he puts forward a statement apparently contrary to fact —" his father and mother we know," say the puzzled Jews—he refuses to explain it, and falls back on his favourite doctrine : " Unless you are of those favoured ones whom God enlightens, you cannot expect to understand me." Little wonder indeed that "many of his disciples walked no more with " a teacher so perplexing and so discouraging ; with one who presented for their belief a mysterious doctrine, contrary to their experience, and then, in answer to their prayer for enlightenment, taunts them with an ignorance he admits was unavoidable. The next important conversation occurs in the temple, and here Jesus, the friend of sinners, the bringer of hope to the despairing—this Jesus has no tenderness for some who " believed on him ;" he ruthlessly tramples on the bruised reed and quenches the smoking flax. First he irritates their Jewish pride with accusations of slavery and low descent ; then, groping after his meaning, they exclaim, " We have one Father, even God," and he—whom we know as the tenderest preacher of that Father's universal love—surely he gladly catches at their struggling appreciation of his favourite topic, and fans the hopeful spark into a flame ? Yes! Jesus of Nazareth would have done so. But Jesus, " according to St John," turns fiercely on them, denying the sonship he elsewhere proclaims, and retorts, " Ye are of your father, the devil." And this to men who " believed on him ; " this from lips which said, " *One* is your Father," and He, in heaven. He argues next with the Pharisees, and we find him arrogantly exclaiming : " *all* that ever came before me were thieves and robbers." What, all ? Moses and Elijah, Isaiah and all the prophets ? At length, after he has once more repulsed some inquirers, the Jews take up stones to stone him, as Moses commanded, because "thou makest thyself God." He escapes by a clever evasion, which neutralises all his apparent assertions of Divinity. "Other men have been called gods, so surely I do not blaspheme by calling myself God's son." Never let us forget that in this gospel, the stronghold of the Divinity of Jesus, Jesus himself explains his strongest assertion "I and my Father are one" in a manner which can only be honest in the mouth of a man.* We pass to the celebrated "last discourse." In this we find the same peculiar style, the same self-assertion, but we must note, in addition, the distinct tri-theism which pervades it. There are three distinct Beings, each necessarily deprived of some attribute of Divinity: thus, the Deity is Infinite, but if He is divided He becomes finite, since two Infinites are an impossible absurdity, and unless they are identical they must bound each other, so becoming finite. Accordingly "the Comforter" cannot be present till Jesus departs, therefore neither Jesus nor the Comforter can be God, since God is omnipresent. Since then prayer is to be addressed to Jesus as God, the low theory of tri-theism, of a plurality of Gods, none of whom is a perfect God, is here taught. In this discourse, also, the Christian horizon is bounded by the figure of Jesus, the office of the Comforter is subservient to this one worship, " he shall glorify me." Jesus, at last, prays for his disciples, markedly excluding from his intercession " the world " he was said to have come to save, and, as throughout this gospel, restrict-

---

* For a good work we stone thee not, but for blasphemy; and because that thou being a man makest thyself God." Jesus answered them, "Is it not written in your law, I said, ye are gods? If he called them gods unto whom the word of God came (and the scripture cannot be broken), say ye of him whom the Father hath sanctified and sent into the world, Thou blasphemest, because I said I am the Son of God?"

ing all his love, all his care, all his tenderness to "these, whom Thou hast given me." Here we come to the essence of the spirit which pervades this whole gospel. "'I pray for them; I pray not for the world:' not for them who are of their father the devil, nor for my betrayer, the son of perdition." This is the spirit which Christians dare to ascribe to Jesus of Nazareth, the tenderest, gentlest, widest-hearted man who has yet graced humanity. This is the spirit, they tell us, which dwelt in *his* bosom, who gave us the parables of the lost sheep and the prodigal son. "No," we answer, "this is not the spirit of the Prophet of Nazareth, but" (Dr Liddon will pardon the appropriation) "this is the temper of a man who will not enter the public baths along with the heretic who has dishonoured his Lord." This is the spirit of the writer of the gospel, not of Jesus: the egotism of the writer is reflected in the words put into the mouth of his master; and thus the preacher of the Father's love is degraded into the seeker of his own glory, and bearing witness of himself, his witness becomes untrue. I must also draw attention to one or two cases of unreality attributed to Jesus by this gospel. He prays, on one occasion, "because of the people who stand by:" he cries on his cross, "I thirst," not because of the burning agony of crucifixion, but in order "that the Scriptures might be fulfilled:" a voice answers his prayer, "not because of me, but for your sakes." This calculation of effect is very foreign to the sincere and open spirit of Jesus. Akin to this is the prevarication attributed to him, when he declines to accompany his brethren to Judæa, but " when his brethren were gone up then went he also up to the feast, not openly but as it were in secret." All this strikes us strangely as part of that simple, fearless life.

We reject this gospel, sixthly, for the cruel spirit, the arrogance, the self-assertion, the bigotry, the un-

Jesus of Nazareth. 21

reality, attributed by it to Jesus, and we denounce it as a slander on his memory and an insult to his noble life.

We may, perhaps, note, as another peculiarity of this gospel—although I do not enter here into the argument of the divinity of Jesus,—that when Dr Liddon, in his celebrated Bampton Lectures, is anxious to prove the Deity of Jesus *from his own mouth*, he is compelled to quote exclusively from this gospel. Such a fact as this cannot be overlooked, when we remember that "St John's gospel is a polemical treatise" written to prove this special point. We cannot avoid noting the coincidence.

We have now gone through this remarkable record and examined it in various lights. At the outset we conceded to our opponents all the advantage which comes from admitting that the gospel *may* be written by the Apostle John; we have left the authorship a moot point, and based our argument on a different ground. Apostolic or non-apostolic, Johannine or Corinthian, we accept it or reject it for itself, and not for its writer. We have found that all its characters speak alike in a marked and peculiar style; a style savouring of the study rather than the street, of Alexandria rather than Jerusalem or Galilee. We have glanced at its immoral partiality. We have noted the numerous discrepancies between the history of this gospel and that of the three synoptics. We have discovered it to be equally opposed to them in morals as in history: in doctrine as in morals. We have seen that, while it degrades God to enthrone Jesus in His stead, it also degrades Jesus, and so lowers his character that it defies recognition. Finally, we have found it stands alone in supporting the Deity of Jesus from his own mouth.

I know not how all this may strike others; to me these arguments are simply overwhelming in their force. I tear out the "Gospel according to St John" from the writings which "are profitable" "for instruction in righteousness." I reject it from beginning to end, as fatally destructive of all true faith towards God, as perilously subversive of all true morality in man, as an outrage on the sacred memory of Jesus of Nazareth, and as an insult to the Justice, the Supremacy, and the Unity of Almighty God.

EVIDENCES OF CHRISTIANITY.

THE MESSIANIC PROPHECIES.

EVIDENCES OF CHRISTIANITY.

THE MESSIANIC PROPHECIES.

BY

WALTER LACY ROGERS.

PUBLISHED BY THOMAS SCOTT,
NO. 11, THE TERRACE, FARQUHAR ROAD,
UPPER NORWOOD, LONDON, S.E.
1876.

Price Sixpence.

THE MESSIANIC PROPHECIES.

THE first in order of time of the evidences of Christianity are the celebrated predictions which gave to the chosen people, in ages long anterior to the event, the expectation of a Messiah. They are the first also in importance, because prophecy is an evidence of Christianity alone. There have been other teachers of religion and morality who have claimed to work miracles, who have suffered martyrdom, and who have received the honours of a posthumous deification. Nor is any religion, while it flourishes, without its seers, its medicine-men, its auguries and oracles. But it was the advent of Jesus alone which is said to have been the subject of previous prophecy, and to have been heralded during a period of four thousand years by the whole literature of an ancient people. Certainly this is evidence indeed. It is true that the people themselves, the fellow-countrymen and lineal descendants of the writers, while clinging fanatically to the prophecy, have always obstinately repudiated the application of it. It is true that they have asserted, with a resolution unparalleled for its trials and endurance, the right of understanding their own language. It is true that for all ecclesiastical purposes that language is with them and them alone a living tongue, and that, if they could conscientiously admit that the words of their old prophets as they still read them have not been unfulfilled, they would escape from a position which is getting every year more desperate, and gain for themselves and their literature a place in the religious scale which would satisfy even the arrogance and patriotism of a Jew. But they will not. Because (it is said) two thousand years ago an excited section of their nation, which was then in a chronic state of disturbance, and was stumbling and wading on through blunders and bloodshed * up to the climax of national and political suicide, mistook the character of a man whom his nearest friends did not understand, and were instrumental in putting him unjustly to death, therefore their descendants prefer still to deny the character of this man, than allow that even under such circumstances their ancestors could have made a mistake. With this theory, however improbable, we are not at the present moment concerned; for it stands to reason that, given an accurate translation of the Bible,† we are as capable of forming an opinion nowadays as any Jew in the first century as to whether the plain and natural meaning of a prophecy was fulfilled in the historical character and career of Jesus. It is only those who interpret the prophecies in a non-natural sense who must bear in mind that the interpretation which they advance is the interpretation of foreigners and aliens from the tongue in which those prophecies were written; and that other than the literal meaning of the words has ever been denied by those who formed and spoke the language, and by teachers whose minute study of every part of the national literature at the time when this new interpretation was first advanced, is a matter of history. Or to put the matter in a different way: No doubt there are in England and Germany scholars capable of interpreting Aristophanes better than any modern Athenian

---

* Acts v. 36, 37.

† With regard to this, it must be remembered that the orthodox octrine of the inspiration of the Bible means not only that each ook of the Bible as originally written was the word of God, but that the compiled volume, and its remote descendant, the version of it that was translated in the days of James I., and our present version of that translation, are equally inspired.

The Messianic Prophecies. 7

can. But who would trust to the criticisms of an English or German professor who discovered in the "Clouds" points and allusions which we know were not recognised at the time the play was represented, nor by any contemporary or immediate successor of Aristophanes, however critically he might have studied the subject? Surely it was for the Jewish contemporaries of Jesus to say whether the Jewish prophecies were or were not fulfilled in him. Their leaders would naturally have come to some conclusion on the subject before they had committed themselves to one side or the other. There must have been at the time many "rulers in Israel" willing to be convinced, like Nicodemus, or like those who accepted the impartial and judicious advice of Gamaliel (Acts v. 34-40). What we propose to do, therefore, is to look at a few of the principal Messianic prophecies, and see for ourselves why it was such men were not convinced; whether, in short, according to the fair and plain meaning of these prophecies as they have come down to us, any one of them has been specifically and exclusively fulfilled in the character and career of Jesus.

Let us begin with the direct prediction of the Almighty himself, Gen. iii. 15: "I will put enmity between thee and the woman, and between thy seed and her seed: it shall bruise thy head, and thou shalt bruise his heel."

This prophecy is said to have been fulfilled so far as it is Messianic—

I. By the mission and teaching of Jesus.

II. By the triumph of Jesus over sin and death.

III. By the temporary humiliation and apparent defeat of Jesus in his trial and crucifixion.

It may be objected, first, that the order of the clauses in the prediction has not been observed in the order of the fulfilment, and that this point, so far from being immaterial, is really of the essence of the case; for it makes all the difference to mankind whether the crowning victory rests with Jesus or with Satan. But waiving this point, has any one a right to say that this prophecy has been fulfilled specifically and exclusively in Jesus? That there always has been and always will be enmity between the seed of the woman (not Jesus only) and the Serpent is clear. The very name of Satan (adversary) or of Devil (confounder) implies this. It is also clear that man, in his progress onwards, is constantly let and hindered by the powers and effects which are represented under the symbol of the Serpent. And who can doubt that those powers are constantly being defeated, and good triumphs over evil? Was not the prophecy fulfilled ages before the Advent in the career of thousands and thousands of good men of all nations struggling against Ignorance, Superstition, and Selfishness—defeated in their own persons and in their own time, but in spite of that defeat, and frequently by their own sacrifice in the cause, ensuring the ultimate victory of those principles for which they had so manfully contended? What did Jesus more than this?

Let us take next the prophecy contained in Jer. xxiii. 5-8: "Behold the days come, saith the Lord, that I will raise unto David a righteous Branch, and a King shall reign and prosper, and shall execute judgment and justice in the earth. In his days Judah shall be saved and Israel shall dwell safely, and this is his name whereby he shall be called, The Lord our Righteousness. Therefore behold the days come, saith the Lord, that they shall no more say, The Lord liveth which brought up the children of Israel out of the land of Egypt: but the Lord liveth which brought up and which led the seed of the house of Israel out of the north country and from all countries whither I had driven them; and they shall dwell in their own land."

It may be objected that this prophecy is one of those which has not yet been fulfilled, but is to be so in due course. To that we reply, that if so, it is not, until

The Messianic Prophecies. 9

fulfilled, any evidence of Christianity, and should not be quoted at all; that if it alludes only to the Second Advent it cannot be adduced as a proof of any special interposition of God in the first Advent; but that, placed as it is in the Epistle for the 25th Sunday after Trinity, it is intended by the Church to commemorate the Feast of the first Advent. Otherwise it would be more appropriately placed for the Sunday after Ascension-day. Has, then, the prophecy been fulfilled by the coming of the Jesus of the gospels? If he was raised up "as a Branch unto David," he must have been the actual, not the putative son of Joseph. It is not here a question what the Jews thought, but what God said. These profess to be the words of the Almighty spoken through one of his chief prophets, and it would be what is called blasphemous to say that God meant, "I will pretend to raise up unto David one who shall be no relation to him; I will foist a child of my own upon the Royal stock, in order that you may listen to him under the belief that he is a lineal descendant of your Hero King." It is a dilemma from which there appears to be no escape, but which does not seem nowadays to create any difficulty, viz., that either Jesus did fulfil the Messianic prophecies, in being the descendant of David, and in that case he was not the Son of God, or that, if he was the Son of God, he did not fulfil the prophecies.* Next, Jesus did not become a "king," nor did he "reign," and certainly he did not "prosper;" and as for executing "justice and judgment upon earth," it was the very part which he indignantly repudiated (Luke xii. 14). In the days of Jesus Judah was not "saved," nor did Israel "dwell safely." On the contrary, they were rapidly preparing for themselves that

---

* This difficulty must have been felt in the first ages of Christianity, and no doubt was the reason why Justin Martyr and the earliest of the fathers trace the genealogy of Jesus up to David through his mother. But the subsequent acceptance by the Church of the gospels of Matthew and Luke in their present form as inspired writings makes this no longer possible.

political destruction which soon after fell upon them. Lastly, when and by whom was Jesus ever called "the Lord our Righteousness?"

The 53d chapter of Isaiah is not a prophecy at all. It is written in the past tense, and professes to be a historical narration of the career of some one who had adopted in public life an unpopular cause and been its martyr. It seems to have been composed by a friend who had sympathised but not suffered with the martyr, and who, after the danger had passed, writes in terms of mild self-reproach of the want of courage of himself and the other followers of his hero. All this may have been written of several popular leaders whose followers have hung back when the cause became a dangerous one. But it must have already happened, and cannot be taken to have any reference to events which did not take place until seven or eight centuries afterwards. In the concluding verses there is a prediction of the ultimate triumph of the cause and of the martyr's reward; but this, if it is to be applied to the case of Jesus, has not yet been fulfilled, and forms no part of the evidence of Christianity. For it is not yet a matter of history that Jesus has "seen his seed" or has "prolonged his days," or that the "pleasure of the Lord hath prospered in his hand" (whatever that may mean). "He shall see of the travail of his soul and be satisfied" will of course be attributed to the historical scene of the Agony in the garden; but it is equally applicable to the last hours of a thousand other martyrs who faced death with more courage and satisfaction than Jesus did.

So too of Isaiah ix. 6. Is this a prophecy—and if so, has it been exclusively fulfilled in Jesus? "Unto us a child is born, unto us a son is given," is a statement of fact, and of a very common one, not a prediction. It is true that a prediction follows, but is it applicable? What "government" ever rested upon the shoulders of Jesus? When was he ever called "Wonderful," or "Counsellor," the "Mighty God,"

The Messianic Prophecies.

the "everlasting Father," the "Prince of Peace?"* All this and the predictions in the next verse are still unfulfilled. The more thoughtful and logical amongst the Christians recognised this, and conceived the Millennium as a period for the realisation of these visions. But the doctrine seems of late years to have fallen into disrepute, and nobody cares to maintain it. With this we have nothing to do more than to point out that such an idea is, at all events, an acknowledgment that these prophecies have not already had a fulfilment.

The prophecy quoted from Micah v. 2 is an important one, because it is said to have been recognised at the time of Jesus' birth by those most competent to form an opinion on the subject (Matt. ii. 4) as applicable to the birth of the Messiah. And the fact that upon a report of the Christ having been born, Herod at once referred to the "chief priests and scribes of the people," proves that both he and they were keenly alive to the importance of the Messianic prophecies, and prepared to recognise as the Christ the person who fulfilled them. This is the prophecy: "And thou Bethlehem, in the land of Juda, art not the least among the princes of Juda; for out of thee shall come a Governor that shall rule my people Israel." But has it been fulfilled in Jesus? The four biographies that we have of him, differing as they do in many other particulars, at least agree in this, that God's chosen Israel—the people who prided themselves on their descent from Abraham, the people who inhabited the land formerly allotted to the tribe of Juda, utterly and consistently rejected Jesus, and his pretensions, and his doctrine, and his disciples after him. "He came unto his own and his own re-received him not" (John i. 11). It is clear that they regarded him, if not as an impostor, at all events as a

---

* As to this title compare what Jesus said of himself, Matt. x. 34, "Think not that I am come to send peace on earth: I came not to send peace but a sword . . ." No one can dispute the fulfilment of *this* prophecy.

crazy and mischievous fanatic (John viii. 48), of no use to them in their schemes of turbulence and rebellion (Luke xx. 26). In no sense did Jesus himself aspire to rule God's people Israel, nor had he the slightest sympathy with them or their rulers, or their projects. His influence was confined to the hybrid population of Galilee, a simple people, ignorant of the old Jewish writings (John vii. 49), without any pride of race or national sympathy with the inhabitants of Judea.

The story of the flight into Egypt is, as is well-known, only given by the author of the first gospel, and it is inconsistent with the history given in the third of Jesus' early days. It winds up with the quotation, "Out of Egypt I have called my son" (Hosea xi. 1). Now this, we must point out, is no prophecy at all. It is like many other so-called prophecies, nothing more than the narration of a simple fact. In this case the fact is a well known one, in Biblical history at all events; but whether it were so or not, the words quoted are an allusion to the past, not an anticipation of the future. Is this so or is it not so? We can point here to no less an authority than that of Dr Farrar, who ("Life of Christ," vol. I. p. 39) says of this passage that the writer of the first gospel finds in this narrative "a new and deeper significance for the words of Hosea," and then adds in a note—

"'Or in other words, totally misunderstands them,' is the marginal comment of a friend who saw these pages. And so no doubt it might at first appear to our Western and Northern conceptions and methods of criticism; but not so to an Oriental and an analogist. Trained to regard every word—nay, every letter of Scripture, as mystical and divine; accustomed to the application of passages in all senses—all of which were supposed to be latent in some mysterious fashion under the original utterance, St Matthew would have regarded his least apparently relevant quotations from, and allusions to, the Old Testament, not in the light of occasional illustrations, but in the light of most solemn prophetic references to the events about which he writes. And in so doing he would be arguing in strict accordance with the views in which those for whom he wrote had been trained from their earliest infancy. Nor is there even to our modern conceptions anything erroneous or unnatural in the fact that the Evangelist transfers to the Messiah the language which Hosea had applied to the ideal Israel."

To our modern conceptions there is nothing erroneous or unnatural in a man's writing what he has been inspired to write. And if the author of the first gospel was supernaturally informed that Joseph was ordered by God to take the child into Egypt and keep him there, in order that a certain prophecy might be fulfilled, he had no option about his narrative. But Dr Farrar does not put the case so high as that, 'and we should like to ask so experienced and conscientious a scholar as Dr Farrar is well known to be, whether there is not to our modern conceptions something very erroneous and unnatural in the fact of a *historian* transferring to his own hero language which had been applied to a totally different character? And whether such a person as Dr Farrar describes the author of the first gospel to have been, can be considered a trustworthy biographer? Were not the natural and acquired tendencies of his mind apt to make him look upon as not sufficiently important the hard and fast lines of historical accuracy? In a word, is it not just possible that the whole story of this Egyptian expedition—upon which the silence of the author of the third gospel cannot be satisfactorily accounted for—was assumed both by writer and readers to have taken place in accordance with "this most solemn prophetic reference?" And though this may not be admitted, it is clear that language which Hosea had applied to the ideal Israel, and which had no objective relation to Christ, is not evidence of Christianity.

The difficulty as to the prophecy quoted in Matthew ii. 23, " He shall be called a Nazarene," is of a different ort altogether. It was spoken "by the prophets." When, and by whom ? No one is able to point out the passage in any book of our Old Testament, and it is mere assumption to say that it is a quotation from some prophetical work or works now lost. The explanation suggested—viz., that it was prophesied generally that Jesus should be a "Nëtser," or "Branch" (of the house of David) is no explanation at all. The statement of the inspired Evangelist is that Joseph went "*and dwelt at Nazareth*" in order that the prophecy which called Jesus a Nazarene (*i.e.*, an inhabitant of Nazareth) might be fulfilled. But if the prophecy did not call Jesus an inhabitant of Nazareth, it was not fulfilled by his dwelling at Nazareth, and Joseph could not have gone there for that purpose. Moreover, it appears to be a historical fact that Jesus was called, perhaps in his lifetime, certainly after death, " the Nazarene," and we have therefore here a curious phenomenon. In other places it would appear that a history has been made to fit into the prophecies ; but in this the reverse has taken place, and a prophecy has been coined to anticipate the history. And whatever explanation is given admits that what we have said of the prophecies in general is true of this one, at all events—viz., that the interpretation of it is the interpretation of foreigners and aliens from the tongue in which the prophecy was written.

Again, let us take the prophecy in Isaiah vii. 14, " Behold, a virgin shall conceive, and bear a son, and shall call his name Immanuel. Butter and honey shall he eat, that he may know to refuse the evil, and choose the good. For before the child shall know to refuse the evil, and choose the good, the land that thou abhorrest shall be forsaken of both her kings."

Here, if anywhere, would the expounders of Scripture have been justified in departing from the harsh literalism of the text; and by accepting a metaphorical interpretation, have avoided the reproduction of the grossest feature in Greek and Roman mythology. But the exposition unfortunately happened at a time when asceticism both in man and woman was looked upon as the height of moral perfection; and the stainless purity of the young wife was supposed to occupy the in estimation of Him who had made woman simply as a helpmeet for man, a lower place than the crude innocence of the inexperienced virgin.

In order to give this passage more apparently the form of a prophecy, the future tense has been substituted for the present in the first paragraph. The proper translation is said to be, "is with child and beareth a son."* Consequently here too what is called a prophecy is the statement of a fact. But is there any analogy here to the case of Jesus? According to the authors of the first and third gospels, Mary while still a virgin became *enceinte*, and bore a son. So far the prophecy may be said to have been fulfilled; but beyond this there is no pretence for such an assertion. Mary did not call his name "Immanuel," nor anything of a similar signification, but called his name "Jesus," and that by the express direction of the angel Gabriel, who seems to have forgotten this prophecy of Isaiah—or, at all events, not to have been struck by its relevancy. As to eating butter and honey that he might know to refuse the evil, and choose the good, if this means the adoption of an ascetic diet (such as John the Baptist's, for instance), in order, according to the popular error of the day, to quicken the spiritual perceptions by mortifying the flesh, the description was singularly inapplicable to a person who was known amongst his contemporaries as "a gluttonous man, and a winebibber." Further, the event which was to happen before the child knew to refuse the evil and choose the

* The Holy Bible, with a Commentary. By Canon Cook. Vol. V. p. 80.

good, happened, as every schoolboy knows, within a very short time of the prediction, and cannot be supposed to have been predicted by reference to another event which was not to happen for seven or eight centuries. The only pretence therefore of fulfilled prophecy here is the alleged virginity of Mary at the birth of Jesus. If this was really fulfilled in his case, we may at once grant that it was exclusively fulfilled, and constitutes evidence for Christianity, in comparison with which the failure of all other evidence would be immaterial.

What proof then have we of this miraculous occurrence? The appearance of Gabriel, according to the third Gospel, the dream of Joseph, according to the first Gospel, are the only occasions on which it was positively asserted. Neither do these two witnesses agree together. According to one, it was announced to the husband and not to the wife, according to the other, it was announced to the wife and not to the husband. Moreover, they are themselves miraculous, and a miracle (it is plain), cannot be evidence of another miracle unless confirmed itself by some independent testimony. We must look, therefore, for some such testimony of these visions. They are never again alluded to by the same evangelists, and never by Jesus nor any of his disciples, nor the two other evangelists. Still, indirect testimony of them it ought not to be difficult to find in the record of their effects. If first the mother and then the father of a child had received from God, before that child's birth, direct revelations of its Divine character, what would—what must—have been the result? Would they not have been themselves, and would they not have brought up their family as his earliest disciples? Any picture gallery of old Masters will answer this question. Look where you will what do you see? The Madonna in an attitude of rapt devotion over, or positive worship of, her wonderful Child. Joseph, Elizabeth, and other relations frequently accompany her, all deeply impressed by the sight of One, whom, ordinary child as he was to others, they knew, on evidence they dared not question, to be the Incarnate God. No wonder the greatest painters could choose no more fitting subject for the highest exercise of their art. No wonder that they should have succeeded so well in a conception at once so natural and so sublime, and that the constant realization of so vivid and deep-rooted an idea never palled from repetition on the profession or the public! At the time when these pictures were executed, art was fostered, patronised, and directed by the Church, and this therefore is the answer which the Church has given over and over again to our question. And being the natural and acknowledged result of these appearances, do we find in the biographies of Jesus (written, be it remembered, by his own friends and disciples), that it ever took place? Quite the reverse. Nothing is clearer from the Gospels than that Jesus' own family and relations were, if at all, among the latest of his disciples. Mary and Joseph "marvelled" at the "Nunc me dimittis" of Simeon. Mary sharply rebuked Jesus, just as an ordinary mother would an ordinary child, for leaving them after the feast, and when by way of reply Jesus asked them if they did not know that he must be about his Father's business, they stared in his face in utter ignorance of what he was talking about! At a very early period of his public career, when his biographers assert that his fame had gone through all Syria, they are forced to acknowledge that Nazareth was not convinced (Luke iv. 23). His friends said "He is beside himself" (Mark iii. 21). His mother is not mentioned as among the women who followed and ministered to him (Luke viii. 3). Indeed, his adversaries could point to his mother, and his brothers and sisters, and say—"Are they not all *with us?*" and that there should be no misunderstanding on the subject, we read, in reply, the bitter sarcasm of the disappointed enthusiast—"A prophet is not without honour, save in his own country, *and among his own kin and in his own house:*" Matt. xiii. 56; Mark vi. 4; see also John vii. 3-10. What other meaning can we attach to the sneers which Jesus was constantly pointing at the obligations of relationship both in his own case—Matt. x. 35-37, xii. 48; Luke xi. 27, 28—and that of others—Matt. viii. 21-22; Luke ix. 59-62, xxi. 16; and his public adoption of the ties of sympathy in preference to those of blood—Matt. xii. 49, 50; Luke viii. 21? Was it not Mary's incredulous curiosity as to the powers of the Prophet which brought upon her the rude rebuke—"Woman! what have I to do with thee;" and her tardy recognition of the suffering Martyr, the curt dismissal from the Cross?*

After this, we are not surprised to find that not one of Jesus' brethren is named among his apostles, and only one, years after, among his disciples. Then, too, his mother is mentioned as being among his followers, Acts i. 14, so it would appear that it was the death of Jesus rather than his birth which converted his own family.

But there is still another quarter in which we should expect to find confirmation of the stories connected with the Miraculous Conception, and that is in the sayings and doings of John the Baptist. He is said to have recognised Jesus before the birth, he publicly proclaimed him before the baptism, he died when Jesus was in the full swing of his career, and by that time he had learned

* It is worthy of remark how invariably distrust of, or disbelief in, the power or mission of Jesus aroused in him the roughness of language, which, when addressed to his mother, seems so unaccountable, Matt. xii. 34, 39. Even his most intimate disciples were not spared, Matt. xvi. 23, Luke xxiv. 25. How else can we account for the cruel speech to the poor broken-hearted Syrophœnician, Matt. xv. 26? And so in contradistinction we may notice the gracious replies which always followed an acknowledgment of his power and position, Matt. xvi. 16-19, xv. 28; Luke xxiii. 43.

The Messianic Prophecies. 19

to doubt, if not to deny, that the Messiah had really come. Is it possible that John, if he had known from his infancy the stories that we have heard—John, whose own birth, whose own name, must have constantly recalled them,—could have ever wavered in his belief? John was, at the time we speak of, in prison, and the events that were going on beyond the walls he could only become acquainted with by the reports and descriptions of others, a very unsatisfactory basis of reasoning, and one never to be adopted in preference to one's own experience. John, it must be remembered, had been no ordinary child. He was "filled with the Holy Ghost even from his mother's womb," and "the hand of the Lord was upon him," Luke i. 15, 16. In his early days he must have heard and appreciated the wonderful stories of Jesus' birth and childhood. Consequently, though he himself did not know Jesus by sight, he announced to the people his coming and greatness (Luke iii. 16), and yet, so little conviction did all these reminiscences carry with them, that he actually sent to ask Jesus whether he was really the Messiah,* or whether, with his sanction and that of the Holy Ghost, John had introduced an impostor to the public? And what said Jesus in reply? Did he appeal to John's experience and faith? Did he remind him of what he must have heard over and over again from their common relations? Did he appeal to John's own life—for if Jesus was not the Messiah, John's career as the Forerunner (John i. 31) was a total mistake. Not at all! He told the disciples to go back and "shew John *again* those things which ye do see and hear." Jesus knew that John had heard it all before (Luke vii. 18), but he had nothing to add, nothing to appeal to, but the sights of

---

* The character of John the Baptist was too honest and straightforward to render possible the ingenious explanations usually given of this question. Besides the little sting added by Jesus to his eulogy on John (Luke vii. 28), proves that Jesus at all events looked upon the question as a simple one and resented it.

the streets and the gossip of the synagogue. This might have been evidence to one who knew no better, but to John, who, as a babe unborn, had acknowledged the Divine Embryo, who had been kept acquainted all along with the Messiah, when he no longer knew the Man, such "signs" as these were very weak. They had failed to convince him before, probably they failed again, and John the Baptist died an unbeliever.

This, then, is some of the indirect negative evidence against the authenticity of the first chapters of the first and third Gospels, in which the Miraculous Conception is respectively asserted. Indirect negative evidence is not evidence of a very strong order, but here there is a good deal of it, and none of a stronger sort on either side. No allusion is ever made afterwards in the New Testament to the story. John would be the best authority on the subject, as being the constant companion of Mary after the Crucifixion, and it is never hinted at in any of the works attributed to him. Paul never notices it, though it would have been a useful foundation upon which to build some of his dogmatic teaching. These chapters might be left out without, in either case, doing the slightest violence to the commencement or contents of the rest of the Gospels of which they now form a part. Taking the prophecy, (Isaiah vii. 14) therefore, as it stands, and acknowledging that it was fulfilled according to its primary signification, we are justified in asking, had it any other, or is the story of the Miraculous Conception an invention and interpolation of a later date by some one "trained to regard every word, nay every letter, of scripture, as mystical and divine, accustomed to the application of passages in all senses," and determined to see in the idea which engrossed his mind, the fulfilment of every allusion in the Old Testament?

That the evangelists took liberties with the histories they professed to be writing, in order to bring them into agreement with the predictions, is clear from two episodes related by them all. The first is the ride of Jesus into Jerusalem. The authors of the second and third gospel relate the story as that of a simple incident. The author of the fourth is struck with the idea that something of the kind had been predicted,* and accordingly (quoting apparently from a very bad memory), adds to the story—"As it is written, 'Fear not, daughter of Sion, behold thy King cometh sitting on an ass' colt.'" Then the author or interpolater of the first gospel takes up the story, with this addition, and referring to the passage, and, not understanding the tautological idiom of Hebrew poetry, fancies that two animals are mentioned. Consequently, looking at every word of scripture as mystical and divine, he not only puts a second ass into the scene, but actually makes Jesus ride upon both at once (Matt. xxi. 7). Again, the authors of the second and third gospels mention that the soldiers divided Jesus' clothes amongst themselves by lot. The author of the first gospel tells the same story, but sees in it the fulfilment of a prophecy, and adds—"That it might be fulfilled which was written: They parted my garments amongst them, and upon my vesture they did cast lots." The author of the fourth gospel takes it up at this stage, but (also misunderstanding the Hebrew idiom), thinks the prediction must have been more exactly fulfilled. Consequently, he makes two separate transactions of it, the soldiers divide the garments, and cast lots for the coat. In order that this may appear reasonable, he minutely describes the coat; and it is but the natural conclusion to the story that we find to this day the preservation of the identical article at Treves, where it has been exhibited for centuries to comfort the faithful and confound the sceptic!

No one supposes that God endows men with supernatural powers except for some purpose, and no one ought to believe that in spite of his supernatural interference that purpose should miscarry. Now, what could have

* Zechariah ix. 9.

been the object of these so-called prophecies, if it were not that when the Messiah came he should be at once recognised by those who were best acquainted with the writings of the prophets? But was this the result? Not at all; these were the very persons upon whom no impression was made! We quote the prophecies as evidences of Christianity, it is true: but to address prophecies to Jews in order eventually to convince Gentiles would surely have been a great waste of power, such as is inconceivable in the God of Nature! Did Jesus ever use these prophecies as a proof of his mission? His object was to seek and to save those who were lost—he was not sent except to the lost sheep of the house of Israel. Would he not, therefore, when exhibiting his credentials to the scribes and rulers of Israel, be likely to appeal to tests the validity of which they would be most anxious to maintain and to see fulfilled? We are told that he did so constantly in support or illustration of his argument. But he never appealed to what have since been looked upon as the great Messianic prophecies in support of his own pretensions.* In their worst treatment of him he asked that they might be forgiven on account of their ignorance (Luke xxiii. 46), but why, with such crushing arguments at his command, had he not taught them better? There must have constantly been among his audience persons old enough to have heard the stories "which were noised about throughout all the hill country of Judea,"—to have remembered the taxing, the visit of the Magi, the Song of Simeon, the witness of Anna. Why, when Jesus was accused of having come out of Nazareth, of being born of fornication, of having a devil, of making himself equal with God, did he not appeal to the pro-

* The quotation from Psalm cx. is hardly a Messianic prophecy, though Jesus claimed it as appropriate to himself. Our idea of the functions of a Messiah is an attitude of constant intercession between an erring people and an angry God—not one of dignified repose while the angry God makes for him a footstool of the erring people.

The Messianic Prophecies.

phecies, and then point triumphantly to their wonderful fulfilment?

There must have been many members of the Sanhedrim before whom Stephen was tried, who remembered, and none who had not heard of, the wonderful child who at twelve years of age was found in the Temple sitting in the midst of the doctors, both hearing them and asking them questions. What better argument could Stephen have used than to show that this child, at whose understanding and answers they had been so astonished, was in reality the Ruler that their prophets had said should come out of Bethlehem, should be born of a virgin, and be the promised Branch of the house of David? He might have reminded them of the voice that "was heard in Ramah," and explained how Jesus was preserved from the massacre, and how, in compliance with the prediction of Hosea, he had returned from Egypt. He might have pointed out that the very name "Jesus of Nazareth," used by his accusers on this occasion, was itself a fulfilment of prophecy, and unimpeachable evidence in his own favour. The events preceding or at the crucifixion, the Betrayal by the friend, the thirty pieces of silver, the being numbered with the transgressors, the parting of the raiment, were all too recent to have been forgotten. He would have shown that, so far from destroying that place, and changing the customs which Moses had delivered, the whole career of Jesus had been to fulfil the spirit of the Law, and all the deep and mysterious sayings of the greatest and wisest of their prophets. If he had had such materials at hand, is it conceivable that he should have made the inane, rambling speech which the writer of the Acts has put into his mouth? As to the result is it possible to blame the Sanhedrim? They had an imperative duty to perform under Deut. xiii. 10. Stephen had it in his power to show by quotations, by facts, by living witnesses, that Jesus was the very Lord God who had brought their ancestors out of the land of Egypt and out of the house of bondage, and thus have ensured his own acquittal—and converted his judges and Paul besides. If he refused to do this, and even to attempt it, he can have no right to the honoured name of Martyr, simply because he refused to bear witness to the Truth, upon the only question which was then at issue.

Had Paul known of the Messianic prophecies we have quoted, how gladly would he have verified the fulfilment of them, how gladly would he have used that fulfilment in his arguments with the Jews, and in his epistles. How valuable they would have been to the author of the Epistle to the Hebrews, who has strung together out of the Old Testament every passage in which he fancies he finds a type of or allusion to Christ —to whom it was "evident that our Lord sprang out of Judah" (Hebrews vii. 14), which obviously he could only do by being the actual son of Joseph. And as they are not used by Jesus himself, nor by his followers after him, we can only conclude that their application to Jesus is the result of ecclesiastical research and ingenuity in post-apostolic ages. The gospels, as we have them now, cannot be identified within a hundred and fifty years of the last events they profess to commemorate, and so far, therefore, from being supported in any way by the old writings of the Prophets, we have every reason to believe that they have themselves been moulded in many of their most important particulars to suit the fancied requirements of those ancient Oracles.

A CONFUTATION

OF

THE DIABOLARCHY.

A CONFUTATION

OF

THE DIABOLARCHY.

AN EXTRACT

FROM "THREE MORE LETTERS" TO THE LORD ARCHBISHOP
OF CANTERBURY.

By THE REV. JOHN OXLEE,
Rector of Molesworth, Hunts.

"Hence it is apparent, even on the indubitable testimony of the devils themselves, that Beelzebub, the Prince of the Devils, died a natural death, nearly eight hundred years ago."
See page 15.

———◆———

PUBLISHED BY THOMAS SCOTT,
MOUNT PLEASANT, RAMSGATE.

———

Price Sixpence.

PREFACE.

Sir,—Although I am well aware, that in sending you the long extract from a letter written by the Rev. John Oxlee, Rector of Molesworth, &c., to His Grace the Archbishop of Canterbury, and published A.D. 1845, you will find in it much that you cannot endorse; yet, I am very sure, that you will approve of the main proofs therein given of his masterly exposure of the false, and sadly misleading translation of the word Satan, in the Old Testament.

That the Rev. John Oxlee was a man of rare parts, a first-rate scholar, a linguist of no mean order—a Hebraist, and, par excellence, a Rabbinical Hebraist of perhaps unequalled attainments in his own day— the various obituary notices appended, sufficiently testify. But, what is still more valuable to us of the present day, (when a man like the Bishop of Natal, who has dared, not only to think for himself, but in the honesty and integrity of his heart, and compelled by his love of Truth to give to the public the benefit of his learning and convictions, has been therefore

Preface.

assailed with the term Heretic, and almost every other un-Christian epithet,) the very books which the said Rev. John Oxlee has published and left behind him *prove his orthodoxy*, while at the same time he was exposing this shameful mistranslation in our Bible, together with various other errors of a similar description.

At all events in 1816, July 10, he was considered orthodox enough to be appointed Preacher, at the Visitation of the Right Worshipful Charles Baillie, held at Thirsk.

They moreover prove, that, had he lived in these our days, his love of truth, his honesty of purpose and his independence of thought and action, would have forced him to range himself on the side of "Free Thinkers," in the proper sense of the word; for he evidently was not a man to keep back the truth in unrighteousness, whether it was to his own advantage or disadvantage, which latter seems to have been his lot in this world—for he passed away to his account almost unknown and unrewarded by the Church which he endeavoured so well to serve.

Having become possessed of most of his now very scarce books, I have, I am happy to say, made the acquaintance, by correspondence, of the present Rev. John Oxlee, Rector of Cowesby, &c., son of the deceased, who is also a Hebraist. This gentleman, in the largeness of his heart, for the sake of Truth (would that I could also add, for the benefit of his pocket, for I should like to see some recompense made to the son for his father's sake, as well as for

Preface.

his own), has granted me permission to have the extract printed—provided it be done faithfully—a favour which I hereby publicly and most gratefully acknowledge. Under these circumstances, as my sole object in asking this favour was to circulate as widely as possible this hitherto almost unknown, or at all events, this almost untaught meaning of the word "Satan," I send the extract for your perusal, and shall rejoice if you consider its republication of sufficient importance to induce you to circulate it with your series of most valuable, but alas! often in the first instance, very unpalatable papers. And if you will consent to do this, I beg that you will at the same time print this letter by way of introduction.

I am, Sir,
Yours faithfully,
JAMES BRIERLEY,
*Incumbent of Holy Trinity, Mossley
near Congleton*

To THOS. SCOTT, Esq.,
*Mount Pleasant,
Ramsgate.*

THE EXTRACT.

My Lord Archbishop,

. . . .

Besides many other fatal misconceptions of the Divine Essence and its attributes, which have been equally productive of polytheism and atheism, of idolatry and fanaticism, there is yet a still greater error to be lamented, the efficient cause of nearly all the grosser superstitions in the present age of the world; and that is, the universal belief, not only in the existence, but in the pluripresence and prepotency of a Diabolarch, commonly called THE DEVIL. *Ne metuas Diabolum—Do not fear the Devil* saith the truly apostolic and venerable Pastor of Hermas; and since the most raving demoniac could never exhort us to love the Devil, it necessarily follows, that he ought to be drummed and driven out of the camp of Israel; that we ought neither to think of him nor mention his name, except as a matter of history, but wholly to discard every designation appropriated to him, from the vocabulary of human speech.

To the best of my recollection, it is Archbishop Usher who has somewhere affirmed that the Devil is God's Hangman. This, unquestionably, is a very proper title for his Satanic Majesty, if he may be allowed to exist at all, and to hold office under God. But if the Devil be really the Divine Hangman, then he ought not to be stigmatized nor reviled, but honoured and respected, as one of the chief servants of God. In the *Sepher Zohar* it is declared, and truly declared, that the world is governed by the two attributes of Justice and Mercy, according to the works of men. But if the world be constantly governed by the divine attribute of Justice, as well as by that of Mercy, then every capital crime must be visited with capital punishment; whilst every culprit about to suffer, whether sentenced to be hung or quartered, must be punctually attended by the Divine Hangman or Executioner; and, since there will be many such like executions, in different parts of the world, at one and the same time, the individual executioner,— no matter whether called the Devil, Satan, or Sammael,—must be possessed of the high prerogative of ubiquity or pluripresence; a flagrant insult to the Supreme Being, in that nothing created can ever be pluripresent, but only the Creator. Nevertheless, however exalted or dignified the Divine Executioner may be, he still ought not to be dreaded. If we neither violate the law, nor offend the Lawgiver, we need not fear the Judge, who has the law to administer; nor yet the sheriff or the gaoler, who have charge of the prisoner; still less need we fear the Hangman, who has the sentence to put into execution; and least of all the halter that has to be coiled round the neck, or the hemp from which it is twisted. But if we shall have confessedly violated the Divine law, and so stand condemned as guilty of death, we need not supplicate the executioner, nor any other agent in the administration of divine justice, for the least grain of mercy, as they have nothing to do with the divine attribute of mercy; but we must supplicate the Divine Lawgiver himself, who alone can pardon the offence and pity the offender. Since God, then, is the sole Destroyer, as well as the sole Saviour of the whole man, I can perceive no godly reason, what-

Confutation of the Diabolarchy. 3

ever, why the Diabolarch or Devil should be retained as the Divine Hangman or Executioner, except as the minister or servant of God ; and, if an efficient servant or minister, then doing the work of God, and to be esteemed for his services.

Before I proceed, however, any further, I must distinguish between *a* devil and *the* devil ; between satan, *a* satan, and *the* satan ; as the whole error of the Diabolarchy, in which both the Jew and the Christian are equally implicated, resolves itself into the want of this distinction. Now there are three sorts of Satans, or Devils, whose existence I by no means deny. The first of these cases is, when either men or angels appear to be the haters of our peace and prosperity, not that they differ in their nature and qualities from other men and angels ; but, because they stand in the way of our plans and movements, and, to the utmost of their power, nullify or frustrate what might otherwise tend to our happiness and comfort. This indeed is the proper signification of the term *Satan;* and the Mikra contains several striking examples of its being so used. The second case is founded on the admission, that there may be a countless multitude of invisible spirits or demons, existing and moving about in the vast ethereal expanse ; and which, occasionally approaching the abodes of men, may, if free agents, wantonly or maliciously injure us ; just in the same manner as we ourselves often wilfully and cruelly crush or strike to death those numerous tribes of living creatures with which we come in contact, without their being permitted to know whence the blow had been inflicted. The third case is that evil nature or propensity to evil, termed by the Rabbinical school, *Hayetser Harang*, which is inherent in every man ; and which, if not effectually checked and subdued, when it first begins to show itself, and to put forth its strength, becomes a deadly enemy, a formidable satan, and the most insidious of devils; nor is there any evil demon, roaming without us, of which we ought to stand in such awe, as that which lurks within us. Lord Brougham, distinguished for the brilliancy and fecundity of his elocution, is reported to have said, that nobody ought ever to be astonished at any slanderous story invented by Malice, and her bastard sister Falsehood—begotten both of them by the Father of Lies on the weakness of human nature; a notable testimony, as well as a beautiful illustration of the procreative energy of *Hayetser Harang*, and not unworthy of that august assemblage in which it was uttered.

These are the three descriptions of evil spirits, satans, demons, or devils, whose real existence I am prepared to admit. Their several appellations being all nouns common, and containing a number of individuals under one and the same form or species, exclude all idea of a Diabolarch, superior to the rest. The Greek, *Diabolos* or *devil*, in the sense of a calumniator, forms no part of the Hebrew Mikra, but appears, for the first time, in certain passages of the Septuagint version, made long after the return from the Babylonish captivity, for the use of the Hellenists, and so rendered in accordance with the prevailing superstitions. The Jewish term for the Diabolarch is not *Satan*, but *Sammael*, the king of the Satans, so called, saith R. Solomon Ephraim, because he blinds the eyes of mortals, so as to prevent them from beholding a divine vision. The notion of such a monster, described by fanatics, as the individual antagonist of God Almighty, assimilated in every respect to the Siva of the Hindoos, and the Ahriman of the Parsees, depicted by the poet, Milton, as carrying hell within himself, wherever he moves; as boasting of his power to subdue the Omnipotent; as holding a divided empire with the King of Heaven; as affecting all equality with God; as denying, that

Confutation of the Diabolarchy. 5

either he or his had been formed or created at all; as seeking to dwell neither in Heaven nor where he was, unless by mastering the Supreme of Heaven; as holding councils with his own angels in the ethereal space, in preference to sitting in hell; called by St. Paul the Prince of the Power of the Air, and the God of this world; by the author of the Apocalypse, the Great Dragon, the Destroyer, the Angel of the bottomless pit; by the Jewish contemporaries of our blessed Lord and his apostles, Beelzebub, the prince of the Devils; by the orthodox Fathers, the Heresiarch, the Prince of the Evil Angels, the Contriver of all Evils, the Prince of Darkness, the Introducer of Death, the Father of every lie, the King of Vices, the First-born Death, the Shadow of Death, the Valiant King, the Ruler of the World before the advent of Christ, the Ape of God among the Gentiles, the President of Evil, the Impudent God of the Heretics, the Head of the Wicked, the Author of Injuries, the Common Enemy of all Mankind, the Destroyer of the Soul, the Father of the Wicked, the King of the Mariners, the Sophist of Ungodliness, the Way of Iniquity, the Beast of the Earth, whose teeth are the persecutors of the good, Destruction of Death, the Proud One, the Crooked Snake, the Corruptor of the Soul, the Morning Star, Lucifer, the efficient Cause both of our natural and spiritual death; by Lactantius, the Spirit created by God the Second, and next to the Son of God; by the heretic, Valentinus, the Offspring of that wisdom which was the last of the thirty Æons or Divinities, and the Parent of those Devils who fabricated the world : the notion of such a monster, I say, was totally unknown by name to Moses and the old prophets of God, who never polluted their speech, nor defiled their minds with any such horrid, damnable, and blasphemous superstition, but everywhere maintained Jehovah himself to be the Supreme and only Destroyer, as well as the

Supreme and only Saviour; the Supreme and only Judge, Ruler, and Governor, not only on the earth, but in the air and the ocean, in hell as well as in heaven. This monstrous and paganic idea of a Diabolarch the Jews first acquired during their captivity, in their intercourse with the Parsees, Hindoos, and other Pagan worshippers; and so, on their return from captivity, brought it along with them into Palestine, where it took deep root, and in the age of the Gospel had become so prevalent that it was impossible to address the Jews on any question relative either to the government of the present world or to the future retribution of rewards and punishments, without instantly adopting it, as the common parlance of the whole nation. Being the vulgar belief of the first converts to Christianity amongst the Jews, and recorded as their diction, in the pages of the New Testament, it naturally passed from them to the Gentile converts of the Western world, so as soon to become, as at present, the universal persuasion of all Christendom; there being always this great difference between the dissemination of truth and of falsehood, that the former, being hitherto unknown, and not easy of comprehension, is propagated with difficulty; whilst the latter, being either congenial or identical with what is already professed and maintained, is diffused with rapidity and eagerly embraced.

That *Satan* is no proper name, but a noun common, implying many individuals of the same class or species; and that the translators of our Bible stand chargeable with great prevarication and dishonesty, in not having deferred to the fact, may easily be shown. In the *Pirke Elijahu*, it is laid down that nouns common may be distinguished from nouns proper by four different marks or characteristics with which they may be accompanied; construction or regimen, plurality of number, affixation, emphasis, or demonstration; none of which marks or signs can

Confutation of the Diabolarchy. 7

accompany proper names. But the term, Satan, to say nothing of its signification, is accompanied with such signs; and, therefore, at all times, a noun common. In the Introduction to the Book of Job, we thus read: "Now the day arrived, that the Sons of the Elohim came to attend on Jehovah; and there came also the Satan in the midst of them. And Jehovah said to the Satan, Whence hast thou come? And the Satan answered Jehovah and said, From moving about in the earth, and walking therein. And Jehovah said to the Satan, Hast thou turned thy attention to my servant, Job; as there is none equal to him in the earth, a man perfect, upright, fearing God, and departing from evil? And the Satan answered Jehovah and said, Is Job fearing God gratuitously? Hast thou not reared up a fence in behalf of himself, his family, and everything belonging to him round about? The work of his hands thou hast blessed, and his property is extended throughout the land. But only put forth thy hand, and smite all that he hath; whether will he not bid thee farewell to thy face? And Jehovah said to the Satan, Behold, all that he hath is in thy hands; only lay not thy hands upon himself. So the Satan went forth from the presence of Jehovah." In this narrative, the angel, called the Satan, must have been himself one of the holy angels of God, attendant on his throne; otherwise, he could never have been admitted into the divine presence at all; and the reason why he is here designated *the* Satan, was not because he was a hater of Jehovah, but because the counsel which he suggested was inimical to the pious patriarch, whose Satan he was, and on whose special account alone he is denominated the Satan. The counsel to tempt and try the integrity of holy Job is elicited from the angel, incidentally, in the divine conference; and though he suggested the counsel, yet the express permission and authority to put it into execution proceeded from God Himself; and, since every express permission from God is a divine commission, yea, a divine command, whatever the Satan did on this special occasion, he did it as the faithful and true servant of God. If the author of the book had ever heard of such an antagonist of the Almighty as a Diabolarch or the Devil, he was too wise and pious a man to introduce such a monster into the history of the holy patriarch. Accordingly, we find that in all the animated discussions instituted between Job and his friends on the cause of his sufferings, not the least intimation escapes from any one of them, that they might possibly have been brought upon him through the malice and contrivance of their common spiritual enemy, the Devil. They evidently knew nothing of the Diabolarch or Devil, as we now entitle him: and well may we envy their happy lot. On the contrary, the pious sufferer everywhere complains of his afflictions being sent to him immediately from God, and laments that he is overwhelmed by an Omnipotency against which he cannot lift up his head. Instead of adopting the superstitious parlance of the apostolic age, and describing Satan as hunting after him, like a lion, and seeking to devour him, he complains of Jehovah himself doing all this, and says: " Thou huntest me like a fierce lion." The Book of Job itself, therefore, contains not the least vestige of a Diabolarch; nor was the integrity of the holy patriarch tested by any Devil whatever, but only by Jehovah himself. The Translators, however, by perverting the rules of grammar, in turning a noun common into a proper name, and so giving us here, as in other places, *Satan*, for *the Satan*, or *a Satan*, have contrived, from the Books of the Old Testament, to establish a Diabolarchy to which the inspired authors themselves were totally strangers.

If we refer to the other passages in which the term occurs, we shall find equal ground for arguing in like manner. Thus, in the prophet Zechariah, we read: "And he let me see Joshua, the Chief Priest, standing before the angel of Jehovah, and the Satan standing on his right to be his Satan. And Jehovah said to the Satan: 'Jehovah rebuke thee, the Satan; yea, Jehovah rebuke thee, who hath chosen Jerusalem.'" By the Jehovah who spake to the Satan, we must understand the angel of Jehovah mentioned at the commencement of the vision. Here, again, we have the term Satan constructed as a noun common; and so far from being understood by any learned Jewish commentator of the Diabolarch, is expounded by Aben Ezra and R. David Kimchi, of Sanballat, and his confederates; by Maimonides and others, *Hayetser Harang* the evil nature in man: but by R. Isaac Abarbinel, of the wicked king, Antiochus, who proved himself the Satan of the Jewish Priesthood, and did his utmost to extinguish it. Supposing, however, this Satan to be meant of a real angel, there will be no need to expound it of the Diabolarch, but of a true angel of God standing up as the Advocate of Divine Justice to impeach the Chief Priest as to certain parts of his conduct, just in the same manner as a learned councillor may be honourably employed in accusing and inculpating the delinquency of a man, as well as in advocating and defending his innocency. So, again, in 1 Chron. xxi. 1, it is said: "And there stood up against Israel a Satan, and he instigated David to take the number of Israel." The Satan here mentioned may well enough be understood of some intimate friend who advised the king to number Israel, and so called a Satan because his counsel proved in the end so disastrous to the nation. R. David Kimchi expounds it of that which is planted in the heart of man from his very youth,—meaning *Hayetser Harang*,—very pertinently remarking at the same time that, in the Second book of Samuel, Jehovah is said to have instigated David to command that the children of Israel and Judah should be numbered. So that Jehovah himself was really the instigator through the means and instrumentality of the Satan, who is afterwards designated the angel of God; and whom David saw with a drawn sword in his hand, committing havoc and destruction, because the children of Israel had offended by their transgressions. In both the preceding passages our Translators, as usual, instead of *the* Satan, and *a* Satan, have given us Satan the Diabolarch. In other places, however, where the very same term occurs, but where their Satan would ill befit the context, they have given us neither Satan nor Devil, but *Adversary*. Thus, in the first book of Kings, we have in the Hebrew, " And Jehovah raised up to Solomon a Satan, Hadad the Edomite"; but in the English version we have, " And the Lord stirred up an adversary to Solomon, Hadad the Edomite." So, again, in the Book of Numbers, we have in the Hebrew, "And the wrath of God was kindled, because he was going; and the angel of Jehovah stood in the road for a Satan to him;" but in the English version we have, " And God's anger was kindled, because he went; and the angel of the Lord stood in the way for an Adversary against him."

This last instance of the use of the term Satan, in the original Hebrew, will suffice of itself to shatter and demolish the Satanic Throne, as well as King Satan himself. For, if the angel of Jehovah, declared by Rashi to be the angel of mercies, who wished to prevent the prophet from doing wrong, for fear he should commit sin and perish; who says to him, " Behold! I have come forth to be a Satan to thee, because the road thou art taking is a bye-road in my sight"; and who further commands him, saying, " Go with the men; only the word which I shall speak unto thee, that same shalt thou speak"; if such an angel, I say, can be called a Satan, and can be allowed to perform the office or function of a Satan; then

Confutation of the Diabolarchy. 11

what opponent will venture to stand up and impugn the truth of the assertion, that all the angels mentioned as Satans by the authors of the Mikra, are the real ministers of God, severally executing their divine commissions, and acknowledging for their Head and Potentate no other Being whatever, except the Supreme Being Himself? Nay, the very angel with whom the patriarch Jacob wrestled, by whom he was first named Israel instead of Jacob, on whose account the place of meeting was called *Peniel*, because he had there seen God face to face, and from whom he craved a blessing before they parted,—is interpreted by R. Solomon Ephraim, of no other personage than of Sammael, the Prince of Esau, the Satan of Joseph, the Angel of Death, the Uncircumcised One, the Diabolarch of the Rabbinical school. This antagonism with the angel is said to have befallen Jacob, because he had not restrained his concupiscence, having acted amiss in marrying two sisters. Moreover, as Sammael, or the Prince of Esau, is called the Satan of Joseph, so also is Joseph designated the Satan of Esau; that is to say, the antagonist of Esau. In like manner, the orthodox Christian Fathers hesitate not to call the Devil the Fury of God, the Beginning of the Ways of God, or the Behemoth, the Questionary of God, the Javelin of God, the Great Mountain, the Day and the Night, the Parching Wind, the Immission of the Whirlwind, the Evil Spirit of the Lord sent to Saul, the Exactor of Tribute for God,—yea, the Perpetual Servant of God, according to compact,—all which titles and designations imply a strict and regular discharge of such celestial functions and offices as are absolutely necessary and indispensable to the exercise of divine justice, and to the due government of the world by God. If, then, we are required to profess a belief in the existence of such a Diabolarch, let him be no longer esteemed as the enemy and antagonist, but as the stern servant of God, causing terror to man, not from any natural enmity to the species, but from promoting the just exercise of the most awful of the Divine Attributes.

Probably, however, I may be called upon to account for the actual admission of such a being as Satan or the Diabolarch, both by Christ and his apostles, according to the evidence of the New Testament. The first reply which I have to make is, that the dogma of a Diabolarchy could have been first revealed to the world, neither by Moses nor by Christ. Not by Moses; as neither he himself, nor the ancient prophets that followed him, have left a single word upon record from which any such dogma can be fairly elicited. Nor yet by Christ; as the superstitious belief of such a monster was already professed and prevalent amongst the Jews before his appearance in the flesh. If, then, we are to admit the truth of the dogma, because it stands uncontradicted in the pages of the New Testament, let Zoroaster and other Parsee divines, from the anterior promulgation of their *Schetan Ahriman*, have assigned to them all the due honour and credit of having first revealed it to mankind; as neither the Jew nor the Christian can arrogate to himself the real merit of any such divine revelation. It does not follow, however, that because a vulgar belief, narrated in the Gospel, remains uncontradicted, it is therefore to be reputed as so much standard divinity. Satan is made to declare to our Lord, that all the kingdoms of the earth had been surrendered into his hands, to be given away and disposed of according to his own will and pleasure; and the wicked lie, in accordance, no doubt, with the superstition of that age and country, is passed over without any denial, whatever, on the part of our Saviour. If it should be remarked, that the Devil, being the father of lies, there could have been no need at any time to contradict his words, then we may extend the like remark

Confutation of the Diabolarchy. 13

to the possessed of the devils; who, on being asked their name, said it was *Legion*, that is, many, yea thousands, in number; for if the Prince himself be accounted a constant liar, well may his minions or subordinates be stigmatised with the very same epithet; and yet it should really appear, from the narrative of the Gospel, that there was a very great number of them, and, consequently, that they had told no lie. The prevailing opinion amongst the Jews of that day was, that all lunatics, maniacs, and other patients, labouring under any seemingly incurable disorder, were possessed of evil spirits or demons; that they carried them in their bellies, just as they believe, at the present day, in Siberia, India, and certain corners of Africa, where Dr Wolff himself appears to have tried his skill at exorcism, but without success. I have already observed, that I am not arguing against the existence of *devils*, nor of *a* devil, but against the existence of any such imaginary individual spirit as the Author of all Evil, the Diabolarch, the Prince of the fallen angels, or the Devil, as he is emphatically styled. The fact appears to be, that our blessed Lord never once condescended to enter into any kind of argument or disputation with the Jews of that age, on the absurdity of any of their superstitious opinions; nor do I recollect a single instance of his upbraiding them with any one of their Paganic errors; but, adopting the common parlance, relative to Gehenna and the Diabolarch, he contented himself with the more important business of inculcating on the minds of his disciples those positive doctrinal truths, whether relating to faith or practice, which never could be contradicted nor refuted; leaving them, gradually, to discard their vulgar errors and superstitions, according as their understandings should become more and more enlightened, and advance in the wisdom and knowledge of the true God. Of this we have a very singular proof in the case of Beelzebub, the Diabolarch of the Ekronites, as well as of the Jews their neighbours. Being accused by his enemies of having a devil, and of casting out devils, by the authority of Beelzebub, the Prince of the Devils, our Lord does not utter a single word to the disparagement of the majesty of Beelzebub; but assuming the existence of such a princely demon, he briefly points out the absurdity of their reasoning in that, if one Satan be empowered by Beelzebub to eject another Satan, then must the kingdom of the Diabolarch soon come to an end. But, because our blessed Lord does not formally deny the existence of this Prince of the Devils, am I therefore bound to admit the reality of it? Surely not. I feel no hesitation in declaring that no such being as Beelzebub ever existed at all, except in the empty pates of the idolatrous Ekronites; and their no less superstitious neighbours, the Jews of that age. Should it even be deemed compulsory on me to admit his actual existence, at the time of our Lord's ministry, I should still have no need to admit it at present. In the *Chronicon Syriacum* of Bar Hebraeus, we have it duly recorded, that in the year of the Hegira 455, or of our Lord 1063, certain Curdean hunters, in the desert, brought a report into Bagdad, how that, as they were hunting in the desert, they saw black tents, with the voice of lamentation, weeping and yelling; that on their approaching them, they heard a voice saying, "To-day died Beelzebub, the Prince of the Devils; and every place where there is not lamentation made for three days, we will erase from its very foundation;" that, when the chief men of Bagdad heard this strange tale, they proceeded to the sepulchres, and there sat for three days, yelling and weeping, tearing their clothes and hair, and blackening their faces with the grime of the kettles, in order that they might hereby pacify the devils, and that they might not slay

Confutation of the Diabolarchy. 15

their friends; that the report thus spread throughout all the land of Senaar; and that the very same thing was done in every other place equally as in Bagdad; in Mosul, for instance, as well as in Armenia. Hence it is apparent, even on the indubitable testimony of the devils themselves, that Beelzebub, the Prince of the Devils, died a natural death, nearly eight hundred years ago, and was lamented and bewailed, with all due honours, by the municipal authorities of Bagdad, Mosul, and other cities in the land of Senaar. There, then, let his mortal remains peaceably rest, never more to be disturbed, in future, by human curiosity.

If we turn to those passages of the Gospel, where Christ himself, in his doctrine, makes mention of a Satan or a Devil, we shall generally find the term used, either in strict accordance with the language of the Mikra, or else capable of being interpreted of, *Hayetser Harang*, the evil nature or evil creature within us, in accordance with the Rabbinical school. In the Greek tongue, as is well known, the definite or prepositive article is made to precede the noun proper, as well as the noun common; and there is just as much idiomatic propriety in saying *the* Cyrus, or *the* Jesus; as there is in saying the Persian, or the Saviour. But in the Hebrew, as well as in the English, the case is quite otherwise: nor does the demonstrative prefix or definite article, *the*, ever come before a proper name, but only before a noun common; and then it limits the signification to one of many. Hence, in the New Testament, wherever the Greek *Satanas*, occurs—preceded, as it constantly is, by the definite article—it ought to be rendered conformably to the Hebrew idiom, *The Satan;* whereas our English translators, carried away by their diabolarchical superstition, and taking undue advantage of the ambiguity of the Greek idiom, invariably give us, *Satan*: making it here a proper name, as they do in the Old Testament. Christ does not say, *Satan cometh*, but, *the Satan cometh;* nor *whom Satan hath bound;* but, *whom the Satan hath bound;* nor, *I beheld Satan fall;* but, *I beheld the Satan fall;* just in the same sense as the prophet was made to behold the Satan standing at the right hand of Joshua; meaning the particular or individual angel, then acting the part of a Satan to him. The like observation will hold good of the Greek term, *Diabolos*, or Devil, employed by the Septuagint translators for the Hebrew, Satan; that it is never used, nor ever ought to have been understood, as the proper designation of a Diabolarch; but only in the sense of *a* Satan, or *the* Satan, accordingly as it may happen to be employed either with or without the definite article. Thus, in the Greek version of the first Book of Chronicles, where our version improperly gives: *and Satan stood up against Israel;* we find very accurately, *and there rose up a Diabolos, or Devil, in Israel;* that is, *a* Satan, according to the Hebrew original. Doubtless, one main cause of this prevalent error throughout our English version is the incompetency of the Latin tongue, from its want of a demonstrative article or prefix, to distinguish between common and proper names; between Satan, *a* Satan, and *the* Satan; so that, in turning the Latin Vulgate into English, our first translators were left at liberty to confirm their espoused dogma of a Diabolarchy by rendering the term, Satan, not as a common, but as a proper designation. In many texts of the New Testament, however, it seems difficult to understand these terms of any evil spirit or demon at all; but merely of *Hayetser Harang*, the Evil Creature within us. Thus our Lord says to his disciples: "Have I not chosen you twelve; and one of you is a devil?" In another place he says to Peter: "Get thee behind me, Satan." Surely, neither Peter nor Judas was actually a Satan or a Devil, that they should be accosted in these terms. But there was within them an active evil principle or nature, always stirring: which unless rebuked, as in the case of Peter, or if left unchecked, as in the case of Judas, soon causes the person to become a hater of that which is good, and an enemy to the doer of that which is good; consequently, a Devil or a Satan. So again our Lord says: "Ye are of your father, the devil, and the lusts of your father ye will do; he was a murderer from the beginning, and abode not in the truth, because there is no truth in him. When he speaketh a lie, he speaketh of his own; for he is a liar, and the father of it." Here we have the supposed Diabolarch or Devil declared to be not only the father or inventor of every lie, and a murderer from the beginning, but possessed, also, of all those carnal lusts and affections, in which we ourselves so frequently and wickedly indulge, by imitating his conduct.

But how, I would ask, is it possible to conceive, that disembodied spirits or angels can be subject to bodily passions and affections, or disturbed by any of those carnal lusts and appetites which are proper, if not peculiar, to the human species? The supposition is too monstrous to be entertained for a moment. If, however, by father Satan, we choose to understand the *Yetser Harang*, as expounded by the author of the *Siphtee Daath*, and other Darshans, this, as well as other texts of the New Testament, will receive a lucid and satisfactory explanation. "Thus (saith R. S. Ephraim) it was the will and pleasure of Jehovah, that the woman should walk after her husband, and not that the husband should walk after the counsel of his wife; because with Eve was created the Satan, as we have it stated in the Medrash; how that the letter, *Samech*, nowhere occurs in the Law until Eve is created, according to that which is written: *and he closed up the flesh in lieu thereof.* Wherefore the Serpent was united, as it were, in matrimony to Eve at the very first; as he was well aware, that she would allure him, and finally prevail." "But of Laban (saith the same author in another place) he Jacob was afraid, and on his guard, lest be should injure him as to his purse, by designing to alter his hire ever so many times; for Laban became the whole of him inverted into a Nabal; and he acted as much the part of a fool, as did Nabal the Carmelite. Then, again, of the Prince of Esau, the Angel of Death, that is, Satan, the same with the *Yetser Harang*, he stood in awe, and was on his guard, lest he should cause him to commit sin; as will hereafter be explained." Hence we clearly perceive, that the learned Darshans, or spiritual expositors of the Jewish Mikra, pursue a method handed down to them, no doubt from their predecessors, very different from that of the illiterate and vulgar professor, in describing the origin and character of their Sammael or Diabolarch; and that, if we adopt this doctrinal course, we shall be at no loss for a suitable exposition of the words of our blessed Saviour. Cain, we know, is the first murderer, as well as the first liar, upon record. Though the *Yetser Harang*, which prompted him to commit the crimes, he may be said to have derived from his father Adam, as well as from his mother Eve; yet, since it stirred, and became an active creature in her the first of any, there is a propriety in making her *Yetser Harang* the parent of that in the first murderer and the first liar; and so the father of all the murderers and liars that ever sprang from the loins of Adam. In this way, the distinction between a child of God and a child of the Devil is quite intelligible: and we can be at no loss in comprehending the language of our blessed Lord, when he designates his revilers as the offspring or seed of the Devil, and as the inheritors of all his lusts. In like manner, the law of which St Pau

Confutation of the Diabolarchy. 19

complains, as warring in his members against the law of his mind, and bringing him into captivity to the law of sin,—which he calls the body of death, that is, according to the Darshan, the angel of death,—could have been nothing else than the *Yetser Harang*, or evil nature within him. So when he apprises the Thessalonians of a future falling away from the faith, and of the revelation of the man of sin, the son of perdition, opposing and exalting himself above all that is called God or is worshipped, so that he will sit as a God in the Temple of God, showing himself, that he is a God; I do not understand by *the man of sin*, a mere individual, such as Nero, Napoleon, or the Pope of Rome, but the *Yetser Harang* in general, enthroned in the heart of man, which is, or ought to be, the temple of God only: thus promoting without restraint infidelity, crime, and apostacy; and doing away with all worship and service, except to himself alone. The orthodox fathers affirm, that Sin is the abode or place of the Devil, and that we bow the knee to him, as often as we do sin: that Satan and the other powers of darkness were seated in the heart, mind, and body of Adam, as their own proper throne, from the time of the principal transgression until the coming of Christ: and that the Devil and the wicked are all one person. These testimonies of the Fathers will appear clear and rational, if we understand by the Devil or Satan the *Yetser Harang*, but in no other manner.

There is one passage in the history of our Lord in which Satan is made to act so distinguished a part, that I am constrained to take some special notice of it; I mean the Temptation in the Wilderness. Since I differ from other expositors in regarding the Temptation itself, not as a literal, but as a parabolical, occurrence, it will be necessary, first of all, to adduce the reasons for so determining it. The first argument

20 Confutation of the Diabolarchy.

in favour of the opinion is, that as Christ was unaccompanied by any of his disciples when he was drawn by the Spirit into the wilderness of Judea, they could have known nothing of themselves as to what happened to him on that occasion, except so far as he himself might afterwards be pleased to communicate it to them ; and, since he constantly availed himself of every opportunity to fetch from actual conferences or occurrences some spiritual or parabolical instruction for the benefit of his followers, I cannot but think that his forty days' fast in the desert must have been turned to the same account. If it should be argued that, in imparting and detailing to his disciples what had there befallen him, he could never have suffered them, however inattentive to the purport of his words, to mistake a parabolical for an historical narrative, I would reply that such an argument is by no means valid. There appears to me always to have been impressed on their minds a feeling of awe and reverence, arising from the solemnity of his divine presence, which checked their verbosity and prevented them from putting further questions as to what he had already said, for fear he should upbraid them with their ignorance and want of comprehension. Besides, if his encounter with Satan were a literal occurrence, how happens it that St Mark, who is supposed to have had his gospel dictated to him from the mouth of St Peter, should have neglected to detail so marvellous a portion of the history, and have contented himself with the brief remark that he was in the wilderness forty days tempted of Satan? How happens it that St John, the prince of the evangelists, should have wholly omitted either to mention or to allude to the fact, had he really been aware of any such conflict literally taking place ; appearing to himself, as it must have done, to be a matter of a much more astonishing and marvellous complexion than many of those occurrences which he has actually

Confutation of the Diabolarchy. 21

detailed ? Secondly, if we compare the two narratives of St Matthew and St Luke, we shall find them differing from each other, so as not to be reconciled, except in the manner proposed. St Matthew makes the devil take Christ, first to the holy city, to place him on a pinnacle of the temple; and then, after that, to the exceedingly high mountain. St Luke, on the contrary, makes the devil take him first to the lofty mountain, and then, afterwards, to the pinnacle of the temple, where he is said to have departed from him. This discrepancy, on the supposition that the temptation was a single occurrence, actually taking place, cannot be accounted for without implicating either St Matthew or St Luke in a charge of error. Their accounts cannot be both correct, if we insist on the historical feature of the detail. But, admit the suggestion of a parable, and that our Lord in rehearsing it a second or third time, had somewhat varied, as he might well do, the order of the narrative, then both the evangelists may be equally correct, and so have duly given what they had duly received. Thirdly, the devil is made to take him to a very high mountain, and from the top of that mountain to point out to him all the kingdoms of the world, and the glory of them, in a moment of time. Now, in an age when the terrestrial globe was believed to be as circular and as flat as a trencher, and wholly in accordance with the visible horizon, such language as this would have been quite admissible in a poem or a parable, but certainly not in a mere historical relation. The Satan thus employed could not have shown him one kingdom, much less all the kingdoms of the earth, with their glory, from any mountain top whatever. Besides, had this encounter with the Devil been a literal occurrence, the particular mountain would have been specified and named, as well as the holy city, and not expressed indefinitely, so as to allow it to be understood of any high mountain whatever, according to the caprice of the reader. Lastly, the Devil is made to take him up into the holy city, and there to place him on a pinnacle of the temple. But is it to be imagined, I would ask, that two bodily or human forms could transport themselves through the air, in broad daylight, and sit on one of the pinnacles of the temple, without being noticed and pointed out by the people in the streets? Had so marvellous an occurrence taken place it would have been duly registered in the annals of the holy city: have been made the subject of inquiry for many subsequent generations: and have been frequently appealed to as a demonstration of the finger of God, as well by Christ himself as his disciples, during their ministry amongst the Jews. Such are the insurmountable difficulties which attend and stand in the way of the temptation in the wilderness, being understood of an historical transaction, whilst, if expounded as a parable, it presents no difficulties at all. Indeed, why should not the Son of Man be made the subject of parabolical instruction, as well as the good Samaritan, or any other personage recorded in the Gospels? The common belief in Demoniacs, and of the diabolical mania, is laid hold of by our blessed Lord, as a suitable material for imparting and inculcating religious instruction. "When (saith he) the unclean spirit is gone out of a man, he walketh through dry places, seeking rest, and findeth none. Then he saith, I will return into my house from which I came out; and when he is come, he findeth it empty, swept, and garnished. Then goeth he, and taketh with himself seven other spirits more wicked than himself: and they enter in and dwell there: and the last state of that man is worse than the first." Here we have strikingly depicted to us the case of an unhappy man, who, for a while, having turned away from his besetting sin, vanquished the *Yetser Harang* or fleshly Satan, and cleansed his soul from all filthiness of flesh and

Confutation of the Diabolarchy. 23

Spirit, returns again to his evil habits, indulging in fresh crimes, adding sin to sin, and so rendering all chance of any future purity of life more hopeless than ever. So likewise, on the other hand, in the account of the Temptation, we have the case of Christ parabolically set forth and admonishing us, how we ought, at all times, to resist every Satanic wile, by rejecting the offered blandishments of all mundane glory, pomp, and power, by implicitly obeying the divine commands, and by evincing contentment as well as a firm reliance on God, under whatever difficulties, troubles, or afflictions we may chance to labour. I would briefly subjoin that, in thus divesting the Temptation in the Wilderness of its literal and historical character, I am under no necessity of doing so to make room for my disbelief in the Diabolarchy: as any angel or satan might have been ordered or permitted to do, what is there related to have been done, without requiring the assistance or presence of a Diabolarch.

Before I bring to a close this part of the subject, it may not be improper to hazard an opinion as to the case of the demoniacs mentioned in the New Testament. The first question suggesting itself is, how it can have happened that we meet with no accounts of demoniacs in the history of the Old Testament, and that from Moses to Malachi we find not a single instance upon record of any prophet, priest or king, casting out devils and curing demoniacs? The only satisfactory answer to be supplied is, that when the Mosaic dispensation was in full vigour, there were no devils to be cast out nor any demoniacs to be healed. The second query suggesting itself is, how we are to account for the fact that at the present day, when the world is quite as wicked now as it was at the commencement of the Gospel dispensation, and when the Devil or Diabolarch has quite as much deference and respect paid to his name now as he had then, we should hear so little of the divine power of casting out devils, or releasing the possessed ; and that, whilst sects and churches multiply, arrogating to themselves the highest spiritual gifts, we should never hear of the gift of ejecting evil spirits being exercised and professed either amongst the followers of Moses or those of Christ? The only answer to be given is, that all such wicked spirits or devils must have long since ceased to exist, having been allowed to die a natural death, like Beelzebub, their prince, in the land of Senaar. In that state, then, let them remain and enjoy a profound sleep. But, if we turn to Jewry, and sift the case of those who are said to have laboured under any demoniacal influence at the time that our Lord exercised his divine ministry amongst them, we shall find that, actuated by that Paganic superstition which they had imbibed during their captivity, the possessed, or their relatives, did not consult our Lord as a sovereign physician : intreating him first to tell them what the malady was, and then to heal it: but they themselves presumed to know, and to inform him what it was, and merely besought him to remove it by the exercise of his superior power. How then, it may be reasonably asked, and by what infallible signs did they ascertain the fact of their being possessed and that devils had entered into their bodies? I would reply, just in the same infallible way that many superstitious individuals of our own times believe themselves to be bewitched, and who have recourse to the wise man, not to inform them whether they are bewitched or not,—for of that they are quite sure,—but to tell them who is the witch and how the spell may be broken. Had our blessed Lord been supplicated to tell them what their mental or bodily infirmities were as well as to remove them, the accounts of the demoniacs in the New Testament, I am persuaded, would have been often different from what they are. He did not always seem to sanction their superstitious ideas, by repeating their own words and expressions. It is a fact, too, which cannot be denied, that the gospel of St John, the beloved disciple and chief of the evangelists, whilst it presents us with historical details both of the miracles and doctrines of Christ, such as are of the very highest importance both to the Church and the world at large, contains not a single instance, upon record, of the Lord casting out devils and healing demoniacs; thus plainly intimating to us, that the exercise of such a power was by no means any requisite sign of his being the predicted and true Messiah. In this I am further confirmed by the answer that was sent to John the Baptist. For, in enumerating the several signs or proofs of his being the expected prophet, Christ makes no mention of the ejection of the evil spirits, but bids the disciples report to their master what, indeed, they themselves both heard and saw: that the blind receive their sight, that the lame walk, that the lepers are cleansed, that the deaf hear, that the dead are raised up, and that the poor have the gospel preached to them. It is true, our Lord commissioned his disciples, amongst other things, to cast out devils; but, by casting out devils, I merely understand curing demoniacs, and healing what were thought by the vulgar to be diabolical maladies. Indeed, exorcism, or the ejection of evil spirits, being closely connected with witchcraft and sorcery, and these things being strictly prohibited by the Mosaic law, would have been a sign or proof of his being a false prophet rather than the true prophet, had it been practised alone by itself unaccompanied with other powers. The wisest determination, therefore, to which we can come in this matter, is simply to say, that as our gracious Lord extended his pity and tender compassion to all the decrepit, diseased and afflicted, without any regard to the distinction of their maladies or complaints, the esteemed demoniacs being egregiously harassed and tormented both in body and mind, equally partook with others of his mercy and favour; but, whether evil demons had literally taken possession of any, or all, or none of them, seeing that we were not present to witness what took place, we cannot presume to decide; nor is it necessary that we should, it being a matter which does not at all interest us at the present day. One thing to me seems quite certain, that had king Saul, upon whom an evil spirit is said to have been sent from God, lived in the middle of the first century, he would have been pronounced a demoniac; whilst so far from the evil demon being considered as sent by God, Beelzebub or Sammael would have been named, and not Jehovah, as the author of the calamity.

But, though we hear less now than formerly of the legionary demons, of such as may be supposed to constitute the rank and file of the Satanic army: and though the monks and hermits have fewer stories to tell us about the tricks and pranks of the devils, such as are to be found in Matthew Paris,—who relates a singular fact of a certain Irish hermit, in whose garden the devils met every night, after sunset, to render an account to their Prince of the various deceptions which, during the day, they had successfully practised on the human race; before whose door, since they could not enter his cell, these same devils had placed naked women to tempt him to violate his vows of chastity,—though stories of this complexion, I say, have ceased to be recorded, yet the titles and designations of the Diabolarch are as current as ever; whilst the prerogatives of his omnipresence, omniscience, and omnipotence cut a figure in the conversation of the first circles, and form parts and parcels of the gravest argumentation. Thus, for instance, in case one man in London and another at Calcutta should happen, at the very same time, to commit murder or suicide, without any apparent motive for perpetrating so foul a deed, the common observation would be, that the Devil had entered into their souls, and instigated them to the act; thus constituting the Diabolarch, not merely pluripresent, but, so far as the human race are concerned, altogether omnipresent; in that no mortal man can be supposed anywhere to subsist and to be thinking either good or evil, without the Devil at the same time standing at his elbow, though he may not be allowed to see him, nor be conscious of the fact. It is only a very short time ago, that I read in a public journal the reported speech of a certain Irish orator, a member of the Latin Church, who is said to have declared, respecting the Irish government, that he knew nothing of their inward thoughts and wishes, as these were known to their own souls and the Devil; thus constituting the Devil, so far as men are concerned, omniscient, in that, if he possesses the prerogative of knowing the secret thoughts and wishes of one set of men, he must be equally cognisant of the very same things in others. In another journal of recent date, there appeared a paragraph on Old Bailey justice, in which the Common Serjeant, on addressing the jury, is said to have told them: "That they must look to the original intent of the prisoner. That the question was, when he hired the horse and chaise, did he intend to convert them to his own use? Or, having obtained possession, was he suddenly tempted by the Devil to do it? That should they be of the latter opinion, then the felony was not made out;"—thus establishing the prepotency and omnidexterity of the Devil, and so doing away with our moral responsibility in that, if one man may be excused punishment because he cannot always be on his guard, nor successful in resisting temptation, the very same consideration ought to be extended to every other individual, who may be equally vigilant enough to defend himself against the attacks of the common enemy at one moment, and yet be ultimately overmatched or outwitted by him at another. Indeed, I am quite at a loss to reconcile the moral responsibility of man for his actions, with the admission of a Diabolarch possessed of such superhuman prerogatives, faculties, and powers; who, being next to God in point of order, called the Beginning of the Ways of God, and the First of the Creation, is thus declared to be the natural and implacable enemy of the whole human race; and who, being so vastly superior to them both in art and might, cannot possibly fail to execute against them, with direful effect, the inevitable explosions of his vengeance and enmity, by diverting them from the path of duty and subjecting them to the censure and anger of the Supreme Judge. If condemned to be eternally punished for what was neither perpetrated nor devised by their own sole agency, how can such a sentence comport with the divine attribute of justice? It will not suffice to tell me that God is merciful and pitiful towards sinners; and that the Word Incarnate, by the sacrifice of the Cross, has made an universal atonement for the sins of the whole world. I freely and fully acknowledge the boundless mercy of God, and am equally thankful for the all-atoning sacrifice of the Cross. But I want to contemplate the wisdom and the providence of God, as well as His mercy and goodness; whereas I am prevented from doing this by that monster, the Diabolarch, standing in my way. If our natural weakness be such that, even were there no invisible and potent enemy meditating an onslaught from without, we should still be inadequate to the full duty of walking at all times uprightly and perfectly maintaining our integrity; for what wise purpose, I would ask, can we imagine the very First of the Creation to be constantly employed in diverting us from

Confutation of the Diabolarchy. 29

serving and pleasing God, as though we had been created capable of doing more than we need to do; and, as though God would be more delighted and satisfied with a part than with the whole of our will and power to honour and obey Him?

Many of our Christian Fathers and Divines were fully sensible of the difficulty of reconciling our moral responsibility with the acknowledged exercise of the prepotency of the Diabolarch; and, in order to make the one dogma consistent with the other, have so defined and limited his energies as to render him a very harmless and inoffensive being, compared with that terrific portrait which is so often given him at other times. Archbishop Usher, for instance, firmly believing in the doctrine of absolute predestination, affirms of Satan, that he may shrewdly guess what we conceive in our minds by our gestures, deportment and outward signs; but to what end or wherefore, or what we think, he cannot certainly understand; for, doubtless, if he were certain of the faith and constancy of the saints, he would never so tempt them in vain; for it is but vain, because they that are truly sanctified and incorporated into the Head, Christ, by his Spirit and their own faith, can never finally fall away from grace given. Thus, the Devil is allowed by our Divines to be either weak or strong, knowing or ignorant, according as the exercise of such prerogatives may interfere or not interfere with the maintenance of their respective creeds. But what an insult to the wisdom and foresight of the Supreme Being, to harbour the thought even for a moment, that he who, according to Lactantius, proceeded prior to the creation from the hands of God, the Second Spirit in existence, being next in order to the Eternal Son, could have been destined from the very first by his Procreator to perform no other functions than to roam about the terrestrial globe, which, being compared with the rest of the universe, is no larger than an acorn : to watch the looks and movements of the human species only, which, if connumerated with the other terrestrial species of living creatures, can scarcely be allowed to possess a millionth portion of that vitality appropriated to their planet, small as it is ; to contend with mortal man in giving a direction to his thoughts, words, and actions, and frequently to be foiled in the encounter ; to be a free agent, and yet to find no other employment nor pleasure in his own existence than that of causing eternal pain, misery, and damnation to mankind ; to be gratified and delighted to the highest pitch, by being able to disturb the harmony, peace, and order of the universe; and all this from no other imaginable cause or motive than some unaccountable and secret enmity to the person of the Supreme Being, an enmity for which no rational mind can account, nor which any tongue can be prompted to depict, except that of a maniac! Fie! and shame! on those ministers of religion and professors of theology—no matter whether Jews or Christians—who can entertain such degrading and ungodly cogitations. If they have nothing more noble than this to intimate to the world, then let them give place to *Boz* and *Punch*, the two grand monkeys of their own age and country, and so cease from dishonouring God, as well as deceiving their fellow creatures.

The final and concluding argument which now remains to be urged against the received dogma of the Diabolarchy, is the important question : How such a monster is to be duly and adequately punished for all the crimes and assaults which he shall have perpetrated both against God and man, so as to be justly and truly dealt with, according to the magnitude and atrocity of his offences? If mortal man, whose moral and intellectual faculties are but weak at the best—to say nothing of his being instigated by the Devil—is to be punished with an

Confutation of the Diabolarchy. 31

eternity of torments for sins committed in the course of a few years; what addition can there be made to that eternity of torments in the case of the Diabolarch himself, whose crimes outweigh and outnumber, both as to their enormity and duration, those of the whole human race put together from the beginning to the end of the world? Surely, if the future punishment of a poor, misguided and neglected sinner, the perpetrator of a few unforgiven sins only, is to last for ever and to extend to eternity; the destined punishment of the Arch-Fiend himself—the instigator to all sin, the Arch-Rebel against God, the Inventor of all crimes and delinquencies—ought to extend still further; even to an eternity of eternities, might such an expression be granted. Is one Gehenna to serve all the damned? And is there to be no distinction made between men and devils—between the devils themselves and the Prince of the Devils? Are the same flames and tortures to suffice for the behemoth as for the adder—for the giant as for the infant, and with the like duration? Alas! we have been copying our theological ideas of Satan and borrowing images—Jews as well as Christians—for the last two thousand years, from the Hindoos and the Parsees; from the former, as to the distinction which they make between their Vishnou and their Shiva, their universal Saviour and their universal Destroyer—from the latter, as to the distinction which they make between their Ormuzd and their Ahriman, their author of all good and their author of all evil; the one absorbed in excellence—the other absorbed in crime, and frequently called Schetan, or Satan, in Parsee compositions. In this way, have we unwittingly succeeded in creating a personal antagonist to the Supreme Being, a Satan to God Almighty; and, as the Izeds of Ormuzd fought battles with the Dews of Ahriman, so the angels and archangels of the Devil are represented by our

Christian poets as fighting pitched battles with the angels and archangels of God, and discomfited only after a most dubious and obstinate conflict; whilst the Diabolarch himself, instead of being chained down in the deep abyss, and there detained to eternity, soon finds means to escape from the place of his punishment, and so bidding fair to play the like trick in future; thus leaving the great Jehovah inefficient and powerless in administering due chastisement—incompetent to restain his hitherto invincible adversary from progressing in mischief—allowing him with all impunity to excite amongst mortals war and tumult, strife and contention, where otherwise might reign peace and concord, harmony and love; whilst the originator of all this evil is left to exult in the successful issue of his plots and devices, unappalled by any distant sign of his being soon called to an account, and undisturbed by any possibility whatever of his being ultimately tortured and punished according to the magnitude and multitude of his crimes and offences. Such is the blasphemous dogma of the Diabolarchy, replete with insult to the majesty of the Supreme Being, as propagated and still retained throughout Christendom in general. The Lord pardon such ignorance and folly!

I have now presented and explained to your Grace, as well as to the Jewish and Christian reader at large, what I mean by the present impure state of Judaism and Christianity, and that, perhaps, in a somewhat unusual course of argumentation; the whole of which may be summed up in these words: that God Himself, the Cause of all Causes, is too little feared and thought of, but the Devil far too much. I can never sufficiently admire and extol the purity and the simplicity of that Mosaic law in which JEHOVAH is everything, and the *Devil* nothing. The legislator Moses, and the prophets that followed him, knew nothing either of *Sammael* or *Gehinnom*, much less did they ever dream of the two goats, upon which the lots fell on the great day of atonements, being destined, the one for Jehovah, and the other for the Devil; but they stood in fear of JEHOVAH and of *Sheol* only, maintaining God to be the King of *Sheol* as well as of *Shammaim*, and that nothing was going on in either locality, except by His special direction and sovereign authority: whereas their less simple, but more superstitious descendants, not only acknowledge *Sammael* and Gehinnom, but have constructed nearly as many hells for the damned as the *Naraka* of the Hindoos is said to contain mansions; all which they have designated with proper appellations, and described with as much minuteness and precision as though they themselves had actually descended into them and explored them personally. Let me, then, invite every pious student and firm believer in the Book of Revelation —every true and sincere worshipper of the Most High, to permit no other Being to be enthroned in the chamber of his soul—no other object to be there adored, feared, and glorified, except Jehovah alone, the only Being who absolutely is, so that God may be all in all, but the Devil, or Diabolarch, nothing at all; to venerate the memories, but not the relics of the departed—no matter whether patriarchs, prophets, or apostles, not even the Virgin Mother herself —but discarding from the mind all other metaphysical inquiries and doctrinal disquisitions, as of inferior consideration, to investigate the Fear of God only; to stand up for His honour, and to perform what He commands, since He alone—not man, nor yet the Devil—can recompense our duty and service, as well with peace and comfort here, as with glory and immortality hereafter.

I have the honour to subscribe myself your Grace's most Obedient and very Humble Servant,

JOHN OXLEE.

BIOGRAPHY

OF

THE REV. JOHN OXLEE.

JEWISH MESSENGER,
New York, December 18*th*, 1857.

We have been advised that it is the intention of the son of the above lamented divine, to publish the biography of his father. We hazard nothing in saying, that so highly interesting a publication will meet with a ready sale amongst Israelites of the United States, The Rev. Mr Oxlee opposed, single-handed, but with the most powerful effect, the whole Conversion Society. He did not enter the battle-field unarmed, but with the best weapons to conquer,—God's law and our time-honoured commentaries,—he fought, he conquered. The Israelites throughout the world owe a debt of gratitude to the divine of another faith who spent the best part of his life to become conversant with the Hebrew law ; who studied the Talmud, and kindred learned works, for the sole purpose of familiarising himself with their laws, their probity, their past chequered condition, and their future glorious prospects. In short, no Israelite who wishes to be informed what the refined mind, the sound Scholar, thinks of his religion, should be without the Biography of the late John Oxlee.

THE JEWISH CHRONICLE AND HEBREW OBSERVER,

January 29*th*, 1858.

The late JOHN OXLEE was an extraordinary scholar. Had preferment in the Church been given by merit, and not favour, John OXLEE would have adorned an episcopal chair, instead of being suffered to go through life unacknowledged by the Church which he so zealously served. We believe that since Buxtorf no Gentile excelled him in Rabbinical lore. But what particularly endears his memory to the Jewish scholar was the candour of the deceased.

Having studied the Scriptures in the original language, he had discovered the groundlessness of many assertions of Christian divines, and candidly and publicly admitted the correctness of the Jewish interpretations of the questions at issue. He was as opposed to the Conversion delusion as the Jews themselves. We, therefore, willingly reproduce the subjoined sketch of the life of the deceased:

Mr OXLEE was born at Guisbro', in September, 1779. Very little is know to me of his early years, more than that, when a youth he removed from Guisbro' to Sunderland, and applied for a time to business, but afterwards quitted it, and devoted himself to study, beginning with that of Mathematics and of the Latin language. In the latter he made very rapid progress; for, when an assistant, able to write Latin with ease and elegance, was wanted by the celebrated Dr Knox, at that time Head-master of the Tunbridge Grammar School, Mr Oxlee wrote to him, in that language, on the subject, and immediately received the appointment of Second Master. Here he spent four years; and commenced his Hebrew, Chaldee, and Syriac studies. At Tunbridge, he partially lost (through an attack of inflammation), the use of one eye; but the other remained strong and clear to the end of his life; and, perhaps, no single eye ever did more work.

Having entered into Holy Orders, he became Curate of Egton, where he married and took pupils. In 1811 he removed to the Curacy of Stonegrave. From 1816 to 1826 he held, also, the Rectory of Scawton, and in 1836 he was presented by the Archbishop of York, to the Rectory of Molesworth, where, in 1854, he died, having nearly up to the day of his death, been engaged in literary labours.

BIOGRAPHICAL NOTICE OF THE REV. JOHN OXLEE,

OF BLESSED MEMORY.

(Abridged from a Lecture by John Dowson, M.D.)

The result of these labours was that he obtained a knowledge, more or less extensive, of 120 languages and dialects. This statement may seem scarcely credible, but rests on authority that cannot be disputed, and it is supported to a considerable extent, by his published works, which furnish abundant proof of his familiarity with the more important languages of the world, and his library supplies evidence that some of the less important were not studied superficially. When a man has a strong natural aptitude for any pursuit, and cultivates it to the utmost, it is difficult to set any bounds to his attainments.

Mr OXLEE was remarkable for zeal and perseverance; thirty-five years elapsed between the publication of the first and third volumes of his great work on the doctrines of Christianity. Of the substance of this work, and of its author's theological opinions, this is not the place to speak; he is merely adduced here as an example of extensive knowledge, derived almost entirely from books, though it seems right to add that Bishop Heber, speaking of his works, says:—"I shall sincerely rejoice to see your labours take the place in public estimation to which their soundness, good sense, and originality, in my opinion, entitle them."

THE CLERICAL JOURNAL,
October 22nd, 1859.

"The Mysterious Stranger; or, Dialogues on Doctrine. Dialogue the first, between the Jew Rabbi and the Stranger By the late Rev. JOHN OXLEE. Edited by his Son, the Rev. John Oxlee, Perpetual Curate of Oversilton, Diocese of York."

"The late Mr OXLEE was a prodigy of Hebrew and Rabbinical learning, and his works ought to be more known than they are. In this posthumous work, which is to be continued, the prejudices of the Jew are met in a scientific manner by one conversant with their modes of thinking. The form of the work is ingenious and the arguments are subtle."

THE ECCLESIASTIC AND THEOLOGIAN,
For October, 1859. Page 489.

Under what seems at first a strange title, ' The Mysterious Stranger,' we find a learned and interesting pamphlet on the Jewish objections to Christianity. It is a relic of the late Rev. JOHN OXLEE's labours, and offers another proof that he was one among that band of original thinkers and deep scholars who prepared the way for the great Church Reviva of our own generation.

THE
SPONTANEOUS DISSOLUTION
OF
ANCIENT CREEDS.

A Lecture

DELIVERED BEFORE THE

SUNDAY LECTURE SOCIETY,

ST. GEORGE'S HALL, LANGHAM PLACE,

ON

SUNDAY AFTERNOON, 23rd *JANUARY*, 1876.

BY

Dr. G. G. ZERFFI, F.R.S.L., F.R. Hist. S.,

One of the Lecturers in H.M. Department of Science and Art.

PUBLISHED BY THOMAS SCOTT,
11 THE TERRACE, FARQUHAR ROAD, UPPER NORWOOD,
LONDON, S.E.

1876.
Price Threepence.

SYLLABUS.

Definition of terms: "Spontaneous" and "Creed."

Constituent elements in Humanity.

Mind and Matter. Imagination and Reason. Superstition and Knowledge. Ignorance and Faith. Intellect and Morals. Emotions and Convictions.

Analogy between Chemical and Intellectual Combinations and Dissolutions.

Religious Reforms. Brahminism and Buddhism. Magism and Zoroastrianism. Hesiod's Theogony and Greek Philosophy. Judaism and Christianity.

Religiousness and Irreligiousness.

St. Paul and St. John.

Christ's Christianity.

Christian Unchristianity.

The Historical development of Religion based on Reason and Science.

Polytheism, Anthropomorphism, Anthropopatism, Acosmism, and Atheism.

Conclusion.

THE SPONTANEOUS DISSOLUTION

OF

ANCIENT CREEDS.

ALL philosophers of ancient and modern times agree that words are the principal instruments of thoughts. A correct knowledge and use of these instruments alone can secure for us profitable results of reasoning as the principal aim of philosophy. I intend to discuss the Spontaneous Dissolution of Ancient Creeds from an entirely objective point of view. In this sentence there are two words which I must beg you to accept in the sense in which I intend to use them. I do not mean to apply the word "spontaneous" colloquially as something "sudden," but scientifically as something "acting, by its own inherent energy, according to a natural law." A spontaneous dissolution will, therefore, be a dissolution to be traced to the inherent constituent elements of the different creeds, as the result of a natural law, according to which antagonistic particles must dissolve in time so soon as they lose the cause or force of cohesion. By the word "creed," I do not signify "a summary of the articles of the Christian faith," but "any system of dogmas which is prescribed as necessary to be believed, or, at least, to be professed." In a former Lecture I endeavoured to trace the influence of natural phenomena on the formation of the different religious systems or creeds. Nature in its *infinity*, and man in his *finiteness*, are then the two principal elements from which the different creeds of all times have sprung; that is, from the very beginning of man's consciousness, his notions concerning the world, its Creator, and himself, spring from two utterly antagonistic sources.

Man is formed of matter and endowed with mind. This must be also the case with the whole universe. Matter is acted upon by an inherent spirit, manifesting itself as law—the law of causation, which pervades *space*, wherever matter is existent, which assumes in *time* different shapes and forms. The further constituent elements in humanity are man's utter helplessness as a single individual, and the necessity that he should enter into a social bond with his fellow-creatures, to render his existence as an individual a possibility.

To make the existence of a collective social state possible, man must submit to laws equally binding on all. Exercising his in-born intellectual power, man will frame such laws to facilitate the existence both of the detached individual and of a collection of individuals, brought together by geographical position, voluntary or forced influences, over which the individual, as such, has little or no control. The laws so framed are in all cases revealed; not revealed directly by the mouth of the Divinity, or by some supernatural agent, but by that self-consciousness which, in its turn, is the result of man's material organisation.

This brings us once more to the never-ending discussion of mind and matter. History illustrates most distinctly the fact that in humanity, as in electricity, there are elements which will be negative, or positive, or static, and dynamic. Neither the negative nor the positive electricity, however, predominates by itself, nor does a machine exist exclusively constructed on the dynamic or static principle. A proper balance between the two forces alone will produce action and reaction, motion and resistance. What is static in electricity or in a machine is moral in humanity—a stationary element. Absolute morality, if there be such a thing, can only be one and the same from eternity to eternity. Relative morality may vary with the intellectual "plus" or "minus" in man's social development; but "wrong," as wrong can only be one in an absolute sense, and must be "wrong" in all times under all circumstances. So it is with virtue. To the philosopher "murder" is murder, whether perpetrated by a single individual to satisfy his passion, or by an army wholesale for the glory of a nation; though relatively war, or wholesale murder, pillaging, robbing and ravaging may be excused under certain circumstances, and even deserve a bright monument. To draw a sharp distinction between the absolute and the relative in dialectics is of the very utmost importance. Absolute morality can only be one immutable, unchangeable element, which renders the existence of humanity as such possible. This existence would be impossible if theft, murder, and adultery were allowed. We trace thus in humanity the existence of one constituent—a static element—morals.

The next element will be intellect—a pushing, dynamic force, ever-changing, ever-growing, ever-varying; to-day different from what it was yesterday, building up slowly the mighty temples of science and art, to which every one may contribute, consciously or even unconsciously, a small pebble or a few grains of sand to form cement; whilst some place the huge corner-stones, others raise a flag-staff on a lofty spire from which a bright banner, floating in the air, shows whence the cosmical wind blows.

These banner-bearers only become possible when every-day working men have dug the foundations, collected materials, mixed the mortar, heaped up stones, constructed the edifice, and crowned it with spires. All work according to the plan of the grand, invisible, and still, through man's intellectual power, ever-present architect, who, in endowing humanity with self-conscious intellect, ordained its use to be continuous, leading to a correct application of morals by an understanding of the aim and purpose of humanity in its component individual particles.

The process of constructing the progressive intellectual development of humanity underwent different phases according as imagination or reason predominated. Both are merely faculties of our intellect; the one engendering superstition and religious creeds, the other science and art. The primary constituent elements begin to be subdivided, and in their subdivision we find the first germs of confusion, but also of activity, of action and reaction. Those who, by their superior intellectual consciousness, assume the lead of humanity, begin to be divided into two divergent groups, each assuming that man has only to cultivate one of its constituent elements.

The moralists presume that, with their superior intellectual power, they have found out for eternity the laws according to which man may be best induced to be virtuous. They proclaim him to be conceived in wrath, created full of wickedness and sin, and propound that ignorance is his birthright and *faith* in the system of the creeds, which they have worked out in the name of the Divinity, his only salvation. They pronounce the innate spirit of inquiry to be of evil, wish us blindly to abide by certain formulæ, separate morals from intellect,

of Ancient Creeds.

mind from matter, the static element from the dynamic, and hinder the progress of our social development, which they try to limit or altogether to check by their dictates. The despotic sway of these dictates they deny, for they consider that their wish to promote the welfare of humanity one-sidedly palliates everything they say or do. They create the first terrible rent in humanity by arbitrarily separating the component parts of our spiritual and material existence; they devote themselves to the exclusive culture of morals and foster an inordinate contempt for intellect. The division is brought about by their remaining stationary, and ignoring the dynamic force as one of the component and indispensable elements in human nature. Wherever this happens, superstition is fostered, and knowledge is only so far promoted as it will serve the general superstition. Faith will be exalted as the best tool with which blind ignorance can be made subservient to the system of an incredible creed. Intellect will be looked down upon as of evil. Morals in the garb of set dogmas thus often become the greatest immorality, for they promote hypocrisy, cowardice, and voluntary stupidity. Emotions are excited, but convictions are silenced. Happily this is a condition of humanity bearing the elements of spontaneous dissolution in its unnatural and one-sided attempts.

In analysing a drop of water we know it to be a compound of hydrogen and oxygen. Add to it any other element, and the water loses its purity. Take only hydrogen by itself, it may burn, but it is not water without oxygen. Taking man as a mere essence of morals, we have as unreal a being as a mere essence of intellect would be. As purely moral or intellectual he might be an angel, an imponderable something, but not man, who is formed of dissoluble matter, endowed with mind. This mind is often assumed to be an entity in itself, through itself, for itself. This may, perhaps, be, but we cannot prove it; we know only that it exists, thinks, reasons, directs our motions, our will, in a certain limited sense, but is nowhere to be found as a separate entity. It has an analogous nature with electricity in an electric battery. We have the machine before us; the proper acids, the metallic elements are there; we hear their working; we take one of the conductors in our hand—no effect—we take the other, and we feel the shocks, gradually and with increasing force, passing through our body. All these circumstances and combinations were indispensable for the production of an effect of electricity on our body. So it is with mind. It is there, under certain circumstances and combinations of the material elements of which we are formed; disturb these particles, change their relative proportion or quantity and quality, and you have an explanation for our different moral and intellectual faculties. Mind is not a cause, but an effect—absolutely, it must exist in the universe and pervade it as well as electricity—relatively, it requires certain conditions, under which it will alone come into entity and activity. If mind be directed one-sidedly, it will become superstition; if filled with mere emotions, it will be driven to madness and engender ghost-seers, spirit-rappers, ritualists, and lunatics; if left uninstructed, it will believe anything, and can be brought, through a long training, to such a state that it will look upon those who are anxious to enlighten or to instruct it as its sworn enemies; hate, persecute, murder, burn, and crucify them. Still, just as in the external world, continuous combinations and dissolutions take place, forming the different phenomena, as air, heat, water, minerals, metals, plants, animals, and human beings, so an intellectual process of the mind, forming and undoing religious systems and scientific theories, has been in operation since the first dawn of human consciousness.

That this is the case no honest and unbiassed student of history can deny. The most spiritual elements in humanity are the different religious systems, by their very nature treating mostly of the unknown and unknowable; and still, though every one of them has been proclaimed as the direct or indirect dictate of the Supreme Being, every one had in the course of time to undergo changes, modifications, to enter into different combinations, or to dissolve into its component parts under the action of the voltaic battery of intellect. All religions are composed of certain elements, partly acting on our moral, emotional, and partly on our intellectual nature. All religions take their origin in the natural tendency of the human mind to explain the surrounding phenomena of nature, and to assign to man his destiny, not only in this but often also in another world. Religions originate in man's imagination, more or less enlightened by knowledge, whether guided, as some teachers assert, by Divine inspiration or revelation, or whether as the mere result of intellectual effort. The position of those who assume a Divine revelation or inspiration is a very difficult one, and requires an immense amount of credulity; for history furnishes us with undeniable proofs that the Divine inspiration and revelation of one period has often been not only contradicted but altogether abolished by an equally Divine inspiration and revelation at another period.

Brahma himself is asserted to have dictated the Vedas, but he has couched his dictates in so unintelligible a language that man, with his limited intellect, had continually to explain, to correct, and to comment upon the utterances of the infinite Spirit. Several times the second person of the Indian Trinity had to assume the human form to save humanity from utter destruction, and we may congratulate ourselves that His Royal Highness the Prince of Wales went to India, because one of the religious enthusiasts has proclaimed him the last " Avatar," or incarnation of Brahma. We may here learn, in reading history backwards, how such incarnations occurred in olden times ; how they were proclaimed by one or several poetical or fanatical enthusiasts, and how by degrees such proclamations were believed, and served as the bases of several Eastern religious creeds.

Manû had in time to step into the world with a new Code of Laws, which, as well as the Vedas, were the breath of the Divinity in every chapter, verse, word, and letter ; and Buddha came at a later period and had to correct again the dictates of Brahma, and to proclaim, quite in opposition to the Divinity, that men were not born in different castes, but that they were all equal. How it could have happened that the divine Being, in proclaiming His will through Manû, should have made such a mistake is perfectly incomprehensible. But the Divinity went even further in its incomprehensible proceedings. For a thousand years the Buddhists had been worshipping Brahma according to the dictates of Buddha, who was Brahma himself; they had constructed temples in honour of that Brahma-Buddha, which, in their splendour and grandeur, are unsurpassed, and yet in the seventh century after Christ this very Brahma-Buddha, who taught his followers a more humane religion, and endowed them with so much virtue, that they are still, though the most numerous, the only sect on the surface of the globe that has not shed one single drop of human blood in the propagation of their faith—this very "Brahma-Buddha" allowed these, his faithful worshippers, to be massacred, and to be driven from the very birth-place of his divine mission. The same occurred with the Magi and Zoroaster. The whole religious system of the Magi was proclaimed by means of the prophet Hom (Homanes), who was also the great tree of life, the source of all bliss and prosperity, the first revealer of the word, the *logos;* the first teacher of the Magi, of the learned in the Scriptures and the prophets; and notwithstanding this another divinely-inspired master was required to purify and to revise the revelation of God made through Hom, and to found the Zoroastrian creed.

In Hesiod we may trace an altogether different process. The Asiatic gods, who assumed for certain purposes, at certain times, human shape or form; who, in fact, represented in monstrous conceptions the different phenomena of nature, were at last deprived by Hesiod of their revolting material and spiritual attributes. They were, for the first time, represented in human shape by the *humane* and poetical Greek mind. Their beautiful outer-forms led to an elevated conception of their spiritual nature, and the Greek gods became mere men and women endowed with higher bodily and intellectual faculties. Through the Greeks, humanity was enabled to leave the regions of the supernatural and to embark on the ocean of inquiry, and provided with the compass of intellect, to make glorious voyages of discovery in the realms of speculative philosophy, and to furnish us with the models of rational inquiry. When the Greeks proclaimed their "γνῶθε σεαυτόν"—"Know thyself," man's spirit became conscious of its own self as part of the eternal divine spirit, but not altogether freed from the fetters of outer-form. Intellect with the Greeks was yet *generalised*, and had to take a beautiful form, as manifested in their immortal works of art; man was not yet unfettered as pure *individual* intellect. We must look for this spiritual development of humanity elsewhere.

The historical importance of the Jews begins with their bondage. In misery and wretchedness they learned their higher aspirations. Their legend about the creation of man in the image of God and the forfeiture of his innocence in eating from the tree of knowledge is a mighty truth, bearing in it all the elements of future dissolution. For if man was created in the image of God, why should the gods have been jealous of Adam becoming as one of them, " knowing good and evil ?" With this antithesis the Jewish misfortune for humanity began. They taught us to be images of God, to long in boundless eagerness for that Godhead, and condemned as sinful this very yearning. Mankind had to undergo endless bodily and intellectual sufferings in consequence of this decomposing composition of heterogeneous elements, placing reality in eternal opposition to the ideal. The Jews always hoped to find a Messiah to reconcile their old oriental antithesis, which they had in reality borrowed from the Persians and Egyptians; they always hoped that somebody would redeem humanity from the fetters of spiritual darkness or sin. It was clearly felt by the Persians, as well as by the Jews, that this redemption could only come through man.

Real religiousness consists in man's consciousness of his double attributes and his attempt to bring harmony into the apparent dissonance of his divine (intellectual) and human (material or animal) nature. This pure process must not be disturbed, interrupted, or checked by any secondary and arbitrary element. Man embodies the eternal divine spirit only in a transitional phase, that is for a limited time. During that limited phase he has to exert all his intellectual and moral powers to promote his own as well as his fellow-creatures' happiness. All those elements that hinder him in this task through obscure verbiage, revealed and re-revealed incongruities, mystic symbolism, or theological hair-splitting, are irreligious.

The contradictions in the conception of God, the transcendent materialism, and the complicated incomprehensible spiritualism with which Jehovah was conceived by the Jews; the half-Assyrian and half-Egyptian mask which he wore—now Osiris, the redeemer, then again Ahriman, the slayer, the destroyer, made him now a mystic tyrant, then again a partial father. He promised his chosen children plenty on earth, and many goodly things, and left them continually in the bondage of the surrounding Gentiles, who were proclaimed to be his abomination. Now he appears in the Psalms, as in the strains of the Vedas, to be a God after whom the soul may thirst to lead us to holiness and righteousness, then again it is "the Lord thy God" who gives away the cities of other people, which they built, the trees which they planted, the wells which they dug and the vineyards which they cultivated, as an inheritance to the Jews, and tells them without cause and reason: "Thou shalt save alive nothing that breatheth, but thou shalt utterly destroy them, namely, the Hittites and the Amorites, the Canaanites and the Perizzites, the Hivites and the Jebusites, as the Lord commanded thee." And if you ask for an explanation of the morality of these enactments, you receive the answer: "the ways of the Lord are mysterious." But this is no answer. The mind of man cannot be satisfied with such replies, it finds them in their very mysteriousness irreligious.

The marble form of Zeus, in spite of its beauty, had to give way to a more ideal conception of the Divinity, and in a similar way the invisible God of Moses had to assume another shape. Mosaism had to undergo a reform after having long before divided the Jews into different sects, who hated one another with that intense fervour which is the natural outgrowth of oppression and long slavery. The records of the religious system of the Jews were more favoured than those of the Indians or Egyptians; for their tenets became sacred not only in the eyes of the privileged priesthood, that kept all sacred and profane knowledge to itself, but also in the eyes and ears of the whole nation. Moses faithfully kept his promise, and made the Jews "a nation of priests;" in telling them, freed from all symbolism, what made the Egyptian priesthood so powerful in their sway over the ignorant masses for thousands of years, he made every Jew a theologian. Notwithstanding all these advantages, the Hebrew records had the element of dissolution as a mere formal creed in them; for the mythic was treated as historical; phenomenal facts were stated with an utter ignorance of science, as was only natural in times in which all sciences were in their infancy, or as yet unborn. Though the spirit of inquiry was fettered for centuries, the reform had to come as a natural sequence of the historical progressive development of humanity. John the Baptist first commenced it, Christ followed.

Christ again was followed by the two apostles, St. Paul and St. John. It is an authenticated fact, that the canonical writings of the New Testament contain different accounts of most important incidents, and are the outgrowth of mighty minds who could but impress with their powerful individuality what they wrote. Next followed the Fathers, who did not content themselves with commenting on Christ's, St. Paul's, or St. John's teachings, but added dogma upon dogma, borrowing them from old forgotten Egyptian mysteries, or from the writings of Greek philosophers; so that in the course of a few centuries, when Christianity became the ruling faith of the Roman empire, it comprised all the elements of spontaneous dissolution in its heterogenous borrowed forms, symbols, dogmas, and articles of faith.

Christ's Christianity, the doctrine of love and forbearance, of humility and self-sacrifice, of common brotherhood, and the harrowing tragedy of his life and death, were all turned into symbolic mysteries. What was simple and intelligible was surrounded by incomprehensible contradictions. Christ was to be the mighty, royal, hoped-for Messiah of the Jews, though he tried as a mere teacher to reform Judaism and to bring vitality into what had decayed into a mere dead formalism. Not to abolish the old law was His mission, but to purify it from its narrow national particularism, and to restore its monotheistic and moral universality.

St. Paul saw in Christ a dying God, who had to atone for the sins of Adam, in order to satisfy the demand of the Jewish law. *Grace* was everything with him. St. John made of Christ the incarnation of Plato's Logos, and added that nobody could come to God except through Christ, which was an uncharitable anathema against all those who were honest and virtuous, but who either knew nothing of Christ, or could not understand the mystic dogmas under which Christ had been buried. Christ's incarnation as the Logos could not have been different to that of Brahma, as Krishna or Rama, or

Buddha, of Amn, as Osiris and Horus. Each of these incarnations took place under very analogous circumstances, and for analogous purposes.

The Divinity to the student of ancient creeds appears continually to assume new shapes and forms and to succeed always only in a very partial redemption of humanity. Did Christ, however, ever assume a Godhead in a Buddhistic or Egyptian sense ? is a question which will, in time, be differently answered than at present. Christ the rigorous Jew who conscientiously kept the spirit of the law, though He opposed its dead meaningless formality, who appeared with scrupulous regularity at the grand festivals at Jerusalem, could He have ever violated the sacred monotheistic basis of the Jews so far as to proclaim Himself as anything else but the " Son of Man," to which title He had every claim, when He declared the whole of humanity to be the children of one Father in heaven ? Did Christ ever intend to make Himself anything but the spiritual redeemer of mankind, by proclaiming on high-ways and in market-places what was kept as a secret by the Esoteric teachers, that there was only one God, and that man had one real aim, to unite whether poor or rich, if only " pure of heart," into one bond of divine love, pervading the universe ?

Love was with Christ the connecting element between the divine and human in man. As attraction is scientifically the vital element of the material cosmos, so love is the binding element which was, is, and will be the fundamental basis of any religion ; and where this element of universal brotherhood is discarded or stifled, by whatever dogmas, our enlightened reason will never be persuaded that the mystery is for our benefit ; for the very assumption, that morals can be fostered and best understood through unintelligible types and symbols in antagonism to intellect, is the very element of a spontaneous dissolution of any creed, and always only a question of time.

The sanguinary persecutions that disgraced the religion of Christ would have horrified no one more than Him, in whose name they were perpetrated. And who were those who were most cruelly treated, robbed, pillaged, insulted, and murdered? Those for whom He prayed in dying with his last breath: " Father, forgive them, for they know not what they do." Christ was said to have established eternal hell-fire. He who commanded us to forgive our enemies " seventy times seven," could He have conceived a Divinity less forbearing in His *infinite* love, wisdom and mercy, than a *finite* human being? In this cruel and contradictory assumption we have another element of spontaneous dissolution, because it is an unchristian dogma borrowed from the Egyptians, with whom Osiris was more an infernal judge, than a loving, supreme Being. With the Egyptians gloomy unconscious fear, and not self-conscious love, was the beginning of wisdom and the motive element of their gloomy creed, which element transferred to Christianity changed its very essence, made Romish idolatry a possibility, and worked as an antagonistic dissolving element in Christ's glorious and simple code of morals.

Day by day the historical ground was cut from under the feet of Christ's Christianity. Dogmas, ceremonies, rituals, and symbolic performances were borrowed by the Christian priesthood from Indians (Brahmans and Buddhists), Egyptians, Greeks, Persians, Hebrews, and Romans. The clergy of the Romish Church strove to become, like the Brahmans and Hierophants, the augurs, magi and bonzes of old, masters of the minds of the ignorant masses, who were kept purposely and systematically in ignorance; for the greater the ignorance of the people, the greater the influence of allegories, symbols, and mystic incomprehensibilities. So it came to pass that the clearest laws of humanity and common sense were trampled under foot with reckless ferocity. From the times of Gregory VII. Christianity became hourly more unchristian.

Unchristian Christianity persecuted, killed and burned for nearly a thousand years, from Charlemagne, the Christian Mahomet, down to the year of grace 1780, when the last witch was publicly burnt at Glarus, in the Roman Catholic part of Switzerland. To whatever Christian country we turn we find the militant Church of Rome desiring prerogatives and immunities. The Church claimed the right to punish those who spoke disrespectfully of the clergy; the right to the luxury of burning heretics; there were continual disputes as to whether emperor or pope, cardinal or king, should be first in authority. Deans and bishops quarrelled in open courts with one another about images, postures, or the right to possess a crucifix. The clear enactment of Christ, " Give unto Cæsar that which is Cæsar's," was distorted and placed under mental reservation. A dignitary of the already half-reformed English Church (Archbishop Sandy) dared to proclaim that we must obey princes " usque ad aras," as the proverb is, "so far as we may without disobeying God." And who had to decide what was considered disobeying God ? The priesthood—which cared more for prerogatives, the right to fell timber, to seize lands in mortmain, to receive such estates as were forfeited for high treason, to have the right of investiture, and to possess authority in lay as well as in ecclesiastical matters, than to educate the masses, to teach them soberness and cleanliness, forbearance, peace, and goodwill.

of Ancient Creeds. 19

The priests loudly proclaimed Christ's law: "Do unto others as you wish that they should do unto you;" but their deeds were in contradiction to the ordinance, and they did unto others as they must have wished that they should never be done unto. They acted like the great mass of the Chinese, to whom Confucius, more than four centuries before Christ, gave the same law: "Do unto others as you wish that they should do unto you"; but as we are cheated, we cheat; as we are calumniated, we calumniate; as we are persecuted, we persecute; as we are robbed, we rob; and as we are served with false measures or sham goods, we do the same. This is certainly not Christianity, and though commentators, exegists, apologists, dogmatists, and inquisitors tried hard to smooth down and explain the contradictions, the creed, that had served humanity for 1,500 years, had to undergo a new reform. Christian unchristianity was once more to become pure, primitive Christianity.

In the eyes of the Romish Church Christianity was no longer the doctrine of Christ, but the enactments of the Church. Christ's personal commands had for a thousand years to give way to the assumed higher wisdom of councils or popes. These councils and popes could, however, not avoid being influenced by the spirit of their times, and were forced unconsciously continually to vary their doctrines, according to the exigencies of the moment, always with one clear aim—to keep the power and the means of being the hieratic masters of the world. So long as the priest could live with a wife, it was Christ's command to have one; so soon as it was found that the priest became too worldly, too humane with a wife and family, it was Christ's command to resign himself to celibacy. So long as Platonism served them the priests were Platonists. In the first three centuries they had no Trinity, they were *de facto* Arians, and then they became Athanasians or Trinitarians, in imitation of the Indo-Egyptians, and cursed all who were not of their incomprehensible opinion. On one day Origen, on another St. Augustine, swayed their minds. They had deadly controversies on the Lord's Supper, and about the use of bread and wine, or the Real Presence, or the Transubstantiation, whilst often thousands were starving around them for want of food. They forgave sins, but only to those who could pay for such remission. They introduced self-abnegation, self-flagellation, and self-torture for the masses, and lived in pomp and vanity. They smiled and cursed in one breath; they spoke immediately before the Reformation, but their language was always ambiguous, for they tried to please all parties; and still they attached more importance to outward ceremonies, vestments, symbols, types, and mere verbal professions without any inward, spiritual meaning, than to moral reality and real religiousness.

Whilst the Romish Church was thus a house divided against itself, many honest monks and more enlightened laymen turned back to the old Greek and Roman classics, and tried to take up the thread of the progressive historical development of humanity, which appeared to have been rent asunder and lost for ever. To re-unite it where it had been broken, they revived sciences and arts; and dogmatists, mystics, and dry school-men were more and more silenced. The Reformation was finally victorious in the terrible struggle; but it had to fight its way through torrents of blood. When the peace of Westphalia left Europe in the possession of religious freedom, Europe sealed her right to scientific progress. The Romish Christian creed was then dissolved, and no Vaticanism will ever revive it. Christianity with the Reformation ceased to be a special creed based on mere outer-signs; it was once more made universal. Christ's God of Love and Reason who was enthroned through the Reformation is the God of the Universe, his existence, in one shape or another, is believed in by Brahmans, Buddhists, Jews, Mahometans and Christians.

Christ, if considered as the incarnate divine spirit of self-sacrifice and love, has freed men of their finiteness by teaching them to surrender their *outerselves* to a pure moral and intellectual consciousness of their *innerselves*, and thus only has redeemed humanity, and dissolved all ancient and modern creeds by establishing real religion based on reason aided by science, promoting real morality, freed of all dogmatic dross and from the unnatural bondage of prejudices and the mystic fetters of ignorance.

Polytheism of old had to yield to a more refined creed of *one* creative power; but Polytheism had already borne the elements or constituent particles of spontaneous dissolution in itself. However poetical the deification of the different phenomena of Nature may be, it was merely the outgrowth of an ignorant and over-heated, an unconscious and unbridled imagination. Bitterly, though poets and artists bewailed this time, they had to surrender their fanciful world of self-created gods. Man, however, wishes at all times to have his emotions taken into consideration. The culture of the emotional element seems to be the last retreat of those who think that dry morals (as if morals did not continually exercise our emotional elements), and mere science (cold, calculating science, as they say in turning up their eyes) cannot suffice to fill man's nature. They then turn to a vague and incomprehensible anthropomorphism, man-worship, which in one form or another, has not yet ceased to be the cherished creed amongst those who crave for the merely emotional.

The Greeks were the first and most cultivated anthropomorphists. Their creed has vanished, but it contained much emotional element that, purified of idolatry, might serve the masses of our modern times as an element of unlimited artistic emotion; for art will and must replace that fervid craving for emotion. Art will yet again shape beautiful forms for their own sake, and ethics and æsthetics will repair our loss of barren phrases referring to supernatural matters. The anthropomorphism of old will revive again, though in another spirit; it will not be sanctified as a creed, but hallowed, because it will lead man, through love, to understand the ideal beauty of everything created, from the tiny and bashful daisy to the lofty-snow covered summits of the Himalayan Mountains.

Ancient Creeds, after having gone through the dissolution of Polytheism and Anthropomorphism, enter upon a species of anthropopatism. The leaders of this creed try to combine revelation and reason, faith and science; they use all possible sophistical contortions to prove that there are no contradictions in the Sacred books of the Eastern nations; that all is clear. You have only to take the different passages in their corresponding allegorical, parabolical, tropological, anagogical or literal meanings. They assert, with a mild gentleness, that there are no difficulties except to the blind, to the heartless, and to those who live to cold science and have no higher aim than the "Fata Morgana" of a dreary materialism. These anthropopatists work out in their own imagination a more or less lofty portrait of the Divinity, and describe, praise, draw, model or paint it according to their individual idiosyncrasies, their sympathies or antipathies. They persecute, hate, despise, or, if they are very kind-hearted, pity those who fail to see a "personal" Father in their dim half-theological, half-rationalistic colours. These men are like some Protestants who deny to the Romish Church the right to have miracles, but keep certain miracles which must be believed in. They do not see that in this very contradiction is a thriving element of spontaneous dissolution. Before a tribunal of logic these half-theologians and half-Rationalists could not pass a "spelling-bee." These men feel that they have lost their historical basis, and to find a new one would necessitate too much study; they could only find it through a correct appreciation of the gradual development of humanity, to attain which they would have to make themselves acquainted with the intellectual pressure of mind brought to bear upon progress. Fortunately the discharges from the electric theological clouds that have gathered, or are gathering, have, since the invention of the lightning conductor of tolerance, become extremely harmless, though they may occasionally be unpleasant. The anthropopatists should base their ethics and metaphysics, if the latter exist, on the ruling principles of the Cosmos, but it is much easier to talk morals than to introduce a new creed in our times, after so many spontaneous dissolutions of ancient creeds.

Who, indeed, wishes for a new creed? We do not want the ridiculous Acosmism which denies the reality of the world, asserting that it had been created out of nothing, and that matter is a nonentity. These modern apostles in tail-coats talk of an "Unseen Universe," as though it could be seen; if it can, then to call it "unseen" is nonsense, and if it is invisible, to waste time in describing it with copious verbiage, is still more absurd. Though we may never know what the absolute essences of matter or life are, we may still study matter in its phenomenal results, and see the aberrations of mind whenever it treats of the so-called supernatural, and its glorious conquests in arts and sciences, when man deals with given forms and quantities, either transforming them into works of ideal beauty, or discovering, after centuries of hard labour and keen observation, more scientific explanations of the secret workings of the hidden forces of nature, than the theologians could find on the easy and lazy path of an assumed revelation. The world belongs in future to another body of priests, to the priests of science and art!

The Indian philosophers already attained the consciousness of creation, preservation, and transformation as the external actions of *one* force, in three equally powerful emanations, and, notwithstanding this philosophical starting point, free of every taint of dogmatism and anthropomorphism, a connecting link of different incarnate gods was worked out by the priesthood to satisfy the emotional ignorance of the masses.

The Jews set up a god of their own, a national, jealous god, who was to be stronger than all the others, which was a silent indirect admission that there were other gods. Jewish monotheism reached merely the notion of a mighty ruler, who was master even over the false gods; and those gods who gave comfort and hope for thousands of years to innumerable generations, saw themselves hurled by Javeh into the abyss of hell, where they had to rule as mighty demons. But the "immanence" or inherence of a pervading spirit in the universe cannot be a person in the sense of an anthropopatist or acosmist, for omniscience and omnipresence is only possible with an impersonal deity. The burning question of modern thought is not, as Renan has it, a contest between Polytheists,—namely, Roman Catholics, Protestants, Buddhists and Brahmans, and Monotheists—namely, Jews and Mahométans; but the struggle is between those who assume an all-pervading infinite spirit, and those who deny the existence of any Deity, between Panmonotheists and Atheists.

But who are those who deny the Divinity? Such men as either cannot or will not understand the cosmos, who can see only matter, but do not grasp the effects produced by matter in the universe as well as in humanity, which is but its reflex. Those who never will draw a line between cause and effect, and most of all those who drag the Divinity down to their own low level, transforming it into an idol of their own, which they wish to force upon humanity at large ; these proud, conceited theologians promote atheism even more than some professed atheists. But who are atheists?

Certainly not the scientific men as physicists, who bow down their heads, and profess, with child-like lips: " We are too humble, too finite to grasp the infinite; we shall be contented to trace here and there some minute workings of the innumerable elements forming phenomena that are, that must have had an origin and must have an aim." Not the philologists who, in languages freed from all the trammels of a paradisiacal tongue, in which God himself spoke, trace and systematize the phases through which languages had to pass to attain their different sounds, alphabets, words, concrete and abstract expressions. Not the geologists, who, unfettered by any Eastern cosmogony, follow up the growth of our globe according to law and order, and find in this very inherent law and order the vestiges of an eternal first cause, which personified becomes utterly unintelligible. Not the historian, who, in the complicated phenomena, of which men are the units with all their passions, yearnings, hopes, and fears, traces the eternal laws of action and reaction, which force humanity onward on the path of continuous progress. To so great an extent is this the case, that if we carefully consider the subject, we are astonished at the relative progress of humanity, and this improvement has been attained since the reformation, since the revival of classic art and philosophy ; since scientific inquiries have silenced the grand inquisition, and stopped the burning of witches and heretics ; since logicians have disproven the false and pernicious principles of the reasoning of an infallible priesthood ; since tolerance and forbearance have clad themselves in ermine and meted out justice with an even hand, regardless of the creed to which those belonged who sought redress for wrongs inflicted upon them ; since even bishops and deans dare to thunder at the gates of narrow-mindedness, and to proclaim the right of free investigation, not only for themselves, but also for those who are under their sway; since the lay-authority took upon itself to spread sciences and arts amongst the ignorant and neglected masses, and to prevent through the strong arm of the law a reactionary and anachronistic movement inaugurated by some of the priesthood, who, craving for the emotional, think to find in tapers, fancy embroideries, monkish dresses, and the most childish mimicry of a creed that went through the process of its spontaneous dissolution more than 350 years ago, a solution of the religious questions of our days.

Mysticism has been for thousands of years the bane of humanity. Ignorance is her cherished foster-sister. Mysticism and ignorance presumed

of Ancient Creeds. 27

not only to lead humanity on the path of emotion to virtue, through different creeds, but also to regulate man's intellectual powers. Ignorance and mysticism built up astronomical, zoological, and geological hypotheses which had to be destroyed; they prescribed to the Divinity how and when the world must have been created; science had to rectify these errors of a natural ignorance. That such errors should have been transformed into articles of creed, indispensable to the salvation of our better intellectual nature, and that this deception should and could have been practised for thousands of years, is not a mysterious riddle, but the natural effect of an equally natural cause. Whenever and wherever ignorance assumes the mask of theological knowledge, it leads men into error. The error once having become, through continuous repetition, an accepted truth (though it may be only *negative* truth, viz., falsehood), it takes the positive shape of an indispensable entity for the happiness of mankind, and it requires thousands of years to remove such falsehoods, and historians testify to the fact that the whole progressive development of humanity consists in the destruction of such falsehoods.

In England and Germany, as the two countries most advanced in civilisation, the one politically, the other intellectually, this process of undoing the past is most apparent. In both countries set dogmas appear to go down the stream of time with ever-diminishing buoyancy, form and bulk, till they must sink altogether. Curates and pastors become rarer and scarcer. In 1831 there were in the eight Prussian Universities 2,203 theological students, and in 1875 there were scarcely 560 (about 70 to a University). In the Universities of Southern and Western Germany the decline of theologians was in the same ratio. In addition to this, *one-third* of the matriculated theological students abandoned theology altogether, and entered other professions, tired of asserting things they could not understand; for they had gone through a scientific training in Logic, Mathematics, and Universal History. The ecclesiastical authorities in Germany had to acknowledge that, in one year or so, *one-sixth* of the vacant benefices would have no clergymen to fill them.

Yet, in the face of this growing dissolution, we have our "Burials Question," as the result of Christ's command, "Love thy neighbour as thyself." After 1875 years of grace and Christian teaching, we find men trying to prevent some of their Christian brothers from lying side by side in the same churchyard, in the same soil from which we have all sprung, to which we all return, from which all our pleasures stream, on which all our woes are concentrated. And why? Because these Christians differ, on certain theological questions without real distinction, from those in power. For this reason Christians of another shade of thinking should be carried in silence to their last resting-place. What tyranny, what cruel tyranny, perpetrated in the name of Christianity! And these cruelties are practised whilst words of piety, fraternal condescension, and humble submission are used on one side, and on the other the stern, indomitable "no surrender" is proclaimed with the blind obstinacy of an Eastern despot. This intolerance is the more remarkable, in the third quarter of the nineteenth century, in our free and enlightened country, whilst in Germany, Russia, and Austria tolerance is practised, at least amongst the different members of the Christian faith. In Germany, Roman Catholics and Protestants often use the same sacred building, the one for his mass, the other for his sermon, and both for their prayers to their common God. In Russia

of Ancient Creeds. 29

and Austria the Christian children of one ruling, pervading spirit, may lie peaceably side by side when fate has sealed their controversies, when they can no more pronounce God's anger and judgment against one another, when they rest from their labours. But we persecute one another even beyond the grave, notwithstanding our great political and social movements. We are trying to bring education into the hovels of our rural population, and to the gutter-children of our over-crowded towns. Our scientific discoveries are teaching us day by day to distrust our preconceived prejudices; our historical inquiries demonstrate how falsehoods were spread; how truth was distorted; how dreams, fancies, myths, and legends were taken for realities; how space and time were filled with the tears and sufferings ot men for the sake of false theories; how nations and individuals lost themselves in dogmatic oyster-shells, and were unable to see beyond their narrow ossified world—and yet we cannot let our fellow men sleep their last long sleep in peace.

Philosophers and physicists may smile at this with tears in their eyes, seeing how the self-contradicting elements in creeds not only lead to irreligiousness, but contain in themselves—through placing the form above the spirit, matter above mind, emotion above reason—the elements of a spontaneous dissolution. This inevitable dissolution can only be directed into the right groove of a higher moral and intellectual phase by a thorough understanding of history, which teaches us that only a synthetical combination of the Indian and Hebrew-Christian creeds and their sublime ethics, divested of all extraneous matter, may furnish us with real religion, as a code of morals binding on the whole of humanity, without fettering in any way our intellectual nature.

The bigoted and credulous, the fanatics and ignorant in the Church and in our Universities, in our colleges and educational establishments, do not tremble in vain at the very name of "Universal History" as the grand store-house of man's immortal deeds, follies, and crimes, committed for thousands of years, partly in the name of the Divinity, and partly to satisfy the religious emotions of a Torquemada, or a Calvin, or some false assumptions based on some imaginary theory or divine revelation. Not in vain have our Universities shut their doors on an honest, unbiassed study of the development of humanity on general principles. Were it not for this, we might lose our insulated position; we might discover a continuous gradual growth and decay of creeds as well as sciences, and see how one system of ancient fallacies served another as basis of development.

Not without grave reason does Cardinal Manning clamour against an appeal to history, and brand it as "heresy and treachery." He does not stand alone, he is supported by our own theologians and the heads of our own Universities, who consider the study of "Universal History" superfluous, pernicious, leading to scepticism; for it might teach us that man formed his own gods and dogmas, influenced by the aspect of nature and his relative amount of brain; that man has wasted his time and energy in trying to answer questions "*à priori*" (out of his imagination) before he could gather information "*à posteriori*" (by experience). We might learn that every step in the progress of humanity had to be fought for single-handed by independent men in whom morals and intellect were well balanced. We might become conscious that dogmatic superstitions in India, China, Assyria, Babylon, Persia, Egypt, Judæa, and Rome, during the Middle Ages and in modern times, had caused the dissolution or stationary state of all these Empires and times.

For man, composed of the two constituent elements of matter and mind, of morals and intellect, must cultivate both; the one according to immutable laws, necessitated by his very organisation, and the other unfettered by any capricious, emotional, and unintelligible self-created and self-imposed creed.

Man's destiny lies in the perfect balance of his moral and intellectual nature.